Drinking In the Culture

TUPPERS' GUIDE TO EXPLORING GREAT BEERS IN EUROPE

Drinking In the Culture

TUPPERS' GUIDE TO EXPLORING GREAT BEERS IN EUROPE

BOB & ELLIE TUPPER

CulturAle Press
Bethesda, Maryland

CulturAle Press
P.O. Box 549
Glen Echo, MD 20812

www.CulturAlePress.com

Library of Congress Cataloging in Publication

Tupper, Bob.
Drinking in the culture: Tuppers' guide to exploring great beers in Europe /
by Bob and Ellie Tupper.
pages : color illustrations ; cm
Includes bibliographical references and index.
ISBN: 978-0-9909610-0-0
1. Beer—Social aspects—Europe. 2. Beer—Europe—Guidebooks.
3. Breweries—Europe—Guidebooks. 4. Europe—Guidebooks. 5. Europe—Social life and customs. I. Tupper, Eleanor S. II. Title. III. Title: Tuppers' guide to exploring great beers in Europe

TP573.E85 T86 2015
338.4/766342/094

ISBN 978-0-9909610-0-0

Design by Susan Schmidler

Cover by Debra Naylor, Naylor Design Inc.

Photography by Robert R. Tupper, Jr. and Eleanor S. Tupper

1 2 3 4 5 6 7 8 9 10

Printed in the United States of America

To Tom:

"Bob! They've got 'em all!!"

Contents

How we got here

It's all Tom's fault.

On a visit to Bob's fraternity house at college, back in the last century, his younger brother Tom spotted the small but choice beer can collection amassed by the members and thought it was the coolest thing since peanut butter. Bob was perfectly happy to pass on an empty from each sixpack, and since there were five left each time, he started collecting too. Ellie joined the family shortly afterward, and it wasn't long before our favorite weekend pastime was to hit the road looking for new cans and the breweries that produced them. (The budget of a starting schoolteacher and a college student didn't allow for much more than that.)

We continued to collect even after Tom reached drinking age and started expanding his collection on his own. More than once, Tom found us good sources, but it was a call very late one Friday night that changed our lives. "BOB!" Tom roared. "They've got them all. They've got them ALL!!" Eventually, more calmly, he explained, and we discovered for ourselves the remarkable efforts of Washington, DC's Brickskeller restaurant to stock every available beer can sold in the United States.

Even with the Brickskeller in our back yard, collecting beers in any form wasn't as easy then as it is now, but we were lucky. In the mid-1970s Bob switched from teaching math to history, including European history. Back then, U.S. tax laws were more generous in granting tax deductions for teachers seeking experiential learning, and the subsidy was just enough to afford our first summer trip in 1974, a hands-on history lesson in England. Later we discovered we could buy—or find—unusual European beer cans and sell them at collectors' prices back in the States, which helped to fund more trips to the continent.

As we approached a thousand cans in our collection, however, it occurred to us that the beers inside were at least as interesting. Even back in the 1970s, with barely more than 40 independent breweries in the U.S., not all of them tasted like Budweiser. Taking notes seemed obvious, not least because a 3×5" notebook made a lot less noise hitting the floor in the middle of the night than a shelf full of empty beer cans. This shift from cans to notes opened up a vast range of new European destinations. By this time we'd learned a fair amount about budget travel in Europe, so in July of 1979, we scraped together a cheap airfare to Luxembourg and a couple of Eurail passes, bought a tiny notebook, and set out on what is now a 35-year jaunt. It's still continuing.

Our first beer notes were on the pilsner from the now, alas, defunct Henri Funck Brewery. Bob commented pithily, "Tastes like beer"; Ellie's cogent note was, "Yes, it does." You have to start somewhere. Over 25,000 beers have entered our database since then, with independent notes and ratings from each one of us. A handful of men in the world have topped this number, including the immortal beer writer and connoisseur Michael Jackson (*not* the pop star); no woman on record has come close.

Our penchant for note taking caught the attention of the owner of the Brickskeller, Maurice Coja, who persuaded us to speak about beer to an upcoming Cornell Alumni Association dinner. Our fee, $5 plus a free meal and all the beer we wanted to drink, seemed like a bonanza at the time, but it led to much more. By 1987, working with Coja and his daughter and son-in-law Diane and Dave Alexander, we were hosting the longest running series of sit-down beer tastings in American history. Every tasting seemed like a graduate level class in the culture of beer, not just for the audience but for us, and we learned from some of the best brewers and beer scholars in the world. (See the acknowledgments for some of them.) We continue to host "Brickskeller" tastings at RFD in Washington, DC, run by the third generation, Josh Alexander, and at Mad Fox Brewery in Vienna, Virginia, and we continue to learn from some of the most interesting people in the brewing business.

Over the years we visited hundreds of breweries, from Anheuser Busch-size monsters to soup kettle nanos, and talked shop with thousands of brewers. Only once did we attempt homebrewing, a memorable experience that firmly taught us our place in the world. But after the first 6,000 tastings or so, we realized that there was A Beer Out There that nobody was making: an amber harvest ale that would be dry hopped, aged for six weeks like a lager, and bottle conditioned, hoppy enough for Bob but balanced enough for Ellie. Our friend Jerry Bailey of Old Dominion Brewing Co. in Ashburn, Virginia—along with his champion brewers Ron Barchet and John Mallet—thought this sounded like a good idea for a small batch one-off. An afternoon of intense comparison of a table full of various bottles resulted, eight weeks later, in Tuppers' Hop Pocket Ale, which won the gold medal for American Pale Ale at the Great American Beer Festival in 1997. The Ale's little sister, Tuppers' Hop Pocket Pils—later Keller Pils—won a gold in 2001 in the German Style Pilsener category and a bronze in 2005 as Cellar or Unfiltered, and before the ride ended in 2007 with the sale of Old Dominion, the two beers made up a significant proportion of Old Dominion's production and paid for most of our daughter's college.

Our early European trips led to more: more travel, more beers, more information, and more great stories. For decades, friends have begged us to publish our tasting notes, and we do hope to put them online someday. But you can get critiques on beers from countless sources these days—for any one beer in our entire list that's currently available, someone's probably posted a rating somewhere. Besides, even we don't always agree on what "best" means. Bob loves sour Flemish red ales; Ellie, not so much. Ellie relishes a nutty brown mild; Bob tolerates them, sometimes.

What we have learned is that the circumstances in which you drink a beer can matter at least as much to your appreciation of it as the beer itself. And that's where this book fits in. There are dozens of travel books that will tell you where to go; there are countless beer books, blogs, and other publications that will tell you what to drink. This guide is designed as the best of both: to help you find the best beer *experiences* in the brewing encyclopedia that is Europe.

For many of our cities we don't talk about specific beers at all, since they'll change by the time you get there. In the back, besides a thorough index, we've included a fairly random but useful glossary and, because Bob is a history teacher, a condensed chronology of European (and brewing) history.

Whatever your taste, in brewing or scenery, there's a good chance that somewhere in this book there is a place that is serving your own "best" beer. Searching for that beer is as good as life gets.

An important caveat. We are two dedicated beer lovers who love to share what we have found with others. Friends and acquaintances have provided valuable tips that are included here, but we have no organization to supply us with up-to-the-minute information on places we haven't seen for a year or two. We have not traveled on every available airline, stayed at every possible hotel, seen every cathedral, or even visited every inviting beer purveyor. We've done our best to make the information in this guide as timely as possible, but even seemingly perpetual institutions do change. *Check online.*

And a disclaimer. Although we have unreservedly endorsed pubs, restaurants, airlines, and hotels, we have not received any compensation from any business mentioned in this book. However, unless we state otherwise, if we mention a business, we've flown on it, slept in it, or guzzled at it. Other than the fact we were pretty obviously taking notes, which you can certainly do too if you think it might help, none of them had any reason to give us special service.

BOB & ELLIE TUPPER

Acknowledgments

We had a draft (sorry) of acknowledgments that ran well over a page, but when we went back to look at it, we realized we had omitted a dozen people who deserved to be on the list as well. We hope to post the full version on our website—there are no page limits online. The shorter version follows, listing barely a handful of those who encouraged us, supported us, and taught us over the years.

Michael Jackson singlehandedly taught us more about beer and beer travel than all other sources combined. His writings, his lectures, and hours of genial conversations helped us develop a framework that lies behind almost every page of this book. Michael blazed the trail to elevate the appreciation of fine and creative beers to the same level of connoisseurship as wine. Countless beer lovers are richer for his dedication.

Our beer career would never have happened without the Brickskeller Restaurant in Washington, DC. We learned there as if we were in beer school, and the tasting gigs over the years financed many of the trips that became the foundation for this book. Maurice and June Coja, Dave and Diane Alexander, and the third generation, Josh Alexander at RFD Washington, made DC a required destination for brewers throughout the western world.

When the lights came on at the Brickskeller tastings, the stage became something of an intimate parlor or seminar. We learned as much as the attendees did about the world of beer from brewing superstars such as Tomme Arthur, Ron Barchet and Bill Covaleski, Larry Bell, Sam Calagione, Pierre Celis, Vinny Cilurzo, Bert Grant, Kris Herteleer, Garrett Oliver, Hugh Sisson, Rob Todd, Bruce Williams, and literally hundreds more pioneers of the craft brewing movement.

Jerry Bailey of the original Old Dominion Brewing Co. brought us into the brewing community when he agreed to make a "little niche beer" that would buy our daughter a couple of textbooks. Tuppers' Hop Pocket Ale and Tuppers' Keller Pils allowed our daughter to attend the college of her choice, did some good for some people who needed the help, and gave us the credibility to pick the brains of dozens of the smartest people we have ever met: brewers. Jerry's brewers included Kenny Allen, Ron Barchet, Favio Garcia, John Mallet, and Rob Mullen, who helped us formulate those and other collaborative beers. Other brewmasters we've had the pleasure and honor of working with include Charlie Buettner, Bill Madden, Jason Oliver, and Andy Rathmann. And to the dozens of skilled and dedicated brewers who have brewed beers for us at all hours of the day and night, *thank you*.

One of the early Brickskeller tastings featured the African beer Ngoma, imported at the time by an "old hippie" named Bill Fadeley. Bill brought some valuable African wood carvings and offered to auction them for charity. His point was, "If wine drinkers can sit, drink, and think about ideas, why can't beer drinkers get together, drink, and think of ways of helping other people?" Since then, Brickskeller auctions have raised over $100,000 for Children's National Medical Center in Washington, and the sales of Hop Pocket beers have helped scores of souls break addiction. Bill, you'll be pleased to know that a portion of the sales of this book will go to local organizations such as Samaritan Ministries, which helps repair broken lives in the DC area, and to organizations trying to make life better for people all over the world, such as those listed at givewell.org.

Before You Go

What this book is, and what it isn't

Over the past 35 years, our search for new beers, and new beer venues, has taken us across the United States and Europe including the United Kingdom. There is good beer almost everywhere else on the globe. Beer is a universal—humankind has noticed for millennia that you can get something, maybe not delicious but certainly mood-altering, by adding water to grain and leaving it alone for a while. But our experience (and our budget) has focused on these two continents because of the sheer variety available in these cultures. Europe is a cornucopia of beer styles and creative developments; brewing in the U.S. reflects all of this country's various immigrant heritages as well as its own unique independence and imagination.

There are guides, both in print and online, that will tell you *all* the places to drink in any one European city (we cite a number of excellent ones below). If you had a lifetime, you could try them all and make your own choices. But you've got a week, maybe; now what? There are also countless travel guides that will tell you all about where to stay, eat, and tour in Europe. But they won't tell you much about where you can get a sample of the local beer.

For this book we've chosen 24 (a "case") of our favorite cities in Europe and the UK, large and small, that have a strong and interesting brewing culture. We're listing them alphabetically because there is no real way to categorize them. Within each city, our tireless research team (that's the two of us) have narrowed down the options to a "sixpack" of—in our opinion—the most interesting or most creative or just plain *nicest* places to drink. Bob has been a history teacher for 45 years, so there's a section on the overall history of each city, along with notes on how that has affected its individual brewing styles and beer-drinking culture. We also offer suggestions, based on our personal experiences, on how to get there, where to stay, what there is to do other than drink beer, and other general travel tips.

Finally, with each city we add suggestions for one or more day trips or excursions. We've found that parking the bags for some days in one city and using it as a base for side trips into the area can save time, headaches, and often money as well.

This book won't cover *all* the pubs or *all* the beers. Just the ones we liked best and that we think will make for a good adventure for anyone who appreciates a fine, fresh beer in a distinctive venue. Good travels, and cheers.

Getting there

Websites and guidebooks more comprehensive than ours provide more information than you can easily digest. Planning's almost the best part—until you actually book the flight, you can go *anywhere.*

That said, here are some tips that took us a while to learn. In our early years we flew as cheaply as we could, including 747 "charters" with 11 people per row. But after a flight in which Bob was wedged for 8 hours between a linebacker for the Giants and a Rush Limbaugh clone, we realized that we are now too old and fat for that, and we'd be willing to go less often if necessary for the luxury of being able to breathe en route.

Fortunately, we (re)discovered Icelandair. Ironically, our first trip in 1979 was with them, landing in their one European hub city, Luxembourg. They now fly to more places than you can shake a TSA scanner wand at—see below. Their Saga Class is the cheapest business class we've found and although it might not quite match Lufthansa's spiffiness, it gives you loads of seat room, above-average food, free drinks, great headphones, and a nicely equipped swag bag. The real deal, though, is the next class down. Icelandair's "Economy Comfort" guarantees that they won't sell the middle seat in the row of three; you and your mate get the whole row. Better yet, if Saga isn't sold out, you can get bumped up to the oversized Saga seats. In either case, you don't get the fancy headphones, Saga food, or the swag bag, but you do get some not-so-bad victuals, free drinks, and use of the business-class lounges.

The lounge is an important perk because all Icelandair flights to Europe require a change in Reykjavik. It's inconvenient to change planes and go through European Union immigration, but the lounge has free drinks (including pleasantly quaffable Icelandic beer) and an impressive buffet of Icelandic specialties such as smoked lamb and the twisted doughnuts called *kleinur.*

The Reykjavik switch allows this relatively small airline to connect a multitude of cities on each side of the Atlantic. Every American Icelandair departure city, and there are many now, connects to literally dozens of European destinations. However, as you book, be very careful to stay within the Icelandair system. They partner with other airlines to reach cities in eastern and southern Europe, but the fares soar once you leave Icelandair's warm embrace.

Travel between the UK and the Continent is much easier than it used to be, but can be more expensive than ever. The Eurostar, a direct train between London and either Brussels or Paris, is by far the quickest … and most boring. The "Chunnel" that runs under the English Channel is an engineering wonder, but the experience is much like being stuck under the East River in a New York rush hour. The trains are cramped and almost always jam-packed. Even when it's above ground, the train uses a high-speed line that runs through a cutting or between fences; these minimize the noise for the neighbors and keep cows off the track, but you can't see anything but walls. Still, you can do in three hours what used to take a full day.

Budget airlines connect England with nearly all the major European cities. You can save several days on a rail pass by grabbing a flight to Vienna or Prague. "Bucket shops," real or online, sometimes offer sensational deals. The down side is that these flights often use minor airports that may be inconvenient to get to or from. But there are always buses and usually trains; for example, four trains an hour run from

London to Stanstead Airport in a bit less than an hour. Note: Luggage restrictions, especially regarding carry-ons, can be much tighter than on the major carriers. Check before you find yourself holding a yard sale in the airport parking lot.

Ferries still connect the UK with ports such as Hoek van Holland. It's been many years since we've made the overnight crossing, but we understand competition with the Chunnel has led to improvements. You can get a combination rail-ferry ticket for well under $100 that will take you from London to Amsterdam. Even booking a cabin for the overnight passage can be cheaper than an equivalent room in a hotel. The classier tickets even include beer in your room, though you might find more pleasure in what you've stashed in your suitcase. What hasn't changed is that connections between rail, boat, and rail are a lot more tolerable if you're traveling light.

Railing

If you haven't been to Europe in a while, you're in for a surprise on the trains. Increasing privatization and some government initiatives have dramatically reduced travel times and often increased comfort, but at a cost. The days of the hop-on-hop-off rail passes aren't quite gone, but supplemental fees and required reservations are increasingly common.

Still, rail passes can save big bucks over individual tickets. Even in first class, just one or two long trips can pay off the cost of a pass. Second class passes are cheaper, but we automatically go for first; apart from the significant spiffiness factor, 2nd class is often (and naturally) far more crowded. RailEurope has the monopoly; you can buy passes through a vendor like Rick Steves or Eurail.com, but if you run into problems you'll deal with the same not-always-helpful RailEurope bureaucrats. When buying online, be very, very careful as you type, and reread your application carefully. The tiniest typo can result in having to cancel and start over, at a hefty fee. Does it sound like we speak from experience?

Many major trains (ICE, Thalys, other high-speed trains) not only require reservations, with supplement charges, but also limit the number of seats available to passholders. It varies. Getting out of France on a pass can be expensive and difficult. Moving through Scandinavia is easier and a bit cheaper.

But in some countries, rail passes are just what they seem to be. In Germany, for example, you can hop onto almost any train and find empty seats in first class. Reservations are cheap and easy to book, so frequent travelers often reserve multiple trains. Seat reservations show on LED signs or bits of paper over the seat; if the seat isn't taken 15 minutes after the train leaves, it's yours. Beware, though: "ggf freiegaben" seats are available for last-minute reservations, and "bahn.comfort" seats are reserved for card holders, so you run a good chance of getting turfed out. If you're flexible enough to get off and try the next train, you'll rarely really need reservations, though for major routes and international travel, booking seats can save you some worry.

In the UK, BritRail passes are nearly twice the price for the same number of days, but worth it. Reservations are free but often unnecessary, and in first class you get complimentary tea, snacks, and even canned beer on longer trips. Our strategy is to get a shorter duration pass to save on the initial outlay. We start in a central location—Sheffield or Manchester, for example—and pay cash for day trips and short hops. We then activate the pass for the big connections and finish in another central spot where we can again pay cash to get around for a few more days. Consider intercity buses, too; they're slower but much cheaper than rail fares.

Many stations have computers that help you plan your route. Sometimes if you have a pass you can use a ticket machine to plan the route—then just not buy the ticket. The Deutsche Bahn website (www.bahn.de) can help you plan not only Germany, but much of Europe as well.

Train stations in Europe often have decent food and sometimes very good beer. In each of our cities we offer you our choice of "Station Breaks"—the best beer we've found within a 10-minute walk of the station exit. Most European stations are in central areas with good accommodations, food, and beer nearby. The exceptions are new stations linked to high-speed lines that bypass inner cities.

Nearly all major European cities have two or more stations. Check and *double check* which station you're leaving from. (You might sense we've learned this from experience, too.) Some trains are made up of sections that go to different destinations; check the sign on the side of the car you're boarding. Fortunately we read the guidebooks before making *that* mistake. Be careful if you get off the train at a longish layover—trains sometimes change platforms. Talk to a conductor before you head into the station to get a beer.

Once there: getting around

It's worth the time, effort, and occasional expense to get a good transit map if you're in a city for more than a couple of days. They always exist, even if your concierge assures you that the photocopied blur he's giving you is the best available. But beware, some cities change transit route numbers more often than the Washington football team changes quarterbacks, and if you're glued to a number you might never see the tram you need. Just ask someone at the stop—and someone will speak enough English to help—if the tram number you're waiting for is the right one. Many stops make it easier with electronic signs that list the next incoming tram or two and a final destination.

European subways, buses, trams, etc. are designed to get people around as conveniently as possible, frequently more so than in the U.S. Our recommended drinking spots are all accessible by public transportation, most of them easily.

Staying

We usually suggest a hotel or two in each of our cities, but you can get far more details and choices from other sources than us. Using the Internet today is almost a necessity. You'll travel with the assurance that you'll have a bed that night—but the down side is that you're choosing from a photo at best. Your feet are still your best ally in getting a feel for a hotel's atmosphere, the nuances of the neighborhood, and whether there's good beer nearby.

Among our suggestions in the chapters are chain hotels and some local lodging options. Staying at a chain hotel deprives you of some of the most memorable and very local experiences you can have. When we were young, the budget didn't cover chains, and we amassed a collection of excellent stories. But at our age, we don't need that many more stories, and sometimes the security of a predictable experience is appealing.

If you travel at all frequently, domestic or abroad, pick one hotel chain and get loyal. The perks soar as you accumulate stays in a given year. At the highest tier, for example, Hilton and Marriott will find you a room even in a "sold out" hotel if you book 48 hours in advance. Room upgrades and breakfast feasts that are priced up to $80 per couple are also complementary. Executive lounges offer happy hours with free, if usually uninspired, food and alcohol. We chose Hilton several years ago, and it's worked out well. We rack up points at moderately priced Hilton properties in the U.S., then soak in the privileges in expensive European Hilton gems. Hilton lounges are still behind the game in consistently offering local beers, but service has generally been outstanding. Their locations vary from spectacular (Munich City, Cologne, and Stockholm) to business-oriented venues (Amsterdam and Dusseldorf), and some summer rates we've found have been steals. Radisson Blu seems to have a knack for the spectacular, but you'll pay for that view over Tivoli or the multistory aquarium built into its Berlin showpiece. Accor is a Euro-centered multilevel chain that runs from the affordable Ibis to the upscale Pullman and always seems to have a hotel within staggering distance of the main train station. Most of the chains give you what you pay for, and again, *more* than what you pay for once you've established loyalty.

We still roll the dice sometimes and find a room after we arrive in a city. It's a game that's at least as much fun as a blackjack table, and winning really matters. Off season, it's easy, but even in season with a huge festival under way, we've always found a room somewhere. The risks are that you'll travel farther away from the center city than you'd like, and pay more than you thought you would, but there is a room if you believe there is. We've learned a few general rules over the years.

- Arrive in the city early in the day: 10 to 11 AM is best. Surprisingly, 7 AM is too early—hotels often don't know for sure who is going to check out.
- Find the tourist office and get a list of hotels, then hit the streets and see what's there. Only as an absolute last resort do we allow them to book a room for us. See the Bamberg chapter for why.
- Or—make a new best friend: a bartender or restaurant staffer near where you want to stay. This advice is not foolproof even if your "friend" is being honest, but you can learn about a fine B&B around the corner that you would never have discovered on your own.
- Hotels near main rail stations in Europe tend to be safe, comfortable, and reasonably affordable. Some inexpensive brands like Ibis have hotels in or adjacent to the station itself. Especially for short stays, it's easier to ditch your luggage immediately.
- The standard star rating system (0 to 5 stars) is pretty reliable, but if you want a specific amenity, ask. Air conditioning, for example, isn't a guarantee even in major chains.

- Always insist on seeing the room. See the room and they'll show you their best; book without seeing, and prepare for their worst. Also, desk clerks don't always know what they're selling. An expensive "palace view" room had a huge tree in front of the window that wasn't that big when the hotel was built; the desk clerk was shocked when we showed him a picture of the "view." In Passau one night, the only window in our room was a ceiling skylight that only opened six inches (and no A/C). Check for dust—you may choose to stay there anyway, but at least you'll know to check the rest of the room more carefully.
- Always, politely, inquire "Is that absolutely your best rate?" If you say it in a sadly-I'm-going-to-have-to-look-elsewhere tone, you can get another 10 or 20 percent off more often than you'd think.
- However, if you arrive late in the day, the tourist office may be your best and quickest bet. If we're staying for several days, we let the office book for one or two nights, then hit the streets the next morning when the hunting is better and less stressful.
- If you hit bad luck—the tourist office is closed and all the nearby hotels are sold out—find a sympathetic-looking desk clerk and look pitiful. He or she may not be able to help you at their property, but they have hearts and will often call around to see what they can find for you. Hotels near the airport can have vacancies when a center city is booked up. If you're really stuck, consider hopping back on a train and trying a different city not too far away. If a major city is completely booked, ask the hotel desk why—then head in the opposite direction from the event.
- If you can, be flexible about dates when you book. Some hotel sites allow you to easily compare rates for different days. If you're traveling in the summer, rates can vary enormously depending on special events or conventions. In 2014 we booked a room at the Hilton Munich City, one of their best, for under $200 a night by nabbing a summer special non-cancellation rate. The same room went for well over twice as much per night a week earlier or a week later.
- Don't assume your hotel will take anything but cash. Most take cards, but some add a fee you'd rather avoid. Travelers checks are so 20th century. If you have to bring them, cash a day or two's value at a bank that doesn't charge a fee.

IMPORTANT: Don't play the "find a room" game on your first day in Europe. Some countries require an address at Immigration. We know of people who have fudged an address, but that strategy is fraught with potential disaster. Also, if you're arriving from the States, your judgment and energy will be impaired by jet lag. Book your first room in advance.

"Left luggage" rooms. Nearly all hotels have some kind of secure space where you can stash your baggage until your late train leaves town. We've left our bags, including obvious computer backpacks, in left luggage rooms all over Europe. With the exception of one clumsy attendant who dropped our soft-sided cooler of beer bottles, we never had a problem. (We were upset, of course, but it was at least a small comfort to realize that the people whose luggage was stacked below ours were going to be more upset.)

Safety

European cities are safer than American cities. Police in some countries still don't routinely carry guns. That said, you are not in an amusement park, and you'll run into the impoverished, the disgruntled, the addicted, and the just plain schemers as you travel. Ordinary precautions, however, can make your trip almost as safe as a visit to Busch Gardens.

As we go to press, isolated incidents of violence across Europe have hit the headlines. But consider the odds. You're more likely to get hit by a car than a bomb. Read the paper, watch for State Department alerts, and just be smart. Trying not to look like an obvious American may not only make you a more welcome tourist, but a safer one. We wouldn't avoid a cathedral tour just because it attracts crowds—but we wouldn't attend a "Fourth of July God Bless America" rally either.

You are not likely to be blown up or shot, or even mugged. You are likely to run into pickpockets. ALWAYS carry your passport, credit cards, rail pass, and whatever money it would pain you to lose in a money belt or pouch inside your clothing. If it makes you look like you have a terrible medical condition, that's better than sounding like you have a terrible medical condition when you find them gone.

- For men from Bob: I still use a wallet for small bills because when I have to partially undress to buy a beer, it disconcerts people. You can keep a wallet in your back pocket relatively safely if you fold a comb, teeth up, inside it; it will hook on the pocket and your pickpocket will be in the next block before you even know he was there. This trick has foiled even Paris's best. The down side, of course, is that it's just as hard for you to get it out in a hurry when you're eager for that beer.
- For women from Ellie: I'm told that thieves on scooters will sometimes drive up onto a sidewalk to snatch a purse, or even use blades to cut the straps. I've never run into this, but don't press your luck. Look around. If the local young women are wearing their backpacks on the front, it's for a reason. Get a purse with a shoulder strap—not a handbag—that zips up, and hang onto it; hook it on your knee or around a chair leg at the table.

Pickpockets rarely look the part. One of a group of "nuns" in a Milan subway got into Bob's back pocket and lifted the contents—a pack of tissues. Amazingly, she put them back before scurrying off the train just as the doors closed. Another trick is for a group of women to surround you as you're getting on the train. The "pregnant" one stops short, then glares at you when her friends shove you into her in the boarding rush. When you get free, you find your bag's been rifled. Keep it zipped and in your arms in crowds.

Check our "scams" section in each city chapter. You might want to read through all of them, since some classic scams migrate as easily as the people who pull them. Brush off panhandlers as firmly as necessary.

Worry about drivers more than you worry about thieves. One study claimed that a pedestrian in Brussels was seven times more likely to be clipped by a car as one in

New York City. Get into the habit of looking both ways even on one-way streets. Never jaywalk in your first 48 hours in a country (obviously *especially* in the UK), and even thereafter obey the lights unless the natives are acting as point men for you. Bicyclists can be more numerous than bees in a beer garden, often faster, and decidedly more dangerous.

Make sure your hotel room door actually latches when you leave the room.

If you want to have some fun playing Sherlock, leave some important-looking fake documents in the bottom of your suitcase and check for them each time you return to your room. A housekeeper once stole our Eurail map because it was in the envelope that the pass came in. We've only occasionally lost items in chain hotels; Hilton, which we use most often, has never let us down. Smaller hotels and B&Bs can have a harder time hiring help wisely; take precautions even when the management have become your best friends.

Most importantly, remember that—except for the traffic—your chances of being actually hurt are tiny. Don't let the bad guys make you paranoid. Before you walk out in a new city, ask the desk clerk or the concierge what areas are safe and which areas might be best to avoid. It is much in their best interest to give you good advice.

Every guide will tell you this, because it's true: *be aware* as you walk in a city. Just your looking around and sizing up your surroundings can persuade some ne'er-do-well to pick on someone else. Talking or texting on your phone as you walk is a good way to wind up getting a new phone—on either side of the Atlantic.

Health

Medical and dental care is usually competent and often at least matches what you'd find traveling in the U.S. Costs to residents are minimal, but costs to you can vary enormously. Ask advice at a good hotel desk.

We've found that probiotics significantly reduce our bouts with viruses. Two recommendations that these big companies have paid us nothing for: TruBiotics from Bayer fits in your suitcase and has served us well. The Danactive probiotic yogurt drink, which for us has been nearly magical, is widely available in Europe under the name Actimel.

Money

Bring at least a little local cash for your first days. Do not get stuck like the hapless couple we met, who'd just gone off for a little sightseeing before taking their luxury North Sea cruise and found themselves stranded when the "day long" on-off tour bus stopped running at 4 PM. We couldn't resist taking a few moments to savor the sight of a millionaire trying to panhandle bus fare before we paid their way back to the dock. You can still buy "tip packs" of foreign currencies; we always keep a little at the end of each trip for the next one.

Currency rates fluctuate. In 1995 the European Union's euro debuted at near parity to the dollar, then dropped to a level that made Europe briefly a real bargain for Americans. However, it strengthened over the next decade, until the cost of a European brew tour reached nearly double when the euro peaked at about $1.60 in 2008. Another swing in the pendulum in 2015 has brought the euro back to near parity, so that beer and breakfasts now cost at least 25% less than they did two years ago.

Several countries declined the opportunity to join the Eurozone. For the most part, that was bad news for you, the outside traveler. In addition to the inconvenience of having to juggle pockets of hard-to-identify coins, the currencies of many of the non-euro countries have held up well. The dollar has made some gains recently against the British pound and even the various Scandinavian crowns, but Denmark is still expensive, Sweden is worse, and Norway makes the other two look cheap. The Swiss franc has held solid at virtual parity with the U.S. buck; if you could get a job there at minimum wage, you could travel anywhere you like.

Most European credit and debit cards feature a "chip and PIN" system rather than the magnetic stripe "swipe and sign" cards prevalent in the U.S. Chip technology is more secure, but it's only slowly gaining ground here at home. Most big city European merchants will, reluctantly, accept a swipe card, but some automated machines, such as rail or metro ticket dispensers and the portable readers used by restaurant waiters, require a chip. If you can get one, it's a good idea.

Shop around before you leave for a debit or credit card that won't cost you an arm and a leg in foreign withdrawal fees. Make sure to tell your bank IN ADVANCE where you're going, so they don't freak out and freeze your card when you buy a beer in Bratislava. ATM machines are plentiful and easy to use. Find ATMs that are bank owned—private companies give poor exchange rates or charge high fees. You will sometimes be given the opportunity to pay in dollars. It's almost always best to turn down the offer.

Packing

Thanks to a firm stance from our daughter a few years ago, we travel pretty light: one small "spinner" wheeled suitcase each, plus a computer (and everything else) bag, a compact backpacker's guitar, and a purse. Ellie does the packing, or we wouldn't be able to move. Advice here is from her.

Wardrobe

Europe is, still, more formal than the U.S. You get a better welcome if you don't look like an *American* (i.e., dangling camera, baggy shorts, logo tee, "mandals," floppy hat and sunglasses). Vacation spots such as beaches and resorts are less formal, but not for dinner. Flipflops are a bad idea. They're disrespectful in cathedrals, hazardous around luggage, painful in museums, and suicidal on cobblestones. Jeans are pretty much universal for any age or gender, but be practical: they're hard to wash, or especially dry, without a laundromat. Bring khakis or a decent skirt and a couple of collared shirts, and just check out who sticks out of a crowd.

Laundry

The key to traveling light, if you care about your personal environment, is washing a lot. Contrary to stereotype, Europeans do not have B.O. to cover up yours. We bring a week of underwear and everything else as lightweight layers, and *nothing white*. Permanent press line-dries faster than knits. Palmolive dishwashing liquid isn't perfect (that's one reason I say no whites) but is compact and concentrated and does the job. And, yes, it's easy on your hands and also does dishes. About 12 feet of stout string and a packet of bobby pins do great for a clothesline. Keep in mind the effect of the weight of wet clothes on whatever you string it from, don't use the balcony (it'll be dirty, and the management objects), and hide everything before the maid comes in. Do not *ever* hang laundry or anything else from a room sprinkler or smoke detector.

Laundromats vary in technology from begging soap and change from the very busy woman in the back, to space-age control panels that regulate every machine in the room. They can be a wonderful quiet time in the middle of a rushed trip. They are rarely cheap and they are never quick, though some places might offer drop-and-fold. The driers can be hellish hot, so don't dry anything that'll shrink. Your hotel might know of one or even have one, depending on the kind of hotel it is: business-traveler hotels often have a guest laundry center; ritzy places have never heard of dirty clothes but offer laundry service at hilarious prices; less expensive hotels are often in apartmenty neighborhoods that have one somewhere within a few blocks. I've found nice laundromats in Salzburg and Munich and one near Gare du Nord in Brussels that has a bar next door. Copenhagen features one that *is* a bar, those practical Danes.

Household (other useful items)

- *An e-reader!!!* (Ellie read 29 books one trip and Bob didn't have to carry them.) HOWEVER, with smart devices, keep in mind that you're on another continent; horror stories abound of people coming home to thousands of dollars' worth of roaming charges.
- Plastic bags: 1-gallon ziplock (ice, wet clothes, clothes not used often); 1-quart ziplock for tasting notes and picnic leftovers; "snack size" for international change, prescriptions, your wet washcloth (not all hotels provide them). Seal *everything* liquid in your suitcase in a ziplock bag. You don't want to spend your first day off the plane dealing with a suitcase full of shampoo. Trust me.
- For picnics, train meals, and carryout in the room, a dozen plastic-coated 8-1/2" paper plates will fit neatly in a 1-gallon zipper food storage bag along with a couple of sturdy plastic knives and spoons. Forks break, you get them with carryout, and people did without them for thousands of years.
- A Swiss Army knife. Be sure to pack it in the suitcase for the flight.
- A small, soft-sided insulated cooler can be folded and packed for the flight and will keep anything cold long enough with a zip bag of Eiswürfels/glaçons/ice cubes begged from a local restaurant. Fast food joints will almost always give you a large cup of ice, especially if you provide the cup and explain that you're American. Alternatively, buy one or two half-liter plastic bottles of water, empty a couple of ounces to allow for expansion, and ask your hotel to put them in the freezer for you overnight. Stored in your cooler, they'll still give you some cold the next afternoon.

- Small light backpack, rain-resistant if possible, for day trips.
- Bottle of White-Out for marking glasses at beer festivals (it scrapes off).

Manners

Look up "please" and "thank you" in every language, and use them. Knowing "Excuse me" is often valuable beyond words.

In self-service establishments, carry your glasses back to the bar.

Stand to the right on escalators; walk on the left. On stairways, keep right, even in Great Britain.

Beer

Beer styles

There are numerous guides to beer that are far more comprehensive than any treatise we could give you here. If you're a novice, get one. Michael Jackson's *World Guide to Beer* is still the most welcoming and readable entry to the world of great beer. Most useful as a glimpse of the beer world when it stood on the cusp of the craft revolution, Jackson's *Guide* can give you the same overall understanding of national styles and beer cultures that countless beer writers and brewers have used as a foundation for their own paths to the 21st century. It's Eurocentric (an orientation that the Great Beer Hunter shied away from later), but for the purposes of this book, that's fine. Some of it is outdated; notably, much of it is not.

We've tried in our "beer culture" section of each chapter to describe iconic styles of the cities you're in, but here's our overview. It's far from definitive; read other writers for their takes as well.

Lagers are fermented at low temperatures and usually conditioned for many weeks—if you're lucky, many months—slowly developing a complex blended flavor like the soup on the back burner of your stove. Our metaphor is a classical string quartet: everyone plays together to create a smooth and gentle experience. Sometimes there's a complexity that only those who really understand what's going on will appreciate.

Ales are fermented at higher temperatures and their flavors act more like jazz bands. Different tastes take turns registering on your palate, and it's OK to applaud them as they go by. Some people find the music edgy; others relish its spontaneity, creativity, and brightness.

Some people who know beer well refer to wild and sour beers interchangeably, but we think there's a world of difference. **Wild beers** include the Lambics, Gueuzes, and Krieks of Belgium as well as farmhouse beers of southern Belgium and northern France. They range from mildly funky saisons to astringent and challenging aged gueuzes. At the mild end, a dry mustiness creates interest; at the other extreme are flavors of horse blanket, barn, and stale urine. Wild beers are an acquired taste. We were never sure why anyone would want to acquire it, yet over the years we've come to . . . appreciate their uniqueness. Lambic brewers range from stubbornly authentic blenders, whose beers even we have had to leave on the table, to those who add fruits, sugar, or artificial sweeteners to make them more accessible. Cantillon's beers are the best at combining integrity with drinkability; Frank Boon's beers, now part of the Palm mini-empire, have also walked the tightrope successfully.

Sour beers include Belgium's classic Rodenbach, a "Flemish Red Ale" fermented with a proprietary yeast (actually a mix of dozens of microbiological agents) and then aged in wood. Some of Rodenbach's single vat releases rank among the best beers ever brewed. Other brewers use a variety of woods and yeasts to produce this style. Some are very successful, such as De Dolle Brouwers; others less so. Sour ales usually evoke the taste of sour cherries, and a few even use cherries to enhance the effect. The result is an enormous range from saccharine sweet to way past "SweeTarts" pucker.

Beer tasters don't spit

But sometimes they dump. Seriously. You've just dropped $8.00 on a beer that is *intensely* unpleasant. Understand the power of the economic term "sunk cost." You paid the money; you can't get it back. Do you want to drink this unspeakable liquid or spend another $8.00 on something you'd like better? You paid thousands to get here; don't waste precious time and liver on a mistake.

Glass matters

It is amazing how much the shape of a glass can affect your experience of what's in it. Belgium and Germany go to apparently ridiculous extremes in the variety of glassware they consider absolutely standard requirements. But a huge generous Belgian sour red would taste like Kool-Aid out of a narrow little Kölsch glass. Note and appreciate the beauty and utility of your beer's presentation. On every trip, we tend to purchase two or three new glasses that we just can't live without. A request: if you encounter a glass you love at a bar, *please* offer to pay for it. If they won't sell it to you, they really need it. More often they'll sell it at cost or give it to you with a smile.

Brewery museums

We've included some of our favorite museums—and warned you away from our least favorite (see Rechenberg under Liepzig day trips)—but there are far more than this volume can include. If you like brewery museums, check the CAMRA guides and go online; they're not hard to find. Many breweries and often pubs are de facto museums. Take time to look at the walls, and sometimes the loos, for pictures and artifacts.

Brewery tours

Most breweries give tours. In the good old days we could walk into almost any brewery, tell them we loved beer, and get a walk-through on the spot, often from the head brewer. No more. You'll usually have to book in advance and hope to get lucky enough to get added to a group tour in English. The good news is that Web pages make that easy. Don't resent the sometimes significant ticket prices. Big brewers can write off the cost of running tours as advertising, but even they have to recoup their investment when they drop several million ducats into providing you sound and lights. The little guys are in business to sell beer—they don't have the margin to give it away or hire people to tell you why it's good.

Vocabulary

So you know what you're drinking:

English	German	French	Dutch	Czech	Italian
beer	Bier	bière	bier	pivo	birra
yeast	Hefe	levure	gist	kvasinky	lievito
malt	Malz	malt	mout	slad	malto
hops	Hopfen	houblon	hop	chmel	luppolo
barley	Gerste	orge	gerst	ječmen	orzo
wheat	Weizen	blé	tarwe	pšenice	frumento
rye	Roggen	siègle	rogge	žito	segale
oats	Hafer	avoine	haver	oves	avena

Diacetyl is a chemical normally produced in the brewing process that makes beer taste creamy, buttery, or even like butterscotch or intense caramel. In lagers, it's a disaster. In ales it can be tasty in moderation. Think of a brewery in Northern England that brews very fine ales with a distinctive "creamy smoothness." That's good diacetyl. Now think of the brewpub lager you had that tasted like stale popcorn butter. That's bad diacetyl. Same stuff, different beers.

Diacetyl usually disappears in lager beers as the beer conditions. Heavy diacetyl in lagers usually means they've been rushed to market. Again, because ales spend much less time aging, diacetyl can remain in even good ones, but the flavors blend better with the more aggressive and estery flavors that characterize ales.

Skunk. When light hits hops, a chemical reaction results in the development of sulfur compounds that make the beer taste like you've just run over a skunk. Clear bottles often offer almost no resistance to skunking, and green bottles aren't much better. Many of the European beers you're used to seeing in green bottles are packaged in brown bottles in Europe: local drinkers care more about the flavor than the packaging. Pilsner Urquell now exports to the U.S. in brown glass; good for them. Today some clear glass supposedly has a light filter that prevents skunking. Right.

Strength. In a few states in the U.S., alcohol is measured as a percentage of the *weight* of the liquid. Most craft brewers—and all the rest of the world—measure alcohol as a percentage of the *volume* of the liquid (alcohol by volume, or ABV). A beer that's 4% alcohol by weight is 5% ABV.

Two other measurements indicate the alcoholic strength fairly reliably. British beers often give an "original gravity," a measure of how much *could* be fermented. It's easy to convert: 1.050 OG refers to a beer of about 5% ABV. Czech beers and some others indicate alcohol using the Balling scale. ("Brix" and "Plato" are slight improvements on Balling's original system.) A rough but functional conversion is to multiply the number by 4 and pop in the decimal. So Pilsner Urquel's 12° calculates out to 4.8% ABV, which is pretty close to right.

Country overviews

We're including a few general bits of advice for these two countries because so many of our cities lie within them. We've put overall advice for other countries in the city chapters.

The United Kingdom

Oscar Wilde observed that British and Americans share almost everything except language. That very much holds true in discussing beer. "Beer" in England means the top-fermented malt beverage that Americans refer to as "ale." "Lager" is what Brits call the bottom-fermented drink that Americans casually term "beer."

But it gets more complicated than that. Word wars have been a part of the English brewing scene for centuries, but today's "cask" versus "craft" brings semantic hostility to a new level. CAMRA (see below) may be the most valuable and successful consumer movement in history, but today it's struggling with the language that defines its identity.

"Real ale" or "cask ale" is beer that breweries put into metal, plastic, or less commonly wooden casks—often with added hops for extra aroma and flavor—where it essentially referments. It is positively, absolutely, *never* pressurized with carbon dioxide, other than what naturally occurs in fermenting and storage. The definition of "real ale" has, in fact, had more to do with dispense than brewing. Cellaring cask ale is a true art.

"Craft beer" in the UK today means whatever the brewery that's making it wants it to mean. But everyone knows that UK Coors is not a "craft" brewery. BrewDog is, and you'll probably never find a BrewDog on cask. Brewers don't have to choose one or the other: Williams Brothers excels at brewing both craft and "real" cask, and Thornbridge, for years a cask brewery, has begun brewing "gassy" CO_2 beers to add to its cask portfolio.

A great deal of all of the controversy is purist puffery. Don't limit your search for good beers by the labels anyone wants to put on them. We'll point you to very good beers, both cask and craft.

CAMRA

You have a choice of an almost uncountable number of good beers in Great Britain in part because of the Campaign for Real Ale, or CAMRA. In 1971, four British lads, faced with the usual slim pickings in an Irish pub, resolved to push pubs throughout the British Isles to offer a better choice of beer. As the campaign evolved, it focused on preserving and resurrecting the traditional cask-conditioned ales. Such "real ales," as CAMRA called them, were fast disappearing in favor of less flavorful, but more stable, CO_2-pressurized keg beers. But CAMRA's concerted pressure forced pubs to change course, and in your journeys you may never encounter a troglodyte of a pub that doesn't serve beer from cask. CAMRA has become one of the most successful consumer movements in history, with nearly 170,000 members as we go to press. While it has continued to focus as much on the way beer is served as the way beer is brewed, it unquestionably made thousands of beer drinkers thoughtful enough of what they were drinking to seek out better beers and pubs with more choices.

We understand why CAMRA traditionalists are so wary of deeming pressurized and filtered beer "quality"—we were there in the 1970s when most keg beer was indeed crap. Still, we're saddened that CAMRA has chosen to sit on the sidelines of such an important part of the craft beer revolution it helped to create. Sooner or later, we think it will have to become more inclusive if it intends to remain relevant. Nevertheless, we're proud to have been members for 35 years; CAMRA's people and publications have led us to more beer adventures than we could relate in a dozen books.

Manners: pubs and elsewhere

You'll usually order food at the bar in a British pub. If you see a number on your table, remember it for when you order. A modest tip is often expected in places where servers deliver the food to you, a bit more if the staff takes your order at the table.

Ask for a taste of a new beer if you wish, but only if you're going to buy a pint of something thereafter. Buying a half pint used to be unmanly, but it's no problem now in bars that feature a wide range of beers.

Children are not always welcome in pubs; the Brits regard the right to an off-color joke with their beer a fundamental part of freedom of speech, and they don't want to have to worry about corrupting your kids or offending protective parents. Pubs that welcome children often say so, displaying a Children's Certificate. The "family" facilities can range from a separate room with toys to a remote corner of the back garden. The best idea is to ask, and if you're going a long way to visit a particular pub, call in advance to see if they'll let you drink your Youngs with a youngster in tow.

A few other suggestions:

- The British queue for almost everything—especially buses. If you hop on a bus without looking for the line, you run the risk of getting an umbrella across the earhole.
- You don't have to learn a new word for "please," so use it, and use it more often than you think you need to.

Language, beyond "ale" and "beer"

It's pretty easy to figure out most of the words that are different in American and British English; here are a few that might make travel easier for you.

- A beer mat is a coaster (to put a beer glass on).
- A biscuit is a cookie—especially important when a malt is described as "biscuity."
- A chemist's shop is a pharmacy.
- Crisps are potato chips; chips are fries.
- A lift is an elevator.
- A rubber can sometimes mean an eraser.
- A torch is usually a flashlight.
- The first floor is the second floor. The ground floor is the first.

- When you're on holiday (not vacation), you'll always ask for the bill (not the check) and go to the cinema (not the movies).
- A serviette is a napkin. Gentlemen, you will not be in need of a "napkin" in England, though infants of either gender will need their nappies changed periodically.

Germany

Germany, like the United States, is a federal republic, and its states retain a measure of sovereign power. Germans also identify with their states at least as closely as Americans do. As a result, a trip to Germany can feel like a trip to several countries, and generalizations should be taken with a grain of salt.

Most beer lovers know of the German purity law, the 1516 Reinheitsgebot that limited beer ingredients to malt, hops, and water. Yeast joined the list later when brewers figured out how God was being so good to them. There were always exceptions to the Reinheitsgebot to allow for local traditions such as Gose beers. More recently, the European Union struck the whole thing down as a restriction on trade. Most German brewers continue to abide by it, however, and you'll see the logo on their labels.

While some German brewers, especially newer ones, have taken advantage of the new brewing freedom to produce adventurous beers, Germany has been slow to join the world beer revolution. It's on its way, but still in an embryonic state. Beer specialty bars in Munich, Berlin, and Hamburg are the bow wave of a more varied future, but most of our favorite places to drink in Germany offer a narrow range of very good local beers. Frankly, on a long European trip through the brewing playgrounds of Belgium, Italy, and Scandinavia, we often welcome a lager-centric break where we can drink more and think less before we go back to the quest for the cutting edge.

Oktober and other fests

If you can, go to Oktoberfest once; then you'll know whether you ever want to go again. We slightly prefer its rival, the larger-in-area Cannstadter Volksfest in Stuttgart—it's easy to do both in a week's trip; Oktoberfest starts slightly earlier—but for glitz and show, there is nothing like the Münchener Oktoberfest.

Oktoberfest began as a wedding celebration in 1820. The main feature was a horse race (horses were scarce after the Napoleonic wars), but enterprising brewers quickly capitalized on the thirst of the crowds. Rides and attractions followed, though the big beer tents didn't start to rise until the end of the century. Today Oktoberfest sells more beer, and chickens, than any event of similar length in the history of the world. The amusement rides are more extensive than Disneyland's. The atmosphere is one gigantic party.

But it's a challenge too. Hotel rooms have to be booked well in advance. The festival itself is free, but if your concierge can help you get table reservations, let him. At night, the nearly 100,000 seats in the tents can be 100% filled. If you go during the day, the music is not as frequent, the crowds are not as exciting, but there are seats—on a hot day, plenty of them indoors—and you can move from tent to tent trying different beers ... by the liter. Even in the evening, if you are alone or with one other person and look plaintive enough, some table of ten will squeeze together for you and make it a table for twelve. But it takes a good deal of both patience and faith.

An alternative, especially if you can't arrange to be free in late September when Oktoberfest occurs, is to find a Volksfest in another city. Check at tourist offices and online, and keep your eyes peeled for the ubiquitous posters that advertise circuses, concerts, and other events. There are a few beer fests in Germany on almost every weekend from early spring to late fall. The Christmas season has its own Weihnachtsfests.

We rate fests by the number of beer tents they feature. A "one-tent fest" is typical of a small town and features the beer of one brewery; a good-sized city like Nuremberg or Straubing might have a four-tent fest; depending on how you count, Oktoberfest is at least a twelve-tent fest. Rarely, two or more breweries will share a tent, but usually it's one brewery per tent. Festbiers always come by the liter, but you can get half liters of Hefeweizen. It's hard to find out the number of tents in advance, but the length of a local festival gives a clue of its size. If it runs longer than a week, it will have many more rides, a wider selection of foods, and more tents (and beers) than a fest that just runs on one weekend.

It's often possible to find a room in a small town when it's having its fest, though booking in advance is advisable. The fest tends to attract locals from a 20-mile radius or more who come for the day in chartered buses. Fest-hunting tourists are rare, and that's why we prefer these local and regional fests to Oktoberfest. At Oktoberfest you'll hear as much Japanese and Amurrikan as you do German—and most of those speaking German are out-of-town tourists as well. But be warned, the first day of any fest can be absolutely jammed; get there very early and be prepared to sit at a marginal table. On midweek mid-festival days, on the other hand, prime tables in front of the bandstand go begging.

Another kind of beer event, more recently, is the "Bier Borse." Organized by the same company, they occur in numerous German cities from spring to late fall. The best we've experienced is Bonn's, which includes one of the best firework displays we've ever seen, but if you're in Germany for more than a few weekdays you can probably find a Borse somewhere. A range of breweries set up specially designed draft carts and wagons on a field or a city street, and you can range among them sampling their wares for a price. The greatest of all of this type of fest is the Berliner "Bier Meile"—see our Berlin chapter for more details.

An increasing number of cities are jumping on the craft beer wagon and hosting worthwhile beer experiences. See the Antwerp chapter for a good one; you'll find others if you look.

Further information

An explosion of books on beer provides you with a great deal of information that we don't have space to include. Some of the most comprehensive can put a dent in your travel budget. The ones below are good value as well as good reads.

CAMRA Guides. If you're just going to one country—the UK, Czech, Germany, or Belgium—order the CAMRA guide and deal with the weight. We've picked our favorite pubs for this guide; the CAMRA guides let you know nearly *every* good possibility. If your time in Europe is short the payoff may not be worth the heft, but they make good planning reading at home. They're too beautiful to cut up, so we photocopy the pages that relate to specific cities we intend to visit.

- The UK: CAMRA's flagship publication, the *Good Beer Guide*, covers every part of the British Isles with up-to-date listings of cask ale pubs and information about the brewers who make them. Editor Roger Protz is currently the best known of the CAMRA stable of fine writers; for something that approaches a telephone book, it's very readable. Its only flaw is that as a CAMRA publication it gives you few clues where to find the rapidly increasing numbers of high quality craft *draft* (as opposd to cask) beers.
- Czech: Witty, knowledgeable, and clear, Evan Rail combines an understanding of beer that rivals the late Michael Jackson's with some of the best travel advice in print. If he had written a guide to all of Europe, we wouldn't have needed to write this one.
- Tim Webb's definitive guide to Belgium is essential when you're there for any length of time, and compelling armchair reading at home. He draws on his own extensive experience, but also coordinates a legion of beer travelers to keep it up to date and inclusive. Includes brewery tours and museums and some information about hotels.
- Steve Thomas's *Good Beer Guide to Germany* is a labor of love and the best complete guide to German brewing in any language. It lists every brewery, almost every brewery tap, and a good many fine pubs, gardens, and beer halls. He's never fully updated it and it's showing its age a bit, but he has a supplement available and he keeps information up to date online at germanbeers.com. The German brewing scene changes slower than that of most other countries in this guide. A seven-year-old guide to Italian breweries would be almost useless; Thomas's German guide still serves as a superb overview of the German brewing scene.

Outside of the CAMRA range, Ron Pattinson has emerged as one of the world's authorities on the history of beer and brewing, collaborating and consulting on pioneering brewing projects in Europe and the United States. His travel guides have the feel of a personal guide and are among the most detailed available—online and in print at http://www.lulu.com/spotlight/andrewsblag; his blog is at http://barclayperkins.blogspot.com/. The thoroughness of his guides is a great strength, but also a limitation; few of his listings can be done in a day or two if you don't have his constitution. However, if you're making an extended visit to any of our towns, his publications are well worth the investment.

Amberg

Quick orientation

You can visit Amberg's breweries in a day, but we strongly recommend you take at least two. Add in an extra day trip or two and you won't be sorry you booked three or four nights.

From the air, the center city's walls and moats roughly form the shape of a football on its side, with the Vils River running north-south down the middle. The railroad station is on the right (east) point. Cross the street in front of the station and proceed straight downhill on Bahnhofstrasse to reach the historical center in the middle of the football. Bahnhofstrasse feeds into Marktplatz near the Rathaus (town hall). From the Marktplatz, Georgenstrasse runs on past the old Gothic Rathaus to the opposite, western end of the football. Most of the breweries are either on Bahnhofstrasse or not far from it on the left (south) as you head through the town, though Bruckmüller is past the center and to the north. You can find hotels near the station, but we prefer to stay closer to the center.

Rathaus Amberg

Station breaks

The Yarma at the station serves a couple of the local Winkler beers on draft (Hell and Dunkel) and another from Regensburg's Bischofshof/Weltenburg. It has a small but adequate bottle selection that is mostly Bischofshof and major breweries. The place has its resident drunks, but it's clean and well managed and friendly enough. If you have the full 10 minutes to walk, however, leave the station and walk into town on Bahnhofstrasse (which in Amberg is perpendicular to the Bahnhof) and on your left just before the central church is the Schloderer brewery and Gasthof, our #4 choice below.

History and culture

It's hard to picture Bavaria without thinking of small towns. Munich is the largest small town in the world, and medium-sized burgs like Regensburg and Passau provide some of the most gemütlich experiences in Germany. But for a true small-town experience you have to go to a village like Amberg. There are hundreds if not thousands of them left in pretty good shape, but Amberg has the additional attraction of at least four functioning breweries in the town and more very close by. Once many towns of its size could have shared the same claim, but Amberg is now very nearly unique.

Amberg has been tied to the state of Bavaria since the Middle Ages. Its food and culture are similar to those of Nuremburg, Bamberg, and even Munich. Unlike most of Bavaria, however, it was a part of the territory of a minor line of Wittelsbachs who sided with the Lutherans in the religious wars that tore Germany apart in the 16th century. The Peace of Augsburg of 1555 stipulated that each of hundreds of princes choose the religion for his domain; Amberg became Protestant. During the 17th century, the stubbornly Lutheran Ambergers successfully resisted an attempt to impose Calvinism, but when the area passed to the major Wittelsbachs the locals had a choice of converting to Catholicism or leaving. Many of the city's residents fled rather than switch religions.

Amberg's past still lives beyond the buildings. A city that won't accept a religion at the point of a gun probably isn't going to accept a Bitburger beer because of a price point. German towns with well-preserved historical sections seem to hold local pride a bit closer to their hearts—and that includes supporting local breweries. Amberg has maintained its small-town character despite the influx of huge numbers of not-always-sober American soldiers from nearby bases who swell the bars on weekend evenings. Somehow, however, even those soldiers have seemed a bit more restrained and a good deal more friendly than GIs we've run into in other German cities. We think Amberg's small-town values and atmosphere shape their behavior.

Today Amberg blends old and new fairly successfully. The city walls are mostly intact, and the entire medieval city perimeter is bounded by beautiful flower gardens and traces of old moats. You're never in doubt whether you're in or outside of the old city. Much of the inner city is nicely preserved or restored with a lovely old feel. The whole town can be walked easily and quickly—even in the rain you can easily get to where you want to go. It's obviously Germany, but it's as easy to navigate as Busch Gardens. Small shop owners take the time to deal with you as an individual.

A visit to Amberg seems to belong to earlier times—not just the Middle Ages, which isn't so hard to find in Germany, but the 1960s and '70s, when Germany still held onto so much tradition in the midst of its remarkable capitalist success. Small towns still supported multiple breweries, and the big guys couldn't get a foot in the door. Salads were pickled cabbage, pickled carrots, and pickled cucumbers rather than fancy greens, and when you ordered a schnitzel, you'd hear the pounding in the kitchen a few minutes later. In Amberg, you still do.

Beer styles and drinking culture

There is no particular specialty here, but Amberg's breweries produce the full range of Bavarian beer styles. Expect to find a half dozen or more styles on most menus. Beer halls tend to be a bit more intimate than in larger towns, and while you'll run into regular patrons, they don't seem to be quite as clubby as in similar places we've visited in other cities. We may have those fairly well-behaved GIs to thank for making Gasthausen a bit more American-friendly.

In the 1980s, Amberg had 10 breweries and rivaled Bamberg as a German brewing capital. Even now, Amberg still has four healthy breweries, and its past lives on in three of the deceased companies that continue to have their own beers contracted in Amberg. You end up tasting at least seven distinctive brewing ranges. Easy day trips yield more brewery visits with little effort. And while it appears that some of Bamberg's breweries are surviving on tourist dollars (God bless those tourists), the Amberg breweries depend mostly on locals.

It's a very small town, but don't rush your visit; we made that mistake decades ago and left unimpressed. Take time to savor the small town atmosphere. Visit the St. Martin church and think about the drama of the centuries of conflict between Protestants and Catholics, and even among Protestants themselves. Visit the small shops—there's just enough English spoken to make it easy. You might be in Ephrata, Pennsylvania, except you're not—this city has been here for nearly a thousand years.

The sixpack of drinking experiences

Kummert Bräu is outside the center city and up a hill. But this is Amberg, not Bamberg, and the walk is not a hard one. You're rewarded with the widest range of beers in the city. We found ten different beers on our last visit; most are average for Germany, which is to say quite good, but the Kummert 27er Urtyp is one of Germany's best Keller Biers. It's a soft-spoken Keller Bier with sweet restrained hops, clean, very pale malt, and a dry, yeasty taste for extra interest. We don't believe this beer travels well at all, so if you've had it in a bottle elsewhere, don't prejudge it. A nice garden provides a fine place to settle in to try these beers and enjoy an above-average brewery Gasthof meal.

Kummert Bräu's garden

The **Bruckmüller** Gasthof is relatively near the city walls at Vilsstrasse 2, though it's only a few minutes walk from the central church. From Georgenstrasse, take Hafnergässchen or any of the small streets that lead to the theater. The Gasthof is next to the brewery just behind the theater. It all used to be a monastery and the Bruckmüller beers still refer to their Franciscan heritage.

The Gasthof is special in part because it is so typical. Lots of wood, four rooms that together can hold a couple of hundred people, plus a courtyard garden for 300 in good weather. One of the rooms is a "winter garden" that's a glassed-in area abutting the garden. The Americans who make their way here are interested in good food and beer and are welcomed by the sympathetic staff, who will welcome you too.

Food is down-home and exceptionally good. Fish tastes fresh; ribs come in a gargantuan mound (that is a bit less daunting than it looks because they're not all that meaty) and are tasty and ridiculously abundant. Pair them with a self-serve buffet of fresh and very German salads. A nice range of nine Bruckmüller/Falk beers, most of them on tap, includes the Bruckmüller Keller Bier. Bottled bock is available when the draft is not.

When we first visited Amberg in the 1970s it had pretty close to the ten operating breweries that were probably its peak in modern times. But daggoned if we could find them. It was really hard in the pre-Internet, pre-Steve Thomas era to find breweries even if you knew they were there. Also in the '70s, almost every Gasthaus in Germany took a 2- to 4-week "Urlaub"—summer vacations which could make it impossible to sample more than one or two breweries even from a town like Amberg at any given time. On our first stop, an old man in the square took pity and directed us, laboriously, to Brauerei Hans Falk. It was open and had a nice range of beers. The wonderful people made it more likely that we would return to Amberg, earning a place in our hearts and a coaster among the few we display in our house. We mourned Falk's demise in 1976.

Bruckmüller is now brewing and marketing Weizen Falk beer. We're pretty sure the old recipes are gone, but the Falk range is decidedly different from Bruckmüller's. Kristall Weizens aren't common any more, and usually aren't very good. Bruckmüller can blame theirs on Falk. But much more interesting was an unusual bottom-fermented Dunkel Weizen. The lemon and crispness of the wheat malt showed, but the lager yeast softened the whole experience. The aroma was subtle to the point of being weak, but it drank really well. We figure Bruckmüller uses the Falk brand to take some risks. Good for them all.

Brauerei Winkler (Schänzgasschen 6): Going down Bahnhofstrasse from the station, take the second left on Obere Nabburgerstrasse for a block to the Winkler Gasthof. Winkler is a tiny brewery by modern standards, no larger than a small American production craft brewery. Their beers are a bit sweet for our taste, but quite professional and well above average in a full German context. The range of beers was exceptional, including a range of lagers and Weizens and a really interesting commercial Zoigl.

Schloderer Bräu is at Bahnhofstrasse 4, a short walk from any hotel—or from the Bahnhof if you're silly enough to try to do Amberg as a day trip from Nuremberg. It opens at 7:30 AM on weekdays and there's a very pleasant courtyard if it's not pouring rain; much if it is sheltered even if it is. It's the closest thing to a tourist brewery you can find in Amberg and even includes a museum-worthy large motif of the brewing process above your head as you leave. The beers are dry and yeasty, not stunningly memorable, but quite competent and professional and better than you'd need to linger a bit in this brewpub that celebrates beer so enthusiastically.

After you visit Winkler (#3 above), mosey down the hill to Untere Nabburgerstrasse 8 to **Schiessl Wirtshaus**, one of Amberg's living ghosts. The brewery closed in the 1990s, but Winkler continues to brew Schiessl beers and you'll have no doubt about their integrity if you've just tasted Winkler's up the street. The two Helleses share a sweet tooth, but the differences in the two Zoigls are striking. The Gasthof is quite spiffy; you'll find nice people and good food.

Maybe we're just fond of **Kate's Irish Pub** (in the Hotel zur Gold'nen Krone, Waisenhausgasse 2) because it has so much better beer than most of the hotel bars we encounter. Don't be too put off by the "Irish Bar" motif. Irish bars have become part of the local drinking scene from Washington, DC, to Zurich, Switzerland, and they seem to take on at least a bit of the local culture. Kate's is less "Irish" than most. The staff is friendly and the beer garden is wood-benched, intimate, and enchanting. In poorer weather the bar area is a fine escape, and Kate has Bruckmüller Keller Bier on tap along with the Guinness.

Other places to explore

We've never been bored drinking in the atmosphere of Amberg's in-town brewery outlets, but if you are, there's a brewpub on the outskirts. If you turn left as you leave the Bahnhof and walk along the path of the city wall, you'll reach Jahnstrasse. A long hike out of town on Jahnstrasse will take you near the Hausbrauerei am Südhang (Am Südhang 7). Call for hours before you schlep all the way out there.

Where to stay

There are a couple of hotels right near the station and they'll do, but we like the **Hotel zur Gold'nen Krone**. Head down Bahnhofstrasse until you're near the main church, then follow the signs left for Kate's Irish Pub, which is in the hotel's ground floor. It's no Hilton, the rooms are simple, but you could do much worse. It's centrally located, the breakfast is quite adequate, the staff is cheerful and helpful, and the Internet is free. The price will allow you to splurge later in your trip.

What to see

Amberg is justifiably proud of its "town spectacles," twin stone bridges that arch over the Vils River whose reflections form a pair of perfect circles. Spend at least a little time following the well-preserved town walls and admiring the gardens that beautify much of the circuit. The Basilika St. Martin in the center of town is a magnificent

15th century Gothic beauty with striking 19th century stained glass windows and some historic bells. If you want to spend more time touring the town, there's plenty to see; get suggestions from the tourist office at Hallplatz 2.

Scams

Of course not.

Further information

The hour-long train trip from Nuremberg on the regional (RE3571) is almost an amusement park ride. It winds up valleys through the hills and rocks back down again. Bring along a Franconian beer if you want—no one objects to beer drinking on German trains.

Day trip

Sulzbach-Rosenberg

A little investigation can produce myriad options to visit neighboring towns and breweries. For convenience, history, and a fine pair of breweries, our top choice is Sulzbach-Rosenberg.

Sulzbach-Rosenberg is barely 10 minutes by rail from Amberg on the way to Nuremberg and gives you two more breweries and more than a millennium of history to ponder as you enjoy them. The town has done a particularly good job of identifying and publicizing its past. If you have the time, you can get a walking guide from the tourist office on Luitpoldplatz 25. Be advised that the office keeps small-town hours: weekday mornings and occasional afternoons. If you arrive outside those hours, though, you can download a PDF version of the city guide from the tourist office's website. Even our brief brewtour will give you a sense of the past as you wander through this 1,200-year-old town. Be prepared for some hilly streets, but you'll be well fortified along the way.

Rich soil and richer iron deposits propelled Sulzbach into prominence by the early Middle Ages. The modern but now abandoned iron works form a striking contrast to the medieval and baroque architecture of the old town. A branch of the Bavarian Wittelsbachs took over in the 14th century and made Su-Ro a truly royal city. Armed with a map from the tourist office (or on your smartphone) you can follow the "mining path" that will show you the rise and demise of the iron and steel industry in the town. Take time to track down the Royal Chapel, or Burgkapelle, parts of which date from around the first millennium. Enough of the original is preserved after restoration to qualify it as one of Germany's oldest church buildings.

Uniquely among the towns of the Holy Roman Empire we've visited, Sulzbach developed a spirit of tolerance that rivaled that of the Dutch. After the religious wars of the 15th and 16th centuries, each of the hundreds of rulers within the Holy Roman Empire chose a single religion for his territory. Choices were Catholicism and

Lutheranism, and eventually Calvinism. According to the town history, the appropriately named Christian August (1622–1708) believed the squabbling Christian branches would eventually unite and in 1652 created the "Simultaneum," an arrangement by which Catholics and Protestants shared churches and public buildings. Even Jews received some protection from the government, and although the Simultaneum was officially canceled in 1957, the town still celebrates its tolerant past.

The castle complex was one of Bavaria's first, and enough of the original foundation walls have survived 17th century renovation to justify your visit. The walking tour map will take you to the city museum and numerous churches and schools.

Brew tour

The railway station has a posted map; take a picture of it with your smartphone and follow the directions below. Also take a picture of the "Abfahrts" (departures) chart; trains out of town are sporadic enough to warrant planning.

With your back to the station, walk along Bahnhofstrasse until it bends right and becomes Neumarkter Strasse. A bit of a jink where it meets Brauhausgasse (alas, no Brauhaus here now) puts you on Bergstrasse, which takes you to the center of town and Luitpoldplatz. The tourist office is a few hundred feet to the right; go there before they close. Otherwise turn left for a couple hundred meters and then right on Hagtor to, a cannonball's arch from the castle, **Fuchsbeck.** The brewery is officially Orth-Bräu, but unless you're the tax collector, it's Zum Fuchsbeck.

When we were there last, the Fuchsbeck beers were among the best in the region. New ownership since our last visit has apparently kept the place in good shape, though we can't guarantee that the beers are identical to those we sampled. Echoes of sweet peas and flowery hops made the Vollbier Helles deliciously distinctive, and the pils also allowed honeyish hops to show. We had never before encountered a low alcohol (2.8% ABV) dark Hefeweizen, and while we wouldn't return to the city for a second half liter, it was a generally successful attempt at a very unusual style. The full strength Weizens were well above average with a nice mix of lemony wheat and clovey esters.

The menu is limited, though the bratwursts are tasty. The brewery dates from the early 18th century. Renovations give it a modern feel, while an arching ceiling pattern recalls a bit of the past. It's a clean and comfortable place to work your way through at least a half dozen beers.

Once you have done so, retrace your steps to the tourist office on Luitpoldplatz and bend right to turn into Rosenberger Strasse. As you pass Frühlingstrasse, keep an eye out for the medieval Weissbeckhaus; nearby at number 14 is **Sperber-Bräu,** the spiffier, if perhaps slightly less atmospheric, of the town's two breweries. Christian Sperber turns out a range of beers that runs from quite respectable to simply marvelous. In high summer, you might run into his Annaberg-Festbier, an unusually complex beer for festing. The Pils is fine, but an exceptionally tasty yeast makes the keller version (Zoiglbier) superb. A Dunkel Zoigl marries hints of maple and chocolate but allows some hops to come through. The Leichte Weisse is one of the best session beers anywhere—full of flavor of clove and a creamy lemon-wheat. The Germans still somehow have a unique knack of crafting light Hefeweizens. We've never had one in the U.S. that could touch the best of them, and Sperber's is one of those best.

In good weather the front terrace is a fine place to enjoy the beers. Sperber's menu is much more extensive than Fuchsbeck's, so save this stop for dinner. If you want to make Sulzbach an excursion, you can stay at Sperber for 80€ in a spiffy modern double that includes a breakfast buffet that can make lunch unnecessary.

Sperber offerings in Sulzbach-Rosenberg

Amsterdam

Quick orientation

As you exit the Central Station, you'll find yourself in the midst of a tram yard. Getting around Amsterdam can take a bit of effort, but a tram map helps; get one at the crowded tourist office just in front of the station. To get into the older part of town, walk perpendicular from the station across the tram tracks, the canal, and the road. From there you can wander along the maze of canals. If you keep going straight away from the station, you'll find yourself at the Dam, the center of hippie culture. The Dam is tame compared to a couple of decades ago, but still fills with street performers and hordes of people.

Amsterdam is about as safe as any other large European city, but it has some distinctive wrinkles. Read our "scam" section before you take it on.

Station break

Grand Café 1e Klas is on the second floor of the central station on platform 2b. The beer list is pretty tame, but the location is right on one of the rail platforms, and you can sit outside in shelter and watch the trains come and go. The inside area is classic European rail station: big, brassy, woody, and hot when the weather is. The food is well above average for train station fare.

In front of the station and across the canal is **Karpenhoek,** the oldest bar in Amsterdam (1606). Nice sidewalk seating area. The inside features ancient dark woods and sanded floor—truly Dutch charm at its best. The beer isn't special, but as a place to pass the time waiting for a train, it's hard to beat.

History and culture

Dutch has just enough cognates to let you think you can understand some of it. Sometimes, as in Amsterdam's name, you can: it started in the 12th century as a collection of fishermen's huts around a dam in the Amstel River. By the late 16th century Amsterdam was taking its place among the major trading cities of the world. During this "Golden Age" the city expanded rapidly; its 14 kilometers of canals were originally intended to drain the surrounding land, but quickly found commercial purposes that continue today.

Amsterdam was the keystone of a Dutch world empire in an age when initiative mattered more than size. Too few to populate other areas of the world, the Dutch established a trading empire that brought them wealth—and some of the best food on the European continent. The influx of foreigners added to the prosperity of the city, and the Dutch learned early that tolerance was good business. They've had their lapses from time to time, but Amsterdam remains one of the most accepting places on earth.

The party ended when the Netherlands was double-teamed in the 1672 "Dutch War"—one of the few instances of British-French cooperation until the 20th century. Nevertheless, Amsterdam recovered well until the pesky French returned in 1795 and Napoleon did a more thorough job of destruction. Long after the French left, empty and decaying buildings reflected an economic downturn that lasted the better part of a century. The city reasserted itself as a financial center, however, and its economy soared during the second industrial revolution of the 19th century.

Somehow, the Netherlands managed to stay out of the First World War, but wasn't so lucky in the second. Resistance to Nazi occupation was primarily nonviolent and at times subtle, including placing the stamp on letters in the left corner (reserving the right corner for the Queen), wearing orange carnations to support the Dutch House of Orange, and boycotting German movies. Some Dutch, including Dutch Communists, were more heroic, hiding Jews and other Nazi targets.

Emerging from the war with a heightened reputation, the Communist Party almost doubled its prewar strength in the Netherlands before fading due to heavy-handed Soviet policies and a billion dollars of U.S. Marshall Plan aid. In 1951 the Netherlands solidified its place in the European economy by joining five other nations in the European Coal and Steel Community, the precursor to today's European Union. Amsterdam resumed its place as a major financial center and, more relevantly to this book, Heineken emerged as one of the world's fastest growing breweries.

Heineken and Amstel completely dominated the post-war Amsterdam beer scene; on our first trip there in 1968, we found absolutely no beer choice. Dutch commercial ties to the rest of the world, however, ensured that the craft beer revolution would find its way to Amsterdam, and today it's a first class beer destination.

Beer styles and drinking culture

"Amsterdam has never been a good city for brewing," our bartender told us, "but it has always been a good city for beer." Amsterdam was the port where brewers upstream on the Rhine transferred their beer from river boats onto larger craft that could carry it to the rest of Europe. So Amsterdamers didn't have to make great beer—they got their pick of the other guys' great beer. (That's very appealing to us, after all.) It's still true today, although shipping patterns have changed. There's a trio of well-respected, Belgian-oriented brew pubs, but the real focus of beer interest in Amsterdam is in the specialist beer bars, including one of Europe's best. It's a wonderful city to be in—worth far more than the two or three days we assume you're giving it.

Try to make time to take Amsterdam on its own terms. Picture yourself as one of the earliest of Europe's powerful capitalists, constructing a fine two-level entrance to your canal-side house. Catch a boat tour and lose yourself in a fantasy of living on one of the houseboats that line the canals. Sit in the Dam and imagine when the place was so filled with hippies that you could hardly breathe without getting high. Then go have a beer from one of the more than three dozen Dutch breweries that have sprung up in what was once a wasteland of unending pale pilsner... and know that just maybe you're there at the best time of all.

The sixpack of drinking experiences

'T Arendsnest. The best places for beer drinking in Amsterdam are the beer bars, because Amsterdam is still a better beer city than a brewing city. A few of the pioneering locals of the 1970s have gone, but others have sprung up to take their place. Amsterdam had already "discovered" Belgian brewing when we were here decades ago and has gone on from there. Now, it has discovered American beers; Flying Dog and Rogue are pretty easy to find if you know where to look. A bar has even opened up with only American beers on draft, most of them very respectable craft brews. But if you're that homesick, go eat at McDonalds and save your drinking time for the Dutch.

If you're not going to go to Brussels, Antwerp, Bruges, or Ghent, then by all means find one of Amsterdam's good Belgian bars and sample some great Belgian beers. But if you live in any population center of the U.S., or have access to a good UK beer-by-mail outlet, save your time and go directly to the signature beer bar for Dutch beers, Proeflokaal 't Arendsnest.

The "Eagle's Nest" tries to carry at least one beer from every brewery in the Netherlands, and it carries only Dutch beers. Its 30 taps rotate frequently, so if by any remote chance you exhaust them on one visit, you can circle back a few days later and find new choices. A huge bottle selection augments the taps. If you're very nice they might, with some reluctance, sell you a bottle or two to go, but you'd be better off provisioning yourself at Bierkoning instead (see #2). The staff is knowledgeable and gracious, and you can either drink inside and gawk at the remarkable collection of beer memorabilia, or sit outside at one of a handful of tables directly on the canal.

Though the beers rotate, you should be able to try the excellent house beer, De Snaterende Arend. Its caramel malt strives to support massive hops that show grapefruit and bitter orange before a long herbal aftertaste.

It's an easy walk to 't Arendsnest from the Central Station if it's not raining. Walk away from the station, cross the water, turn right on Prins Hendrikkade, turn left on Singel, and enjoy a canal-side stroll until you get to Herenstraat. Turn right across the bridge, then cross one more canal after that and look left as you do. It's at Herengracht 90, on the canal just below Herenstraat.

Amsterdam has some first class bottle shops. DePrael (see #4 below) is a good start, but don't miss the dazzling range at **De Bierkoning** (Paleisstraat 125). Pick up some brews you've never heard of; a canal bank or a city park becomes one of the world's best beer bars with a bag from Bierkoning. It advertises over 900 bottles, but we think it had about 1,200 when we were there. Or maybe the 1,200 referred to the number of beer glasses for sale. Or maybe it was the number of minutes it took us to make up our minds about what to bring back to the hotel for an evening's tasting session.

***Some* of the selection at De Bierkoning**

We opted to taste the full range of beers from a brewery we had never heard of. We could have as easily filled the evening with a single style. Happily, their plastic shopping bags are strong. We had splurged on a particularly expensive hotel that had ice machines, and while we don't recommend icing Dutch beers, having them cooled is nice. We tuned in our favorite Internet radio music show and had a lovely night of it. We were sharing the hotel with a Tommy Hilfinger convention, and we were certain of two things. First, we definitely didn't look like the other guests, and second, we definitely were having more fun.

Every certified beer geek who visits Amsterdam makes a pilgrimage to **In de Wildeman** (Kolksteeg 3). Located in an old distillery, it's an old narrow bar on an old narrow street and it's atmospheric down to every board and every beer. The feel reminds us of Brussels's Morte Subite, but smaller and without the hordes of tourists. Eighteen taps and over a hundred bottles ensure a great drinking experience. You'll find beers you don't see elsewhere, but it's the bar itself that will bring you back time after time.

Numbers 4, 5, and 6 are the three brewpubs of Amsterdam. If you're short of time you don't really have to do all three, but it isn't hard to do all of them in an afternoon. They're different enough from each other to be interesting and give different glimpses of what Amsterdam is and was.

Our favorite brewpub for a number of reasons, including some that have little to do with beer, is **DePrael** (Oudezijds Armsteeg 26), an easy enough walk from the city center. Visit during the day to catch the tours that normally run from 10 to 2, but you can visit the beer shop anytime. A nice array of other Dutch craft brewers complements the full range of DePrael beers. The staff couldn't be more welcoming and friendly. The brewery is run by a couple of former psychologists, who undoubtedly have come to understand that two people can do as much to improve world mental health by making beer as any other activity. They've continued to do more than just brew, however—they've hired dozens of people who have had mental health issues to work in the brewery. You can sense that the place is run by people who care about doing the right thing.

And they've got a definite sense of style as well. The café backs up to the brewery, though the brewery entrance is in another street. DePrael beers on tap seem to go perfectly with the 1950s recordings on the sound system—the beers are all named for the Dutch artists you're listening to. A larger pub may be open by the time you read this; we hope it won't lose the something of a hole-in-the-wall atmosphere. They serve a limited but adequate lunchtime menu and sometimes, but not at all reliably, make a dinner special.

Some of the DePrael beers seemed to us to have picked up a wildness that might not be intended, but the best of them are exceptional. The Willy Quadrupel was our top pick. We'll grant it's not hard to brew a beer with a great deal of flavor if you're going to hit 11%, but it isn't easy to craft a beer with this much *good* flavor at any strength. Sweet, chewy, rich dark roast malts with chocolate accents dominate, especially at first, but herbal, vinous, woody and cherry fruit flavors give the beer an exceptional complexity as it drinks.

A short if rather remarkable walk from DePrael, **De Bekeerde Suster** (Kloveniersburgwal 6) is in the heart of the town's red light district (see separate entry under Sights). The "Converted Sister" is not a dramatically distinctive beer experience, and if we were going to have to skip a stop, this might be it. But the beers are among the most accessible of the three Amsterdam breweries, and it's a very accomplished beer bar in its own right. Its range of around 50 bottles included three new ones for us, and about a dozen beers on tap should provide something for most tastes. It's a multi-room, multi-level, sprawling sort of a place, quite sizable for downtown. It features a wider array of food than the other breweries, and a local specialty sometimes joins the more expected fare. The gleaming brewhouse in the back seems usable, if not frequently used; in short, the Suster is a good basic boozer.

The best known of the brewpub trio is **'t IJ** (Funenkade 7), which exports bottles to the U.S. and elsewhere. Its attraction is the well-preserved windmill next door that features on its label. Pick from a half a dozen beers on tap. The beers are dominated by the yeast, which some of those who love the wild beers of Belgium will enjoy—we have friends who can't get enough of them. We found them something of a challenge. We'd give the edge to the Struis, a dark, sour barley wine which at 9% alcohol has a

Brewpub 't IJ

good deal going for it other than the yeast. The tavern is pleasant with a very nice garden area in front that gives an excellent view of the mill if the weather is good. Snacks are very limited; peanuts and hard-boiled eggs are standard. An abbey cheese could make the beer taste boring by comparison—there was no problem smelling it at a distance of 20 paces.

Get there by tram bus #22 from the Central Station, tram #14 from the Dam—or tram #10 from the Heineken Experience, if you're seeking a completely different drinking experience.

Other places to explore

If for some bizarre reason you have a longing for American craft beer, **The Beer Temple** (Nieuwezijds Voorburgwal 250) has 30 taps, most of which feature American beers ranging from Anchor to Three Floyds. It's the creation of Peter van der Arend, who also owns our top-rated 't Arendsnest. The founders of Brew Dog were making an appearance on our last visit, and you might have a better chance of meeting Mikkeller here than in his bar in Copenhagen. Still, we come to Amsterdam for a Dutch experience, and we pick 't Arendsnest over this import emporium every time.

Gollem (Raamsteeg 4) is a welcoming and rewarding beer bar. It doesn't have quite the panache of De Wildeman or the range of 't Arendsnest, but it's had seats for us at times the other pubs have not, and we've found beers that were new to us among its nicely selected range. It's an easy detour if you're walking from Bierkoning to In de Wildeman.

Where to eat: a "must do" dinner experience

Present day Indonesia was a key part of the Dutch commercial empire for nearly three centuries; the Indonesian influence continues in some of Amsterdam's best culinary experiences. Satays and rice dishes such as nasi goreng abound, but the rijsttafel is the star of this crown. Although it's based on Indonesian cuisine, this buffet-on-a-table seems to have been a Dutch invention to avoid having to decide on an entrée. The fuller versions feature dozens of small dishes of meats and vegetables served with a large helping of white rice. While it's not a bargain experience, you generally get quite good value for money. Prices vary, but we've never had a bad rijsttafel in Amsterdam; you can probably find one close to your hotel in Amsterdam or Haarlem.

Where to stay

We strongly recommend staying in nearby Haarlem, our excursion city for Amsterdam, for much lower prices…and less noise. But if you want to go drinking late at night, you'll probably want to spend some time (and a great deal of money) in Amsterdam itself.

Don't use the tourist office except to buy their overpriced but necessary map (the map you'll get from your hotel is nearly useless) and, if you wish, the large booklet of hotels. They'll try to sell you a small book with only some hotels, but if you insist, there's a better guide with a wide range of places arranged by levels of luxury. We've had success just walking away from the station and looking around. If you get a 24-hour tram card, you can ride the tram outside the inner city to find hotels in abundance that the tourist office won't tell you about.

Hotels dot the city. Some are located across the bus/tram plaza and canal and stretch down the hill towards the center city area. The Crown Plaza is a budget buster, but very convenient to the train station and to trams headed downtown. The Doubletree is right at the station, but we prefer to get a bit closer to the bars.

If you want to get away from the downtown energy, or the ubiquitous red light window displays, the Apolloplan area sports a half dozen business-oriented hotels, most of them set back from the street and several of them with canal views. Rooms here are quiet if pricey, but if you're traveling with children, the "working girls" in this area don't advertise. An easy tram ride: get off the #5 or #24 tram at Apolloplan, turn right on Apolloplan, and look around. Still, by the time you've trammed all the way out here, you could have bedded down in Haarlem just as quickly for half the cost.

What to see

The Heineken Experience

You probably have to visit the Heineken Experience. Our first draft of this chapter listed it, reluctantly, in the top six beer spots, but it's really a tourist attraction more than a beer-drinking opportunity. It's overpriced, over-commercialized, and over the top, but you still have to do it. Because if you're a real beer enthusiast it's a must—sort of like visiting Karl Marx's house if you're a free market economist—and if you're a casual beer tourist, you'll learn enough about the history of the industry and the process of making beer to make the visit worthwhile. And it is, despite the commercials—and in some ways because of them—entertaining.

Brew kettles at Heineken

The first time we "experienced" Heineken here it still looked like a brewery. We won't soon forget the huge brewing and mashing kettles that formed its heart. Heineken started in Amsterdam and held on as long as it could in the middle of an increasingly traffic-clogged city, delivering grain by canal boats. In 1975 they gave up and transferred Dutch production to a larger and more shipping-accessible location in Zoeterwoude. If you want to see Heineken actually brewed now, you could try for a group tour in Zoeterwoude, but in Amsterdam, you have to settle for the "Experience."

Tram lines #16 and 24 will take you there from the Dam. Your 15€ buys you entrance and two beers at the end with a mini-taste along the way. (Beer for those over 18, of course.) Much of the show consists of displays, clever animations, old footage projected inside brewing tanks, and an amusement park-style moving theater/ride that bounces you around as you "experience" what it's like to be transformed from barley into a bottle of beer. The front row gets wettest. Afterwards, you're entertained with, or subjected to, a variety of Heineken advertisements and movie product placements, reminding you what a big business big brewing is. The heart of the tour, however, is a gem: a walk in and around the old "Brew House #2" that really hasn't changed since we were there in the '70s. On the lower level you can taste some wort that's still made on site—in a tiny mash tun there for the purpose—and you can grind the grist that will go into the next batch of it.

Heineken isn't much better or worse than most other Euro-lagers, but you have to respect the business savvy of the three generations of Heineken men who transformed a failing 19th brewery into a 20th century business empire.

Other sights

The main sights in Amsterdam are easy enough to identify. For art seekers, the newly refurbished Rijksmuseum has finally reopened and the "Night Watch" is back on post. The Van Gogh Museum is another must. There's a good zoo and a flower market. The tourist board offers plenty of information at http://www.iamsterdam.com/en/visiting, though it takes a bit of digging around to find the less obvious attractions.

A visit to the Anne Frank House is sobering, but also uplifting. Anne Frank and nearly all of her family did perish in the Holocaust, but the sad ending of the tale is well known and comes as no surprise. The house, however, stands as a monument to the human spirit and, especially, to the exceptional courage of many Dutch as they worked to protect Jews during the Nazi occupation. The Dutch Resistance Museum provides a broader view of the extent of the challenges of daily life. A new children's section may be open by the time you read this (http://www.verzetsmuseum.org/museum/en/museum).

The country's largest science center is quite close to the Central Station and impossible to miss with its huge sloping roof area that serves as a relaxing observation deck. It's kid-centered with English summaries of the Dutch explanations.

Whatever your itinerary, save time and money for one of the narrated canal tours that leave from several different places in the city. We've been on several and if there's a significant difference between them, we haven't found it. You'll get a good overview of the city's history, a memorable lesson in architecture, and a sense of the city life that has earned Amsterdam the moniker of "Venice of the North." Keep your eye out for the perfect canal-side pub to return to.

Scams and alerts

Your bartender or waiter returns change for a smaller bill than the one you presented. When called on it, he graciously says, "Well, if you're *sure*, then here's the difference. I won't know until tonight when I count the till, of course, but if you're *sure*, you may be right." We saw this done in two separate places within a two-hour period, one a very touristy place and the other from someone we never, ever would have suspected.

So just pay careful attention when you hand over a bill—look at it for a second so he sees you notice it, then hand it to him…and everyone stays friends.

The Pilgrims who gave us our "puritanical" culture fled from creeping Catholicism in England to the Netherlands. It was one of the few places that would put up with them—the Dutch practically invented the concept of tolerance. The Puritans quickly moved on, however, as they found that the society that so happily tolerated them tolerated everyone else too. Their teenagers, in particular, were having way too much fun learning things that challenged both canonical and anatomical laws, so off to moralistic Massachusetts they went. The broad-minded Dutch remained to offer a welcome to almost everyone since, except the Nazis. Today in Amsterdam, "coffee shops" still sell weed, though they can't advertise their business as openly as the "working girls" in their red-lit windows. The city is trying to concentrate these sometimes startling displays into a couple of designated districts, but on our last visit, there was still plenty of, ahem, window-shopping in other parts of the city. The official red light district is a part of the historic downtown area, and many of the best bars, brewpubs, and restaurants are located on the edge of, or even within, the neighborhood. The bottom line: you probably can't escape it, so if you're traveling with small children, have your explanations ready.

The good news is that businesses that are unregulated and dangerous in New York are here about as safe as they can be.

Further information: tourist Amsterdam

Language. If you've traveled much in Europe, you'll know that the generalization "they speak English everywhere" just isn't close to true, and the more you know of a language, the more options you'll have. But in Dutch cities, it is true. If they greet you in Dutch, ask politely if they speak English, but most of the time they'll just greet you in English ("hallo" is universal). However, "please" and thank you" are always appreciated, and at least one of them isn't hard:

- Please (the hard one): If you mumble "*All* stew bleef" really really fast, they'll recognize it as "please."
- Thank you: "Dank U wel" is quite easy if you're at all familiar with the German "danke."

Day trip/excursion: Haarlem

An evening at 't Arendsnest will show you well the range of Dutch beers. With your notes and a map you can scout out a number of relatively easy excursions from the capital. Our choice is Haarlem for several reasons. It's less than 20 minutes from Amsterdam, it's very walkable, the museums are making it a tourist destination for "normal" travelers, and it has one of the most interesting and vibrant house breweries on the continent. We've grown so fond of it that we've actually reversed the excursion, staying in Haarlem and venturing into Amsterdam when we want the big city's attractions.

Catch the train to Haarlem from platform 1 of Amsterdam's Centraal Station. (Behind you, by the way, is our Station Break, Café 1e Klas.) You'll be in Haarlem in 17 minutes. Be sure to wait for Haarlem's central station; if you see an Ikea, stay on the train. Take a look around before you head into town. The train station, a listed building, is probably the most beautiful in the Netherlands.

Roads lead away from the station from either side of the plaza in front of the exit. Both take you to the main square. Janisstraat on the left is a bit more direct. Kruisweg on the right passes a gift shop with an "i" information sign. It's not a tourist office, but you can buy a 1€ map of the city that's a near necessity. If you want to go to the real tourist office you'll have to go through the city center and continue to Verwulft near the Botermarkt. The office looks like a large trolley car set in the middle of traffic.

Haarlem was a major trading center in the Middle Ages, richer and more important than nearby Amsterdam. Specifically, it was a major brewing center, and brewers were among the city's richest and most influential citizens. Their chapels in the Grote Kerk attest to their power and wealth. At one time there were more than 150 commercial breweries in town, most of them along the Spaarne river and the Bakenesser Canal. One of the largest, the Elephant Brewery, still stands, but hasn't brewed in centuries.

Haarlem's brewing fortunes declined after the Middle Ages, as changing tastes made wine, tea, and coffee more profitable. Even more problematic was the water supply. As early as the 16th century, canal water became too polluted to use. Brewers responded by creating a "brewers' pool" near Overveen and shipping the water by boat to the town. It's hard to imagine how they could have stayed competitive with other brewing cities, and of the more than 150 Haarlem breweries in the 15th century, only 55 survived by 1640. Commercial brewing continued to dwindle through the 19th century, and the city's last brewery closed in 1916.

Loss of brewing isn't the only hardship Haarlemers have had to face through the years. Starving townspeople hacked the sheriff to bits in the Cheese and Bread revolt of 1492. The Spanish Duke of Alba laid siege to the city during the 80-year struggle for Dutch independence. The city held out heroically, but Alba eventually prevailed and slew a slew of the resisters. In 1576 more than a third of the city burned.

Still, most of the time Haarlem remained wealthy—it produced more works of silver than Amsterdam, extensive linen-bleaching fields surrounded the city, and in the 17th century tulip craze, acres upon acres produced bulbs, the rarest of which could fetch up to ten times a man's annual wages. Haarlem was a thriving artistic center during the Dutch "Golden Age" of painting.

The beer

There's one overarching reason for beer geeks to explore Haarlem. The **Jopenkerk** brewpub (Gedempte Voldersgracht 2) is one of the most interesting places to drink anywhere. It's set in a former church and uses the building's history in many of its beer names. Look for the hymn boards over the bar that list what's on tap. Many of the staff are beer fanatics who work there as much for pleasure as for profit.

Jopen beers began with the 750-year celebration of the city in 1994. Well aware of the city's brewing past, a handful of locals decided to commission a beer based on an old Haarlem brewing recipe from the 15th century—modified a bit for today's tastes—and scored a huge hit. They continued to make Jopenbier and other spiced

The brew house at Jopen

ales under contract until 2010, when they opened Jopenkerk, Haarlem's first new brewery in over two centuries. Jopen continues to make historical beers, as well as beers that no one in the Middle Ages could have imagined.

The brewery is housed in the old Jacobskerk. The owners bought the church from the city for 1€ and a promise to restore it, a promise they have fulfilled magnificently. The hall is cavernous and uses the full height of the church and much of its size. (Note the fabulous arched wooden rafters.) The gleaming copper kettles of the substantial German-built 20-hl brewing system dominate the space behind and above the bar. The downstairs drinking area is a mix of tables, bean bags, and sofas, with a library of sorts at one end with dozens of magazines. It attracts a young crowd, though at the other end of our long table was a couple of our own advanced age who'd dropped in for a quick cup of coffee.

There were about a dozen beers on tap at our last visit, including one guest beer. Several more appear on the bottle list. They don't publicize it, but if you eat in the upstairs restaurant you can order 75 cl bottles of Jopen brews that they don't sell anywhere else. The beers range from acceptable to exceptionally good and from ordinary strength to extraordinarily strong. The original 1407 recipe, Jopen Koyt, is a traditional Dutch gruit beer, a spiced specialty. Today's version is a masterpiece, a rich red wine of a beer with a gentle spicing that intrigues rather than dominates.

The restaurant isn't cheap, but well worth the splurge. A small menu is in a sense "reverse engineered"—the chef prepares foods designed to go with specific Jopen beers. They expect you to take their pairings seriously, and doing so is actually a good idea. The Russian Imperial Stout paired with chocolate is to die for.

If you're just in Haarlem for the day, you won't need to go anywhere but Jopenkerk. But if you must, there are a few good beer cafés in town.

Café De Roemer is on the Botermarkt, a few blocks southwest of the Grote Markt. A dark inner bar contrasts with a big glass-enclosed patio and open-air tables stretching into the market square. It won't match Brussels's Delirium, but it has a respectable beer menu and several taps, some of them very interesting. Den Dorstigen Tijger India Pale Ale could have come from San Diego, and you don't see La Trappe Trippel on tap at ordinary bars. The menu features about 60 bottled beers, including 15 of the usual Trappists, along with a reasonable range of food choices for lunch and dinner.

The **Studio,** right on the market square at Grote Markt 25, fancies itself a beer café, but its beer list pales in comparison to the heavy hitters in Amsterdam. A couple of owners ago it was "the" spot in town for good beer; current management's efforts to bring it back seem half-hearted. It has a great location on the square, however, and some of its draft lines rotate to provide some interesting choice.

Café Briljant (Lange Annastraat 33) is popular among local beer geeks. The menu offers about 40 beers, three of them on tap, but other than the Jopen beers, which you can get at the brewery a few blocks away, most of them are the usual suspects. Closed Monday and Tuesday.

Other than Jopenkerk, the gem in Harlem's beer crown is **Melger's** beer shop, located at 13-15 Barrevoetestraat. Dennis De Leeuw stocks over 800 beers, and by the time you read this he will have added room for 300 more. Ask him for recommendations if you don't know where to start. He's in close touch with brewers and beer moguls throughout the Netherlands and even supplies some beers to Bierkoning in Amsterdam. He'll also sell you bags of ice cubes to chill your evening's fare. De Leeuw also commissions his own beers from Jopen, including a better than average rich dark barley wine featuring dark sugar flavors and a big floral finish.

Where to stay

Look hard right as you come out of the station. The Golden Tulip Lion D'Or (Kruisweg 34-36) is an upscale hotel just a few minutes' walk away. It's been full whenever we've been there; we'll book it in advance next time. If you're specifically visiting Haarlem, a downtown hotel is a better bet, but if you're using Haarlem as a base for Amsterdam, the location simply can't be beat. More central hotels include the Carillon, which is literally in the shadow of the towering Bavo Church. In the front rooms, which we love, you'll be serenaded by the bells 24 hours a day, though mercifully infrequently in the dead of night. A few other hotels are in the neighborhood. If these are full, the tourist office near Verwulft will find you a room, though if you arrive on a festival weekend you may find yourself staying in a nearby town. A good double with bath and without breakfast should cost about a hundred bucks—less than half what you'd pay in Amsterdam for the same quality.

What to see

The center of Haarlem is well preserved; the old meat market next to the St. Bavo Church hasn't changed in almost 500 years. City Hall is even older, and the art deco sign for a fish market over the inviting old pub at the end of the square pays tribute to the fish stalls that once stood there. The price for keeping the center intact and relatively traffic free was the destruction of the city walls to expand the commercial areas of the city. Only the "Amsterdam Gate" remains.

The St. Bavo Church has dominated the city's skyline for centuries. Officially it's the "Grote Kerk" but everyone refers to it as "Bavo," which causes some confusion since there is a relatively new Catholic St. Bavo Cathedral on the canal not far from the Jopenkerk Brewery. The huge Gothic edifice is still the center of the city in many ways. The soaring ceiling and vast stone columns are well worth the small admission charge. Note how much simpler and less ornate it is than the Catholic cathedrals further south. You can get in for free by attending one of the gratis organ concerts. On Mondays and Fridays, the church bells peal a substantial concert of their own.

The Franz Hals museum is a short walk south from the city center and only a couple of blocks from the tourist office. Your ticket gets you half off at the Haarlem History Museum across the street as well. Set in a building created as a home for old men and later used as an orphanage, the Hals museum shows a range of local painters and culminates with some spectacular works by Hals. Furnishings, clocks, and silverware augment the substantial art collection. Don't miss the doll's house if you're bringing kids, or are one at heart. We liked the experience—it can be done in a couple of hours, though if you want to linger, there's plenty to ponder. Much of the museum building still has a sense of the old men's home. An old poster emphasizes the strict rules—doors were locked at 7 PM, quarreling at the table was strictly forbidden, and the men were "only" allowed to take one jug of beer to their rooms. We thought that sounded like a pretty good deal.

The nearby Haarlem History Museum is a modest display of the city's past and about worth the $3 to get in. You start with a short English language film on the history of Haarlem—with a few clever special effects (you never know when some Fokker is going to surprise you). Be sure to get the English translation sheet for the museum's two rooms; most of the exhibits are only in Dutch. Don't miss the stereoscope machine and the wooden model of the Grote Kerk in the main room.

You can get a guided tour of the Adriaan windmill, an iconic sight along the Spaarne River that includes a striking view of the river from the observation area. The original burned down in 1932, but this recreation is supposedly quite authentic.

The Ten Boom museum is dedicated to Corrie Ten Boom, whose family hid refugees from the Nazis. Discovered late in the war, all of them died except Corrie, whose writings became famous. Guided tours only—look at the door to find out when the next one is.

❦ *Antwerp*

Quick orientation

Antwerp introduced us to great Belgian beer a long time ago, but it's in this book for one reason: the Kulminator beer bar is one of the very best in the world. If we had one last night to drink, this is where we'd spend it.

But there's lots to do while you're not settled in at Kulminator, and most people come here for other reasons. The Beer Passion Weekend at the end of June is a good way to taste a range of beers and gawk at central Antwerp at the same time. Beyond that, Antwerp's one of the great museum towns of Belgium and even Europe.

The train station is a fair distance from the heart of the city. Take a cab or a bus to town.

Station breaks

Unlike most European cities, there's not much good drinking around the train station. If you're stuck there, you might as well hunt up the station bar. If you have the

time, though, catch a bus or a cab to the old town and do your drinking there. If you're stuck in the station for a while, you might consider a visit to the zoo next door.

History and culture

Romans inhabited the area that makes up modern Antwerp and provided one of the possible origins of the city's name. The villainous giant Antigoon supposedly cut off the hands of the captains of river boats who refused to pay his tax. (There's a modern allegorical statement here, we're pretty sure.) The Roman soldier Brabo turned the tables on Antigoon, handing him, as it were, his first defeat. In addition to a pair of disconnected hands on the city crest, there's a fountain in the Grote Markt showing a nude Brabo heaving the giant's severed and spouting hand into the river.

In the Middle Ages, Antwerp became a part of the Holy Roman Empire, and eventually part of the Spanish Empire of Philip II. As a fortress town with a deep river, it became a major trading center, replacing Bruges as the center of Flemish economic activity. Its 16th century population of nearly 100,000 ranked it as one of the major cities of Europe; some consider it the center of the world's economy at that time. However, the religious wars of the 17th century hit Antwerp hard. The Dutch closed the Scheldt River to navigation, and the merchants fled to more profitable and accessible ports. Even after the Peace of Westphalia brought an end to most of the Thirty Years War, continued fighting between Catholic Spanish and Protestant Dutch restricted economic growth.

Protestants and Catholics found a point of unity during the wars of the French Revolution: both groups hated the French. However, the conquering French did open up the Scheldt and paved the way for an economic renaissance into the 19th century. Germans made even more enemies than the French during the two occupations of the 20th century, yet Antwerp remained an important mercantile center. As one of the largest seaports in Europe, it prides itself on being something of a working man's city, and some of the areas away from the center, devastated by German attacks in WWII, do look pretty ordinary. But Antwerp isn't ordinary in what it has to offer the casual tourist, and especially in what's here for those who are mixing seeing grand sights with drinking grand beers.

Beer styles and drinking culture

It's Belgium. There's beer. The local beer is De Koninck Amber, usually designated in bars simply with the name of the brewery. In the 1980s we thought it was one of the best beers in the world. We don't think it has changed, but we know we have. Nowdays, in a much more crowded field, De Koninck comes across as a reliable, pleasant, but understated amber ale. In fairness, other beer critics continue to rave; not long before his death in 2007, beer connoisseur Michael Jackson called it "perilously drinkable." In a sense it's a perfect beer to symbolize the charm of Antwerp. If Antwerp is a working man's city, this is a working man's beer.

For years De Koninck only made one beer, but they've branched out lately. We've found the specially packaged Cuvée to be inconsistent, but superb at its best.

De Koninck makes at least two blond ales, one of which is the house beer at the Gollem Pub in Amsterdam. The well balanced 6% blond makes a good, though strong, session beer. The 8% Gusto 1833 is a sipper whose yeast smooths an already understated gold flavor, though some notes of lemon and metal give it a bit of character. An 8% Ruby Red offers dark and berry fruits before a dry ending, but falls short of memorable. The 7.2% Strubbe Keyte Tripel is a gentle but pleasant interpretation of the style; soft-spoken pear and green grape notes give way to a dryish finish.

The sixpack of drinking experiences

Kulminator (Vleminckveld 32). There are several good beer pubs in Antwerp, but Kulminator still rules the roost. Since Kulminator is the reason you've come to Antwerp, it's probably worth at least three visits. It closes on Sunday and much of Monday so you'll have time to explore other exceptional drinkeries, but you'll be brought back to Kulminator again and again. In fact, the thought of (hm... six nights a week times 52 weeks...) 300 visits a year makes us wonder whether Antwerp wouldn't be a pretty good place to retire. We're giving you the required six beer experiences in Antwerp, but more than in most cities, there's a world of difference between the top and the bottom of the list. Kulminator rises over the next two, and those two tower over the rest.

To say Kulminator is one of the best beer bars in the world really doesn't do it justice. It's like visiting your great-aunt who just happens to have a thousand or two vintage aged beers. The place is small, shabby, and jammed with beer paraphernalia, mismatched old furniture, and cats. But, oh my goodness, the beers.

Kulminator played a significant part in the world beer revolution. Dirk and Leen will be happy to show you early Michael Jackson books with several pictures taken there—everyone looking much younger than now. As you work your way through vintages of Belgian beers, you can imagine the Bard of Beer sitting across the table doing the same thing. His spirit certainly is.

There's no food that we know of, but a very good sushi restaurant just across the street can fortify you for the drinking to come.

It's worth spending a night exploring the vintage aged beer. You may have to ask for the telephone book-sized listing of vertical tastings, and we're not sure how many are left. On one visit, beers from the 1980s such as Thomas Hardy's and a huge range of De Dolle Oerbier and Stille Nacht were just a beginning. The earliest De Dolles—early 1980s—were available only in a vertical tasting. It cost €15 to €20 a bottle but gave us a tasting we simply couldn't get anywhere else. If you haven't had a vintage Thomas Hardy—one brewed in the 1970s and 1980s at the Eldridge Pope Brewery—you need to splurge and have the experience. The oldest years are starting to show a bit of oxidation that passes pretty quickly. The sherry notes and deep vinous flavors are unlike those of any other beers we have tried.

But you don't have to sell your car to have a vintage experience. While you can manage to drop a bunch of euros on Thomas Hardy and some of the rare years of other specialties, most of the beers are surprisingly reasonable. Reasonable prices, in fact, are the norm in nearly all the bars in Antwerp. If you're used to $6 "pints" of craft beer in American cities, 4€ just seems cheap for beer that is often truly exceptional.

You could spend a second night on the huge beer menu; it lists more beers than we could taste in weeks of trying. We didn't realize that the Duvel Triple Hop changed the focal hop each year until we had missed several. We caught up quickly at Kulminator. (Who'd have thought Duvel would be buying up Citra hops?) Take a stab in the dark and just have some fun trying beers you didn't know existed. If you're with friends, pick different ones, share them and score them, and see who can pick the best beers over the course of an evening.

If you hit the right time, the draft offerings could make an evening's entertainment by themselves. Be sure to note small words that can make a common beer very uncommon. In 2010 the La Trappe Quernicus (10% ABV) seemed like one we'd had before, but an "Eik!" on the chalkboard showed it had been aged in oak and is one of Belgium's rarest beers. Apparently a 33 cl bottle goes for €30. A mere €6.50 brought a 33 cl glass from the tap that was one of the best beers we've had in this century.

The Kasteel Cuvée de Chateau from 2009 was a blend that included a 10-year-old vintage—a sort of Belgian Entire Butt. Only the comparison to the La Trappe kept it from blowing us away.

You'll find different beers, of course, by the time you get there, but there will be plenty to interest.

'T Antwerps Bierhuyske (Hoogstraat 14) is one of Belgium's best bars and might make Antwerp a destination city even if Kulminator were not there. Some of the drafts are ordinary, but some are decidedly not. A Struise Double Black was, at 26%, a staggering experience in many ways, but well worth the $12 it set us back for a tiny glass of it. The beer list is arranged by brewery, but be sure to ask Dylan what's new or special and not on the menu. We grabbed one of the last of his Orval Green—if you can imagine the taste of Orval in a true lambic, you have an idea of it. Those will be long gone by the time you read this, but you can be sure he's hiding something special for people who really appreciate beer. He also dug us up a bottle of a White Pony dark ale, Dark Signs, that had been brewed by an Italian at Gaverhopke. The 13% ale was special in itself, but several months in first a Sassicaia wine barrel and then in a scotch whisky barrel produced a remarkably successful complexity. It was one of our top rated beers of 2014.

Dylan is the son of the owner of Kelk, our favorite bar in Bruges. Some talents obviously run in families.

Right around the corner from 't Antwerps Bierhuyske is **Bier & Eetcafé Gollem** on Suikerrui 28. Gollem features an unusually large number of taps for a Belgian bar, and its bottle list, while shorter than the previous two stops, should keep you amused as you nosh on their "Bapas" snacks and giant hamburgers and watch the shoppers wander by. Both places are just a short walk from the main square.

Save an evening to have dinner at the **Grand Café Horta** (Hopland 2), in the fashion district, around the corner from the mammoth Rubens Café. Victor, Baron Horta, was a Belgian Art Nouveau architect at the turn of the century. His iconic Maison du Peuple (1895–1899) was demolished amid international protest in 1965. Some of the ornate ironwork was sold for scrap to Japan and the rest sat in a field until

Grand Café Horta

the Palm Brewery won the contract to build the Grand Café (and museum) Horta and used the gorgeous white iron to frame it. Walk around inside while you're waiting for dinner to arrive, or just enjoy the beers. It's a Palm house, which means beers from Palm, Rodenbach, and more recently Boon. But the unfiltered Palm is smooth and interesting, the Royale is strong if sugary, and the Palm Dobbel is a wonder of smooth caramel malt and balancing hops, a perfect pairing with their superb menu.

There is no shortage of decent beer bars in Antwerp. One of them, **Paters' Vaetje,** is just up from the Cathedral (Blauwmoezelstraat 1). The outside tables are great for people-watching on a pleasant evening; the beer list is a little above average for a Belgian beer bar. You probably won't find much you haven't seen elsewhere, but you won't go thirsty either. It was the top recommendation of the generally helpful and well-meaning tourist office, but if you just wanted to go to bars recommended by tourist offices you wouldn't be reading this book.

't Pakhuis (Vlaamsekaai 76) is Antwerp's brewpub. It's a pleasant place, and it gets you out of the old town for a few minutes. It has an appealing décor with lots of brick and glass and a welcoming brew house as you enter. The fermenting cellars are on display as you go to the WCs downstairs. We didn't eat, but the family next to us was clearly there for the food and not the beer…which kind of made sense. It's not bad beer, but it's yeasty and a bit clumsy. We'd have no problem drinking it for an evening if we were meeting friends there, but if they really were our friends, they would have asked us to meet them at Kulminator. Skip the brown ale unless you're bent on trying them all. The star of the show is the Tripel. It shares the house character of fruity, metallic, and sugary flavors, but the yeast seems to work here better than in the other beers. It's not a world classic, but it's decidedly above average.

A special weekend

Beer Passion Weekend at the end of June is vaguely reminiscent of the World Beer Festivals that *All About Beer* hosts in the U.S. *Beer Passion* magazine holds a center place and it's quite commercial. There are fewer beers—200, more or less—but it's a more sedate event than the sometimes boisterous WBFs. The Groenplats is a big stone-paved plaza with a statue of Rubens holding out his hand (ask a native about his secret) in the shadow of the cathedral. It disappears under a ring of tents for three days in June.

Beer Passion Weekend

Admission is free; you buy a beautiful little (actual glass) glass, plus 1.5€ tokens to exchange for samples of about a quarter liter—usually one token, though the Deus was two. This isn't the Great British Beer Festival where beers average 4.5% ABV: your token is getting you 8% as often as not. But the beauty of it is that many of the beers are only produced in 750 ml bottles, and your token gets you a sample for a fraction of the bottle price. There are some interesting local food stalls—sausages, sandwiches, cheese—and barely enough tables, but those that are there have a view of the medieval cathedral.

Where to stay

We splurge on the Hilton; summer rates are often fairly reasonable. It's right on Groenplats, so if you're there for Beer Passion weekend, the hotel overlooks the festival and a dash to your room can save the unpleasantness and expense of the portapotties on the square. It's Antwerp, so you can have a Hilton experience at a well-below-Brussels price, especially in the summer.

There are plenty of other hotels. As you travel from the train station to the center of town, the standards of the hotels generally rise—as do the prices.

What to see

Enough of Antwerp's center escaped damage from the past 400 years of war to yield surprises around every corner. The striking town hall dates from the 1500s; the Butchers Guild, with its typical Lowlands horizontal-striped brickwork, is now a musical instrument museum. Museums seem to pop up on every corner. Antwerp was and is the European hub of the diamond trade; the Diamond Museum, next to the Centraal Station, glitters with displays and history. (Alexander the Great mined them by throwing sheep carcasses into the pit, then robbing the nests of carrion birds that flew off with the meat; diamonds adhere to fat and repel water, principles still used in mining. Who knew?) The National Maritime Museum, on the Scheldt River by a more modern statue of Antigoon looking daunting, has a vast open shed sheltering an amazing array of historic regional watercraft. The zoo is expensive but it has a wonderful 19th century feel to it and its programs are world-renowned. You can stroll around with a Maes pils and watch the animals eyeing you enviously.

The good news is that if you really want to see all the museums, just book an extra few days guilt free—there are enough beers to fill your evenings.

Also of intense interest to Ellie were the Quetzal Chocolade Bar (Lijnwaadmarkt, in the shadow of the Cathedral), with an awesome menu of hot chocolate drinks, and the Profijtelijk "tweedehands boeken" second-hand bookstore on Wolstraat. The Cathedral is old and gorgeous but modernized inside; when we were there it included a Rubens exhibit. There are a variety of horse carriage tours out of the Grote Markt that clatter sedately around the old town and along the river.

Helpful words here: *aus d'blief* (ows de bleef) = please; *hoog'e dag* (ho-[ghgh]e dahg—with a bit of gargle in the middle) is the Flemish "howdy," distinct from the Dutch "hoog de dag"; *look* is garlic and *room* (there's a lot of it around here) is cream. But everyone speaks English, if you're polite about asking.

Scams and alerts

Scam-free in our experience. Even the cab drivers appear to be honest—far from a guaranteed experience in Belgium. The tourist office is helpful and, in our experience, professional, which also isn't guaranteed in most cities.

Day trip

Ghent

Before you jump on the train for our day trip, pay a visit to Bruges or even Brussels (see that chapter). If you've been to both, a trip to Belgium's second largest city makes sense.

Ghent, like Bruges, is a pleasant city in which to drink beer. There's lots of river and canal frontage, huge church buildings, and old narrow cobblestone streets for atmosphere. Bruges offers a greater diversity of choice in beers, but with a bit of poking, you can find some very fine drinking experiences in Ghent.

You have three good options in the downtown area. **Waterhuis aan de Bierkant** has a great waterside location just off the Groentenmarkt. The tiny pub's windows and good-sized patio both overhang the Leie River. Inside is snug, about eight tables. Most of the bar is restricted to the servers—with a 2€ fine for encroachment—but there's plenty of room outside. Sixteen taps pour mostly the usual suspects, though the pub commissions three of their own beers from a couple of different breweries.

A short way away on the opposite side of the river, **Aba-Jour** is more of a restaurant than a beer house. Its beer list isn't as extensive as it is thoughtful. Half a dozen drafts offer a couple of rotating taps, and the 100 or so bottles, if standard, offer good choices to go with your food. Aba-Jour is owned by a beer enthusiast who maintains good enough relations with Orval to be one of the bars to serve both a fresh and aged version. An increasing number of Belgian pubs offer the comparison, and it's worth seeking out. We've always noted a note of orange in Orval—from the yeast rather than the new antipodean hops—and the fruitiness steps forward with age. The young Orval has a hint of peppery spice that recedes as it matures. A bit of rawness to the alcohol in young Orval also disappears in a year. Aba-Jour inspired us to start an Orval cellar of our own.

Aba-Jour's food is quite good. Stooverij is a Flemish specialty, a beer-based beef stew, and Aba-Jour cooks up a fine version made with three different dark beers. It's

The Waterhuis has a beer for each of these glasses

worth waiting for a table on the downstairs riverside patio. Another good choice for food and view is **Oude Vismijn,** just up the street at Sint-Veerleplein 5 and again right on the water. Draft Rodenbach goes beautifully with seafood and Oude Vismijn does seafood well. Neither of these choices is budget friendly, but you'd pay more for less in New York or Paris.

Our favorite bar downtown is **Café de Trollekelder,** by Sint-Jacobskerke. It's become so popular that it underwent an expansion in 2014, but it's kept its character well. Multiple levels give a small pub feel to a fairly good-sized drinking venue. The accordion-like beer list is quite respectable: in winter it grows to near 200 beers while during the Ghent Festivities in the summer it shrinks to closer to 20. Trollekelder is a great place to drink; it's where many of the bartenders in Ghent go to drink after their own bars close. It's open until 2 AM and a staggering 3 AM on weekends.

To get the best Ghent has to offer, however, you have to move out of the old center area. Before you get to our top bar selections below, stop in at the town's brewery, **Gentse Gruut,** at Grote Huidevettershoek 10. You can find their beers around town, but they're a bit better at the source. As a bonus, it's a great place to drink. It sits on a canal, and the water theme comes right into the pub itself in the form of a tiny artificial creek that runs along the floor. Copper tanks are clearly evident from the bar or the tables. All the beers are drinkable, seasoned with a special blend of spices ("gruut") instead of hops, but the Inferno, a strong Belgian blonde that pushes 9%, tops the field. Bottles of it in town were interesting, but the draft at the brewery was magnificent, somehow managing an artistic blend of chalky yeast and very clean flavors. From here, if you could swim the canal you'd be only a couple of blocks from your next stop, but you have to retrace your steps west and then north to reach Brabantdam, which will take you to Trappistenhuis.

On the edge of touristy Ghent, **Trappistenhuis** (Brabantdam 164) has a superb selection of about 150 beers and will almost certainly have at least a few that you haven't seen. Service is superb—helpful and very knowledgeable. Trappistenhuis has a well-deserved stellar reputation among Belgian beer aficionados, and while it won't in itself make Ghent a beer destination, it's a can't-miss once you're here. It doesn't open until 5 PM, so go to the Gruut brewery first, then settle in. The beer list is huge and sports color pictures of many of the beers or their labels. You'll get more out of it if you read Flemish, but there are enough cognates to pick up some information from the extensive text entries. At the very least, it shows clearly how seriously these people take beer.

Less well known but well worth the effort to find are a couple of side-by-side charmers. **De Brouwzaele** and **De Planck** are almost opposite each other on Ter Platen, which runs parallel to the canal where it crosses under Sint-Lievenstaan. The #2 tram gets you pretty close—it's about a 10 minute walk from the Gent-Sint-Lievenspoort stop. Look right just before you cross the bridge.

De Brouwzaele and De Planck have similar beer lists but provide very different drinking experiences. **De Brouwzaele** is the older of the two and the more conventional—if you can regard a huge canopy over the bar made from a brew kettle as conventional. Service is friendly and the food is quite good; if you haven't had your fill of mussels yet, they're a specialty here. A bit more than 100 beers are available and include some that aren't on everyone else's list.

Across the street, opposite the gigantic movie complex, is **De Planck.** It's on a real boat, permanently moored in the canal. In good weather the upper deck gives a great view of trees and some water. In cold or rain, downstairs is warm, dry, and romantic. The open windows lie just a few inches above the water, and you can say hello to the inquiring ducks that paddle by. Like De Brouwzaele, the beer menu stretches to about 100, but there are several you can't get across the street. De Planck is another pub with close ties to Orval, and you can do your vertical tasting here if you haven't been to Aba-Jour. They're quite proud of the commissioned house beer as well. One word of caution—the stairway down to the lower rooms and the bathrooms is very steep and somewhat treacherous. We were in awe of the staff who seemed to glide up and down effortlessly, but we've heard of a number of patrons who haven't been so graceful and had to be helped back up the steps that they traversed so quickly on the way down.

Bamberg

Quick orientation

While Bamberg's old town is a long walk from the station, once you're there, it's compact. It was laid out in the shape of a cross, with four churches defining the original settlement. It's grown a great deal since then, of course, and our pub crawl will take you out into the suburbs. Other important sights and Kellers grace the tops of the hills on the edge of town.

Although we'll give you our top six, you'd need at least a week in Bamberg to visit even a majority of the good drinking venues, and dozens of wonderful beer

The Bamberg Rathaus: left and right banks couldn't agree on location so they parked it in the middle

River views are everywhere

adventures lie within an easy day's excursion. Like an Ivy League admissions officer, we've excluded choices virtually identical to the ones we picked.

The number of Bamberg breweries briefly hit single digits not long ago, but Weyermann's pilot brewery has brought them back to ten. That's enough for any city in the world other than Portland, Oregon, but you still can't help but notice the clear traces of the dozen or so breweries of the lost past. Still, ten breweries will do, and if you're manic enough, you can visit them all in one stupor of a day—about as good a pub crawl as Germany has to offer. But to keep consistent with other chapters, and because we're arrogant or foolish or both, we'll tell you the six places where you have to have a beer if you only have limited time.

Station breaks

Bamberg's great pubs are a hike from the station. There's a café across the street that will do if your time is very limited. Otherwise a very brisk 15-minute walk or, more sensibly, a cab ride takes you to Spezial or Fässla, across the street from each other on Obere Königstrasse. It's pretty easy to catch a bus back to the station.

History and culture

At the end of the first millennium AD, Bamberg was a small town in a sparsely populated area. Henry II, who managed to conduct wars against both Poland and Italy and force the Pope to crown him Holy Roman Emperor, created a new bishopric in

Bamberg to spur development in the center of his realm. The plan worked: the magnificent cathedral and church offices drew population and wealth. Henry continued to support art and culture there, and a visit from the Pope in 1020 furthered its fame. By the high Middle Ages, Bamberg had emerged as one of the major cities of central Europe.

Bamberg continued to prosper in the Middle Ages since it was the northern starting point for shipping down the Main River. It also continued to attract artists and authors into the Enlightenment. You'll find plenty of reminders that E.T.A. Hoffmann lived there, and Hegel spent time in the city as well. Bamberg largely missed the Industrial Revolution, however, and its role as a religious center declined after the fall of the Holy Roman Empire.

The economic decline during the Depression of the 1920s–1930s might have been the best thing that happened to Bamberg. There just wasn't enough of value to make it worth the cost of bombing it in WWII, and it remains one of the best preserved medieval towns in Germany. UNESCO named it a World Heritage Site, celebrating its well-preserved architecture from three eras.

Bamberg's relative isolation during the modern era may explain why it alone continued to brew the smoked beers that typified brewing in many other places in Germany during the Middle Ages. Bamberg, while quite modern in many ways, seems more content than most other cities of its size in savoring its distant past. Lucky us.

Beer styles and drinking culture

Rauchbier

Many breweries in the U.S. and some other countries now make some form of Rauchbier, usually using smoked malt from Bamberg's Weyermann malt factory. Bamberg is still the place to drink it at its best, however. Rauchbiers were once common. Barley malt is dried by kilning—heating—and the amount of kilning determines how dark the grain, and thus the beer, will be. To accomplish the kilning, malteries used a three-chamber process. In the bottom room, huge fires burned to heat the air in the room above, and that heated air was then channeled into a third-floor room where the malt was kilned. Some brewers skipped the step of the air chamber and used the fires, smoke and all, to heat the malt directly. Brauerei Heller (Schlenkerla Rauchbier) now has purpose-built machines that control the amount of smoke the malt absorbs.

If you get adventurous and take some bus trips into the area around Bamberg, you'll run into several versions of smoked beer, but of the city's ten breweries, only two specialize in the style, Spezial and Heller. Both have flagship beers and also produce seasonals, but there are significant differences in style. When we were younger, the Spezial beers appealed to us more than those from Heller. They're sweeter, a bit cleaner, and not so overwhelmingly smoky.

Heller's Schlenkerla Rauch Märzen, its flagship, is darker than most of the smoked beers in the area and has a richer, deeper smoke. The first taste can be overwhelming: dry ash, very woody and intense, almost creosote. While some hops are evident, much of the balance comes from the smoke. It cannot be appreciated on a first taste. However, the human brain has a wonderful way of masking flavors and aromas over a relatively short period of time to allow other perceptions through. Remember the old days when you could drink in a smoky bar for hours and never notice the stink till the next morning when you decided to throw your clothes away? The annoying whine in your air conditioner that drives you nuts when you arrive at work is simply gone by coffee break—for you. The human palate masks the smoke in Schlenkerla in the same way. On the second liter, and especially the third (we still don't know why people laugh when we explain this), the smoke nearly disappears and you're left with an exquisite balance of malt, hops, and only a touch of smoke for balance and breadth. One could argue that the second liter of any beer tastes good, but trust us, not every beer does.

Aside from the smoked beers, most of Bamberg's breweries produce an expected German range of lagers and weizens. Ambräusianum is a bit more adventurous, and there's no telling what you might discover at Weyermann.

The sixpack of drinking experiences

The sixpack of gems if you're really short of time. See below for directions on how to find them.

❖ **Schlenkerla.** See above. Slam dunk "can't miss" even if every tourist to the city knows it too. The Kellerbier here is almost impossible to find elsewhere.

❖ **Spezial Keller.** See Brews with a View below. Perhaps the best view in Bamberg.

❖ **Michaelsberg.** The brewery museum and beer garden on Michaelsberg is one of Germany's best. Also below.

❖ **Fässla.** No beer lover will believe you've been to Bamberg if you haven't been there.

❖ **Klosterbräu,** especially if the weather's nice and you can snag a riverside table.

❖ Either **Keesman** or **Mahrs,** or both—they're on opposite sides of the street.

The full tour

Our crawl of ten breweries in one day is, we admit, a theory. We've never had the discipline to leave a brewery fast enough to do them all in a day. Still, we've listed them in an order that reflects opening times and bus schedules. You definitely can't do them all if you insist on tasting every beer they brew, and we don't guarantee that you will actually be able to get all this done in one try—or that you will remember much of it if you do.

Start with the pair of breweries between the Bahnhof and the old town on Obere Königstrasse. **Fässla** opens at 9:30 in the morning and if you really want to do all the breweries, your throat had better open then too. Fässla beers tend to be a bit

Fässla's garden

stronger than most in the region, which may explain their remarkable popularity among our serious beer-drinking friends. If it's crowded, or you want a bit of time to yourselves, go into the self-service garden, turn left along the dark paneled wall, and left again into a forgotten corner with a tiny potted plant next to the fire escape for the rooms above. A round table will seat eight in a pinch or two quite comfortably, and it's where we type these words. Beers vary widely. The strong dunkel Zwergla is the best of the bunch, a rich, strong dark lager. The Pils is quite commendable and remarkably clean. The Helles is an under-attenuated buttery unpleasantness, unless you like diacetyl. Weizens are fine: the hell showing a bit of banana candy and the dunkel featuring very mild roast and only a hint of Weizen character.

Cross the street to **Spezial,** one of our favorite breweries from our early years of sixpacking adventures. The wooden barrels are gone (if they don't tilt they ain't real), but the beer is fresh and the people have been wonderful to us over the years. When we've had the luck to find a vacancy, the hotel upstairs has been quite comfortable. In back is one of the smallest beer gardens in Bamberg, but a couple of rooms accommodate more. Actually, it's good you're here in the morning, because trying to find a seat at dinner can be a challenge inside or out. The Spezial Lager is a classic smoked beer, sweet for the style but, for some tastes, the best there is. The Märzen is deeper and richer, though still gentler and sweeter than Schlenkerla. In recent years, they've branched out to a Weizen and several seasonals.

Hop the 906 bus to Gaustadt and **Kaiserdom's Gastätte** at 26 Gaustadter Hauptstrasse. Take the bus to the second Gaustadt stop if you want to overlook the brewery on the way to lunch; get off at the Rathaus if you want to save time. Warning: the Gastätte now closes for a couple of weeks in the summer (they must be quite profitable), usually the end of July. They also close for a few hours in the afternoon (on reflection, they must be *very* profitable), which is why we have them slated for the morning part of the tour; get there well before 2 or wait until after 5. They have a small, pleasant garden and several, but not all, of the Kaiserdom beers. You can stay in the hotel, which apparently continues to operate, sort of, during their summer vacation.

Now back to the city. The 906 bus runs fairly frequently. (In case you've slept late and started with Kaiserdom, the 906 stops right in front of Fässla and Spezial.) Change at the ZOB (main bus station) to the 912 or 918 and ride up the hill to Laurenziplatz and **Greifenklau.** (Don't get off at Laurenzistrasse unless you're missing your usual date at the gym.) Greifenklau has been there for nearly 300 years—another brewery keller, Röckeleins, shared the hill a few doors down until 2003, but an office building has taken its place. Greifenklau is a good hotel-restaurant, sporting a classic cellar garden with a good view. Lager and Weizenbiers are commendable.

Take the 912 or 918 back down the hill to Schillerstrasse for the short walk to **Klosterbräu.** Walk straight back in the direction the bus has come from, then cross a small canal; pause if you wish, to check out the gondoliers. Then continue straight across Geyerswörth and across another small bridge over the rocketing river channel. Turn right, and before you is Bamberg's Kloster Brauerei. If you can, grab a table by the water—it's one of the best drinking views you can find without a 20-minute climb up a mountain. They have begun to specialize in darker beers in recent years and do a pretty good job with them. The beers are smoke-free. The garden is not.

Walk back to Schillerstrasse and catch the 912 or 918 to the central bus station, the ZOB. You're playing Beat the Clock with the bus system in Bamberg as the evening approaches. The main lines stop at 8 PM, and while there are good night lines that run until 1 or so, they don't run very frequently. So it's worth the effort to get the peripheral breweries done before the chariot turns into a functional but slower pumpkin.

A quick detour to **Weyermann** allows you to visit during their daytime-only hours. Take any of the buses that go past the train station to Brennerstrasse, or take a bus to the station and walk under the tracks to the Brennerstrasse exit, then walk left to Weyermann's magnificent red-brick complex at number 17-19. A gift shop is open most days, though it tends to close early in the afternoon. It sells a dazzling array of beers from the Weyermann pilot brewery. Grab a couple, sample them discreetly on the street, then get your €2.50 Pfand (deposit) back and move on.

Take any of the myriad buses back to the ZOB and pick up the 905 to Wonderburg, a suburb that is now part of Bamberg itself. Get off at the main stop and there before you are **Keesman** and **Mahrs** breweries. (Maisel used to be a short walk away. Sigh.) Pick one—each has its own charms—and settle in. Food is good at each and the beer range is pretty extensive for Bamberg. We started at **Mahrs** mostly because we didn't expect to find a new beer there, as they're exported to the States. But we did, a nicely dark Heath Bar of a beer named for E.T.A. Hoffman, who wrote his Tales in Bamberg 200 years ago. A very pleasant garden winds around the Gasthaus and the required dark wood-paneled rooms are inviting in a north German sort of way.

Across the street, **Keesmann** has a lovely garden that backs up to the brewery. You can see their so-spiffy-I-wish-we-had-one bottling line from the tables. Beers are clean and good and the food can be exceptionally good if you order from the most, but still not very, expensive part of the menu. Dark but inviting rooms beckon within. If you want to linger in the area you're only a few minutes' walk from the Fässla beer cellar on the grounds of the former Maisel brewery.

Back on the 905 (a late bus also runs this route) and you're ready for the final assault on the breweries of the city. Don't dawdle; some of them close at 10:30 or 11. From the ZOB, walk or take a bus to the Dom. It's almost impossible to approach the Dom without bumping into Schlenkerla's massive Gasthof. If you're early enough, walk past it just a couple of doors to **Ambräusianum,** Bamberg's newest brewery-restaurant. We recommend visiting Ambräusianum before Schlenkerla because the beers are not smoked and you won't be able to perceive much after you've assaulted your palate with a full Rauchmärzen. In many ways Ambräusianum is a typical German modern city center brewpub; the beers are unfiltered and you get a light, a dark, or a wheat. But seasonals can set it apart and make it seem worthy of its Bamberg setting. We tasted a summer spelt beer (Dinkel) that made the best use of spelt that we had tasted anywhere.

Now on to the palace of Rauchbier. The brewery is Heller; the beers are named for the beer hall, **Schlenkerla.** (If you follow our advice to climb the hill to the Spezial garden, you'll pass the Heller Brewery.) In recent years the brewery has become much more adventurous in producing a wider range that includes seasonals, and they're good at what they do. But the original smoked Märzen set a standard that not even the new Heller brewers can match. Try the seasonals, but try at least a half liter of the smoked Märzen as well. If this is really your ninth stop, a half liter is probably all you'll want, but if you've stretched the tour out into a more sensible three or more days, make time to spend time with "the" Schlenkerla. It is, after all, the reason you're here. Warning—Schlenkerla closes earlier than Ambräusianum and they have no sympathy for the pleas of tourists who don't show up on time.

Other places to explore

Brews with a view: the Keller experience

Beer cellars are on hills. Or sometimes *in* hills. In Bamberg they're in the tops of hills. In the Middle Ages, Bambergers mined sand from the mountains to use as scouring material. By the 18th century, brewers had figured out that these abandoned sand mines were perfect for keeping beer at a relatively constant temperature. Some clever fellow discovered if you planted trees and spread white gravel on the top of the hill, the temperature in the caves stayed even more constant in the summer. It didn't take long for them to realize they had created a perfect environment to consume what they were cellaring. By the 19th century Bamberg's hills were riddled with nearly two dozen of these Kellers. Often tappings were held with little notice—just a brewer's symbol on a tree to indicate that the cellared beer was going to be poured—but regular hours, sort of, emerged in time. Today the handful of remaining cellars open in "fine weather," which means whatever the beer houses want it to. Each has a smaller Gasthof attached, however, that does sell beer predictably.

The best one, far and away, is the **Spezial Keller**. Climb the steep Alter Graben, turn left on Oberer Stephansberg, catch your breath, and turn left again on Sternwartstrasse when you reach the well-marked Heller Brewery. Bear right (still up) and look for the sign that takes you across a large field (and more up) to the garden. Get a table along the edge that stretches all the way to the parking lot behind the Gasthof for a magnificent view of Michaelsberg, especially at night. The beer range is limited to Spezial's smoked Helles and their non-smoked Weizen, but you could happily drink Heineken here if you had to.

The biggest of the gardens is the **Wilde Rose** garden. To get to it, continue—you guessed it—up Oberer Stephansberg, past where you would turn to get to the Spezial cellar, and keep climbing until you see the old lagering house with a sign for the beer cellar. Then, because that entrance is closed, walk up some more until you get to the main entrance. Wilde Rose is a former brewery, and the garden still commissions beers they claim are their own, though they don't say who brews for them. Keesman Pils is also available, so you can taste that side by side with the Wilde Rose and see what you think. It's all self-service. You can get a liter Mass, but almost no one does. Don't forget to turn in your mug to get the hefty 3€ deposit back. The potential for an exceptional view is lost to a fairly tall fence around the entire perimeter and the food is very, very limited. But it has a great garden "hum" and an imaginative and extensive playground if you've got the kids with you.

Though it doesn't really advertise itself as a cellar, the garden at **Greifenklau** apparently started as one. It's a fine garden with a view that doesn't match Spezial's, but is very nice nonetheless. A full menu and two well-brewed beers make it all the more attractive. See #4 in our brewery tours for directions. At least to get to this cellar you don't have to walk uphill.

And, though it's not strictly a cellar, the beer garden at **Michaelsberg** has the feel of one. Forty years ago you would have been drinking beers from the oldest brewery in the world: the Michaelsberg brewery was founded in 1015. But in 1969, some collection of nitwits failed to come up with a way to keep the brewery going and shut it down. Almost 20 years later, a largely volunteer effort turned it into the museum that it is now. The museum is first rate, but that decision meant that everyone our age is never going to be able to taste a beer at a thousand-year-old brewery. It's good there's a church on premises; those folks need a whole lot of forgiveness.

Maisel brewed a Michaelsberg beer for a while, but there is no pretense any more. An Italian restaurant now occupies the space where we remember drinking 30 years ago; walk past it to the other side of the church and the beer garden. It has better views and much better beer.

The **Maisel** brewery closed only a few years ago, a sad tale of underinvestment and ownership discord. The brewery stands almost untouched today, a 10 to 15 minute walk past Keesman and Mahrs. The former tap is open again, however, at Moosstrasse 32 selling Fässla beers and is a lovely place to drink. It bills itself as Fässla's keller, but it's better described as a modest beer garden. A charcoal fire grills fish on Friday. A bus will take you nearly to the door, but beware, it runs infrequently and stops altogether in the early evening. The walk downhill to Keesman and the more frequent 905, however, is an easy one.

Where to stay

Bamberg is a very, very popular tourist destination. It's a charming enough city in its own right, but it has also gained enough brewing prominence to wind up on the itinerary of beer seekers from all over the world. In short, it's jammed. Book online before you come, or call one of the brewery guest houses for reservations.

If you arrive without a reservation, there are so many hotels in Bamberg that you'll almost certainly find a room if you're clever and persistent, but you may spend more time and much more money than you intended. We recommend you find the tourist office, get their hotel list (which they say won't do you any good), and then wear out your shoes. There are a good number of hotels within a several-block radius of the tourist office.

A recent Bamberg visit epitomized what can go wrong by trusting a tourist office to find a room. "You don't need a list, you need ME! Bamberg is *completely* sold out!" warned the fellow at the desk. What did we know? Perhaps we did need him, so we let him book our room. First he offered us a hotel in a distant suburb south of Forchheim, "quite nearby" (see day trips below), then a 300-euro room in a different suburb barely served by bus. Finally he "found" a room at a nearby Ibis and booked it on his computer, giving us the confirmation sheet. When we showed up at the Ibis, the hotel had never heard of the reservation and were indeed completely sold out. By then the tourist office was closed. The Ibis desk clerk called around to neighboring hotels, explained our plight, and somehow Hotel Villa Geyerswörth squeezed us in for the entire three days we wanted. The next morning, Bob toured several nearby hotels to see how many would have been able to find a room for us at least for the night. Forty percent said they would have found us something. When we relayed this information to the tourist office guru, he said, "I only have what I see on my computer." At least *that* was a true statement.

Hotel Villa Geyerswörth turned out to be a wonderful splurge and is now our hotel of choice in Bamberg. A 10 minute walk to the Dom and Schlenkerla, it's even closer to Klosterhof.

What to see

For beer lovers, the museum on Michaelsberg is a must. It's in the old Michaelsberg brewery that would have been the oldest in the world had not the cretins who managed it in the 1960s shut it down before we could get to it.

Today, you can wander through the brew rooms and cellars of memorabilia. Highlights include unusual brewing equipment and one of the most extensive collections of brewery memorabilia we've seen anywhere, but the best part of the experience is just wandering though the maze of rooms and thinking about the richness of the brewing history on this hill.

Back in town, you can get a sense of the heritage of Bamberg's brewing past by keeping an eye out as you walk for the remnants of the many dozens of breweries that once operated here. Look for the large arched doorways that once allowed horse carts to deliver malt to the brewery and beer to the rest of town; Obere Sandstrasse contains several. You'll see the old Lowenbräu brewery on the way up to the Wilde Rose Keller, and the name of the Polar Bear brewery still ornaments the doorway of the Bolero restaurant on Judenstrasse. The Bamberger Hofbrau restaurant near the tourist office used to be the tap for what was Bamberg's largest brewery, located near the train station. Röckelein's old brewery was near the Dom, and their Keller shared the hilltop with Greifenklau.

The Bamberger Dom is a vast, gaunt, millennium-old grande dame featuring an imperial tomb by the amazing 15th century sculptor Tilman Riemenschneider. The Neue Residenz rose garden nearby held Ellie, not normally a garden freak, entranced for an hour.

Weyermann Malt Factory

The Weyermann specialty maltery gives public tours on Wednesday afternoons at 2 PM. If you can arrange your schedule, it's well worth the time. It's hard to find a craft brewery from Sweden to Italy to the U.S. that doesn't have some sacks of Weyermann malts in the storeroom.

In 1879, Johann Baptist Weyermann bought a roasting machine for "malt coffee" and invented the first indirect firing for a malt roaster. He also roasted grain for brewers, building a plant in the hills above Bamberg. In 1888 the railroad came to Bamberg, and Johann Baptist moved his plant down to its present site by the rails. In 1906 he built the first "pneumatic" malthouse in Europe. "He was very lucky": he married the daughter of the local pharmacist, who became the maltery's chemist, and another in-law, a famous architect, designed the current building complex (late 1800s) including the Villa. Today, Weyermann is in the hands of the fourth generation and is growing fast. A second maltery in Hassfurt produces their pils malt and they now export to 135 countries.

What you see on the tour depends in part on what's going on at the time you're there. Even our VIP tour had to skip a room because of high CO_2 levels, but the history of the place and the variety of products they make are really interesting. The tiny but humming-busy pilot brewhouse shares a rebuilt stable with a mini-maltery, a test bakery, and a distillery, and the tour ends with samples of beers made on the spot by Bamberg's smallest brewery.

Scams and alerts

Other than maybe a hapless tourist office clerk, you're likely to encounter only honest and helpful people in Bamberg. Exercise normal caution in crowds.

Further information

Once you have found a room, the tourist office is a helpful place for maps and information, and most of the staff are as friendly as they can be. They'll sell you a package ticket that gives directions to each brewery and is good for a beer in almost all of them. Some of the books they sell on German breweries (in German) are hard to find in bookstores.

Bamberg hosts several festivals during the year; some are major city events, others are closer to neighborhood affairs.

One of the cutest is the Canalissimo canal fest at the end of July, a three-day fest of music, beer, and some food along the little canal that, serendipitously, runs by the back garden of the Hotel Villa Geyerswörth. You can do a mini Franconian beer tour by visiting the small draft tents along the water. The best food is just outside the festival area: a tent about a hundred yards along the canal, at the opposite end of the festival from the tourist office, offers fresh fish grilled over live coals and a small beer garden in which to enjoy the feast.

You can book gondola rides on the canal; the longer rides take you out to the main river areas. Your hotel's desk can give you information.

Day trips

You could spend an entire vacation based in Bamberg and never run out of day trips. We'll give you a couple; the tourist office will give you more if you ask. The guides to Franconian breweries may make you decide to quit your job and move.

Forchheim

Forchheim is just a few stops south of Bamberg on the Nuremberg S Bahn. You can visit three of the town's four breweries and taste a few others from nearby and get back to Bamberg in time for a Rauchbier nightcap.

From the Forchheim Bahnhof, turn right on the Bahnhofsplatz and then left to follow the signs to the Altstadt. Bear right at the fork and continue downhill until you can turn left on Wiesentstrasse and it will take you to Bambergerstrasse. Turn right, and you're only a few yards from the tiny **Eichhorn** brewery and its half-timbered Gasthof: standard German food and Eichhorn's very fresh beer. Even after selling tanks of their beer at the Annafest, they barely break 2,000 barrels a year; essentially it's a nearly 200-year-old brewpub.

Leave Eichhorn and turn right to retrace your steps and keep going straight towards the well-signed Rathaus. It would be worth the trip even were there not two breweries directly across the street. **Neder** has a plain front and a simple interior. **Hebendanz** isn't any bigger. Next door is the original brewery site for **Greif,** though they moved outside the city walls some years ago. You get a feeling of how things used to be in late medieval Europe, with breweries lining the streets competing for custom with none of them dominating. Large cities such as Munich could have 30 or more along a few blocks; here a tiny town could still support a handful of them. A stop in any of the three downtown Forchheim breweries gives you a sense of how so many can be sustained—they're really small, but they all have regulars. We got the impression there isn't a great deal of pub crawling here except by sixpacking tourists like us.

Take the street away from the breweries to the right of the Rathaus and you'll pass a couple more pubs with beers from not far away. Wolfshöher beers are brewed near enough to have a garden at the Annafest. St. Georgenbräu has a presence in town as well. If you want to visit Greif, get a better map than the one they post around town, or better yet a cab, and head for Serlbacher Strasse 18. Be warned, they open early and close very early—by 2 PM most days except when they close earlier.

Blümlein: the best seat at Forchheim's Annafest

If you can possibly arrange it, get to Forchheim for the **Annafest.** The party runs for the last two weeks of July so it's better for summer travelers than many of the major German fests. Even if the weather stinks it will still be humming. The fest ranges all over the Annaberg, a steep little mountainette that has so many beer cellars dug into the sides that one almost expects it to collapse under the weight of the beer and partyers there for the fest. A bus will take you from the Bahnhof every half hour for a couple of euros. A cab will get you there faster and closer for 6€, including a decent tip.

The "Festgelende" starts at the base of the hill and winds its way to the top. Along the way are myriad food stands, carnival games, and rides, including a medium-sized Ferris wheel that gets most of its height from being installed on the edge of the hill halfway up. As you reach the upper parts of the hill, beer gardens line the path on both sides. At least a couple of dozen operate during the fest, several are open all summer, and a few hardy ones serve in good weather year round. The actual cellars are more for show than for cellaring now, but the number of them—and the fact that most of them are in use as service and keg-holding areas—gives you an unusually good opportunity to get a sense of what the Keller concept is about. The number of Kellers in the Annaberg is more or less what you would have found in Bamberg a century and a half ago.

Our secret mini drinking Keller is the Blümlein, at the very top of the hill, past the bands as far as you can go. When you see the exit signs you're close; you'll think you're leaving the festival but keep going, past the rent-a-truck bathrooms and past the fest tables arrayed in what is a pretty typical cellar garden. A small path leads to the right and down to the cellar itself, now used as a dispensing area, and on your left is a tiny square microcave with a rustic wood table and benches carved from the stone walls. There's space for six or maybe nine very close friends. You can still hear the music from the bandstands back on the main path, and otherwise it is a died-and-gone-to-heaven scout camping expedition.

We absolutely loved the Eichhorn 2008 festbier here; the 2011 version seemed a bit edgy, though still quite clean. Unless you crave crowds and noise, Blümlein is the best Festplatz in Bavaria. But get here early to get the cave—then watch the sad and envious parade go by of Germans who thought they were the only ones who knew about it.

Memmelsdorf

Memmelsdorf is the kind of small town many people believe every small town in Germany is like: 8,959 people, a rather fabulous Schloss, and two breweries, **Höhn** and **Drei Kronen.** It's a quieter town now than the last time we stayed in it—not so much because the people who live there are more restrained, but because no one has to put up any longer with the 20-minute-long tank convoys that used to rattle the dishes off the shelves during the Cold War. Reach it easily by bus from Bamberg, but watch the schedules to be sure of getting back.

Berlin

Quick orientation

Berlin is a huge city, in population but especially in geographic area. The brewpubs and best beer bars are scattered all over the city. Most of our recommendations are within reasonable distances of each other, but if you go beyond the reach of this guide, allow plenty of time to get to the more far-flung locations.

You'll probably arrive at the humongous and relatively new Hauptbahnhof. It's one of the few main stations in Europe that are not ringed with hotels (yet), so count on having to ride the rails or hire a cab to get to where you're staying.

Once you're settled in, public transportation will get you almost anywhere and a day pass is only 6.50€; you can buy passes on trams or in vending machines in subway stations. If you buy it from a machine, be sure to validate it on your first ride. If you're doing the grand tour of the city, an investment in a good map is wise, but the free maps hotels give you are unusually good and show bus, tram, and subway lines.

Station breaks

Berlin has a trainload of stations. You'll find beer in or near all of them. The Hauptbahnhof has a faux brewpub, Hopfingerbräu, on the top level that's a pleasant place to drink while you're waiting for a train. The decorative brewing equipment has never produced a drop of beer, but a Hausbier from the pub's cousin at Potzdamer Platz (see below) gives it a bit of a brewpub feel. If you have some time you can catch a regional train to the Alexanderplatz station. Exit and look around, and you'll see Brauhaus Mitte, which is one of Berlin's better brewpubs (see below).

History and culture

Berlin traces its origins to the 11th century, but even in the late Middle Ages, Berlin was a small town—actually a pair of towns, Berlin and the somewhat smaller Cölln on the other bank of the Spree River. The two towns shared some administration and belonged to the Hanseatic League for a time, but apparently never made it off the junior varsity team and bowed out in the 16th century. The Elector Frederick III used some fancy semantics to acquire the title "King" Frederick I in 1701. In a move similar to New

York's 1898 borough consolidation, Frederick merged Berlin-Cölln with three other neighboring towns to make a Greater Berlin, suitable to be the new capital of Prussia.

Frederick II, the Great, Frederick I's grandson, brought Berlin into the modern Age of Enlightenment beginning in 1740. Even while fighting a war with Austria, he found the resources to build palaces, the opera house, and cathedrals. By the end of the century, more public buildings, the Brandenburg gate, and the broad Unter Den Linden boulevard had given Berlin much of its current magnificence.

Libraries and universities helped Berlin become an intellectual center by the early 18th century. When Karl Marx's father discovered his son was having too much fun at the relatively easy-going atmosphere of the University at Bonn, he forced Karl to transfer to a more disciplined life in Berlin. Apparently it worked, although the key difference seems to have been that Berliner students—while drinking the same copious amounts of beer—talked as much about philosophy as they did about girls.

In 1848 Berlin became a revolutionary center, as liberal opponents of monarchy tried to establish a business-friendly unified Germany. A popularly elected parliament meeting in Frankfurt offered to make Frederick-William IV ruler of a new and powerful German state. Fred toyed with the idea, but then declined to pick up "a crown from the gutter" and instead sent in Prussian troops to quell the uprising—inspiring the future chancellor Otto von Bismarck to observe that great questions are resolved "not by speeches and majorities" but "by blood and iron."

When Bismarck was the de facto leader of Prussia, he tricked first Austria and then France into providing the blood for his iron, launching wars that resulted in a new German Empire by the end of 1871. Berlin was now the capital of one of the world's great powers. William II, however, in 1890 "dropped the pilot"—firing Bismarck—to chart his own incompetent course for the ship of state, leading to World War I. At the end of the war, Willy scooted off safely to the Netherlands, leaving a starving capital to deal with revolutionaries from both the left and the right. A parliamentary government emerged, however, and despite some bumps in the road Germany had returned to the family of nations by the late 1920s.

The 1920s roared in Berlin perhaps even more than they did in the United States. The movie *Cabaret* does not exaggerate. As in the U.S., however, the avant garde elements lived side by side with grumpy right-wingers who yearned for a return to the values and stability of the 19th century. The global Depression paved the way for a particularly grumpy failed Austrian painter (and one of the world's worst writers) to finagle his way to the head of the German government.

Hitler charted his own course of disaster to another devastating war loss, and this time the victors occupied Germany, split it up, and restructured its government. In 1949 the Western allies reunited their respective occupied sectors to form a Federal Republic of Germany, or West Germany. The Russians, however, who had experienced unimaginable devastation from uninvited German guests twice in 35 years, left nothing to chance; their troops sustained a Communist East Germany, the DDR, for another half century.

Berlin, although geographically entirely within the Russian sector after the war, was split among the four victorious powers. For a few years, the four city sectors shared administration, but that soon came to a halt. In 1948 Stalin tried to force the Allies out by blocking all highway and rail access to the city. The West responded by supplying the entire city by air for almost a year (the Berlin Airlift). By the end of that time, East and West Berlin were decidedly two separate cities.

Movement between the two halves was relatively easy, however, until the East tried to stanch the flood of over 30,000 people a month who were fleeing the "workers' paradise" in hopes of being "exploited" at vastly higher wages in the west. In August 1961, work began on another of history's many great and futile walls.

During the divided years Berlin felt like a city under siege, which in essence it was. West Berlin, maybe as a result, seemed to push the cultural envelope in all sorts of interesting ways. On visit in 1984 we were struck by marquees advertising movies that were banned in the U.S., as well as kiosk posters flaunting such cultural triumphs as female mud wrestling festivals. East Germany, which was easy for an American to enter—and even fairly easy to get out of—was a different story. We've seen more joy at Episcopalian funerals than we saw in East German beer halls. East Germans rarely got drunk in public for fear they might say something that the secret police would note. (See our chapter on Prague for where they did go to get drunk in public.)

By the late 1980s, however, changes elsewhere created new opportunities for East Germans. Mikhail Gorbachev, the Soviet Premier, visited Berlin on October 7, 1989, to celebrate the 40th anniversary of the DDR. Its authority lasted only five more weeks. Gorbachev's reform government no longer provided Russian troops to prop up East Germany's authoritarian rule. Increasing opposition to travel restrictions led the Communists to consider ways to moderate this political pressure. On November 9, a misinterpretation of an order easing travel rules led to the premature opening of the Berlin Wall, and 20,000 people poured through the gates. The Communist government could either make civil war on its own people or capitulate. Free elections the following March paved the way for German unification in October of 1990.

Ampelmänner

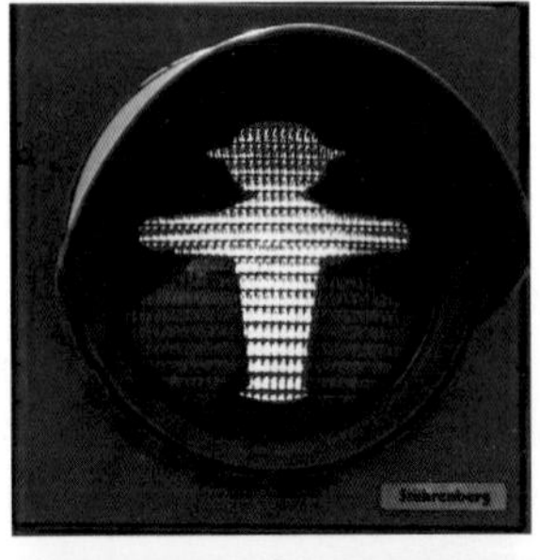

Since then, western capital has poured into the former East Germany, gobbling up many of the larger corporations and most of the larger breweries. Ironically, some of the smaller breweries that survived the Communist era through personal connections or by submitting to nominal Communist control couldn't compete with the Carlsberg and Heineken subsidiaries cranking out ordinary, but clean and inexpensive, mass market yellow suds.

In the quarter century since the fall of the Wall, the obvious divisions between East and West Berlin have nearly disappeared, though demographic studies show profound differences remain. The population of the former East Berlin is poorer, older, and more agrarian than the former West, more likely to get flu shots and put their young children in day care. More obvious signs include the city's architecture and layout. Much of the influx of western capital went to new building, resulting often in elegant skyscrapers towering next to some of the lousiest quality construction of the 20th century. Main streets in the East can be heroically huge and city blocks go on forever. The surest way to tell which sector you're in, however, is the pedestrian crossing signs. The eastern sector featured a "working man" with a proper hat, while the western sector used the generic humanoids you find anywhere in Western Europe. After unification, the city government moved to standardize the signs until protests from the former East Berliners persuaded them to keep this symbol of their distinctive past. "Ampelmann" souvenir stores throughout the city now feature the dapper pedestrian on everything from pencils to lawn chairs. (Ampelmänner make great Christmas decorations, for starters.)

Thus, for the visitor, Berlin is again one city. The siege atmosphere is gone, the transportation is seamless, and Berliners relish their city's role as capital of a reunited Germany.

Beer styles and drinking culture

For centuries a visit to Berlin meant drinking the iconic Berliner Weisse. If you hunt for it, you still can find it. It's brewed in a somewhat commercialized form, but is probably pretty similar to what Berliners drank copious amounts of at the beginning of the 20th century. No one is entirely certain how the style evolved. One theory posits that it was basically a mistake that tasted good; another links it to migrating Huguenots who supposedly brought a Belgian influence to the north of Germany. Wheat beers were common in northern Germany at least since the Middle Ages, and while most brewers switched over to the easier-to-handle barley, some regional wheat specialties remained. A handful of these were tart and dry, not unlike the wild lambic beers of Belgium. Until relatively recently, Beck's Brewery in Bremen produced a Bremer Weisse under the Haake-Beck label that was similar to Berliner Weisse, and Leipzig currently has at least two revivals of Gose in production.

Although in the past Berlin's breweries brewed stronger, darker wheat beers, Berliner Weisse has been primarily a summer drink. A 3% thirst quencher, it won't do

Berliner Weiss, rot und grön

much to warm you in the icy winters. It's never served on draft; even before glass bottles became affordable in the 19th century, Berliner Weisse came in thick crocks designed to withstand high pressure. Berliners would store it in cellars or dig a hole in their yards and let it mature over a winter or two. We've never tried aging it, but some of the beer's fans still do.

It's possible to enjoy Berliner Weisse's tart astringency unadulterated, but it is traditionally served "mit Schuss," a shot of raspberry or woodruff flavored sweet syrup. "Ein Rotes" will get you the former; "ein Grönes" will produce the latter. Once ubiquitous, the style suffered a slow decline in the 20th century as pilsners and Bavarian Weizens grew in popularity. The two large-brewery examples of the style, Berliner Kindl and Schultheiss, are now produced by the same brewery, but we believe they still use slightly different processes to achieve the distinctive tartness.

The sixpack of drinking experiences

It's not hard to find good places to drink in Berlin. Few tower over the others, however, and you may want to consider making your choice based more on location than our rankings. You can lose a great deal of drinking time on long U Bahn rides. If, on the other hand, you're there for a while and intend to explore several parts of the city, go online for the latest information and you can find some treasures beyond the scope of this guide.

We've changed the "top six" every time we've visited the city. Except for Das Meisterstück, if you replace any of the other six with an entry from our "other" list, your experience in Berlin won't be any poorer.

A true "top" six might have you spending longer in the U Bahn tubes than in the pubs. The six we give you here are close enough so you can, if you wish, get a view of the city by using the double-decker buses that creep through the streets. These pubs are all in or very near the Mitte section of the city. Thirty years ago we wouldn't have sent you anywhere near here—our selections are all in the former East Berlin.

One of the few bars in Germany that could as easily be in Copenhagen or Baltimore, **Das Meisterstück** (Hausvogteiplatz 3) is just a few yards from the Hausvogteiplatz U stop. It's not a typical Berlin experience, or even a German one, but it's the best way to see the future of craft brewing in a country that's just starting to move from its back seat in the world craft beer revolution. Meisterstück has close ties to BraufactuM and serves a huge (for Germany) range of styles. Four taps pour craft beer, but the bottle selection is the reason to come. On our last visit, about 100 different beers ranged from an affordable four bucks to house-mortgaging rarities. More than enough were in the \$6 to \$10 range to keep us busy for an evening.

The best beer we had there, and one of the best of our time in Germany, was a Simcoe 3 Hopfiges from Riegele Bier Manufaktur in Augsburg. We've known Riegele for years as a producer of good but very predictable German beers. This one was indeed good, but not at all predictable: essentially a hop-centered session IPA with a judicious use of Simcoe that provided enormous flavor while maintaining drinkability.

Few U.S. brewers have nailed the style as well as Riegele. Berlin's Heidenpeters and Munich's Crew Republic joined the sort-of-haus BraufactuM (brewed in Frankurt am Main, at least for now) in giving us tasting experiences at Meisterstück that we hadn't encountered in weeks. Also, more alcohol and lots more hops, that gave us hangovers we hadn't had in weeks. Sigh.

Treffpunkt Berlin (Mittelstrasse 55/Ecke Friedrichstrasse). The area from the Gendarmenmarkt near the Stadtmitte U Bahn north to the Friedrichsrasse U Bahn stop hosts a range of German-themed restaurants. The Treffpunkt is an unassuming pub, but is our favorite place to drink Berliner Weisse. Treffpunkt gives an authentic presentation; try it all three ways. The food is well prepared and affordable and the English-speaking wait staff is friendly and welcoming. You'll share the place with some tourists, but Berliners eat here too, and if you block out the sounds of English you can imagine yourself in as true a "local" as Berlin is likely to offer these days. An alternative is Berliner Kindl Bistro Am Gendarmenmarkt.

A far cry in location and ambience from GeorgBräu (see #5), **Hausbrauerei Hops und Barley** (Wühlischstrasse 22-23) is a small brewpub in an increasingly trendy neighborhood that's easier to find if you don't put it off until after dark. The beers are better than most of the new wave of urban brewpubs; the Dunkel balances four malts well and even finds room for a few hops. But the reason to go is the "local" atmosphere and exceptionally friendly welcome in a city that doesn't always provide one. It felt clubby when we first entered the smallish bar, but when it was clear we were there for the beer, we had lots of new best friends.

Brauhaus Lemke and **Mitte** (no. 4 and 4a) are under the same ownership and pour similar beers, but they're both worth a visit for the striking settings. They're within an easy walk of each other. **Lemke** (Dirksenstrasse 143) is tucked away in the arch of an elevated railroad—the place shakes when the trains go overhead, but that's part of the charm. Lots of bricks frame several rooms and there are even some outdoor tables off the beaten track. An unadventurous Weizen and a wildish sugary Copper are adequate. The floral hops and chalky yeast of the unfiltered Pils make it more flavorful than smooth, but the Original achieves a pretty nice balance after a sweet start. All are a welcome contrast to the boring big-kettle pilsners that used to dominate the city.

Mitte (Karl-Liebknecht-Strasse 13) is a flight up in a multi-purpose building just off Alexanderplatz. A deck area allows for fine people-watching. The Hefeweizen was a mild yet muddy disappointment, but the other three beers were well above average for a city brewpub. A well-crafted Keller Pils and a roasty-toasty Dunkel are fine session beers, though the unfiltered and sweetly yeasty Zwickel is the most interesting if you're just having one.

GeorgBräu Brauhaus (Spreeufer 4) is right on the Spree River and you can watch the tour boats ply the river as you ply your beer. Inside is wood and tile with bottles and glasses and old photos. The bar sports big copper pipes and tap. Tall tables fill a large bar area and surrounding rooms feature booths and low tables. The semi-open kitchen is clean; the staff is attentive and as welcoming as the decor. In short, it's a lovely place to drink, and it broke our hearts not to love the beer as much as we did the pub that makes it. But there's the rub. The Pils can be so overloaded with diacetyl as to be almost undrinkable. The Dunkel Pils—no mistake, that's what they call it—was a bit better on both our trips, but it won't make anyone's classic list. It's almost amber in color, though some roast and chocolate last well beyond the finish. While there's still some diacetyl, especially in the finish, it's not as pronounced as it is in the Helles and it blends with the chocolate malt reasonably well. The aftertaste is really quite nice if you can get to it.

Hofbräuhaus Berlin (Karl-Liebknecht-Strasse 30) is so much of a Tourist Institution that we were tempted not to include it even in our Munich chapter. We almost skipped visiting the Berlin version, but after dutifully checking it out, we've returned a few times, though we recommend avoiding it during the "Beer Mile" and on Saturday nights.

It claims to be the largest beer hall in Germany, though it's hard to see how it tops its Munich sibling. Jam-packed with tourists, groups, and bachelor/hen parties, it can be hard to find a seat on a Saturday night in the summer. Or to hear yourself think. Many of the customers are trying to drink as much of the Hofbräu beer as they can, and the decibels reflect considerable success. But the food is surprisingly good for

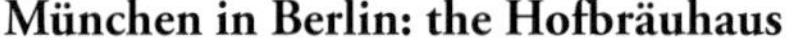
München in Berlin: the Hofbräuhaus

what must be a factory of a kitchen. The goulash soup was one of the better versions we've had in years, the Hax'n are among the largest we've ever seen (almost certainly enough for two if you have soup first), and the schnitzels are reliable. So, of course, is the beer. If you've been living the adventures of yeasticity—brewpub hopping—you might find the strikingly clean Hofbräu Hell a pleasant change of pace. Don't be put off when the band strikes up "Country Roads" and everyone bellows along. According to one survey, it's the number one song at Oktoberfest.

Other places to explore

The Berlin drinking scene doesn't change as rapidly as London's, but it's picking up steam, and we run into a new "find" each time we visit. By the time you read this, the new Berlin outpost of California's hop-centered Stone Brewery may be helping to change the scene even faster. For a fuller listing, visit Steve Thomas's germanbreweries.com and don't ignore the "news" page.

We've enjoyed each of the following for very different reasons. Our eating recommendations are also good places to drink.

Brewbaker is at Sickingerstraße 9-13, a short walk from the Beusselstrasse S Bahn stop. Maybe. A peripatetic nanobrewery, Brewbaker is probably still brewing somewhere by the time you read this. The beers vary enormously, but they aren't boring. The brewer, Michael Schwab, speaks excellent English, so take the time to say hello if you can find him. We encountered Michael and his brew kit in the Arminius Market Hall (Arminiusstrasse 2-4, near the Turmstrasse U Bahn), which was an attraction in itself. We believe the tap at Arminius still serves Brewbaker beers, and it's worth the trip to see this superb example of 19th century market architecture.

A stone's throw, but a longer roundabout walk, from the Zoo takes you to perhaps the city's most picturesque Biergarten, **Café am Neuen See** (Liechtensteinallee 2), on the edge of a small lake just off Liechtensteinallee. You can find better pizza and

Café am Neuen See

salads back home, but it's a relatively cheap meal. The beers are ordinary German lagers and weizens, which is to say pretty good. It's the lakeside setting, however, that brings us back on a warm summer evening. Trees, water, and the beer garden buzz make for a perfect place to cool off with a cold beer. For 10€ you can hire a boat to paddle around in the small lake if you wish. The 200 bus will get you close, but your best bet is to get to the west end of the Tiergarten and look at the maps posted on the paths that lead into the garden.

Another park garden, **Volkspark Friedrichshain** is more compact than the vast Tiergarten, but also more distinctive in its own way. Founded to celebrate the centennial of Frederick II (the Great) of Prussia, it provided a park for workers who weren't allowed in the snobbier Tiergarten areas. In World War II, a pair of massive anti-aircraft batteries set up in the park were a prime target for Allied bombing. The two heaps of wreckage left were too big to clear away, so instead the East Berliners trucked in rubble from the rest of the city to add to the piles. Today "Grosser Bunkerberg" and "Kleiner Bunkerberg" are densely wooded "mountains" that look entirely natural, though if you look closely at an eroded area in the woods you can see that what's under the soil is mostly a pile of bricks. Sunbathers, most of them with beers, take to the fields that alternate with the woods below the hills, and there's nary a sound of the English language anywhere—with one exception. An outdoor theater shows movies at 9 PM (entry 7€) and while they are mostly dubbed German, several are in English. A few beer gardens are scattered about. The main restaurant's garden is modest by Munich standards, but it overlooks a small lake with a tall gushing fountain and abuts a big playground for the kids. The half-dozen beers aren't surprises, but they'll do. We prefer the much smaller garden of Pavillon just off the car park on Fredrichshainstrasse. The view is only OK if you look away from the cars, but we like its intimacy. It features light and dark draft beer from the Czech Jarosover and a small menu that will feed you if you need it to.

Brauerei am RollBerg (Am Sudhaus 3) is a pain to get to and it's only open Thursday through Sunday in the evenings, but it's worth the trek. It's located in a part of the old Berliner Kindl brewery, so you'll catch a piece of history. When you get inside the pub, have them turn on the lights so you can see. The small brewpub system sits directly under the bottom of the huge brew kettle that still remains in the old brewery building. No one gets to see what's still left upstairs, but the looming copper is a dramatic sight from beneath, like an alien landing gone wrong. Of the one seasonal and three regular beers, the Hell is the most professional; all are organic. If you're so inclined, stop at a grocery and pick up a good steak or sausage and whatever fixings appeal. The brewpub keeps a grill going to cook your own food in good weather.

To get there take the U8 subway line to the Boddinstrasse stop, exit the station at the front of the train, and keep walking on Hermannstrasse until you get to Werbellinstrasse and turn left. Go just past the big grocery store and, at Werbellinstrasse 50, enter what looks like an abandoned warehouse project. You'll recognize the classic shape of a 19th century tower brewery. Walk towards the brewery circle and around counter clockwise, and you'll bump into the entrance on ground level.

Marcus Bräu (Münzstr. 1-3) claims to be the smallest brewpub in the city and we have no reason to doubt it. If you want to take a look, it's not far from Alexanderplatz and the Lemke and Mitte brewpubs.

Am RollBerg: the old (look up) and new

Lindenbräu (Bellevuestrasse 3) is a towering brewpub in a new building near Potsdamer Platz, so it's not far off a very well beaten path. Lindenbräu Hofbräu Weisse is the one house beer, and while it teems with flavors, not all of them are pleasant. Lindenbräu is actually a Hofbräuhaus Traunstein outlet, however, and the Bavarian imports are pretty good. The Pils, for example, is one of the better beers you can find in Berlin. Food is reliable and it's worth a visit just to see what may be the world's only silver brew kettle. We've read a report that they've stopped brewing, however, and their website is suspiciously silent about the origin of their "fresh" beer.

Where to eat

Zur Letzen Instanz (Waisenstrasse 14-16) is a short but tricky walk from U Bahn Klosterstrasse Station (a map will help). Nearly all drinking places offer good food in Berlin. Happily, exceptional restaurants usually offer good beer as well. Zur Letzen Instanz claims to be the city's oldest restaurant, dating from 1621. The beer menu isn't bad and holds a few surprises. One of them for us was Raschhofer Zwicklbier, an unfiltered gem from Altheim that more than matches its sweet malt with a dry, yeasty, and nicely bitter finish. The echt German menu was worth the effort to find the place.

Pfefferbräu Restraunt und Bergbrauerei (Schönhauser Allee 176) just missed out on our top six drinking experiences and it's easy to get to. We think it's worth the considerable time you might spend waiting for service. Take the U2 to Senefelderplatz; Pfefferbräu is exactly across the street from the station, through a stone archway and up a flight of steps to a garden perched on the hillside. When you don't see it, look harder.

The newpub-style house beers are clottingly yeasty, but mercifully it's a good-tasting yeast. The view from a window table overlooks the street below and gets prettier and prettier as the sun sets. In good weather a large (by Berlin standards) patio-garden hums. It's an unusually good place to drink. But food is the star. It's an arts-themed eatery (there's a comedy theater upstairs), and the artistry conveys to the kitchen. A fish soup was the best single dish of our latest trip to Europe: a delicate fish broth served as a palette for the flavors of a dazzling array of very fresh fish and shellfish. The kitchen also handles handle ordinary extraordinary well. Veal liver is a Berliner specialty and here it's as tender as foie gras. A schnitzel is properly massive, though the potato salad tasted as if it came from an institution-sized bucket.

If you're in the Mitte area and want a taste of Bavaria, **Augustiner am Gendarmenmarkt** is just a few blocks east of Meisterstück on Charlottenstrasse 55. They tap a wooden keg at 6 PM and it's gone in an hour. A second might last a little longer, but when it's gone, you're drinking draft—which is still OK. The Bier vom Holzfass is decidedly sweeter than the draft version: CO_2 in the keg adds a hint of bitter bite the cask doesn't have. Food is reliably Bavarian; the limited menu made us feel, for better or worse, that we had never left Munich. We almost never make reservations, but you should here unless you don't mind eating at the bar. It's not Munich-large and completely fills even on a Monday night. Even with a reservation, be prepared to wait 45 minutes or more for your food, though when we've been there for the Holzfass we've never found the wait a serious problem. You can sit and drink at the bar, but they expect tables to turn in the dining area.

Maximillian's, a tourist-oriented Paulaner outlet at Friedrichstrasse 185-190, is another Stadtmitte possibility—you'll probably see signs on pickup trucks pointing you to it. Prices are pretty good for a big city.

Where to stay

Go online and book in advance. The tourist office in the station will assure you that the city is full when it is decidedly not, but you can waste hours proving them wrong. The Berlin Hilton isn't the chain's best, but the location on the Gendarmenmarkt is superb and the breakfast can hold you until dinner. In summer you can sometimes get a room for about 100€ if you book online and agree to a non-cancellation policy. Some other major chains that cater to businessmen also give huge discounts during the summer. Be skeptical about location claims and check the addresses on an Internet map site. One example: the Mercure "am Alexanderplatz" is an affordable and pleasant reincarnation of a Communist architectural disaster, but you can just barely see its rooftop sign from Alexanderplatz—a good 15 minute walk away.

What to see

Trying to guide you to the sights in a city of this size is as futile as it would be in Paris or London, but as with those capitals of the world, there are a few things you have to see or face the scorn of your friends back home. The Museuminsel (Museum Island) can cost you a full day, but you won't regret it. The Pergamon has one of the greatest collections of ancient artifacts in the world; German archeologists were as acquisitive as their British counterparts.

The Brandenburg Gate gives you a striking opportunity to see how far the eastern sector has come in a generation with the infusion of western capital. The museum at Checkpoint Charlie shows devices East Germans used to escape to the west. It's a wonderful tribute to human ingenuity and courage in the face of authority. The Berlin City Museum, tracing the history of the city, is just east of Freidrichstrasse on Unter den Linden. It won't cost much time or money but gives a decent historical orientation, with some memorable photos of the divided years.

The zoo is a great change of pace and you can end your visit in the city's best beer garden (see above). The Charlottenburg Palace is striking if you haven't overdosed on others of its kind. A trip to Potsdam and Frederick II's Sans Souci will teach you more about the Enlightenment than most semester college courses.

The elevated sections of the U Bahn and the rattling streetcars in the outer sections are tourist attractions in themselves. At night on some U Bahn lines you'll be serenaded by bands of rolling buskers, some of which are actually worth the coins they expect from you.

Scams and alerts

There are a few areas that you'd not be so welcome in—your desk clerk can advise if you're particularly adventurous after dark. The places we send you to are in safe areas, though if you stay really late in a remote pub you might consider a cab to the U Bahn. The panhandlers in the subway can be edgy, and note our cautions about pickpockets in the introduction.

Further information

The "Bier Meile" (Beer Mile) in early August is one of the most remarkable beer festivals in the world. It's very, very commercial, but on a nearly unimaginable scale. It stretches along Karl-Marx-Allee for a full two subway stops—a true mile if you pace it off—on one of the eastern sector's massively wide sidewalks. Breweries from all over Germany and from many parts of Europe set up shop in wagons, carts, and small portable beer gardens. A .2 liter tasting glass allows you to purchase 2€ samples of most of the beers. For more serious or focused drinking you pay a deposit for a glass and drink whatever that stall is selling, then get your deposit back and move on. If you want to keep the glass, the deposit becomes the purchase price. Get a festival map if you care what country's beer you drink. There's music in 20 stages up and down the strip that peak in the evening. In the evening the crowds teem, but with persistence you'll get beer—though probably not a seat.

We like the Sunday session. The festival observes "Mittagsuhr," a quiet time when bands are forbidden to play until 3 PM. Crowds are light and the serving staff has a chance to be friendlier. Unlike British festivals, few vendors run out of beer until very late: better to have a leftover keg than lose the potential sales at 10€ a liter.

Day trips and excursions

Lutherstadt Wittenberg

Our colleague Joel, who knows far more history than we do, broke our hearts by assuring us that Martin Luther did not, in fact, nail 97 theses to the church door in Wittenberg. But happily, Joel hasn't lectured to the people of Wittenberg, so they'll show you where and how Luther did the hammering, even if he didn't.

Luther used this door even if he didn't nail things on it

The church itself is easy to visit and has a simple elegance that's worth your time. Luther may not have nailed here but he did preach here, and he did set off the Protestant Reformation from this spot. Thomas Friedman calls our own global era a time of the "super-empowered individual," but Wittenberg can remind you that individuals in the right time and place have long been able to change the world. The Protestant Reformation may have led to a "work ethic" that contributed to Europe's global domination a century or two later. It certainly sparked peasant revolts in the short run, and centuries of devastating European international and civil wars. All this from a small-town priest who just wanted to encourage some big guys to clean up their act.

Of course we wouldn't send you there just to see a church. **Brauhaus Wittenberg** is an unusually attractive two-story newpub. The bar surrounds the gleaming brew vessels, whose venting stacks extend up through the ceiling for diners on the second level to admire. A courtyard garden is a lovely respite on nice days. The beers aren't spectacular, but the Dunkles is pretty good, and the setting is superb. Fortified by a few decent local beers and a good lunch, you'll be set to wander the streets of this walkable-sized town. There's enough of the old left standing to make for a pleasant and most un-Berlin-like afternoon.

Leipzig

Leipzig (see the chapter) is an 80 minute rail jaunt from Berlin. We strongly recommend giving it a couple of days, but if you don't have time, you can do some highlights in a day trip. Visit the Thomaskirche and have a beer and a bite at the Brauerei an der Thomaskirche, see a museum, and end the day with a Gose at either Ohne Bedenken or Bayerischer Bahnhof. Trains run late, but check the "Abfahrts" at the station to be sure of getting back to Berlin. Chemnitz, our day trip from Leipzig, is another easy reach from Berlin.

Birmingham

Quick orientation

Birmingham is a modern city stuffed into a small Victorian core. Some of it is crumbling, some of it is under construction, but for England's second largest city, most of it is surprisingly close together. The advantage is that with a bit of luck you can walk nearly anywhere. The disadvantage is that cars can't move on the circuitous, gridlocked streets. A friend from London remarked, "If you learn to drive in Birmingham, you can drive anywhere in the world."

You'll probably arrive at the New Street Station. When it opened in 1854, it had the largest roof in the world. Renovations have left it thoroughly modern and almost as impressive, and its central location puts it close to much of what you'll want to see.

When you arrive, go to the WH Smith bookstore and buy yourself the best map you can find—never mind the cost or the weight, you can leave it in your hotel room when you leave. (Actually the pocket size AA map will do.) Make sure it shows the canals as well as the roads. You'll still get lost, but at least with a good map you can find your way back to where you started more quickly. Maybe.

Canal narrowboats

Station breaks

Several of the best pubs are within a very walkable 10-minute radius of the New Street station. If you know what you're doing and are relatively luggage free, three of our top six picks, The Briar Rose, The Wellington, and The Post Office Vaults, are well within our 10-minute limit. The station pub is The Shakespeare; it's very expensive and keg only. Don't even think about it; you're three minutes from a good pub and five from one of our favorites in the world.

To reach all of our station breaks, take the New Street exit. You'll actually be on Stephenson. Turn left and then right on Lower Temple Street, to find a much better Shakespeare on your left. This Shakespeare opens at 10 AM and serves good cask ale. It's a Nicholson house, but carries a nice range of guest beers, often local and sometimes hard to find. For some reason it tends to be a bit more sedate than some of the other bars in the area. Food is good quality pub grub and probably a cut above the Briar Rose. If you have more time, proceed uphill past the Shakespeare, turn left on New Street at the top of the hill for a block, and then turn right on Bennetts Hill. Heading up the hill, first the Briar Rose in half a block, then the Wellington in the next block, are a short walk. If you stay on New Street, the Post Office Vaults is on the left through a tiny door a few doors from #81. The Vaults could make you miss your train. The Wellington, for us, already has.

History and culture

Birmingham (pronounced Birmingum, *not* the U.S. "Birming-ham"; "Brum" if you're in a hurry) was, and still is, a working man's city, but it is emerging from its grimy past. The youth unemployment is still too high and the unemployed youth get too drunk too early in the afternoon, but it's also a city with a vibrant intellectual life as well. It can get raucous, but it's safe.

Birmingham started as a Saxon village in the early Middle Ages. In the 12th century it was granted the right to a market, then a fair, attracting people from throughout the Midlands. By the 17th century, with 5,000 residents, it had become a significant textile center. The Industrial Revolution started early here, and by the turn of the 19th century, the population had swollen to 73,000. By the early 1800s it was an economic powerhouse.

James Watt was Scottish, but did much of his best work in Birmingham. Watt, often credited with inventing the steam engine, actually only improved the work of others, but those improvements raised the steam engine from an inefficient behemoth, good for little more than pumping water out of the mines that produced the coal it gobbled up, to a world-changing tool. Watt made it smaller, simpler, and safer—compact enough to fit on a car on rails, and efficient enough to power a factory. The Industrial Revolution began.

Birmingham's history has long been entwined with transportation. Today it remains a major rail hub. We know a railroad projects engineer who realized it was easier to live in Birmingham and commute all over the UK than to move from city to city at the end of each project. It's barely over an hour to London or York, and only four to Glasgow.

Birmingham also became one of the world's great jewelry centers, with hundreds of independent businesses crowded into the "Jewellery Quarter" along with other high-end manufacturing companies. ("Brummagem" is still a mild pejorative for inexpensive, flashy jewelry.) Heavier industries lined the canals of the center city. Birmingham was also the world's most important city for pen manufacturing; 100 companies exported to nearly everywhere. Many of them located in the Jewellery Quarter and some of the original buildings still stand.

The canals that still thread the city were a key to its 18th and 19th century growth. In 1768, James Brindley received a £50,000 contract to build the city's first major canal system. Unfortunately he needed another £20,000 to do the job right with embankments and tunnels. Brindley delivered by looking at a contour map and realizing he could build a complete system at exactly 450 feet above sea level. His pioneering "contour canals" cut through the city to reach the nearby major coal fields. The routes were long and twisting, but when the canals opened, the price of coal in Birmingham dropped by 50% overnight. Later improvements added the bridges, tunnels, and locks that Brindley couldn't afford. The tunnels, some of them over three miles long, were unpleasant to traverse, lit with tallow candles and oil lamps, but these improvements spurred even more economic development. At one time Birmingham's canals extended over 150 miles. About 100 miles are still in use for transport or recreation; the nifty and distinctive narrow canal boats are everywhere. The waters look dirty, but what you see is the coal silt on the bottom; if you scoop out a glassful, it's perfectly clear.

New industries are helping Birmingham emerge from the economic doldrums of the late 20th century. A major university, theaters and performing arts centers, one of England's premier aquariums, and a range of museums help define its identity. Birmingham's cultural and physical center is its massive new library.

Beer styles and drinking culture

The "Big Boys"—in this case primarily Holts and Mitchells & Butlers—so dominated the town that the city had a less-than-average selection of beer in the 20th century. But M&B is gone and Holts no longer brews within the city, and there doesn't seem to be a brewery that has developed a "home town" following. Many pubs now post "local" stickers on the tap handles; however, "local" is a tough word to define in the West Midland's packed brewing scene. CAMRA defines it as within 30 miles, but is a brewery 32 miles away really any less local? Birmingham's central location has made it easy for publicans to obtain beers from an exceptionally wide range of small but ambitious craft breweries.

The beer range is typical for much of England. Gold ales rule in the summer; darker, heavier beers help get Brummies through the winter. Increasingly, though, you'll find "out of season" darker beers in the summer. A local CAMRA branch sponsors social events and publishes pub news in *Out Inn Brum*—you'll find a copy at the Wellington.

A recent trip coincided with a sort of informal cider festival. We're not sure whether it was simply suggestion, or if some pubs were running ciders and beers through the same taps, but many of the beers had a distinct apple-y flavor. We think the city has a bit of a sweet tooth and likes the taste of apple. Many ale yeasts throw apple flavors, but these were sweeter and more cider-like than we expected. You can find some hoppy beers, especially in the Wellington and the Post Office Vaults, but the usual pint of bitter isn't very. We don't list specific beers in this chapter because the attraction of nearly all our favorite places is the constant turnover of a vast range of beer. Anything we could recommend would be long gone by the time you got there.

The sixpack of drinking experiences

As you read this book, you'll see cities that are so crammed with phenomenal places to drink that we've had to include double lists of six. Not here. While there are some up-and-coming new beer bars, to the best of our knowledge the top four here stand in a group by themselves. Lots of other bars in Brum are good places to drink, but the top four make Birmingham a destination for beer fanatics.

The Wellington Specialist Real Ale Pub (37 Bennetts Hill). From New Street Station, walk out the New Street exit and take the directions above. This is the bar that made us include Birmingham in this guide. Once quite unassuming, it received a significant face lift in 2013 that's changed the overall feel from slum to spiff. (Remember we like slum, but we can deal with spiff if the beer is good.) A welcoming drinking area as you enter includes comfortable seating and a working fireplace with lovely tiles. The longish, rather narrow bar area leads to a second, equally decent drinking area. Out in the alley, a flower-framed staircase provides the ouside access to a small sheltered terrace for smokers. There's a new upstairs bar and drinking spaces including another pretty fireplace. A new ladies' WC changes the experience of the place for women with flowers and complimentary toiletries; don't worry, guys, it's still pretty basic for us downstairs.

The Wellington: thirsty yet?

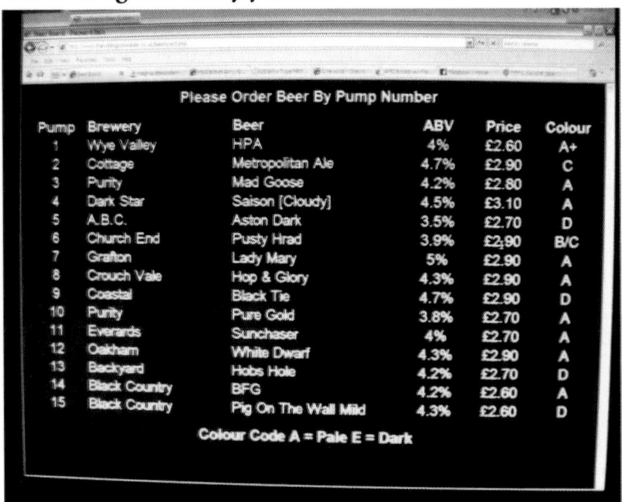

Please Order Beer By Pump Number

Pump	Brewery	Beer	ABV	Price	Colour
1	Wye Valley	HPA	4%	£2.60	A+
2	Cottage	Metropolitan Ale	4.7%	£2.90	C
3	Purity	Mad Goose	4.2%	£2.80	A
4	Dark Star	Saison [Cloudy]	4.5%	£3.10	A
5	A.B.C.	Aston Dark	3.5%	£2.70	D
6	Church End	Pusty Hrad	3.9%	£2.90	B/C
7	Grafton	Lady Mary	5%	£2.90	A
8	Crouch Vale	Hop & Glory	4.3%	£2.90	A
9	Coastal	Black Tie	4.7%	£2.90	D
10	Purity	Pure Gold	3.8%	£2.70	A
11	Everards	Sunchaser	4%	£2.70	A
12	Oakham	White Dwarf	4.3%	£2.90	A
13	Backyard	Hobs Hole	4.2%	£2.70	D
14	Black Country	BFG	4.2%	£2.60	A
15	Black Country	Pig On The Wall Mild	4.3%	£2.60	D

Colour Code A = Pale E = Dark

The most distinctive feature remains untouched: several flat-screen monitors over the bar project a computer table that lists the 16 cask ales by name, brewery, ABV, and darkness; an icon indicates if the beer is local. In this beer mecca, taps change sometimes hourly and even the staff can't keep up, so you're asked to order by tap number.

The beer is nearly always in superb condition, and the Wellington's range provides a festival experience. In keeping with their beer-only philosophy, they don't serve food, but they do provide plates and cutlery. They don't just allow, but "welcome" you to bring your own food. You'll have no trouble finding good grub to bring in during the day. A Philpotts sandwich shop is almost next door; they'll make a huge range of sandwiches to order, put together a salad, or carve you a roast to go. At night stray farther: the Briar Rose will let you carry out, and if you get to the "M Local" market before it closes, you'll find a wide range of take away foods including rotisserie chicken and salad. Other food shops abound on New Street. We do not recommend the McDonald's.

The Wellington staff is well informed and friendly even at the busiest of times. Not surprisingly, the place tends to draw good people interested in good beer. If you don't strike up a conversation with someone around you, it's because you don't want to.

In one of our many visits, three kegs changed in a two-hour period. We've never moved in at the 10 AM opening and closed it up to find out how many beers we could get in a day, but that plan is on our bucket list. We sleep a block downhill at the Briar Rose, but there's also a Premier Inn on Waterloo Street, just downhill and around the corner.

Our second and third choices are here in part because almost every experienced beer drinker we encountered in the city said these were the top two. And because we really did like them. But they take more work to get to than most pubs in this guide. Both have the two distinctive bar areas—the "public" in front and the posher "private" or "saloon bar" in back—that used to be a hallmark of British pubs. Lots of dark wood, red carpets, velvet curtains, and brass fittings create the ambience that "pubs" in the U.S. try so hard and so unsuccessfully to imitate.

The Old Moseley Arms (53 Tindal Street, Balsall Heath), a 15 minute ride (bus #50—you'll have to ask where to get off), is a gem. The owners dropped the better part of a hundred grand not long ago to return it to its 19th century ambience. It's especially worth the effort to get there during the four seasonal festivals it holds each year—an array of 10 casks makes the garden in back a destination. It's run by a relatively new Brummy who cares passionately about beer and about presenting beer in a traditional atmosphere. Be sure to read the four-page history of the pub on the wall in the front lounge.

The Black Eagle (16 Factory Road, Hockley). Take the Metro—the "tram"—to Benson Road, Soho, and turn right and walk downhill. Have faith. It's on the left just about when you think you're in the wrong place.

This "trad" pub features beautiful frosted front windows and a horsey theme. A small snug is on the left, and to the right is the bar, leading to a dining room at the back. They take their food seriously here. Beer selection is good, not great, but they're in good condition. The staff couldn't be friendlier, but use the Internet if you have questions about the beer. To paraphrase Mark Twain, "It ain't what they don't know, it's what they know for sure that just ain't so." If you're hauling yourself out there for a beer seminar, you've come for the wrong reason. It's a great pub with great beer and great people: enjoy both.

The Post Office Vaults (New Street). If you continue on New Street past Bennets Hill and the Wellington you'll see Victoria Square and the grand old Post Office building. Before you get there, look left. Hard. At #85, which is to say about 17 inches from the end, there's a single red edged door with, if you're lucky, a small marquee signboard in front. We walked past it at least six times before some kindly 20-year-olds gave us directions (it was right behind us). It's not hard to spot if you know it's between #81 and #86, both of which are clearly marked. Downstairs is the Wellington's sister pub. With eight taps compared to the Wellington's 16, they seem to try even harder to find beers you won't see anywhere else. And if by any chance you're bored by the cask offerings, a small telephone directory of several hundred Belgian beers includes some that aren't easy to find in their own home country. The Vaults have some American rarities as well. The bartender is a beer fanatic and can talk beer all night, if you want and it's not too busy. A young crowd fills the place late, but as is so true of almost everywhere in Birmingham, they couldn't be friendlier. They'll even kid you a bit—which, if you've traveled at all, you'll know is the ultimate greeting. You're a regular on your first visit if you care about beer.

The Briar Rose (25 Bennetts Hill Road) is a JD Wetherspoon pub. Wetherspoon operates over 800 pubs in the UK; the name came from one of the founder's teachers (Wetherspoon) and, we're not making this up, Sheriff J.D. Hogg from the American TV series "Dukes of Hazzard." All Wetherspoons feature cask ales and many offer a decent range. We've found the quality to vary, but if you're stuck in an airport and find a Wetherspoon, count yourself lucky.

You could do worse than the Briar Rose, too. Just downhill from the Wellington, it's a big and sometimes raucous boozer, but a solid value and a bargain food stop before you settle in at the Wellington. It used to have a more extensive beer range, but it still has some guests of interest, they're in good shape, and they change every day or two. On a 2012 trip, a "two-for" special on the dinner menu fed two people nicely for the equivalent of $15—including two UK pints of cask ale.

Wetherspoon operates a half a dozen other pubs in the city and many are at least as good for beer drinkers as the Briar Rose. But they're not located on your route between the Wellington and the Post Office Vaults. For that matter, many of the pubs we've listed for the Jewellery Quarter and the canals probably match the experience of drinking here. But they're not on the way…

Pennyblacks in the Mailbox (132-134 Wharfside St.). The Mailbox is a gigantic multiuse (offices, restaurants, boutiques) structure with a distinctive solid red front—you can see it from all over the city. Pennyblacks underwent a total refurbishment which we haven't seen. Some of it needed improvement: CAMRA beer geeks disapproved of its commercial brassiness and the fair lack of knowledge on the part of the staff. Admittedly the place was pretty hokey—the casks and copper dispense pipes behind the bar were fake—but they did have up to eight real casks on real hand pull. We've never been there without finding beers that were new to us. The food wasn't dramatic, but reliable. You could do much worse in the area (for example, the "Handmade

Burger Company" that evidently cared much more about its cows than it did about its customers).

Other places to explore

The **Two Towers Brewery** is the more accessible of Birmingham's two breweries; check the Web for information about their sporadic £10 tours. You can find the beers in several of Birmingham's beer spots including the Rose Villa and Malt House below. The name refers to J.R.R. Tolkien's work, of course, but specifically to two Birmingham "towers" that supposedly inspired Tolkien, who lived in Birmingham for 15 years. The towers are Perrot's Folly and the water works tower near the Edgbaston Reservoir. Fanciful stories abound explaining the Folly, though the most credible explanation is simply that Perrot built it as a good place to party. You can still see them, though Perrot's Folly is now closed to the public.

The other Birmingham brewery, **Aston Manor Brewery**, despite its name produces far more cider than beer.

You can get brochures at the library for some pub tours in sections of Birmingham. We picked up a couple at the Wellington (you have to ask); the Jewellery Quarter guide proved invaluable in discovering the pubs below. The Jewellery Quarter not only is a wonderful pub tour, but also takes you to some of the city's best sights.

We suggest you include the following in a Jewellery crawl, and check out our "what to see" section before you head out.

The Drop Forge (10 Hockley Street) is very near the Jewellery Museum. It still has a good portion of the forge behind glass. It's a very handsome gastropub with industrial iron, pale woods, skylights, and angular steel stairs leading to upper levels with some of the machinery still in place. The bar itself seems something of an afterthought, but overall it's a good reclamation and its four rotating handpulls serve quite good cask ale. Skip the Jewellers Arms a block away. At a distance it's an attraction, but inside it's clubby with a narrow range of beer.

The Rose Villa Tavern (172 Warstone Lane) is also quite close to the Jewellery Museum. It's a renovated old Mitchells & Butlers pub that has been reborn as a gastropub. It's spacious, with more room upstairs, but the small rooms give it a sense of intimacy. The floors and stained glass windows are original. It's sort of an ordinary pub for Birmingham, but we'd give both right arms to have it within walking distance of our house.

The Lord Clifden (Great Hampton Street) has some cask ales, but is most proud of its "Yeast Budweiser"—the stuff from Czech, not St. Louis. It's unfiltered and worth the effort to find if you're not going to Prague or Budweis. They also have dark Budweiser and a tap that pours a blend of gold and dark. A long series of bars leads to a nice garden in the back, a great place to drink if it's not raining. On Sundays they feature a traditional English roast lunch that is well worth the 15- to 20-minute walk from the city center.

Not far away, **The Church** (22 Great Hampton Street) is an attractive corner pub serving cask ales. It's not worth the walk from the center by itself, but can fill out a

Jewellery Quarter pub crawl nicely. It's an Everards tied house, and the new owner and menu feature "down home Louisiana cookin'." (?!) **The Queens Arms** is closer to the city center (150 Newhall Street), a few blocks toward town from St. Paul's. It has one of the most charming facades we've ever seen and just reeks of traditional British pubbery. The inside doesn't disappoint.

Some other city center taps are more commercial, but worth a visit if you have time.

The Malt House (75 King Edwards Road), a Taylor Walker house, is a sprawling, rather commercial pub, but its location is fantastic: smack on an intersection of two canals with some of the best drinking views in the city. It's wedged between the National Indoor Arena and Symphony Hall and across the canal from the aquarium. They serve decent food and cask ale. It's a good stop if you're waiting for the one-hour canal tour that leaves from just down the quay.

Walk along the canal toward Broad Street, cross the canal there, and keep going along the water; the **Canalside Café** is near Gas Street about halfway from the Malt House to the Mailbox. It's just off Broad Street, though if you're on Broad Street you'd never know. Three handpulls serve good beer, but the story is the canalside tables.

This stretch of canal is studded with waterside gardens, pubs, and cafés. The largest beer garden in Birmingham, according to themselves, is **The Figure Eight** on Broad Street, a Wetherspoon tavern that blends in with an array of lager-oriented binge bars, but the garden is fairly echt. **The Tap and Spile's** upstairs bar can be a bit clubby, but in good weather, its quieter lower level has tables right on the canal.

The Queens Arms

Where to eat

Balti is a type of Indian cuisine in which marinated meats and vegetables are cooked quickly; the spice blend was supposedly developed in Birmingham, and there are numerous Balti restaurants. Some are BYOB places; you might want to consider bringing Aston Manor's Balti Beer, a brew that is supposed to enhance the richness of the spices.

Where to stay

We've stayed at the Briar Rose and the Hampton Inn, and they both have their attractions, but plenty of other choices abound. You should be able to find a room even in high season, but your choices may be limited if you don't book in advance.

The Briar Rose has accommodations at £59, but if you book online through Wetherspoon's website or at laterooms.com, you can sometimes do much better. If you stay there, you can roll out of bed and get breakfast and a beer at 7 AM while you're waiting for the Wellington to open. Rooms are well appointed—not huge but comfortable, and all have bathrooms. An adequate British breakfast is available in the pub at an additional but very reasonable charge. Try for a room on the second or third floor. You'll be able to get to your room during the frequent elevator outages, and you're still high enough to avoid some of the street noise (Bennetts Hill is a challenge for truck [sorry, "lorry"] transmissions). It isn't perfect, but it's very good value in a good part of town, and a brief walk to the trains at New Street Station.

Sometimes cheaper is the "Hampton by Hilton" on Broad Street, where a AAA card can get you a room for as little as £51. Several other chain hotels including a Hilton Garden Inn are nearby. The Briar Rose is much more of a British experience, though the Hampton (the largest outside the U.S.) folds in some European elements such as a hot, if pre-fabbed, English-style breakfast: sausages, beans, tomatoes etc.

Major hotel chains abound; the Bull Ring area is convenient, but noisy at night. Hotels on or near canals include the Hyatt, the Premier Inn, and the Ramada, which occupies the upper floors of the Mailbox, the canal-side shopping center that includes Pennyblacks (above).

The Paragon Hotel in Digbeth is about a 15 minute walk from the city and has an interesting history. It was built as one of the Rowton Houses, inexpensive but decent hostels for working men built by a Victorian philanthropist in the 19th century. For a shilling a day, residents had a place to stay, access to cheap meals, and an information service listing job openings. You'll now pay closer to $100 for a refurbished en suite double, which still isn't too bad for city prices.

What to see

The main art museum has some 19th century gems and, like nearly every major art museum in Europe, some other surprises. One of the surprises is that it's free.

The Jewellery Museum is rated as one of the best free museums in Europe. Note opening hours carefully. It's closed Sunday and Monday, which of course is when we tried to go.

The pen museum in the Jewellery Quarter is free, though they ask for a donation. It's not the Smithsonian, but it's a nice two-room glimpse into a specialized, lucrative industry that helped change the world. How can there be so many different kinds of pen tips?

To get a far more detailed history and sense of Birmingham's past, take one of the narrated hour-long canal tours on a traditional narrowboat. Sherbourne's Wharf (don't go to the wharf, it's just where they keep their boats) runs tours from the Convention Center several times a day. Other companies leave from the Mailbox area. Prices run £6 to £8 per person. If you're a folkie, you'll like the piped-in music, although much of it, oddly, is from the American canal song repertoire.

Churches: Rising out of the shopping center, St. Martin in the Bull Ring is easy to reach and open from 10:00 to 16:30 daily as well as on Sunday. There has been a church on the site since at least the 14th century, though the current gothic Victorian building dates from 1873. The architecture and stained glass make it worth a look. St. Paul's is a century older and a natural stopoff on a Jewellery Quarter visit. If you can get in, note the east window.

The Science Center has hands-on exhibits for the kids and one of the most extensive aquatic life museums in England.

Vintage Trains runs excursions, including a "Shakespeare Express" on summer Sundays to Stratford-upon-Avon (http://www.vintagetrains.co.uk).

Scams and alerts

Taxis don't have it easy in this maze of congested one-way streets, but the drivers are almost as inventive as the ones in Brussels in finding long circular routes to "avoid the traffic," which, of course, in Birmingham only means a longer circular route through more traffic. Walk or take a bus if you possibly can.

The rate of actual street crime is low, but be sensible about dark canals and dark streets at night. Well-lit areas are populated and safe.

The "lager louts" come out in full force in the evening, or even the afternoon. They mostly bother each other, but occasionally out of boredom turn to harassing other passersby. We've found if you stop and ask directions, they'll usually turn into your best friends—and sometimes they'll even know how to get you where you want to go.

Day trip

Burton-upon-Trent

We were tempted to include Burton-upon-Trent as one of our 24 cities. It was the definitive home of Pale Ale for decades and rightfully has a place among iconic brewing cities like Pilsen, Bamberg, Amsterdam, and Munich. However, the number of great pubs and the range of beers on offer in the city is narrow, not only for the cities in our 24, but compared to other cities in this part of the UK, such as Huddersfield and York, which have a better range of beer specialty bars. Still, Burton is a doable and most rewarding day trip. You can reach it easily from Birmingham or Sheffield, and there's plenty enough beer to enjoy while you take a trip into brewing history.

We've learned a great deal about water by visiting Burton breweries over the years. The famous gypsum-rich Burton water, which attracted brewing companies in flocks back in the 19th century, has been so depleted that the increased mineral content of the city's well water would make undrinkable beer. Hence, local breweries now strip the water of whatever minerals are left, then add the right ones back in—a process called "Burtonization"—to create the same water as in Burton's history. The irony is that Burton brewers now have to do the same thing as any other brewer around the world, from London to Las Vegas, to get the water where they need it to be. Marstons claims they use original source Burton water, but we were told by another brewery that you can't brew in Burton without Burtonizing. In any event, water is more engineering than location these days.

At its peak Burton had 30 breweries, most of them production facilities that sent beer far afield. At one point, Burton produced almost 25% of all the beer brewed in Britain, but the glory days are gone. Bass decided to become a pub company instead of a brewery, branched out to include hotels, and as a result almost committed corporate suicide. Bass Ale is now made by Marstons. The old Bass brewery is a museum, and the somewhat newer Bass brewery is now a Molson-Coors mass-market operation making Carling, which for a while was the largest selling beer in England. You can be sure the brewery does not import Rocky Mountain spring water for its Coors.

If you want a tour of a real brewery, call in advance to the **Marston's Brewery visitor center.** The normal minimum tour size is 50, but they'll pack you in with a group if they know you're coming. The reason to make the effort to do the tour is that it's unlike any other in the world. Marstons operates the last remaining Burton Union system of brewing, a process that defined Bass for nearly a century. A phalanx of 26 or 52 wooden fermentation vessels are linked together; the actively fermenting beer, thick with yeast, bubbles up into a trough that funnels it back into the casks, until finally all the yeast collects in the trough and the beer in the casks is clear. You kind of have to see it to understand how it works. The process is isn't all that different from Samuel Smith's Yorkshire Slate system. Both systems are kept going out of a respect for tradition rather than any economic reason—they're tremendously labor-intensive. You can see one of the last of Bass's Burton Unions between the road and the parking lot of the National Brewery Centre.

If you can't get into Marston's you'll still have a fine and productive day visiting the **National Brewery Centre**, on the grounds of the old Bass Brewery, and following it up with several superb pubs. The Centre has guided tours, but you can work your way through at your own pace quite nicely. Most of it comprises the old Bass Museum, which Bass established when it was still brewing beer. The first building takes you through the history of beer with some operating machinery from the early 20th century. Other buildings house an operating early steam engine (which runs sporadically), nice displays of brewery transport vehicles, some real live draft horses, and exhibits about the brewing industry's place in Burton-on-Trent. The brewery on the ground floor of the Worthington Brewery building looks functional ... because it is.

Cross section of a Burton Union system

The **Brewery Tap,** the last stop on the National Brewery Centre tour (and also open to people from outside), is a fine pub. You can sample the Worthington White Shield, one of the country's original IPAs, fresh from the "cow." If you've paid for the tour, you'll get four tokens which get you four "single pull" samples or can be combined for a half pint.

You get more beer with the singles, but we'd suggest buying a full pint of the White Shield. We've had it in bottles in London and on cask in a number of pubs, but it's never seemed to us to be worth the fuss. Here, it is. The rich, chewy malt is remarkably delicate for a 5.6% beer. We understand now why it doesn't travel well, but shows so well at the brewery. It's been around since the 19th century, and savoring it here after the tour lets you take a step back in time.

The largest locally owned brewery in the city is **Burton Bridge,** a small but successful brewery with about six tied pubs. Exit the National Brewery Centre visitors center and jog left and then right on Bridge Road. You'll pass "The Malthouse," a reuse project of one of the old malteries. As you go down Bridge Road, look for the round blue plaques on buildings on both sides of the street. You're on the "brewery trail" (see the tourist office for more information) which takes you past several of the dozens of breweries that once thrived in Burton. Before you get to the bridge, opposite the Three Queens Hotel, is the Burton Bridge Brewery. Established in 1982 at the dawn of the craft movement in England, it remains a destination for beer lovers from Burton and around the world. Be sure to take note of the "Gold Medal Beer"—it changes monthly, with new hops and a new name. The "guest beer" is from Burton Bridge, but one that is usually not on tap. The brewery and a garden are out back.

There are a few tiny production breweries in the city, one of which has a brewery tap which makes it, in effect, a brewpub. The **Burton Old Cottage** brewery outlet is the **Cottage Tavern.** To find it, exit the station, turn left, and walk until you see the unmistakable Town Hall. It has two-foot-high brick replicas of old town walls around it. Walk past it, turn right and go to the end of the block. The Cottage is on your right. It's a lovely typical British pub, with three rooms and several handpulls. They have several regulars from the brewery plus rotating guest beers from a wide area in England as well as other Burton micros.

The best pub in Burton is **Coopers.** It was, long ago, a home for the brewmaster, then was used to store Bass Porter. Those in the know would sneak over and help themselves from the cooperage—the name is a pun—and eventually the company gave up and turned it into a Bass brewery tap. The massive brewery across the street is now Coors, and Coopers is now the brewery tap for Joules Ales in Shropshire. They feature several guest beers, some of which are served on gravity pour. Ironically, Joules was one of the breweries that Bass swallowed up, but it has regained its independence.

The bar area is unique. In a tiny room, hand pulls and gravity guest beers fringe a compact serving bar, and lining the walls of the room are high benches where the regulars perch like crows on a telephone line. Fortunately they're quite friendly, though they'll have you on a bit at the start. The rest of the pub is more normal, but still pleasantly pubby and filled with memorabilia and Joules advertising material. The draught Bass, we believe, is always on gravity and probably as authentic as you can find anywhere any more. No food, but you can take beer from Coopers to the Indian restaurant next door.

A few other good pubs are close enough to the rail station to include in a crawl. The **Roebuck** has three casks and has the advantage of being within sight of the train station. A block past it is the **Devonshire:** comfortable, well respected, and a good source of Burton Bridge ales if you're not going as far as the brewery.

If you chose to make Burton an overnight, the Travelodge is right at the station; come out, turn left. The Three Queens Hotel is opposite the Burton Bridge Brewery. Breweries use it to house out-of-town clients, so we assume the quality is good.

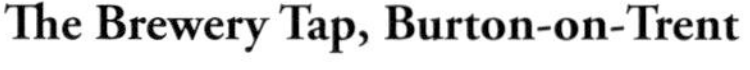
The Brewery Tap, Burton-on-Trent

❧ *Brussels*

Quick orientation

You'll probably arrive at Midi/Zuid, which will quickly demonstrate that everything in Brussels has both a French and Flemish name. Brussels has two other stations: some major trains stop at Nord; only local hoppers bother with the well-named but underused Centraal.

There's a tiny tourist office in Zuid that will sell you a so-worth-it 50 cent map and give you a free but invaluable map of all the bus and tram routes that don't show up on the city map. A larger tourist office is a block off the Grand Place to the east. Very little of the transportation system penetrates the old city center, but the Bourse and Centraal metro stops get you close.

A 24 hour pass on trams, metro, and buses costs €6.50 and is usually worth it, especially if you're staying near Zuid. The old town, happily, is nicely compact.

Restaurants line St. Catherine's Square

Station breaks

You'll want to get away from Midi/Zuid as soon as possible, but if you're stuck waiting for a Eurostar or Thalis, exit the station near the Eurostar terminal onto Horta. Nearly a dozen nearly identical restaurants line the long block that parallels the track. None has a stellar beer selection, but altogether they offer at least 25 different, though pretty usual, Belgian beers. Prices are better than you'd expect given the high tourist traffic.

From Centraal, head downhill on Keizerinlaan, then left on Schildknaaps; the two-block walk takes you to Morte Subite.

The Gare du Nord neighborhood is a beer wasteland, filled with offices on one side of the tracks and rather startling "working girl" displays on the other. You might as well grab a mass-market ersatz Abbey at the coffee shop in the station.

History and culture

Belgium is a political amalgamation of bits of territory that various coalitions over the centuries have fought hard to keep out of the hands of someone else. For much of its history, the area was more or less content to be ruled by Spain, and enough of a tie remains to cause the Bruxellois to go wild in celebrating the Spanish 2010 World Cup victory. The penultimate ping-pong left Belgium in French hands (though not happily; Brigand Beer commemorates the brief but ferocious Peasants War of 1798), but when the English defeated Napoleon at Waterloo in 1815 the Congress of Vienna created the United Kingdom of the Netherlands, under a Protestant German prince, William I. By 1830 the French-speaking Catholics or Walloons in the south were fed up with William's bigotry and the fierce Belgian Revolution erupted in Brussels, triggered (in true Belgian irony) by an opera. The major European powers were sympathetic and eventually split the whole region into the modern Netherlands, Luxembourg, and Belgium. Belgium became a constitutional monarchy ruled by Leopold I of Saxe-Coburg—conveniently, the uncle of Queen Victoria. Independence Day, June 21, celebrates his accession and the acceptance of the national constitution.

Divided by language and religion, but at least both blessed with good resources and a strong work ethic, the French and Flemish Belgians got along just well enough to prosper. As true of any self-respecting 19th century European nation, Belgium became an Imperial power. However, Leopold II made the Belgian Congo his personal possession and exacted its wealth by means of unspeakable abuses. How much Belgium actually gained for the mess they left behind is debatable, but the Empire did result in Brussels becoming one of the most racially diverse cities in Europe.

In 1914, Kaiser Wilhelm of Germany disregarded the 1839 Treaty of London guaranteeing Belgium's neutrality (his chancellor called it a "scrap of paper") and barged through on his way to invade France. Though Belgium found a measure of revenge abroad, beating the Germans in Tanzania (German South West Africa), World War I wrecked the country. Reparations from Germany patched things up some, but in 1940 Germany tackled France again, with Belgium once more a sort of inconvenient roadbump. After that, avoiding another European war was a matter of survival, and Belgium took a leading role in creating the Coal and Steel Community, which evolved into today's European Union. The headquarters of the EU is in Brussels, and few countries celebrate their European ties as enthusiastically.

Beer styles and drinking culture

Belgium's role as a leader in Europeanization and then globalization probably hastened the process of the beer world's "discovery" of its remarkable beer culture. Michael Jackson's writings did even more, earning him an honorary knighthood of the Belgian Brewers Guild (Ridderschap van de Roerstok). While consolidation of the beer market happened here as elsewhere in the 1960s and '70s, it may have been that the Belgian market just wasn't big enough for the big boys to bother trying to conquer. Breweries that owned a significant number of pubs vanished quickly, but independents like Rodenbach held on by selling a unique product to other breweries' pubs. Small local breweries produced beers that big brewers couldn't understand, much less match, and when the world woke up to beer with flavor, the Belgian time capsule stood in remarkably good shape. Today, the Belgians know what they've got. Brands are celebrated on postcards and in souvenir shops.

A curious side effect of those small breweries clinging to tiny market segments is that most interesting beers were sold only in bottles. That's changing some, and the specialty bars now get beers that have only recently become available on draft. The drafts are good, of course, but it's still a good idea in Belgium to think twice before automatically ordering whatever's on tap.

For a tiny country, it's remarkable how localized and regional the beers can be. Most of the really adventurous breweries are in the northern, Flemish section, though many of the abbeys are in the southern French-speaking section.

There can be some confusion over Belgian beer styles. The area around Brussels, the Zenne (Senne) river valley, is known for the unique wild yeasts that produce the authentic lambic beers: spontaneously fermented, astringently dry and acidic, often with enteric notes (horse, poop, urine, etc.). The term "Flemish Red Ale," on the other hand, usually refers to a beer of fruity character and varying sourness. It may or may not have an element of spontaneous fermentation, but the yeasts used are often decidedly unconventional. Both lambics and Flemish reds are puckery, but there's a world of difference between the two. We refer to the Flemish ales as "sour" and the lambics as "wild."

The sixpack of drinking experiences

We remember when **Delirium Village** (Impasse de la Fidelité 4) was just a bar (but a remarkable one), little more than a decade ago. It's now not just a village but an empire. It has a cocktail bar, a monastery bar, a draft bar, a craft beer bar, a tequila bar, an absinthe and gin bar, a Guinness record for most types of beer available ever, and a separate offshoot on the other side of the Grand Place.

But the heart of the place remains the taphouse downstairs, with a beer menu more massive than most telephone books. Astonishingly, nearly the entire menu is in stock. Some are vintages from breweries that have long gone out of business—you have the feeling you're drinking beer from a dead star. Since most Belgian beers hold up pretty well, especially in Delirium's cellars, you can usually get a sense of what the brewery was about. DeProef, and a few others like it, also swell the numbers by producing distinctive beers for almost anyone who walks in their door with a sufficiently fat wallet.

The cellar is good sized and usually very crowded—impossibly so on weekends, but the staff heroically seems to get to everyone in a reasonable time, and once you're seated you can focus on your beer odyssey. Be prepared for the loud and young clientele, who often appear much more interested in how much they can drink rather than how well. Eat before you go; the cold plates of meats and cheeses are fine for snacking but won't keep you out of trouble.

Just above street level is the café. About 30 taps rotate, though they offer less imagination and variety than you'd find in Denmark or England. Tasting glasses at €2 allow you to try beers you know you're not going to want in liter quantities. (Fleurette's Cactus Wit beer topped our list of that sort on our last visit. Never trust a green beer.) The crowd is even younger and louder than downstairs and spills out into what is in essence a smoking alley outside.

Another floor higher is the Hoppy Loft, their craft beer tasting room. The beers are pricier, but the selection of craft beers from all over the world is stunning. It gets crowded on weekends, but early in the week tables are easy to find and the atmosphere is conducive to conversation about the beers you're savoring. The bartenders know beer; trust their recommendations.

The Monasterium is a recent addition that features the monastery and Trappist beers you'd expect, with one significant exception. Most of the drafts are from the Lost Abbey, which isn't an abbey at all, but a line of beers from Port Brewing in San Marcos, California. Don't be disappointed—Tomme Arthur, the Lost Abbey brewer, is one of America's best.

A real functioning lambic brewery in the heart of Brussels, **Cantillon** (Musée Bruxellois de la Gueuze; Metro stop Clemenceau or Gare du Midi) is the best place in the city to taste lambic beers. It also offers one of the best brewery tours anywhere. Cantillon still relies on spontaneous fermentation, in which the bacteria and yeasts that create so much of the flavor just drop out of the atmosphere into the beer as it sits in open vats called cool ships. A handful of exceptionally talented American brewers have created positive-pressure rooms dedicated to the production of wild beers; Jean Paul Van Roy just has to open his window. Jean Paul is a great guy and an international brewing star, and if you're lucky you may get a chance to meet him. The tour gives you a chance to see up close how much art still tops science in making world-class beers. Sitting around in the tasting area—even the new spiffed-up version which has replaced the handful of busted barrels that used to suffice—is an experience to be savored. Check online to find out opening times and tours.

The cool ship at Cantillon

"I want a local like that, and if I can't have one, I want to move here." Ellie rarely waxes as enthusiastic as she did when we reluctantly left the tiny paradise of the original **Moeder Lambic.** "Mother Lambic" began 25 years ago as one of the first bars to celebrate the vast number of Belgian beers available. A thousand bottles filled the place, there was no refrigeration, and the bathrooms were outside. Several near-bankruptcies and changes of ownership later, the emphasis is more on quality than quantity, and the bar obtains exclusive offerings you won't find elsewhere. Weekly specials augment a beer menu with hundreds of regular choices. Go early; the handful of solid wooden tables and benches fill quickly even on weekdays, though outside tables increase capacity in good weather. The staff is friendly and welcoming, playing cards and board games are available at the bar, and bins of comic books, in French naturally, entertain children and adults alike.

The location, Rue de Savoie 68 in the Saint-Gilles section of the city, can seem daunting, but it's not hard to get to. From Zuid, take the 81 tram toward Montgomery and get off at Lombardie. Walk a half block further, uphill, turn right on Rue de Savoie, and it's one block along on the left. Continue on the 81 to Janson, then transfer to the 92 to Congress, and you'll be within a couple of blocks of Bier Circus or the restaurant Titanic.

A few years ago, Moeder Lambic expanded to another bar at Place Fontainas 8, a few blocks south of the Bourse. Follow Blvd. Anspach toward Zuid, and you'll see it hiding behind umbrellas on the left side of the sort-of-square. It has the advantage of a central location, much more space, and about 40 taps, but despite the friendly and helpful staff, we couldn't warm to it the way we did with the original. If you can't get to the original, though, you'll find some of the same exclusive offers here, and you're more likely, though far from guaranteed, to find a seat. (No comic books, though.)

Le Bier Circus claims to be two steps from the Grand Place, and if you're Goliath, it's probably not too many more than that—vertically. At Rue l'Enseignement 57, neatly located three or four blocks from four different Metro stops, it's not hard to get to. We recommend you use the Madou station, cross the square to Rue du Congrès/

Congresstraat, walk downhill, and turn left at Onderrichtsstraat. The food would be worth the visit even without the well-chosen beer list, and the hearty welcome can make you feel like a regular by the end of your first visit. Drafts can include rarities and sometimes include beers made for the house. If this bar were in most other cities, it would be at the top of everyone's list; in Brussels, it's just what you expect. Our only complaint is that it's only open five days a week and closes altogether for three weeks in the height of summer. When you're done, it's a downhill walk, 15 minutes with normal legs, to the Gare Centrale and eventually the Grand Place.

If **Café de la Poechenellekelder** (Rue du Chêne, 5) adds one more piece of period art there won't be room for customers. Monks and casks hang from the ceiling, and the two old regulars in the corner of the bar never leave. It's more than cuteness on steroids, though. Waiters know their beer and serve it with care. Eight interesting drafts rotate weekly, and over a hundred bottles should be able to keep you well amused. La Poechenellekelder overlooks the classic Manneken Pis fountain, and if you can tear yourself away from the museum-like interior, a busy terrace in front puts you within feet of the Pis-gawkers hovering around the fountain. The Manneken apparently offers an especially vigorous pis at 6 PM; all in all we prefer Munich's Glockenspiel. We understand it's not a noble thought, but we can't help a sense of rich superiority as we sip our draft La Trappe next to the busload of Fredonian tourists deeply engaged in watching a little statue pee—and who a few hours later will be washing down their tourist menus with a similar-looking liquid. Be warned, though: there are many tables at La Poechenellekelder and few waiters; don't go if you're in a hurry.

We hold our breath a bit in recommending **In 't Spinnekopke** (Place du Jardin aux Fleurs, 1), an historic inn dating to 1762, but at its best, it's one of Brussels's best kept secrets. Even the staff at Delirium haven't heard of the place—partly because it's not well suited to a barkeep's budget. A list of 80 or so beers includes some surprises, including some drafts from the Tubize brewery and their own house-blended gueuze lambic. After visiting La Bécasse and Mort Subite you might think the only other real lambics come from Maine and California, but you'll be quickly reminded here of the striking astringency of the real thing. On a good night, the food can be as much of an attraction as the beer, though recent entrees have fallen victim to overcooking. Still, sauces are good and you'll usually get good value for your money. Walk west from the Bourse until you reach the Place des Jardins aux Fleurs; it's at most a 15 minute walk from La Bécasse and not hard to find if you use a map. Our most recent visit featured the overcooked food, but we'd still give it another chance.

Other places to explore

Touristy but fun

All of these are in the tiny alleys and streets between the gigantic Mint (La Monnaie; de Munt) and Theatre Royal de la Monnaie, and the Grand Place.

Au Bon Vieux Temps's door (at Impasse Saint-Nicolas, 4) is a stone's throw from La Bécasse, though you'd have to be Cy Young to hit it. Follow Rue des Fripiers from

Place de la Monnaie/Muntplaan, turn left on Kiekenmarkt (Marché aux Poulets) just before you get to La Bécasse, and look for a tiny passage on the left that takes you to the pub. Vieux Temps much reminds us of the historic pubs of downtown London, with wood and lots of nooks and corners in its tiny wonderful space. It's clubby, and service is polite at best (though it can warm if you invest a few smiles and a word or two of French), but this pub can provide something almost no other beer bar in Brussels can: a bottle of Westvleteren at a bargain price of 10€. The menu doesn't specify which one; they had both the 10 and the 12 on our last visit. The 12 was rich and deep and enormously complex. It may not be "the best beer in the world," but it's in the running, and is probably the most difficult regular production beer for ordinary people to obtain. It's a sipper. Take the time to savor the dark gentle yeast-driven fruits, the dark malt that almost tastes like a wooden spoon that's been stored with dark rich chocolate, and the exceptional creamy balance at the end. We've seen this beer priced at 60€ and above (closer to 25€ in bottle shops), but this is the first café we've seen where it's a regular menu item.

À la Mort Subite just misses our top six; it's a sentimental favorite. Michael Jackson's writings brought us here on our first trip to Belgium, and we always seem to make it back even though the kriek is now so sugary sweet it barely retains a lambic character at all. The tall ceiling and huge mirrors of the hall, however, give reassurance that the place itself hasn't changed a whit since it opened in 1928, and if you sit at a table near the front, a look down the street takes you back a century as well. The beer menu is limited to well-known major brands, though a "beer of the month" can be a surprise. Snacks and sandwiches might do for lunch. From the Mint, walk left up Schildknaps Straat and take your first left after Léopoldstraat. From Delirium, walk uphill past the classic mussel restaurant Chez Léon and turn left into the Galéries du Roi (Konings); Mort Subite is across the street from the end. From Centraal Station, walk down Rue d'Arenberg and it's on your right. If you start here, find Delirium by going through the first half of the Galéries and turning right at the end; Delirium is up its own tiny alley a block past Chez Léon.

À la Bécasse

À la Bécasse is another Michael Jackson find that would easily have made our top six 20 years ago. In recent years, however, they've given up any pretense of having their own house beer and the Timmermans Witte and Doux Lambics they now offer are a pale sweet shadow not only of the lambics they once were, but even paler compared to good American wild beers. The family-owned bar is still charming, though; lots of wood fills a small drinking hall that that dates directly to the 19th century when Great-Grandfather Steppe acquired it. It had been in existence as a coaching inn for many years before that and once faced the street before newly built housing relegated it to the end of a narrow pedestrian passage. Find it by turning right out of Au Bon Vieux Temps and taking a left on Rue de Tabora, then look down at the sidewalk or up at the building for La Bécasse's signs (a bird sitting on a jug).

And finally

Even some tobacco shops stock about 200 beers that mostly can withstand the several months they spend on a shelf. A few stores far exceed the usual suspects, however. One of them is **Beer Planet,** just a couple of blocks from Delirium (www.beerplanet.eu). The friendly owner speaks just enough English if you don't speak French, and he's eager to ship whatever you want back home. We've seen him pack huge boxes headed to the U.S. You can put together a nice range of tasters at below bar prices, get a picnic lunch from a Stop and Go, and head for a park. Most Belgian beers don't require refrigeration, but as long as you're there, buy a couple of tulip glasses; you don't want to drink your treasures out of the bottle.

Les Brasseurs de la Grande Place still had a brew kettle in the window in our 2013 visit, but no signs of life. Putting a brewpub on the Grand Place in sight of the Brewers' Guild was brilliant. Producing achingly ordinary newpub beers in the epicenter of global creative brewing was not.

A cluster of bars just off the Grand Place cater to beer guzzlers and tasters alike. Brouwers Straat, appropriately, leads you to them; turn right and go uphill about halfway from La Poechenellekelder to the Grand Place. **Au Brasseur** occupies one corner, **Golden Bar** the other. Their beer menus are not extensive, but they offer some "buy two get one free" deals on decent beer and a set of six good-sized tasting glasses for about 2 euros a shot. A small notch above their sidewalk fray is **Little Delirium**, the empire's newest venture, with about 30 not-so-adventurous taps.

Where to eat

If you want to eat well and enjoy unusual beer, go to Bier Circus if it's not in its summer shutdown period; otherwise try your luck at In 't Spinnekopke. Most of the best beer bars offer no more than cheese or cold meat plates.

We've asked everyone we know if there is a better or worse choice in deciding among the morass of restaurants (and their noisy touts) that fill the back streets near Delirium. The most frequent responses have been "go somewhere else," or a recommendation of a restaurant that's closed for the summer. You can look for Michelin stickers if you have the cash to pay the premium; otherwise, if you have to eat close to Delirium to preserve valuable drinking time, **Chez Léon** suffices. Léon started here and now has multiple branches in Paris and other cities. The down side of their success is that the charm of the place, if it ever really had it, has gone touristy, but the up side is that you'll get reliable food at no more than 20% higher prices than you really should pay for food-factory cuisine. We have found the mussels safe and competently prepared. Go on Sunday after 6 PM and get an all-you-can-eat deal on moules-frites that is hard to beat.

The best places to eat that we have found have been away from the downtown tourist areas. Tourist restaurants don't depend on return business; neighborhood restaurants do. Our favorite is **Titanic,** at Rue du Congrès 31 about two blocks toward the city from the Madou metro station. The décor is clever if a bit puzzling, with a bow-shaped balcony eating area, portholes for windows, and no life boats in sight. The curious theme seems to have little impact on the cooking, which is very Belgian, very good, and quite reasonably priced. It's only a short walk to Bier Circus, and a major tram stop lies at the base of the hill near the monument to Belgium's unknown soldier.

The area around **St. Catherine's Church** (Place Sainte-Catherine; Sint-Katelijneplein) sports a slew of restaurants surrounding a large square with canal-like reflecting pools. You'll find a wide variety of places to eat and, for Brussels, reasonable prices. Vistro is one of the few with a respectable beer menu, but we've been very well fed in several of the others. Most restaurants are filled with locals and knowledgeable travelers; tourist groups don't get this far off the beaten path. It's right on top of a Metro stop or a 15 minute walk back to Delirium.

If you walk uphill from La Poechenellekelder you'll hit a small square with a half a dozen restaurants—again off a bit off the normal tourist track, but still quite close to the beer bars of the center. We've had mixed experiences here, but at least you won't be shanghaied by the strong-armed barkers in the small streets near the Grand Place who earn their living by putting your seat in theirs.

Where to stay

As you walk from Gare du Nord to the old part of the city (don't go the other direction), a host of hotels, including some major chains, dot the first several blocks. Sheraton, Hilton, Crowne Plaza, and a bevy of three-star independents ring Place Rogier, a site of endless construction but good if confusing Metro access. If you're traveling on Eurostar to England, your ticket is good for passage from Nord Station to Zuid, though some of the rail personnel aren't aware of that; hold your ground and you'll ride for free.

Le Meridien, if you're a lottery winner, is almost a part of the Centraal Station; Novotel, Best Western, and Ibis are just downhill. Some very fancy boutique hotels with unsurprising prices are close to the Grand Place.

Radisson's Park Inn and a range of Accor hotels including Ibis are right at Midi/Zuid. Pullman Hotel, Accor's top of the line, is actually *in* the station, and the trip from your room to the Eurostar departure gate is about 100 yards. Pullman's 23€ breakfast is worth the splurge (catch the Rube Goldberg orange juice machine).

What to see

Brussels has its share of great art and some remarkable buildings to gawk at. It also has some sights that are distinctly Belgian.

The Brewers Museum (Grand Place) isn't the most extensive on the planet—it's dwarfed by the one in Bamberg and by those of many commercial breweries—but it's a pleasant recap of brewing in this brewing city and you get a tasty, if unidentified, beer at the end. Most of all, you'll spend time in the Brewers' Guild Building. In Brussels, as in most of Europe, guilds at one time controlled almost all economic activity; this is the last guild that still functions, albeit no longer as a monopoly.

The Museum of the City of Brussels, also on the Grand Place, contains changing exhibits and some information about the town, but its biggest draw is a section celebrating the Manneken Pis. It's a custom to dress the kid up, and the collection of past costumes here is mind boggling.

The Museum of Costume and Lace, just outside the Grand Place, behind the Brewers Museum, celebrates Brussels's textile industries with collections of lace, fabrics, and fashion. A recent display on women's styles from 1950-58 was notable chiefly in that the actual dresses on display had more human waist sizes than the 1950s movie stars did. Ellie notes that it would have been nice to include lingerie, as it's always been a mystery to her how women got to be that shape.

Scams and alerts

Taxis are legally required to use meters, but many don't. If you take a cab to your hotel and the driver says it's a flat fee, take the ride, then get out, get your luggage in hand, and explain that you're going to have the hotel desk call the police to help determine a fair price. He'll be gone like a flash and your ride is free. We are half-joking, but this happened to us. The police actually appreciate it if you take this approach—if all tourists did the same, the cabbies would start using the meters.

The downtown area can get very crowded. Secure your belongings. Between Place Rogier and downtown, the Rue Neuve is a major pedestrian-only shopping street. Returning to the Gare du Nord area late at night, however, it's a deserted canyon and we feel safer on the parallel Bd. Adolphe Maxlaan, which is lined with cheap hotels and tired adult entertainment venues but at least is always busy. We've been told to use a cab or the train to get back to Midi/Zuid at night.

Day trip

Bruges

Bruges (Brugge) is a two or three day excursion, not a day trip, though if you must you can spend a day there profitably. But some of the best bars don't open until late afternoon and you'll miss some of the best of the city if you're trying to get a train back to Brussels. The train station is a long haul from the center; take a bus.

Bruges has been a commercial center for centuries. Brugians have become experts in taking your money, which means you're going to find good food, good places to stay, and very good beer. None of it comes cheap, but at least you're not in Stockholm.

Bruges has museums and some very attractive churches and old buildings, but the main reason to go is just to soak up the atmosphere of a beautifully preserved city. Happily you can soak up a great deal of good beer at the same time. Our ranking is, of course, subjective. Our most recent visit reminded us how much circumstances

Bruges

affect one's opinion of an establishment. Go on a crowded Saturday night and you might have trouble getting served at all; go to the same place early on a weekday and the owner will be making suggestions and fishing out beers from the back that aren't on the menu. Our list reflects our own experiences, but we've also taken into account information from several people who live and drink in Bruges year round.

Our top pick for beer bars is **De Kelk** (Langestraat 69). Located several blocks below Berg, it's on the left as you walk away from the center. It doesn't open until 4 PM; when it does the four bright lights on the front will catch your attention. You're likely to find Kelk's owner Jeroen tending bar and he's knowledgeable and enthusiastic about beer. (His charm is heritable; see our writeup of Ghent, in the Antwerp chapter.) His recommendations are worth taking seriously. If he has time, get him to talk about his plans for the upstairs hall, which used to be used as a theater.

There may be a couple of places in town with longer beer lists, but we found Kelk's the most interesting. If you live in a place where good beer is relatively hard to find, you'll find plenty to like at any of our recommended places. But if you live near stores that specialize in importing unusual beers, you'll be surprised at how many of the beers in the specialist cafes are ones you've seen before. Kelk had so many beers we had never seen, we never really finished studying the menu.

'T Brugs Beertje (Kemelstraat 5) makes every connoisseur's top list. We were impressed, but less captivated by it than other beerfolk; perhaps our expectations were too high. Located in a 17th century building, this is the sort of bar that was nearly unique when it opened in 1983, but finding a place with 300 beers where people like to drink and talk about beer just isn't all that hard any more. We're sure any opinion of the place depends largely upon who you meet there rather than what you drink there. The knowledgeable staff, a cozy atmosphere, and rich history make Brugs Beertje a required stop on a complete Bruges pub crawl.

The next two on the list are clearly aimed at catching tourist dollars—and do so with great success—but each of them was recommended to us by permanent residents.

Bierbrasserie Cambrinus is just off the market square at Philipstockstraat 16. One of the city's newest beer specialty cafes, it's also one of the slickest; we were warned that it is a tourist-centered bar. A wooden plank holds the menu and huge beer list, dishes of nuts and snacks come with each round of drinks, and the décor is beer-focused, dressy and new. You'll hear a great deal more English than Flemish. Our intention was to have a beer just to say we did, then get out. But the beer list held a number of surprises for us, and as we waited out one of Bruges's "normal" showers, we saw the kitchen producing some very impressive meals. We're glad we stayed. Our dinner was among the best we've had in Belgium, the service was amazingly effective on a jammed Saturday night, and the beers were a delight. You won't get the personal service you'll have at Kelk or Brugs Beerje and the noise level can be staggering, but it offers a fun night of good beer and food. It's also one of the few places to drink that's open day and night.

Another tourist-oriented beer experience is **2be** (53 Wollestraat), located on the other side of the market from Cambrinus and overlooking a canal. You enter by passing the "Beer Wall" that supposedly displays all 1,300 Belgian beers and a proper glass for each. On your right are gift emporiums that sell all sorts of locally themed products from honeys and chocolates to Tin Tin action figures. Downstairs in the cellar is a very respectable bottle shop. At the end of the Beer Wall is a small bar area. The emphasis is on draft beers; the selection changes often and you can read about what's on tap by pulling down the draft lists that are suspended on elastic strings from the ceiling. The featured drafts can include some unusual brews. But this isn't the best place to taste beer, it's just one of the best places to *drink* beer. When the weather is nice, customers stretch out over a large patio that runs along two sides of the building, and all of it overlooks water. Look for the bean bags at the very end. Kwak, a way-too-smooth-for-8.4% brown ale, comes not only in the characteristic quarter-meter hourglass-shaped glass but in a larger half-meter size as well. The secret of not getting soaked as you tilt to get to the beer in the bottom part is to slowly rotate the glass as you drink from it. Note that 2be, unlike most drinking spots in Belgium, is open only during the day—it closes at 7 PM.

Two cellar beer cafes are directly opposite each other on Vlamingstraat well away from the market square. **'T Poetersgat** (Vlamingstraat 82) is where our local friends take out-of-town guests for the "wow factor." Watch your head as you descend into the cavernous basement room with stone archways festooned with dried hops (and a skeleton at the end of the bar). It's dark and seems well removed from reality in time and distance—a former bartender remarked that it was disconcerting never to know whether it was night or day, sunny or raining. Across the street a similar head-challenging set of stairs takes you down to the **Comptoir des Arts** (Vlamingstraat 53). It's much posher, a jazz/blues/soul venue: smaller, wood instead of stone, and there is a window. Even without performers, the jazz on the sound system is first rate. Both places have very limited food—eat elsewhere—and both have beer menus

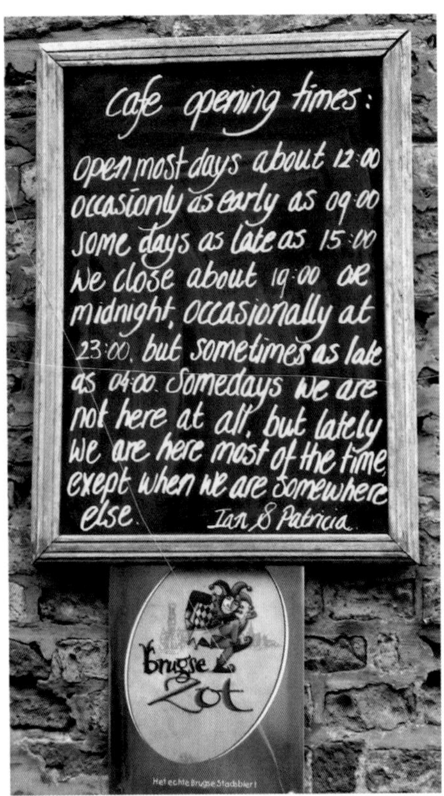

At 't Terrastje

of nearly 100 beers, some of them interesting, and a reasonable range of whiskies, if you want a break from 9% beers.

In 't Niew Museum isn't really a beer café, though they have a respectable selection, a variable "beer of the month," and a close working relationship with Chimay that sometimes gets them something rare. The food is the draw here. Logs burning in a rack drop hot coals down to a bed over which ribs and steaks sizzle and pop—we've never seen anything quite like it. All-you-can-eat ribs aren't fall-off-the-bone: they're fire grilled, not smoked and basted, but they're lean and tasty and come with three sauces to play with. And the management is serious about the all-you-can-eat part. A full rack is just the start—all you want follows freely. Steaks are perfectly cooked and the welcome couldn't be warmer. In the dark of winter, it's even nicer—candles light the interior and the live fire warms the room. The beer list tends to include darker beers, too.

Our final café recommendation, **Café Bistro Terrastje** (Genthof 45), near where Genthof intersects Langerei, isn't really a beer specialist café, but it's a great place to drink. Family run, it's just across the road from a canal. The inside is welcoming and intimate. By the time we left we felt we had made several new best friends. You should be able to find a beer you like among the six drafts and couple of dozen bottles; three of the taps are from the local Halve Maan brewery. This was another café we hopped into just to avoid torrential rain, but we'll return to drink Brugse Zot on the outside deck. Walkable from the center, or take the 4, 14, 43, or 91 buses that drop you off at Gouden Handstraat a block or so away.

There's only one brewery left in Bruges, the **Halve Maan** (Walplein 26), which also brews Straffe Hendrick. The 45 minute tour is worth the ten bucks, and includes a couple of samples. You get some great views of the city from the upper levels of the brewery and have a chance to see some fairly unusual brewing equipment, including a square brew kettle. The brewery café courtyard is sunny, umbrella'ed, and ringed with plants and flowers, a very pleasant place to drink even if you're not doing the tour. "De Halve Maan," which as you can tell from their logo means "half moon," opens daily for tours between 11 and 4 in the summer. Ironically, you may find the best of the Halve Maan beers back home. Their De Halve Maan Straffe Hendrik Heritage 2011 was absolutely superb, but we saw no signs of the killer specialties on our last visit. The blonde on tap was sweet but nicely complex and the dubbel had some flavorful roast along with some tannic fruit and hints of toffee. Neither, however, would be worth the effort to get there were it not for the brewery tour.

While the Beer Wall at 2be has the feel of a museum, Bruges's real brewing museum is a short walk away at Breidelstraat 3 near the Grote Markt in a fine old building. We were too occupied with the café scene to carve out time for it, but we've added it to our to-do list as a result of rave reviews from our friends. An audio tour (separate one for kids) takes you around lots of pictures and antique tanks; the impressive-looking tap room overlooks the square.

The **Struise Brewery** has set up a tiny shop on the Burg Square. Struise produces some of the most sought-after beers on the planet now, and at times we understand why. Face the tall tower and look right—there's a neon "miracle" sign in the window. Inside are dozens of different Struise beers and a few more on draft from collapsible beer balls. You can taste beers (the shop actually functions as a tiny bar) and learn anything you want to know about Struise and about Belgian beer in general. Be sure to get there before the 7 PM closing time.

As you exit, turn right and go through the passageway, and you'll be only a block or so from 2be. On your way, you'll pass **Erasmus**, which has very expensive food and a better reputation for beers than it probably deserves. We felt we were treated brusquely there; our resident friends said no, they're actually just rude.

If you're planning on staying in Bruges, it's a good idea to book in advance. The **Crown Plaza** on the Burg has an absolutely wonderful location with some rooms in the $200 range, though you'll pay plenty for a "medieval" view. The tourist office will usually be able to find you a room for a small fee; we think they're better and more honest than most. Be prepared for "bed and breakfast" if you haven't reserved a hotel. On our next trip, we're headed for the **Barge Hotel** (Bargeweg 15), an easy walk from the station. The life vests laid carefully on each neatly made bed are somehow very appealing.

Bruges has some sights, but it speaks volumes to note that the three biggest draws are museums dedicated to chocolate, lamps, and French fries. About ten bucks gets you in the door of each one. We chose to spend our money on fries we could eat. Canal tour boats whip through the waterways that crisscross the city. You can hire a horse-drawn carriage to give you a briskly paced tour for a bit over $50. Or just look around as you follow our pub crawl, and enjoy this beautiful city knowing that, unlike nearly all of the many thousands of people you're sharing it with, you know where to get the good beer.

Cologne

Quick orientation

First, Cologne is Köln is Cologne. On the Munich/München principle, we're reluctantly using the Anglicized name. However, keep in mind that "Cologne" doesn't show up on any European train schedules except maybe English ones. If you're looking in the index for anything but "Köln" you'll miss your train.

You can't mistake where you are when you come into the city. The Dom (Cathedral) soars into the sky, and trains take a curved route across the Rhine bridge into the station that gives you the chance to see this magnificent structure from different angles. In fact the curve *forces* you to view the Dom in its entire splendor, an intentional design that slows entry and exit of the station to a crawl in peak periods. The locals hate it; we love it.

On the far side of the station from the Dom, a modern shopping area leads eventually to the old town. As you walk down toward the river, the buildings get older and more interesting. The Kölsch restaurants—the reason you're here—cluster mostly in the old town. You'll have no problem getting more suggestions from your hotel than we give you; Colners know what they've got.

Station breaks

There's a Sion kiosk in the Hauptbahnhof plaza, but if you have even a few minutes to spare, skip it. The Dom looms over the square in front of the station—head towards it. Before you enter the Dom plaza, up the street a little way on your right is **Gaffel Am Dom.** It's new and modern with a Munich beer hall feel to it. The crowd is very young, but still mostly drinking Gaffel Kölsch; here it's drawn from a tap rather than barrels. See if there are seasonals—on our last visit, the Sonnen Hopfen featured an American boatload of Citra hop. It was probably the hoppiest German beer we have ever had, yet the blend of hops they used tamed the Citra to a lemony sweetness. Well worth the effort to find.

Alternatively, follow our directions below to get to **Früh.** On a fine day tables stretch outside, and if the weather's cruddy, the woody oldish feeling inside gives welcome respite. The inside is a virtual museum of the brewery's history and the role this building played in it.

History and culture

If you're going to spend a while in Cologne, invest in a better history guide than we can give you here. Cologne isn't the only city in this guide with Roman ancestry, but it's one of the best cities on the continent to trace the path of European civilization from antiquity to globalization.

Cologne flourished as one of the Roman Empire's premier trading cities north of the Alps, and its association with the Hanseatic League centuries later ensured its continuing economic success through the Middle Ages. The mix of profit seekers and pilgrims made Cologne one of the most successful Imperial Free Cities; its population of 50,000 at one time was larger than London or Berlin. A thriving Jewish community was well integrated into the greater society. But the Black Plague ended the ethnic harmony, and the beginning of the Age of Exploration in the 15th century opened new trade routes that avoided Cologne, causing a long, slow economic decline. The Rhineland was the heart of the Industrial Revolution in Germany, however, and Cologne returned to its status as a major economic player even before Germany's unification in 1871. The city's economic prominence almost doomed it, as it was a prime target of Allied bombing attacks during World War II. By the end of the war, 90% of central Cologne was rubble, the population had dropped below what it was in the 11th century, and some suggested simply walking away from the giant pile of wreckage that used to be the old town.

Reconstruction took decades, but today it's hard to believe that except for the Dom, almost everything you see downtown is postwar construction. Cologne again prospers as a center for world trade and hosts myriad international conferences. Today's pilgrims are the hundreds of thousands of tourists with whom you'll share the city. Happily, the biggest beer halls accommodate these numbers pretty well, and the tourists leave the smaller Kölsch houses alone.

Beer styles and drinking culture

Most brewing histories say that Cologne continued to brew ales even when the lager revolution swept Europe in the 19th century. What they often don't mention is how great a range of light and dark styles there were here until very recent times. It took the hardships of the post-World War II era to standardize the Kölsch style as we know it.

The postwar years were horrific for ordinary Germans. Cities like Cologne lay in absolute ruins; bridges flopped like overdone spaghetti. The Dom looked more like a window screen than a building. Food was scarce all over Europe, and the Allies certainly weren't inclined to make life easier for the Germans than for the Belgians or French. Beer production was often simply impossible. According to a brewery publication, Hans Sion, of the Sion Kölsch fame, managed to rustle up enough grain to make a very pale light ale, and got permission from the occupying U.S. troops to do it. He convinced his fellow brewers to produce a similar brew, and began promoting it all over Germany as distinctively "Kölsch." The appellation means that if you're drinking a Kölsch in Germany, it's brewed in or near Cologne.

Until a few decades ago, though, Kölsch was an iconoclastic and rare style of beer. Eventually, Americans traveling to the city brought home tales, Michael Jackson enthused, and some bottles found their way to the States in marginally acceptable condition; the result was an explosion of brewpub "kolsches" in the U.S. Unfortunately, many of the brewpubs hadn't the slightest idea what the beer was supposed to taste like, and started to use the term "kolsch" (with or without the umlaut) for any golden light ale. Worse, a fair number of them use wheat, which the brewers of Cologne do not. Most of these American kolsches are actually closer to British gold ales, an entirely different creature, than they are to genuine Kölsch Bier. When you get the real thing in the city of its birth, you're in for a treat.

Kölsch is an all barley malt, top-fermented brew, light colored, light in body, exceptionally finely balanced, and perhaps the most delicate-tasting beer in the world. The only beers really close are the darker Altbiers of Düsseldorf up the river a bit. Served in slim, cylindrical 2-centiliter glasses and replenished constantly by roving waiters, Kölsch is always at the proper temperature—no "warm and horrible" dregs like the last of a Munich liter. It's aged as if it were a lager and served, at its best, from small, constantly changing barrels. (Even a decade ago, the barrels were wood; the only "wooden" ones we saw on our last trip were plastic jackets, but the presentation is still tempting.) Hops vary from barely perceptible to spritzy and inviting. The real secret of Kölsch, we believe, is the yeast. You can buy "kölsch" yeast at a homebrew store in any U.S. city, but it won't make a true Kölsch for you. True story: A friend of ours endured the full three-year brewmaster's course at Weihenstephan in Freising, Bavaria, the foremost brewing school in the world. (He is, of course, an absolutely fabulous brewer and, happily, a very successful one as well.) During his stay, he roomed with a member of a Kölsch brewery family. The Colner, apparently, could get roaring-senseless drunk and was a barrel of laughs, but even then if you asked him how, exactly, to brew a Kölsch, he'd clam up into instant sobriety. We're pretty sure the severed head of a large Rhine fish would show up on the bed of a brewer who blabbed.

The bottom line is that to taste Kölsch, you have to go to Cologne. It legally can't be sold in Germany as Kölsch if it's made anywhere else, and while you can find Colner Kölsches in Munich or Berlin, they don't travel very well. The good news is that the small portions mean that with a little legwork you can sample nearly all the major Kölsch beers in one good night of pub crawling in Cologne.

The variety isn't what it once was, and you'll rarely drink your beer in the place where it's brewed any more. Gradually the house brewers have discovered that serving beers pays better than making beers, and several of the brands are now produced at a single central production facility. We find it hard to believe they're all still using different yeasts, but the recipes clearly do still vary from brand to brand.

The multipack of drinking experiences: an old town Bier tour

We've included more than six spots here because the portion sizes are tiny and the total crawling distance is quite short. You can visit all the pubs we list in an evening. That said, we recommend you take a few days to enjoy the city's history and limit your kölsching to two or three pubs a night. It takes more than a single 0.2-liter portion to really sense the subtlety in this very delicate style. If you're in the city for more than one night, you'll be able to find all the major brands and a few other outliers on your own; get a decent map (20 euro cents from the tourist office), get an online list, and circle the brewery restaurants.

Most breweries are represented in the old town, and just in case you've planned one staggering evening, here's the route we took on our last visit. The order is vaguely from high ground to the river. There are interesting breweries further out from the center, but you'll get a good sense of what Kölsch is all about by following the route below.

From the station walk towards, then around the Dom. It's under construction. It will be under construction when your grandchildren find this book in your attic. If you could walk straight through it, you'd emerge on a plaza that is framed by the Römer Museum and the Dom Hotel. Walk along the front of the Dom Hotel toward the museum; look right as you get to the end of it, and **Früh** stands in front of you. Früh used to be bigger, and they don't brew onsite any more, but it's still a good place to start your crawl. Bar 19, to the left of the Früh entrance, used to be part of the beer hall and is now Früh's attempt to present some upscale dining and drinking. Still, the patio out front is a good place for a typical meal, and enough of the inside is left to give a good sense of a classic Colner beer hall. The beer is a good start too. It's light and delicate and well balanced; it shows off the slight hint of apple that characterizes the yeast-fruit component of Kölsch.

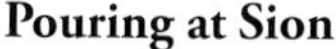

Pouring at Sion

Emerge from Früh and, looking at the Dom (quite impossible not to do), turn right and go downhill on Am Hof to the mostly pedestrian Unter Taschenmacher. Halfway along on your right is the substantial **Brauhaus Sion.** The prominent "Since 1310" clearly does not refer to this modern edifice, but there's wood and benches and a basic Gastätte feel to it. Sit in the front and watch the groups of fifty or sixty 50- or 60-year-olders traipse in and out for their one-per-person 0.2-liter quaff of "house beer." Give thanks and order another one for yourself. The menu is one of the biggest in town, which usually means some of it is coming out of packages. If it's factory food, though, it's pretty good factory food. From the tables just to the left inside in the bar area, you'll have a chance to see their mechanized pulley system for replacing the kegs. The beer is clean and pleasant. In one sense, the postwar "original" Kölsch is a bit malty for the style, but some apple peeks through at the end.

As you come out, turn right to the end of the block and then left (downhill) to the Alter Markt. There seem to be fewer Kölsch houses and more Irish pubs here every time we come, but a couple of classics remain. **PeterS Brauhaus** never brewed PeterS's beers, but the building was a brewery at the turn of the century and, after a period of neglect, PeterS has created a beautiful beer hall that looks like it's been there far longer than it has. At peak times it's packed, for good reason. The beer shows a distinctive touch of herbs, and a bit of bready, though clean, malt lingers into the aftertaste. The food is good, too.

Return to the Alter Markt and at the far end on the left is the **Brauerei Ausschank Gaffel Haus.** It's woody and old and has an aura of authenticity we like, even if the beer does come from draft taps rather than the usual barrels. Our samples seemed especially fresh even by Cologne standards. Some grassy hops are a bit more evident than most others and the taste ends dryly. Every time we come to Cologne we find a new favorite beer; on our most recent trip, Gaffel was the winner.

As you walk out, you're on the end of the Alter Markt. Staying at this end, go across to exit at the opposite corner, pass the youth-bars, and curve uphill to Marsplatz, and you'll see the striking red brick **Gasthaus Brungs.** It's really a wine bar rather than a beer keller, but it's a quiet, atmospheric place to sip a Kölsch. Though the buildings date from the 16th century, much of what you see is postwar reconstruction done with an artist's touch. The garden is inviting and off the beaten path, and a magnificent wooden spiral staircase that really does date from the 17th century leads up to a balcony area inside. The old romantic cellar includes a piece of the Roman city walls—worth a peek even if the room isn't in use. **Reissdorf** is a big brewery Kölsch, but carves out its own niche: just a bit estery with a hint of citrus. If someone told us they sneaked in a bit of wheat, we wouldn't be surprised. Most of the Kölsches feature a bit of Juicy Fruit, but this has more of it, along with a touch of green apple skins.

Walk straight downhill to the Heumarkt. As you enter the plaza, to your right is the big corner bar **Gilden im Zims.** "No!" the old man called to us, scurrying over as we surveyed the outside. "It isn't a real Kölsch bar any more, it's just a business; don't go there." But of course we went in despite his warning—we owe you the tough research. We don't begrudge the old man's attitude. The place was spiffy beyond words and money, and beer poured from the only fake barrels we saw on our crawl. (They're former barrels converted to tap coverings. You can spot a fake barrel when the spigot is anywhere but the very bottom of the cask—you can't drain a keg from a hole one-quarter of the way up.) Still, all in all, it was a good experience, enhanced significantly by a tome of a menu that described in German and English all the heroes of the city. In addition to contributing to the history section of this guide, it was enormously valuable in helping us understand how at least some of the Colners see themselves. Gilden is one of the beers brewed at the coop shared brewery, but it's a good Kölsch, exceptionally clean and not heavy handed at all, yet with some distinctive flavors. Balanced malt, fruit, and hops left space for a touch of metal and bit of green grapes that reminded us of some of the beers using Nelson Sauvin (though we'd be very surprised if Gilden did). Some residual sugar and graininess suggested that it might have been a bit rushed.

Return to Heumarkt; walk down the Dom side towards the river. In the far corner on the left is **Max Päffgen**'s tavern selling Pfaffen Kölsch, which Max makes in a suburb south of town. Max's place features a series of small drinking areas connected by low arches and leading to a small garden in the back. It's small, but it feels bigger than it is. The front room seems to center on wheels: there's a winch resting on an oak trellis, a big iron wheel above you, and lots of clocks. Almost uniquely in this part of town, Max offers a bottled seasonal beer in addition to the Kölsch. His Hefeweizen is almost a Hefeweizen Dunkel, with some roast to go along with a good deal of spiciness. There's a Bock in winter.

Bierhaus Päffgen

Two doors down, at Salzgasse 5-7, is **Bierhaus en d'r Salzgass,** one of the few outlets for Päffgen Kölsch and a beautiful place to stop for a beer. Drinking in Germany can approach a religious experience and the bar area has the feel of a chapel.

We don't have space to relate how these two very similarly named brews came to occupy this part of the world, but the Päffgen wars made Hatfield-McCoy gatherings look like fraternity reunions. Päffgen (versus Pfaffen) has at times been our favorite of the Kölsches, mostly because the hops are so nicely evident. A hoppy and slightly grassy noble hop start finishes cleanly, but the hops return for an aftertaste that is, by Cologne standards, actually a bit bitter.

One of **Sunner**'s better outlets is on the same street, but it closes for a big chunk of the summer and looked endangered on our last visit. You'll have no trouble finding the beer in the area, though.

You can end the crawl here, but if you've held yourself to just one at each place, you might still have the stamina to pack in a few more as you loop back toward the Dom. Turning left at the bottom of the hill onto Buttermarkt gives you a chance to sample the **Mühlen** Kölsch. Across the street is another opportunity for Päffgen, the **Bierhaus am Rhein,** which is worth a stop in itself; the river view from the back terrace, as with several similar bars and restaurants in this section of town, is unusually good.

Further along, the Bier Museum's 18 ordinary beers are pretty skippable unless you're trying to find Becks or Guinness. At the end of the stretch, however, the **Stapelhaus,** a Dom Ausschank that can let you taste the relatively well-known but still clean and brisk Dom Kölsch, gives another first-rate river view. The menu's attempt to provide traditional Colner cooking is a bit touristy, but meaty and substantial. We've always found any food tastes better when you can watch barges going by.

Almost across the street from Stapelhaus is **Wirtshaus Schweik,** named after the hero of a darkly humorous book by Kafka's rival Jaroslav Hašek. It once was a breath of Prague on the banks of the Rhine, but the beer range has dwindled to a few taps of well-known beers. When the weather's hot, though, a cold Czech Budweiser can be refreshing: the chilling bars that divide the shelves of glasses inside are also featured at Toro Negro, between the feuding Päffgens.

Off the beaten track

Weiss-Bräu am Barbarossaplatz (Am Weidenbach 24) is a ways from the old town, but worth the effort if you're in the city for a few days. Located in an attractive brewpub in a section of the city you're not likely to see otherwise, the brewery produces beers that are a blend of Cologne tradition and well-above-average newpub modern. You don't expect to find a big estery Hefeweizen in this land of delicate barley, but Weiss-Bräu's take on the style includes a bracing pepper along with the clove before a chewy soft yeasty finish.

Where to stay

After a few bargain basement misfortunes, we now stay at the Hilton. In the summer you can luck into good rates, and it's probably the best location of any Hilton on the Continent: you can schlep there from the train station in five minutes max, and some of the rooms have views of the Dom. Over the years we've needed to make a few unusual requests of the staff, and they've bent over backwards to take good care of us. The breakfast, as usual, is spectacular—try to get a rate that includes it. If you're using Cologne as a base to explore this area of the Rhineland, the location simply can't be beat.

What to see

The Dom

The Dom is breathtaking in its sweep—even before you enter. If your camera has a panorama feature that you've never used, you'll be trying to figure out how to use it here. The city's website points out that it's as tall as 26 giraffes, but unless you've gotten up close and personal to a giraffe recently, you'll still be stunned by its magnificence. The site also says "prepare to meet God"—while the phrase actually is intended to suggest appropriate clothing, you can take it any way you want.

While Christian artifacts in the city date to Roman times, by the 9th century Cologne had the wealth and power to play an important role in the Holy Roman Empire and built a cathedral worthy of the city's status. Three hundred years later, the large "old Dom" wasn't large enough, and the powers that be wrestled with the task of finding a site for a new, larger structure. We've read of no such accusations, but can't help wondering if the devastating fire of 1248 wasn't the medieval counterpart of the modern "insurance fire." However it started, the fire opened up the space for the current building. Consecrated in 1322, the new Dom took another 200 years to complete—sort of. Take a look at the huge north entrance: it's the same design as the entrance you'll use today. Until the 19th century it was the entry into the church—everything to your left as you look at it has been added later.

A few euros will get you a tour, currently at 10 AM with an additional tour at 2:30 PM on Sundays and holidays. The tour is worth the hour it takes. Our tour guide said we had special permission just that day to enter the sanctuary where the bones of the Three Magi are housed in one of Europe's largest reliquaries, but you may be similarly blessed. The skulls were a gift from the bishop of Milan to Frederic Barbarossa in 1164; "freely given," apparently, in gratitude that Barbarossa didn't slaughter him. But by hook or crook, the relics put the Cologne cathedral on the religious map and led to pilgrimages so plentiful it required the massive Dom to hold them all. The money the pilgrims spent on housing, food, and beer ensured Cologne's economic growth until modern times.

Cologne is spitting distance (on horseback) from France and was an early target of French Revolutionary armies. Napoleon's secular occupation brought hard times for the Cathedral, which became a camp, a barn, and a prison before the Little Corporal's early retirement to St. Helena allowed it to return to its religious purpose. In the 19th century, some academic sleuthing and civic pride led to the discovery of the medieval architectural plans and a campaign to finally complete the original design. Private funds helped, but the key was a chunk of change from a Prussian government looking for ways of instilling nationalist German pride. The final design with the enormous twin towers reached completion in 1880. Alas, 14 massive Allied bombs undid much of the work of centuries, and some of the damage is still in the process of being repaired. You can see some of the not-so-medieval decorations near the organ.

Other sights

Take the cable car across the Rhine for a great view of the river that unites so much of Europe. It passes over a clothing-optional spa, but it's high enough so the kids won't see much. On the other side you can walk along the river or take a mini-railroad ride through the park.

The Roman museum is one of the finest of its kind in Germany and attracts more tourists today than the Romans sent troops. Even if you don't go into the museum, you'll see evidence of Rome throughout the city in the remnants of walls, aqueducts, and sewers. The Romans constructed one of the most sophisticated sanitary systems in the ancient world in Cologne, bringing in water from a hundred kilometers away through aqueducts as impressive as those in Italy. The clean water and the giant sewer now known as the Rhine sustained one of the larger Roman outposts in Europe.

The little tourist trolley that rolls through the streets is pretty good way to get a quick orientation and it can get you to the zoo or other sites that are a bit of a hike. Pick it up just off the Dom.

Near the Rathaus you can see a working archeological dig that's discovering more about the medieval Jewish community every year. A few steps away is the Farina House where you can sniff the development of Eau de Cologne, although the 4711 outlet store is nearer the Dom.

Scams and alerts

SPECIAL ALERT! Many years ago, Cologne introduced us to the beer mat misle ("misle," you may not know, is the present tense of "misled"). We've seen it here and elsewhere many times since. Kölsch bier is served in tiny glasses which are constantly replaced until you signify an end by placing your coaster on top of your glass. The waiter makes a mark on your coaster each time you have a beer, and determines the bill by the number of marks at the end. Nice system—except that the waiter sometimes provides a coaster with a couple of innocent-looking marks around the edges that turn out to cost you when it's time to settle up. Get a perfectly pristine coaster; stare down your waiter if he gives you anything else. He may be so embarrassed (and probably afraid of you reporting him), he'll give you fine service for the time you're there.

Day trips and excursions

Düsseldorf

You could spend a night or two in Düsseldorf, but we prefer to stay in Cologne and commute by train. On our last visit to Düsseldorf, we realized we could reach the city center faster by rail from Cologne than by street car from our Düsseldorf hotel. It seemed like the trains were more frequent too.

Düsseldorf shares much with Cologne, and at least some of the citizens enjoy a cordial mutual disdain that recalls that of New Yorkers and Bostonians, albeit on a smaller scale. The Düsseldorf specialty beer is the "Alt" style, brown, light, and fruity. We've had brewers tell us that, other than a difference in roast and color, the process is nearly identical, and the results are more similar than different. The Altbiers are a bit less standardized than the Kölsches, though, and the city never got an appellation for them (it's hard to copyright the word "old") so you'll find lots of interpretations of what an "Altbier" is in Germany. Still, a tour of the Altbier breweries of Düsseldorf gives you variations on a style that will remind you of your old town Kölsch crawl.

Downtown Düsseldorf is more compact even than Cologne, and you can hit most of the high points on a day trip. Start with a visit to the tourist office, open Monday to Saturday in the main train station and every day in the old town. Get a map and head to the old town. You don't really need us, or anyone else, to find good beer in the maze of taverns, bars, and restaurants.

When we're there, though, we generally hang out in one or more of the city's most traditional alt houses. **Brauerei Uerige** is on Berger Strasse 1. The first time we were there in the late '70s, we thought the Germans were the luckiest people on earth to be able to eat and drink in a comfortable pub which brewed its own beer. Now, of course, even small-town Americans have the same the same pleasure—and sometimes with beer that's about as good. But we still like returning to a place that made us dream about a beer revolution, and the beer is still really, really good. Uerige beer isn't all that hard to find in the U.S., but what gets to the States can't match what's served at the brewery. You can't go wrong with any of the four fine Alts in the places we list here, but Uerige's gets our edge. Chewy, roasty, nutty, chocolate caramel malt is beautifully balanced by a long hop finish. A delicate fruitiness testifies to the fact it's an ale, but nothing overwhelms.

Fuchschen Alt beer

The city's other traditional brewpubs are within scampering distance. **Hausbrauerei Zum Schlüssel** (Bolkerstr. 41-47) brews another good Alt. Toasty with caramel and brown sugars, it sports a slight ale fruit in the finish. It's slightly nutty but nicely clean.

Find Schumacher's interpretation at their old town outlet, **Brauereiausschank im Goldenen Kessel** (Bolkerstrasse 44). The beer is malty with soft caramel in the finish and a bit of ale fruit, then good hops, and all of it smooth even for this style. A low alcohol version was OK, but the unfermented sugars made it edgy.

Brauerei im Füchschen (Ratinger Straße 28) has a typically delicious Alt beer, characterized by even, toasty malt with ale fruit and toffee in the finish. Hops are balanced and dry.

Wuppertal

A trip to Wuppertal can be done in a day and is well worth the time and effort; trains from Cologne are frequent. Wuppertal's brewery is worth a visit, but the reason to go there is to experience a real-world amusement park ride, the Schwebebahn. Built in 1901, it's the oldest monorail in the world. It's no Loch Ness Monster, but it's no staid Busch Garden monorail either; it swings freely beneath the track and although it claims a "comfortable 15 degree sway" it's enough to scare the schrudd out of some of the unsuspecting tourists. And not without some reason: a 1999 mishap killed four people—the only monorail deaths anywhere in the 20th century. We figure it'll be another 85 years before the next accident, so we love the ride. It's a trip.

The Schwebebahn will take you near the **Wuppertal Brauhaus** at Kleine Flurstraße 5, in the Barmen section of town. A converted swimming pool now provides a different form of liquid indulgence. From the outside it looks more like a school than a pool—red brick and slightly imposing. Inside, a huge wood-topped oval bar occupies the center of what once was the pool. Fermenting tanks sit behind glass on the second level. Wooden carvings of oversized bathers strike a tone that's somewhere between comical and surreal. And for the men—one of the most serene trips to the pissoir ever. Outside fest tables, some under cover, occupy a sizeable patio-garden area. The beers wouldn't be worth a trip on their own, but they're decent enough not to get in the way of a pleasant time. Soft, sweet, and yeasty, they're pretty typical of German "newpub" styles. We found the Dunkel the best balanced of the three: roasty,

The Schwebebahn

Hanging out at Wuppertal Brauhaus

chewy malt, sweetish but a far cry from Malz, with some fruit and a dry chalky yeast. Pretty easy to drink.

A side note—the historical museum at Wuppertal has a particularly good model of Arkwright's water frame, one of the pivotal inventions of the Industrial Revolution. See the Manchester chapter.

A ride on the Rhine

If you have a Eurail pass, one of the prime add-ons is the KD boats that ply the Rhine. You can meander someplace and back or plan an overnight. We don't guarantee you'll have the same luck, but we've never had any trouble finding a Gasthaus or Zimmer Frei in any of the Rhine towns as long as we (a) got off the boat before late afternoon and (b) didn't even *try* it during the "Rhine in Flames" fireworks festival.

A recent excursion included a night in Oberlahnstein. On weekdays, you can talk your way into the brewery and their small museum, and it's not hard to find their beers. Sometimes sold under the St. Martin label, they include an exceptional range. They're all drinkable, the Weizens better than average, and the fest beer actually has some hop character to it. It's really more of an export than a typical Festbier. If you're there outside of normal hours, **Zum Rebstock** seems to serve later than most; the schnitzel seemed to come from a freezer, the portions are a bit less than German, but the prices are a bargain. It's a good local with very nice local beer and wonderfully friendly welcome.

From Oberlahnstein you can get to Niederlahnstein and **Maximilians Brauwiesen.** The boats don't go, but trains do, and it is walkable in good weather. The brewery is on the river, and its garden grounds sloping down to the water give a memorable Rhine experience. Ellie called it "one of the best drinking spots ever," and we spent a full afternoon gawking at the river. The beers were not quite as memorable—on our last trip the unfiltered Dunkel had the telltale diacetyl signature of hurried lagering—but the Helles Naturtrüb was pretty good, especially if you like their yeast strain, and the Hefeweizen was more than respectable. They're good enough to wash down a range of decent snacks. Currywurst, if you haven't had one, is a must try; the chili was loaded with meat and beans and sported a very un-German bit of heat.

It was at Maximilians, by the way, that we made the remarkable discovery that yellow jacket wasps don't like lemon or clove. The garden was swarming with them—except at the Hefeweizen tap. We always carry cloves with us now as a repellent, and they've worked remarkably well.

Copenhagen

Quick orientation

Copenhagen's main station is indeed "central"; you're no more than 15 minutes from most of our sixpack favorites, and really only a few minutes' walk from anything else you're looking for. Outside one entrance, past the bus depot, is Tivoli Gardens, one of the world's oldest and most beautiful amusement parks. Beyond Tivoli are the main shopping areas and several of the best bars and brewpubs. The harbor, museums, and some of the scenic parts of the city are further off. On the opposite side of the station from Tivoli is a seedy "adult" district, mild compared to Amsterdam, that nonetheless leads to the most recent hotbed of craft beer activity and a couple more of our top six. While you're in the station, admire the magnificent traditional longhouse-style raftered roof.

Nyhavn harbor

Station breaks

Exit the station on the Tivoli side, turn left to the main drag, Vesterbrogade, and then go right. Just past the Tivoli main entrance is Apollo, Copenhagen's first brewpub. Facing it across Vesterbrogade, just a short way farther, is Streckers and in that is the Vesterbro Bryghus. Five minutes more, across the square (which is semipermanently under construction), is BrewPub. But if you have just a bit longer, make the 15 minute trek in the opposite direction to Mikkeller—though if you do, check alternate departures before you leave the station. You'll have a hard time keeping your visit a short one.

History and culture

The Danes revel in their Viking past, and make good money at a number of authentic and recreated Viking sites (not to mention the souvenir shops). It's been almost a millennium since the Viking era ended its course, however, and it's pretty hard to make a case for a direct influence on modern Danish culture. Perhaps a spirit of adventure and risk taking has lingered, albeit rather latently during some of the years since.

The name Denmark appears for the first time on the 10th century Jelling stones, making the country a newcomer by European standards, though Vikings had been making their mark on other people for some time. Scandinavians roamed as far as France and Russia, and for some time much of England was ruled by invading Danes. But most Vikings were farmers, not raiders, and over the centuries even the voyagers grew fonder of profit than plunder and developed into reasonably respectable traders. Denmark's rulers found they had to cope with an increasingly influential clergy and nobility, and the country's expansive period ground to a halt.

The savage wars of the 16th and 17th centuries fostered the establishment of strong monarchies in many European countries. The Danish absolutist monarchy's adventures included a costly participation in the Thirty Years War, in which Danes alternately united with and fought against other Scandinavian nations. Ultimately a weakened Denmark limped away with the loss of about a third of its lands. The 19th century wasn't much easier, Denmark being located uncomfortably near various German states. Among the three wars that Otto von Bismarck used to create the modern state of Germany was the Danish War, in which a couple of disputably Danish provinces became Bismarck's breakfast.

By the 20th century the Danes wanted nothing more than to stay out of others' conflicts while they focused on new industrial economic opportunities at home. Personal wealth soared even as the state edged toward a mild form of socialism. Neutral in World War I, the Danish government clung to "independence" even during the first years of Nazi occupation in the Second World War. But when the Germans ended that myth of autonomy, Danish pride seems to have arisen spontaneously. The Danes became more successful than most in making occupation uncomfortable for the Germans. Stories that the Danish king threatened to wear the Star of David, or that massive numbers of Danes actually did, are apocryphal, but the rescue of nearly 7,000 Jews by an ad hoc flotilla to Sweden is not. Someone should write a book on the collective drain on German resources caused by resistance movements in the Netherlands, Denmark,

Yugoslavia, and Finland. None was really "successful," but together, we suspect, they may have kept just enough German troops away from Normandy when it mattered.

The Danish resistance movement was substantial enough to earn the country status among the victors, and Denmark was a founding member of the U.N. It eventually joined the European Union in a razor-close vote, but opponents of the European connection were able to defeat adoption of the euro. You'll need to cough up crowns during your stay here.

In lore and legend, as well as a multitude of tourist attractions, Danes love to celebrate their Viking roots of independence and adventure, though the Viking gift of commerce is no less important. Whatever its origin, a spirit of independence and adventure certainly plays a huge part in the Danish beer culture today.

Beer styles and drinking culture

Denmark's role in the history of modern brewing may not have been swashbuckling, but it was vitally important. Louis Pasteur discovered what yeast was and what it did, but it was the labs at Carlsberg that really turned brewing into a science. The big breakthrough came in 1883 when Emil Christian Hansen developed a method to propagate pure yeast. *Saccharomyces carlsbergensis* became the global standard of lager yeast.

The Carlsberg brewery turned into a papa and son story. J.C., the dad, hung on to traditional brewing methods; son Carl cut fermentation times and modernized marketing. Carlsberg probably deserved to become a brewing giant—they actually contributed to the art as well as the science of brewing—but today its global reach has made it almost indistinguishable from other huge brewing conglomerates.

By the 1970s, Tuborg, Carlsberg, and a handful of other Danish breweries had succeeded in convincing the Danes that bottom-fermented yellow fizz was about all there was to beer. Copenhagen had some fine places to drink, but nothing much to try once you got there. Today, however, the craft brewing movement has grown strong enough in Denmark to prompt Carlsberg to start its own line of craft beers. Husbryggeriet Jacobsen is a small modern brewery tucked within the Danish behemoth that produces abbey style beers and a number of other interesting ales and lagers. Some of these "crafty" creations are pretty ordinary, but there are also some winners. A 2013 batch of Carls Porter, a 7.8% imperial porter, was almost shockingly complex for Carlsberg and showed a remarkable balance of serious flavors.

The real adventures in brewing in Copenhagen, however, have left Carlsberg behind. Serious beer bars are proliferating faster than we can visit them. The Copenhagen beer scene is very much a part of the global craft movement. Mikkeller and several other Danes brew beers in Belgium and Norway, but you have to go to Copenhagen to find some of them. Without question, the world's beer culture would be poorer today without Mikkeller and friends, wherever and however they brew.

The sixpack of drinking experiences

Lord Nelson (Hyskenstræde 9). We're not sure we've ever encountered a bar that was more of a beer club, but it's a club that anyone can walk off the street and join. Look like you're really interested in beer, and you'll have a new best friend in no time at all (the clientele is multinational, but the central language is English). It's a one-room gem of a pub that has just enough regulars to keep it safely in business but not so many you can't find a seat, except at the very busiest times of the week. Eclectic soft vintage rock provides a background for conversation and there are no TVs or fruit machines to distract. Two of the dozen taps are cider; the ten beers emphasize the best of Danish brewing, including the work of Danish brewers at breweries in Belgium and Norway. Among the taps are usually a few rarities. The Lord Nelson is one of the pubs that get a very limited production "beer of the month" from Amager. Fermentoren (see below) is another.

Lord Nelson is not elegant: it's a dim, foodless, shabby, sometimes smoky downstairs boozer with a definite "no pretentions" attitude. There are many more sophisticated drinking establishments in Copenhagen and several places that have more beers, but this is still where we always start and usually finish. They have a small picture of us posted behind the bar. Point at it, say we sent you, and you'll be treated especially well.

A digression. On our first visit, we were writing up no more than our third beer when a strapping fellow from the bar sidled over to ask what we were doing. We explained and gave him our "We've tasted…" card, which at that time counted about 19,300 beers. "Oh no! You are seventeen hundred ahead of me!" he exclaimed. We looked at him askance. "No, not seventeen *thousand*," he said, reading our minds. It was Jens Ungstrup, who at the time was #1 on RateBeer and had planned on being the first person in the world to record 20,000 beers. (Michael Jackson far exceeded that figure, but never kept count. We've now topped 25,000, but we still think we're far behind the one and only Beer Hunter.) But Jens couldn't have been nicer, and pointed us to Mikkeller and some other places where we could run up our numbers, showing a truly generous spirit. When we met again by chance at the Great British Beer Festival, he told us we didn't have a chance to get to 20,000 before he did because he lived in Europe and therefore had access to vastly more beers than we did. In a narrow sense he was wrong; we beat him to 20,000 by a few weeks. He passed us shortly afterward and achieved the status of having notes on the greatest number of beers of any living person… for a few months until someone passed him. We both agreed the chase was getting in the way of having fun drinking; we've slowed down a bit and he may have too. It's impressive how many of the very top raters on RateBeer are Scandinavian, in a sense proving Jens's point.

Mikkeller is Copenhagen's bucket list bar for beer drinkers. Mikkel (Keller dropped out of the partnership early on) is a phenomenon—a brewer without a brewery, just a former teacher with a bunch of outrageous ideas, some of which work really well and some of which don't work at all. Most of the Mikkeller beers have been brewed at the Belgian brewery De Proef at Lochristi, a brewery that specializes in making other people's beer fantasies become reality. If the idea is good, De Proef usually does it well; if the idea is crap, that's what the beer is going to taste like. Fortunately, they don't accept many crappy ideas. Some Mikkeller beers, especially the dark ones, come from Norway, and Mikkel has also collaborated with brewers in the U.S. and the UK.

Find Mikkeller at Viktoriagade 8, about a 10- to 15-minute walk from the station. The two smallish rooms, down a steep half-flight of steps in the semi-basement common to Copenhagen architecture, offer a basic design, kind of funky, that matches Mikkeller's drink-it-or-leave-it attitude. The bar can get very crowded, but if you get here in early evening or late afternoon, you can have a bartender for a new best friend who will guide you through a beer adventure. Relatively few Danes show up here to drink—Swedes and Americans comprise the bulk of the patronage—so the bartenders are used to English speakers and are exceptionally patient with neophytes just discovering how interesting beer can be. English is the norm for customers and you may well wind up talking beer to the people next to you longer than you intended.

A big range of Mikkeller beers is on offer, rotating constantly enough to make you dizzy. When we were there they also sported a telephone book of bottles, though they may have moved many to the bottle shop in Nørrebro. They've apparently saved a few of everything they've done that keeps well, which is most of what they've done, and you can get it—at a price.

Like many of Copenhagen's classic beer bars, the most serious food you can get is sesame cashews or an assortment of artisanal cured sausages, but a few doors down Mikkeller has opened a beer café, **Øl & Brød,** featuring beer and food pairings. The menu is sophisticated, ambitious, and *not* cheap. After two days of paying Copenhagen prices of up to $12 a beer, we settled for cashews.

To get there, exit the Central Station and turn left on Vesterbrogade, then walk a few blocks and turn left on Viktoriagade, just before the you-really-can't-miss-it red sign of the Loven Hotel. The bar is on the right a block along, just past Øl & Brød—keep looking down the steps.

Mikkeller and Friends (Stefansgade 35). If the Mikkeller folks weren't so interested in making an impact on the rest of the world, they would probably have the creativity to open enough different beer bars to shove almost every other bar out of anyone's top list. Less funky than their basement emporium near the station, And Friends also serves as an exclusive Danish outlet for the iconic Three Floyds beers as well as a big range from Mikkel's former students who produce To Øl. In addition to 40 taps featuring Mikkeller, Three Floyds, and other interesting drafts, there's a bottle shop next door where you can get a good sense of how busy Mikkeller has been over the past few years.

Located in the increasingly hip Nørrebro section of town, it's three times bigger than the original Mikkeller, with lots of pale pine and cool blue colors. The floor plan is unique. Shutters can close in small semiprivate drinking areas or open them up to the center floor; the intent is to allow you to have a bit of your own space while drawing you into conversation with others. In common with the Vesterbro location, Jonathan and the rest of the English-speaking staff couldn't be nicer.

Take the 5A bus up Nørrebrogade, alight at the Stefansgade stop, and walk a few blocks down Stefansgade to number 35.

Nørrebro Bryghuis (Ryesgade 3). Nørrebro's beers are usually well made and often interesting, and it's very much a part of the global craft beer movement. The brown ale, for example, seems heavily influenced by Garrett Oliver's work at Brooklyn. If

Nørrebro Brygghuis

you've tried Nørrebro beers in the U.S., you'll find them fresher and better here. If you haven't, set aside a good chunk of time to work your way through the extensive menu. Downstairs is a relatively informal bar, but consider saving up some crowns to splurge for a meal in the upstairs restaurant. A small but excellent menu emphasizes Danish cooking and local ingredients. Some tables out on the sidewalk, if you get there early enough to get them, are a fair-weather option.

When Nørrebro opened, it was a lone brewing standout in a part of the city that tourists don't usually find. Now it's part of one of the most interesting areas for beer in the city. **Ølsnedkeren,** the newest of Copenhagen's brewpubs, is in the same general neighborhood, and a few stops on the 5A bus drops you within a short walk of Mikkeller and Friends.

Fermentoren (Halmtorvet 29C) is the bar where Mikkeller bartenders drink when they're off duty. The owners have brewing experience and collaborate with a number of breweries under the name of Crooked Moon. Another downstairs and funky-welcoming single-room bar, it offers a small, sheltered terrace for mid-range weather as well as a larger picnic-table garden at street level. No kitchen, but the management is perfectly comfortable with your bringing in pizza from one of the local shops. You'll find some beers among the 20 taps that you won't see anywhere else, and the smallish bar encourages making new friends. Three different serving sizes can either save your budget or slake your thirst. Most bars are reasonably happy to let you have a small taste before you buy; Fermentoren has tiny, free tasting glasses that they offer without being asked if you even inquire about a beer. Nice touch. For something completely different, try their coffee of the month.

Fermentoren is a relatively short walk from Mikkeller. Walk down Viktoriagade to Halmtorvet, turn right, and keep on going past the big fish and meat market area; it's on the left. If you're coming from anywhere else, take the S train one stop west of the Central Station to Dybbølsgade, go right on Skelbækgade perpendicular to the track, and walk north one looong block; the garden is on your right at the T intersection with Halmtorvet.

While you're in the area you might want to check out **Ølbutikken** at Istedgade 44. A bottle shop-cum-tasting room, it sports four or five glass-front coolers of craft bottles from the U.S. and Europe. You can drink there, sometimes at a bit of a premium, or take them with you—the train station is within walking distance. The very knowledgeable staff have links to Fermentoren and Lord Nelson and it's a very low-key way to play around with some very good beers.

You could walk past **Vesterbro Bryghus** (Vesterbrogade 2B) thirty times and just think it was "Streckers Bar," which is the only sign you'll easily see from the front. It's not a Mikkeller sort of beer geek paradise, but it's an enormously welcoming bar with a staff that loves Americans, and a kitchen that produces good meaty meals at a fair price—for Scandanavia. Beers can vary somewhat, but the spicy Hefeweizen alone is worth a visit. Vesterbro's brewmaster also crafts the beers for **Færgekroen Bryghus,** a small brewpub that perches on a lake in the middle of Tivoli, close enough to the thrill rides to hear the screams. Sipping a beer there may be the best "ride" of any amusement park you'll ever visit.

Other places to explore

In Copenhagen, the following are relegated to the also-ran list, but they'd make our top six in many other cities.

By the time you read this, Mikkeller's latest venture should be up and running. **Wall Pigs** is a joint venture between Three Floyds from Illinois and Mikkeller from everywhere. It will feature American barbecue and American style beers—whatever that means these days. The location is in the meat packing area quite close to the original Mikkeller bar, Fermentoren, and Ølbutikken.

BrewPub København is the city's largest…brewpub. Located on Vestergade (*not* Vesterbrogade) just north of the main shopping area, it's exactly 100 steps from Rådhuspladsen and no more than 10 minutes from Tivoli. It offers a range of eight beers, some of which rotate pretty quickly. We've found their beers a bit inconsistent, but quite good at their best, and continuing to improve. They don't do any better than most U.S. brewpubs in their attempt at a Kölsch, but the German-style dunkel is quite respectable and the IPA at the time (it rotates) was better than most we've had in the States. BrewPub also has good food at, for Copenhagen, decent prices. Their long, snug semi-basement rooms are empty in the summer in favor of the big open courtyard in the center of a 17th century building; patio umbrellas and lap blankets provide shelter in iffy weather. The brewery offers tours on Monday evenings, but you have to book in advance and they don't always run if enough people don't sign up.

The courtyard at BrewPub

Save yourself the time and money by taking a squint at the brew kit through the glass panels on the right as you come in.

Ølsnedkeren (Griffenfeldsgade 52), in the same general part of town as Mikkeller and Friends and Nørrebro Bryghuis, keeps such short hours we wonder how they stay in business. They open as late as 7 PM and only five days a week. But if you can meet their schedule, it's a good stop. Their hop-handed brewer would be at home in the U.S., and his version of a smoked rye pale ale was daring and successful. Some beers are ordinary (there ought to be a term for ersatz kölsch beers—maybe "fälsch"?).

Charlie's Bar, just off the pedestrian shopping area at Pilestræde 33, is a Scandinavian favorite because it's an affordable way to almost visit England. It's small, actually cramped, and sometimes crowded. We respect its independence and dedication to real ale in a region of the world in which cask is rare. However, Charlie's unabashedly English orientation means you'll be trading good Danish drinking time for your quick trip to the UK.

The **Apollo** brewpub sits just outside the walls of Tivoli next to the Hard Rock Café. It was the first of Copenhagen's brew pubs and did its share in helping to shift Copenhagen from a big-brewery city to a craft beer town. It's a bright, touristy, but well-run restaurant with quaffable beers that have improved in recent years, but we've never found it as welcoming as Vesterbro across the street, nor as interesting as BrewPub, which is an easy walk away. It's still a good option, though, if you're waiting for a train. Its range of beers has increased in recent years—three of the four now rotate in season—and the food, while pricey even by Danish standards, is a carnivore's delight.

Ofelia, in the Nyhavn area, sports a harborside terrace under the eaves of the Royal Danish Theatre that is one of our favorite places to drink on a warm summer afternoon. The beer selection is tiny compared to a real beer bar, but a trio of drafts from the Skands brewery in nearby Brøndby provides a tasty alternative to mass-marketed

Brew house at Apollo

Carlsberg. Mostly it's a great retreat from the jam-packed Nyhavn area around the corner and an airy respite from the basement bars that harbor so many of the city's best beers.

Where to stay

The **Radisson Blu** is a tremendous splurge, but sometimes in summer you might not actually have to win the lottery to afford it. The rooms overlooking Tivoli provide the best reason to stay here. You'll see the spectacular Saturday night fireworks display at least as well as those who are packed together in the park. Wheedle yourself into the VIP breakfast on the top floor if you can, just for the view, though the same excellent spread is available on the ground floor. The location is very convenient—a few steps from the tourist office, it's within sight of the Central Station and walking distance to Mikkeller and Fermentoren. A short walk in the other direction takes you to Rådhuspladsen and the city center pedestrian streets that lead to BrewPub København and the Lord Nelson. The **Copenhagen Plaza,** a four-star hotel a few steps from the Central Station entrance, is on our list for a future stay.

Hotel 71 Nyhavn is a converted spice warehouse in uber-scenic Nyhavn. You pay an extra $50 to look at the water through a not-so-large window, but the view is spectacular—one person at a time. Rooms are tiny (but charming) and walls are thin, but the hotel has earned its four stars by doing some of the details well. The **Admiral Hotel** is in the same area. You can walk to Lord Nelson, and Ofelia is virtually out the back door, but it's a long haul from Mikkeller and some of the other top beer destinations in the city. The 66 bus is much faster to the Central Station than the 11A; from the station you can walk to the original Mikkeller or pick up the 5A to the Nørrebro area pubs.

Big hotel chains line the water a long walk south from the main station and sometimes have room when others don't. They're sometimes listed as "Tivoli area"; you might be able to see Tivoli from a roof if you have binoculars.

The tourist office is near the station, across Vesterbrogade from Tivoli and next to the Radisson, and can get you a room quick in high season. It works with a limited number of hotels and charges you $20 to make a reservation. They freely admit there may be empty rooms they don't know about within 500 yards as they send you to a hotel that's a couple of miles away.

Tivoli at night

What to see

Tivoli is a must. We've never seen a more beautiful amusement park; there are parts of it where you'll forget you're anywhere near a big city. Just a stroll around is worth the price of admission. Linger into the night when the lights make it really special. If you have kids in tow, or if you just like rides, there are a few for thrill seekers, and some of the entertainment can feature well-known performers. Fireworks and lasers light up the skies almost every Saturday night. Enough restaurants provide acceptable food at, well, Copenhagen prices. Lunch at the Færgekroen brewpub on the lake is a great option, though.

You have to see the Little Mermaid in the same sense that you have to visit the Hofbräuhaus in Munich or the Eiffel Tower in Paris—people will wonder about you if you don't. It's a surprisingly small statue a few feet offshore in the harbor by the Kastellet. You can buy a map and figure out how to walk there, or take a city boat tour (which you ought to do anyway).

The Carlsberg brewery is well outside the city center and worth the bus ride. There's a daily tour which shows you some brewing equipment and a good look at the Husbryggeriet Jacobsen. If you miss the organized tour you'll have an informative museum visit anyway. The detailed history of the brewery captures a good deal of social history in its narrative, and there are just enough displays of artifacts to keep it interesting. The price of the visit includes a couple of small plastic cups of beer in the courtyard, which on a good day is a fine place to drink. You can find a pretty good selection of Carlsberg's more adventurous beers in the well-stocked brewery store at the end of the visit. A horse cart will jostle you around the grounds for a small additional fee; we actually preferred it to the tour.

For something completely different, spend a couple of hours in the Workers' Museum at Rømersgade 22. A socialist-friendly look at the past, it gives a good insight into why ordinary people have been attracted to a collective society. It includes the entire apartment of a working class family from the 1930s. Also fun is the Copenhagen City Museum.

Scams and alerts

Once the Danes stopped burning, raping, and looting—apparently the same old stuff got boring after a few hundred years—they became hard-working, honest, and very friendly. So no scams here. The exchange rate is so nasty, though, you'll think you've been Vikinged...until you go farther north into Scandinavia and find it even worse. Remember, when you are tempted to grouse about paying over $30 a liter for beer, that Copenhagen is where vast numbers of Swedes come to drink "cheaply."

Be careful of "Viking Excursions" that include dinner, beer, and a show. It's possible to land one that's entirely in Danish and limits you to two smallish Carlsbergs. The Vikings themselves weren't much nastier than that.

Day trips and excursions

Bakken

If you want a more ride-centered amusement park, especially if you have youngish children with you, take the local line that takes you to Helsingor and spend a day in Bakken. The beer isn't great, but you can find some variety if you look hard, and some of the all-you-can-eat deals are a pretty good bargain for Scandinavia. The rides won't make the Travel Channel's Ten Greatest, but are sufficient to amuse.

Malmö

Malmö, even though it's in Sweden, is only about a 20 minute train ride away and it's our top beer-centered day trip from Copenhagen. A combination of local breweries and great beer bars has made it one of our favorite drinking cities. Bring your transit pass from Copenhagen—it's good on Malmö buses. Your currency, however, is not good; you'll have to get some Swedish crowns.

The train station sits quite close to the water on one side of the very walkable center of town. Your first stop is the **Malmö Brygghus Hamnmästaren** (harbormaster's house), a new project of the Malmö brewery. You have the sense that you are indeed entering the harbormaster's house: the main bar looks like someone's parlor. If the weather is at all decent, the good-sized garden, with some water views, is a wonderful place to relax. They serve a wide range of the brewery's beers, of course, but also feature up to a dozen beers from other local craft breweries. Malmö is so close to Copenhagen and the bar so close to the station, it's still worth a few hours just to train over, drink at the Hamnmästaren, and train back. If you can, try to visit for a meal; the smørrebrød offers the most generous portion of shrimp we've ever seen in a Scandinavian meal, and they have an outdoor grill at dinner during good weather. Among

Malmö Bryghus Hamnmästaren

many good house beers, the Brown Out stood out—soft sweet roast with just a touch of finishing chocolate, complemented by sweet fruity and herbal leaf hops. You'll find something just as special.

Further out on the water, the **Green Lion** was once one of the premier beer bars of the area, and its waterfront location ought to make it a destination drinkery. It carries a decent range of beers, though many of its taps are duplicates, and you'll drink them in a modern gastropub with what must be several million dollars worth of dark woods, plush, and brass, with some mounted heads of dead things looming down from the walls. A corner library actually has books, and a fireplace and armchairs beckon beyond the separate dining area. All that atmosphere comes at a price—beers are never cheap in Sweden, but the Green Lion's prices are almost double those of some of the other pubs in town. We doubt the pull taps actually produce cask ale; the brands are all British and usually kegged in this part of the world. Astronomical prices and mediocre background music seemed to explain the small Saturday crowd, but if you have the budget for $25 pints, the service is friendly, and at least there's no problem finding a seat.

On the other side of the canal that separates the station from the main town is one of two **Bishops Arms** (Norra Vallgatan 62). It's a relatively small pub on the ground floor of a hotel, with the British décor you'd expect from the chain. Fifteen taps and a few handpulls offer a good range. If you have the liver for it, an impressive lineup of single malt scotches includes a 40-year-old Highland Park. The basic bar food offers a few surprises including lamb loin and an affordable 185 SK salmon.

The other **Bishops Arms** is a short walk away at Gustav Adolfs Torg 49 near the center of town. Conventional wisdom says the town center location is the better of the two, but we found the station-side branch had the edge in both the welcome and the range of beers. The chain imposes a few restrictions, requiring sale of the high-profit big brewery beers, but individual managers have much influence in choosing the craft beers that make the bars special. It's worth visiting both, therefore, if you have the time.

Malmö Brygghus is near the Triangelns station on Bergsgatan 33, but you can walk it from the in-town Bishops Arms at Gustav Adolfs Torg. It's a big place by Swedish standards, with narrow rooms wrapping around the brewing equipment and making clever use of space inside a former chocolate factory. (The chocolate factory still functions upstairs. You can take a tour if you get there early enough in the afternoon, and they offer the chocolates for sale in the pub. They are *fantastic.*) The brewery features beers that you can't get at the Hamnmästaren branch. A simple pub menu will feed you, if not elegantly, on burgers and pulled pork. The indie acoustic is easy to drink to—we wondered if the Green Lion wouldn't draw better crowds if they stole the Malmö Brygghus soundtrack.

A short walk to the Triangelns station can put you on a train back either to the harbor or to Copenhagen, but if you have time, make a stop at **Söder om Småland** (Claesgatan 8) if it's open. Malmö bartenders tell us that the selection of a dozen and a half rotating drafts is extremely well chosen.

Malmö can't rival Copenhagen for sights, but it's an attractive town. An easy way to see much of what there is to see is to take the canal boat ride that leaves almost from the door of the station-side Bishops Arms. The "Twisted Man" is one of the most unusual skyscraper designs you're likely to see anywhere and you might as well see it from the boat—if you haven't booked the upper floor for a private corporate event, you can't get in the door. The other principal sight is the bridge that got you here.

A brewpub in the Opera claims to be the "world's smallest brewery," though we don't know how much research they've done to know. You can only try their beers on days when the Fat Lady is singing.

Glasgow

Quick orientation

A disclaimer: Glasgow is not one of the great brewing cities of the world, but it still squeaks into this book—partly because the Scots have a beer culture that is too interesting to ignore, and partly because it's just a lovely city in which to drink beer. You can find many Scottish brews south of the border, but they're in better shape when you get them closer to home.

Not you, of course, but someone who reads this book, will benefit from the following warning. Do not ever say something like "We're here traveling in England for two weeks." While the Scots rejected secession from the UK in September 2014, they did so only after securing promises of more autonomy, and even with that, a strong majority in Glasgow voted to go. You're speaking English in a "United Kingdom" built on brutalities that would today invite U.N. intervention. The Scots have not forgotten. See below for how it happened.

The Scots can have an edge that ironically they often save for their best friends, so if someone seems edgy, take it as a compliment. For the most part, you'll have to go a long way to find people more honest and welcoming than the Scots, and that's especially true for those you'll meet in pubs. A local writer made the observation that his co-Glaswegians "love to chat." They sure do; desk clerks, bartenders, taxi drivers, and random strangers will happily talk your ear off.

(P.S. It's pronounced *Glozz-go* though the local accent will warp it into Glesca, Glasgie, and other affectionate diminutives.)

Glasgow has a tight inner core. Most of the places you'll want to drink are walking distance from each other, though you won't be sorry if you make the journey from the city center to the West End by bus. The bus day pass is a £4 bargain you can buy from the driver. Note: Almost uniquely in Europe, the bus day pass and the metro day pass are entirely separate. To use both systems, you have to buy both tickets. Your BritRail pass, however, takes you to many of the outer areas on local trains.

If you get to Glasgow from the south you come into the charming Central Station. The Queen Street station, a walkable few blocks away, is a smaller, less picturesque but functional depot serving northern destinations. The ticket windows at Central Station will, if you ask nicely, give you directions to Queen Street and maybe even a map, but if they're closed, here's how. Exit the north end of Central Station at the end of the tracks. Turn right on Gordon, go three blocks and turn left at the Post Office onto Buchanan; go two blocks and turn right on West George Street. Two blocks beyond is Queen Street station on your left. If you look uphill on Buchanan before you turn on West George, you'll see the new tourist office. Some of the signs still lead you to the abandoned space on George Square.

Station breaks

Finding beer in most UK rail stations is about as hard as finding sand on a beach, though there's no guarantee of quality. Central Station has a couple of bars. Arrol, on the main floor, is OK if you have a very short time. It has three hand pulls and a warm pub atmosphere, though similar to what you could probably find in New York.

Better is the Crystal Palace, an enormous Wetherspoon emporium barely a block from Central Station. Go down to the lower level and cross under the tracks to Jamaica Street. Less than a half a block on your right is the Crystal Palace at #36, with several handpulls in good condition at bargain prices. Food is cheap, chain, and reliable.

The Queen Street station has a couple of options. Exit to George Square, and a stone's throw hits The Counting House, a Wetherspoon pub featuring a half a dozen cask ales, most of them Scottish; it almost made our top six pubs. Drop the stone instead of throwing it, and just on the right downstairs as you exit the station is Camperdown Place with four handpulls. Camperdown is another Wetherspoon; the Counting House is the better of the two.

History and culture

Scotland and England were separate countries until the death of Elizabeth I in 1603. The heir to the British throne was Elizabeth's nephew James, the king of Scotland. He jumped at the chance to take the more prestigious seat to the south and moved to London to become James I of England, as well as James V of Scotland, and begin the Stuart dynasty. No one was happy. The Scots had lost a live-at-home king, and the British had inherited a crude Scotsman who spoke poor English (in part because his tongue was too big for his mouth) and occasionally cut off people's ears. Worse, James was an autocrat and virtually ignored Parliament, where Elizabeth had skillfully manipulated her legislators to ensure public support for her policies. James's reign endured political turmoil and the occasional plot: our term "cabal" comes from the first letters of the names of his advisors. Although James alienated a fair portion of his new subjects, he was careful enough to avoid full-scale rebellion. His son Charles I was not.

The Scots started the trouble. John Knox brought Calvinism to the churches of Scotland, and Charles, who was still king of Scotland, tried to repress the movement with English troops. Parliament didn't mind the idea of killing off some Scots, but insisted on the right to raise the tax money to do it. Charles saw that as a threat to his authority and sent them home. They refused to go and instead stuck around to set off the English Civil War in 1640. The Scots found themselves in a tough position: the prospect of being ruled by a foreign nation's parliament was even worse than being ruled by a nominally Scottish king they didn't like. The parliamentary leader Oliver

Cromwell emerged as "Lord Protector" of England, got Charles beheaded, and laid claim to Scotland. He probably would have caused even more trouble for the Scots if he hadn't been so busy killing Irish. Cromwell died in 1657 and his son Richard took over as Lord Protector. But like today's Kim clan in North Korea, Richard had a hard time explaining why he should inherit the helm of a government that was established in opposition to hereditary rule. The English made him go away in 1660 and restored the Stuart Dynasty. Charles II promised to play nicely with Parliament and not hold grudges, and for the most part kept his promise. The Scots heaved a sigh of relief as Charles became Charles (conveniently II) of Scotland as well.

Charles and his brother James had sought refuge in France during the Civil War and had grown ominously tolerant of Catholicism. Charles was smart enough to stay in the Church of England until just before his death—he took the C of E Last Rites, then converted to Catholicism to take the Catholic Last Rites (to cover his bases), and died before anyone could get upset with him. He died childless, which left his brother to inherit the throne as James III. But James had converted to Catholicism earlier, which might have been marginally acceptable if he hadn't had the misfortune to have a son (another Charles, of course). The English would have no part of a Catholic dynasty and instead offered the crown to a Protestant, James's older daughter Mary, wife of William III of the Netherlands' House of Orange. She wouldn't come without her hubby, so England got William and Mary—and Virginia got a fine name for a university.

James, having learned from his father what happens to Stuarts who lose civil wars, scurried to France and the bloodless "Glorious Revolution" was complete. The Scots, however, were now cut out of the loop, with a Dutchman ruling England and laying claim to Scotland.

In a few years Parliament legally combined the two kingdoms in a forced marriage that many Scots still refer to as the "wanchancie [unlucky] covenant." Despite Bonnie Prince Charlie and "the '45" rebellion, the union endured, while the British continued to try to wipe out Scottish cultural as well as political independence, even outlawing kilts, Gaelic, and bagpipes. Traditional Scottish ales, many of which did not use hops, also faded in favor of English-style hopped beer.

As with so much of Scottish culture, however, Scottish beers are making a comeback.

Beer styles and drinking culture

In the lexicon of beer, a "Scottish ale" still means a darker than pale, sweet ale that may or may not contain a bit of peat in the taste. Such ales are classified by a number that used to indicate the tax, and therefore the strength, of the ale. A 60 shilling ale, or "60/-," is a lightweight session ale, 70/- has a bit more oomph, and 80/- is a beer of some substance. Sometimes you'll see a 90/-, or "wee heavy," most often at a festival, but in general they're easier to find in brewpubs in the U.S.

Long ago, Scottish beers weren't hopped, and in the last century or two they've been hopped only enough to make their sweetness bearable over an evening's session. In the past couple of decades, however, an English invasion of highly hopped beers has had a profound influence on a steadily increasing number of small craft brewers in Scotland.

American beers with an even more pronounced hop intensity have made their mark as well. BrewDog beers from Fraserburgh (now Ellon) reach unique extremes.

Bruce and Scott Williams have led a revolution against creeping hoppism and its English overtones. Starting with a homebrew shop, then moving on to small contract operations and eventually to operating their own brewery, they have revived ancient Scottish brewing traditions and made their mark on brewing all over the world. Starting with a heather ale, Fraoch, and moving on to elderberries, gooseberries, pine, and even seaweed, they turn out a range unlike any other in the world. The Williams Brothers Brewery, now in Alloa, also produces a range of more standard ales, though even these often feature honey and herbs.

Scottish pub etiquette is similar to that in England. Tables in crowded pubs are shared; beer, and usually food, is ordered at the bar (be sure to say "please"). Alcoholic strengths, if you're not in a BrewDog pub, tend to be low, so the imperial 20 oz. pint isn't as formidable as it looks.

The sixpack of drinking experiences

Clockwork Beer Company (1153-1155 Cathcart Road, Mount Florida). We first tried Clockwork beers in a tasting Bruce Williams set up at Washington's Brickskeller in the late 1990s. Those memories are another reason we chose Glasgow for this book. Our trip to the source confirmed our impressions. It's a good-sized, rambling pub with separate drinking and eating areas. Food is well above average for a pub. If you're just there drinking and the dining area is empty, you can ask to sit there; if they've got the space they'll be quite gracious about making the exception.

An impressive array of cask ales can keep you busy for an evening. Clockwork, like many brewpubs in the UK, is confident enough in its own beer to offer several guest beers as well; you may find a few you won't see anywhere else. But the Clockwork beers more than hold their own. If you drink the lagers and spiced beers such as their ginger, you get what you deserve. But if you choose what Scots do best—darks, ambers, and strong ales—you'll be rewarded with some of the best brews in the city. Clockwork is more willing to use hops than some others in Scotland, but there's always a firm malt foundation that contributes to the complexity of their beers.

The welcoming décor features the eponymous clocks, but also flags and lots of wood; a small garden is out back. A friendly and remarkably efficient bar staff make the crowds seem to melt away when you go up to order your beer.

Trains will get you close, and it's easier to get to than it sounds; these directions will help: Take a train to the Mount Florida station. Exit south to your right, take a left on Bolton, go two blocks to Cathcart, then right to head south on Cathcart. The pub is just past the split at Kings Park Road.

One of the great cask houses in the city, **The Bon Accord** (153 North Street) is also, if you look for it, something of a museum. Between the front windows a stag dressed in a scarf and tie gazes down at the long, two-level bar. Old cartoons on the front side wall and rows of "Best Pub" awards stretch a bit farther back. Barrels and bottles and pots and stoves, sports pictures, an array of soccer balls, and more different styles of furniture than Granny's attic—all in all nearly as many artifacts as in the Tenement House (see "Sights") and you can spend your £12 on four UK pints of beer instead of an admission price.

Not that four pints is necessarily enough. Ten cask beers and a cider, plus the requisite lager taps, give plenty of choice. Beers in good condition at proper temperatures are no surprise. This place takes beer seriously. Periodic beer festivals feature brews from specific regions of the British Isles and will have beers you have never seen before—promise. The welcome is always warm from the staff as well as from many of the patrons.

The Three Judges (141 Dumbarton Road, Partick, in the West End) is on everyone's list of the best beer bars in the city, and rightly so. Small, woody, and atmospheric, it keeps almost a dozen hand pulls in very nice condition. In the summer it runs a series of "festivals" that focus on beers from all over Scotland and include England as well. It's a much lower-key pub than some you'll run into; it seems to draw people who are serious about beer, and we all know those sorts are very well behaved. It's one of the best places in Glasgow to sit back and enjoy a first-class pint and some conversation. Although snacks are very limited, the staff is happy to let you bring in food. The Indian take-away next door is well above average at a very affordable price.

Inn Deep (445 Great Western Rd., also in the West End) is a relatively new venture by Williams Brothers Brewery of Alloa, the guys who resurrected the heather ale style. Second-generation Williamses run the place and do a bang-up job of it. Down more steps than you think you'll be able to reclimb, it sits on the river with a waterside deck and somewhat cave-like rooms with original art painted on the walls. Some of the

The Three Judges

Williams Brothers beers are always on tap, of course, but they also serve a good range of rotating beers from around the UK and even the United States. The burgers are not only phenomenal for Scotland, but would hold their own in a U.S. pub as well.

BrewDog (1397-1403 Argyle Street, West End). If you know much about beer, you know the BrewDog beers. So you won't be surprised by what BrewDog envisions as a good place to drink. Industrial décor, Spartan, but oddly welcoming, the place is almost as off-the-wall as the beers. A dozen or so taps (and they are taps, not casks) include guest beers from funky European breweries, including Mikkeller and Mikkeller's friends. But while you're there, try the beers you can't afford to buy by the bottle. When we visited, the ridiculously strong BrewDogs included the stunning 32% Tactical Nuclear Penguin and the stunninger 41% Sink the Bismarck!. Both were produced by the "ice beer" technique of freezing and removing water. Some purists argue that they're not really beer, but we don't remember any serious beer critics claiming that the Eisbier from Kulmbach wasn't really beer. The Penguin tasted like a liqueur, but the Bismarck really did retain a great deal of the flavor of beer, albeit at a devastating strength.

BrewDog guys aren't dumb and they don't want you to guzzle their powerfuller stuff, so buying a bottle will cost you your car (and Hertz hates it when you do that). But at "only" £5 for 5 cl, about one seventh of a bottle, we got a pretty reasonable taste of each one. Save their liverkillers for the end, though; drink, nosh, and enjoy the funk before you impair yourself.

When you're planning your time in Glasgow, check early to find out if there's music at **Blackfriars Bar** (36 Bell Street). Blackfriars has the reputation of being one of the better music venues in the city, and if you hit a good music night you can't do better than their range of beers to accompany the entertainment. They also have a comedy club if you want to take a stab at Scottish humor. But even if the house is dark, the beers are in great condition and this is a good part of the city to explore. See "Sights" below for a couple of attractions nearby.

Other places to explore

The Counting House (9 St. Vincent Place) is a JD Wetherspoon house, with all the faults and glories that entails. It has a greater range of casks than other Wetherspoons in the city, but you have to semi-circumnavigate the bar to find them, or spot the not-too-easy-to-spot chalkboard. Its cavernous space nearly fills at the peak of lunch, but if you're persistent you'll find a table while other people stand around feeling sorry for themselves. The décor is more bank-like than even other converted-bank Wetherspoons. Food is, um, Wetherspoonful. UK cask fans disagree about the chain. It is indeed a chain, but they work pretty hard to support breweries that usually can't get in the door of operations of their size. For us it's an easy call—they've dug up beers for us we haven't had. Thanks, JD.

If you walk out the back of the Bon Accord and keep going straight, you'll emerge onto Argyle Street and have a chance to do some fine pub hopping on your way to BrewDog and the Three Judges. Our favorite of the new pubs that are springing up in the area is **The Pourhouse** (1038-1042 Argyl Street, Finnieston). Three handpulls offer beers we haven't seen elsewhere; the 20 or so bottles include a few Belgians. A bright, airy high-ceilinged room holds no more than seven or eight tables; the cooking is imaginative. A bit farther on is the **Islay Inn,** which is one of the most likely places to find folk music in the city.

The **Inn at the Cross,** formerly Bruadar, is a draft-only house that tries to celebrate both craft and cold beer with mixed success. People do go there. In our view, if you're looking for bare décor, appallingly cramped bathroom stalls, and cold keg beer, this is just about perfect. It's just behind the Three Judges and it does serve food. A recent visit found the service much improved from its Bruadar days.

Uisge Beatha (22/246 Woodlands Road) still shows up on Web lists as one of the best pubs in the city, but it's now fully a part of **DRAM!** DRAM! tends to modern, with wifi and flat screens, but it has its charms: a few handpulls, lots of wood and stone, and a set of church stalls as a sort of a snug. A nice range of whiskies if you want to digress. North of the West End, it's on several bus routes and it's not a bad walk through the park from BrewDog.

If you find yourself in the club and restaurant area along Sauchiehall Street in the city center, **Hengler's Circus** is another of Glasgow's dozen or so Wetherspoon pubs. It's not worth a separate trip, but it can offer a good pint before or after dinner at the Kama Sutra, a well-above-average Indian restaurant a few doors up towards the Buchanan center.

West Brewing Company is at The Green. The Green is the city's oldest part, stretching along the river just southeast of the city center, and West (just "West") overlooks the park. The location alone almost placed it in our top six. On a fine day it's well worth the effort to get there (the 62 bus stops a few feet away). The lightest beer, West 4, was a clean, more or less German, 4% lager, a pleasant session beer you can quaff by the liter if you're so inclined. Their other beers have their fans in Glasgow and feature in several of the city's pubs. There's no doubt about the Germanic yeast used to produce the hefeweizen; they're very fond of the heavy banana flavor. (We aren't.) The remaining two lagers are a bit stronger and sweetly unmemorable.

A great hangout for young groups, **Republic Bier Halle** (7-9 Gordon Street) is more a series of basement caverns than a hall. It concentrates on pizzas and pushes out hundreds of them in an evening with "buy one get one free" pricing. They're not bad, and you can't find a haggis pizza just anywhere. Mixed olives, reubens, and deli boards are alternatives, and there are vegetarian options. A pair of Fraoch Heather Ales, two pizzas, and the non-included tip will leave you with change from $40. A few lonely Scottish drafts join about 10 Continental taps and 80 or so bottles, but you won't find many that you can't get at a good beer bar in a typical American city. A change of pace from the "real ale" scene—if you need a change of pace.

Where to eat

Pub food sometimes exceeds expectations. Even when menus are limited, standard pub fare can excel; the burgers at Inn Deep are an example. There are some marvelous dinners to be had in Glasgow, however, if you don't mind drinking conventional beers.

If you walk north on Hope from Central Station you'll find a slew of ethnic restaurants and the classy **Mussel Inn.** Scotland has some of the best seafood in the world, and the Mussel Inn prides itself on fresh and local. Mussels are sweeter even than those of Belgium, and the fish and other shellfish are as fresh as you'll ever find in a city. After your meal, walk uphill a block and cross the street to the **Pot Still,** one of Glagow's premier whisky bars. On a good day you can find four cask ales, but whisky is the star: hundreds of bottles line the towering shelves behind the bar. The welcome couldn't be friendlier; you get to expect that in Glasgow.

Where to stay

The tourist office in Glasgow will give you a book of hotels and B&Bs. They'll also book a room for you, if you insist, at £4 plus 10% and a great deal of your time. Even the people at the office often say to go find the room yourself.

A good B&B in England and Scotland is a delight to stay in. While you trade some luxuries for personal service, a B&B provides a fine mix of a home stay's charm and a hotel's anonymity. Finding a good B&B without a car, however, is a dicey proposition, and city B&Bs rarely measure up to their country cousins.

The tourist office gave us their highest recommendations for the Newton Hotel on Bath Street and we offer this description as illustrative of the type. We paid about $100 for a quiet, smallish room in the back of the hotel. Booking a "family room used as a double" is worth the extra twenty bucks for the space you get. The pork-free "traditional" Scottish breakfast wasn't bad and the hotel's location is fine—it's a block away from the Novotel and a block in the other direction from Sauchiehall's shops, restaurants, and clubs. But there's the rub. The club-goers that stay in a place like this often wreck it, and management are reluctant to put money into furniture that could well be in the rubbish bin in a fortnight. A rock-hard mattress was beyond annoying, a fellow guest raided the kitchen and found badly outdated supplies, and the Internet didn't really work (but maybe that doesn't matter since the "working desk" had no chair you could possibly use for working). Even with all its faults, however, we'd consider a return. The breakfast-room and cleaning staff couldn't have been friendlier or more helpful, and it was cheap. We would test the mattress before paying for the room. Alternatively, hotel chains abound.

What to see

Glasgow's eight main museums are easy to identify, and they're all free; pick up a brochure or map at the tourist office. The Kelvingrove is the jewel of the crown—it looks like the Smithsonian and sort of encompasses the Smithsonian's range in one building. Art, animals, and industrial artifacts fill this something-for-everyone experience. A riverside museum, 10 to 15 minutes' walk beyond Kelvingrove, focuses on transportation.

The Tenement House is a near-perfectly preserved worker's flat from the early 20th century. A botched bequest left it sitting untouched until someone realized it had become historically significant. A couple of rooms on the ground floor document the history of tenement living in Glasgow. Upstairs is Mrs. Forward's flat just as she left it when she died. While she lived into the 1960s, she never really left the '20s in lifestyle, sleeping in the kitchen near the coal stove and shopping daily to avoid the need to buy a refrigerator. It's part of the National Heritage and will set you back £6, a bit less if you're old enough. We are old enough, and it came as a shock to us that half the content of this historical display consists of artifacts and events from our own lifespans. If you're not that old, don't laugh—you're next.

If, and only if, you're going to Blackfriars pub during the day, pop in to the Police Museum next door. It's free, though they extract a donation. The curator will talk your ears off (we warned you above), but that's a good part of the charm. If you admire police uniforms, then this is your museum; otherwise your visit won't be long, though the stories of past crimes (who stole the Stone of Scone??) told in placards and displays are entertaining.

Across the street from Blackfriars is Merchant Square, a collection of upscalish restaurants sharing an old market building. We were underwhelmed, but some of our Glaswegian friends say it's "the" place to eat. A craft and design market on Sundays has the breadth and depth of a small church bazaar.

Scams and alerts

Our friend Skye told us that Glasgow is "one of the scariest places to grow up and one of the worst," but if you're already grown up and are clearly a tourist, you'll almost certainly never see the harsh side of the city.

Scots here and anywhere else will almost always treat you well. Drop a £20 note on the floor of a pub and it will be in your hand before you know you've lost it. We've been randomly high-fived by tattooed 20-somethings walking through the pedestrian zone. Almost without exception, Glaswegians will know where you want to go better than you do. Sometimes they're right.

Cabs may occasionally "avoid traffic" to add kilometers—but the marginal increments are so small that we doubt it happens often. Many Glasgow streets run one way, but some change the direction of flow every few blocks. If you note where you're going as you ride a downtown bus you'd swear the bus was "adding kilometers" too. Most cab rides we had were as direct as possible and not expensive.

Scotrail bans drinking on trains after 9 PM, though in our experience enforcement is minimal. Cross-border trains are exempted from the restriction.

Further information

Bottle shops

You can find more beers than even the good pubs of Glasgow make available at a good bottle shop. Three of the best cluster in the West End. **Valhalla's Goat** (449 Great Western Road) is a Williams Brothers venture just up the road from their Inn Deep. A selection of several hundred bottles features small brands that are delivered

Valhalla's Goat

to the shop by one-man brewery operations as well as some of the new London craft ventures. Ask Jin for advice and tell her we sent you. The selection is exceptional, but it's also worth noting that no one is getting really rich here: most beers were under £3 and a few well less than that. **The Cave** is on Great Western on the other side of the ravine from Inn Deep; AD will help you find some gems. **Hippo Beers,** on Queen Margaret Drive, a ten minute walk away from the city and off Great Western, also carries exceptional ranges; Aleck and Derrick know their beer well.

In town, the **Good Spirits Co.** (23 Bath Street) is just a couple of blocks from the Queen Street Station. Their selection is small, but they give it a good deal of thought, and if you're putting together a picnic, some are kept cold. You can find some very small breweries represented and some rare (and expensive) bottles. They stock a few American craft beers as well, including some Goose Island beers we haven't seen in the States.

Brewery tours

Clockwork does tours; arrange them in advance, but it's a pretty small operation. Tennent's does not do tours, but you can get into the building on "Doors Open Days" if you book well in advance and can time your visit to *the* weekend it's open. We wouldn't change our schedule to do it—big industrial tours are common in the U.S. and Europe and you won't see much you wouldn't get elsewhere. But if you're interested, the website is http://www.doorsopendays.org.uk/opendays/ The same scheme gets you into a number of other buildings in Glasgow that are shut the rest of the year.

Entertainment

Glasgow works hard to bring a range of musical and theatrical experiences from around the world. "They've tried so hard," a Glaswegian lamented, "to bring in events that will bring people to Glasgow. But the only thing they can't bring here is good weather." Keep an eye out for festival events. Even when there is no festival, there's lots going on. Pick up a copy of *The Gig Guide* in many pubs or at the tourist office. King Tut's prides itself on booking acts you'll know six months later. The Islay Inn, on the way from Bon Accord to the Three Judges, has weekend live music including a Sunday open mike.

Day trips

Buses range far into the countryside from Glasgow and there are myriad worthwhile sights ranging from ancient castles to industrial heritage museums. Arran, though a bit touristy, gives you a view of Scotland that's very different from Glasgow.

Arran

You can have a Hebridean island experience in one day if you take a train from Central Station to Ardrossan Harbor and take the ferry to Arran. There's much to do on the island. Buses are timed perfectly for a visit to the distillery tour in the morning and the brewery in the afternoon; there are also a pottery and a perfumery that makes its own cosmetics from local ingredients. For a more leisurely pace, take the mile-plus walk over to the brewery, have a pub lunch at the Wine Port, take the brewery tour, and pub your way back to the boat afterwards. If you follow the Fisherman's Walk along the shore to the brewery you'll be rewarded by a dramatically beautiful journey

Arran harbor from Fisherman's Walk

through unspoiled seashore and tidal wetlands. If you make time, you can visit the castle that is next to the brewery.

Arran produces good to absolutely excellent beers. Their Arran Ale is a summer 3.8% gem, but the others are well worth trying as well. Four pounds gets you the 2 PM tour. Gerald is a brewer and an historian and his tour informs and entertains; small samples of five of their beers follow. You won't have to walk far—the "tour" consists of three sets of windows along a corridor—but you'll get more information about the history of brewing both on Arran and in general than you would expect. You can get lunch at **The Wine Port,** next to the brewery; it has two handpulls of Arran beers as well as take-away growler offerings from the brewery. Food is pub grub with some imagination and good local sourcing. The décor is bus station coffee bar, but in good weather plenty of tables fill the courtyard.

A pub crawl on Arran is limited, but can keep you amused until the ferry leaves. The **Ormidale Hotel** is uphill behind the athletic fields on your left as you leave the village—look for the big "BAR" sign at the edge of the woods. More conventionally, find it by turning left opposite the drug store, go a quarter mile or so past the church, and look left into the woods. Take the time to appreciate the absolutely stunning tropical trees and plants as you make your way up the drive; the Gulf Stream runs up the west coast of Scotland and the island climate can be surprisingly gentle. The pub has several rooms: an orangery of sorts, a comfy pub bar, and a living room. The solid carved wood tables are works of art, and no matter where you sit, you can view the magnificently maintained grounds. The smaller rooms invite conversation, and you'll almost certainly be included. You won't find hand pulls at the bar; it's one of a relatively few pubs to still use "tall fonts" that essentially push the beer from the cask instead of pull it. It looks like a CO_2 system at first glance, but the cask ale that flows is CAMRA approved. Meals exceed pub expectations.

It seems as if everyone on the island gathers for happy hour between 5 and 5:45 at **Brodick Bar.** Occupying an easy-to-miss building behind the post office, it fills with family-friendly energy. The modern bar features checked carpet, tartan curtains, and pale woods. Plenty of pillows and benches provide seating, but almost everyone—all of whom know everyone else—gathers at the bar. Deuchars IPA is on a "tall font" cask, along with a handful of mass market foreigners. Like the Ormidale, their attached restaurant offers food that goes beyond minimal pub fare.

Karlsruhe

Quick orientation

Karlsruhe likes to call itself "the fan-shaped city," and many roads do emanate from the Karlsruher Schloss, but you're better off thinking of it as a rectangle with a fan-shaped Schloss park sitting on top of it. At the bottom of the rectangle is the Haup-bahnhof, which also serves as one of the main trolley hubs.

Exit the Bahnhof on the "city" side, not the south/Sud side. Directly across from the Bahnhof is the Zoo, stretching away from the station towards the Schloss. To the left is a pedestrian walkway that runs the 3 kilometers to the front door of the Schloss; to the right of the Zoo is Ettlinger Strasse, the main tram route to the market and city center. A day pass on the trams is easy to buy at multi-language ticket machines in the tram boarding area for about 5 bucks.

The tourist office is also directly across the street from the station. They'll give you maps and brochures, tell you what parts of the city have been dug up or shut down due to construction, and provide you with a very helpful brochure of all the city's hotels.

Karlsruhe is off the usual tourist path, but attractive enough that they have to deal with foreigners anyway. In the breweries and brewpubs, you'll find some of the nicest

Schloss Karlsruhe

people you'll ever meet. In some of the other places you find people who remind us of beach personnel in August—they're just plain tired of the same old questions every day. Ask if they speak English and they'll deny they know a word. But start by trying to limp through in German, and they'll suddenly remember they learned more English in high school than you'll ever learn German. That said, you'll run into more people here than in most cities who really don't remember the English they learned because they haven't had a chance to use it. In our experience, when you find these people, you're far enough off the conference/tourist circuit for them to be wonderfully gracious in speaking sign language and cognate-groping.

Station breaks

The few decent options near the Bahnhof close early in the evening. Am Tiergarten (Bahnhofplatz 6) has a lovely patio right on the zoo entrance where a grumpy staff serves draft beer until 8 PM; if you need food, however, keep moving. The other option is the bar of the Residenz Hotel just to the west (the McDonalds side) of the station, which serves Ketterer beers from Pforzheim (see "Day trip," below). The hotel is a pleasant place, but the bar closes for much of the summer.

If you're hanging around the station after 8 PM for some reason, buy your beer in the station market and drink it on the platform. After 10 PM the market won't sell beer, but you can get it from a small cooler in the coffee shop a few doors away. Neither has much in the way of good local beers.

History and culture

Unlike most of the German cities in this guide, Karlsruhe has a relatively short past. Karl III Wilhelm, Margrave of Baden-Durlach, had it built in 1715. Karl, one of the most forgotten of many forgotten European Charleses, was one of about 2,000 virtually absolute rulers in the area that now makes up Germany. He didn't rule much of an area, but within it he most definitely ruled.

Supposedly, he went out hunting one day to avoid the stress of so much absolute authority—as well as the absolute lack of authority he apparently had around the house—and fell asleep in a peaceful grove. When he awoke, he decided to build a new palace in this wonderfully quiet place—Karls Ruhe: "Charles's Rest" (*ruhe* also means peaceful in German). Ordering the construction was easy. Attracting a population large enough to build and sustain a royal Schloss, however, was a challenge. Karl hoped to entice people from many parts of Europe with the promise of low taxes and, remarkably for the time, freedom of religion. It worked.

Today, the town maintains its prosperity by using its central location to attract a wide variety of conferences and trade shows. At sneezing distance from France, it's only an hour from Strasbourg and Frankfurt and three from Paris and Munich.

You'll see the term "Badisch" or a form of it on everything from beer to museums. It just means "of Baden"—this part of the large German state of Baden-Wurttemburg.

Beer styles and drinking culture

Karlsruhe lacks any particular drinking style, though most of its breweries seem to do very good work with Weizens. Otherwise, you'll find the same styles and the same fads that roll through the rest of Germany. You won't find the liter Masses of Bavaria or the delicate Kölsch glasses of Cologne and Düsseldorf—Karlsruhe makes this book because its relative modernity gives it a different feel and it does have more breweries than most German towns. Especially, we've found that the range of brewpubs and brewery taps shows a good deal more variety than we've found in other cities. You can drink in a big, well-financed brewery-restaurant, a slick modern brewpub, or a brewery restaurant that is itself a work of art, or spend an evening in a place that feels like someone's home. You'll have to work a bit to find the good drinking spots here, but it's worth the effort.

This is Germany, and not Berlin, which means that some of the places you'll want to go close relatively early. Ask when you get there, or call in advance, and get an early start to your evening drinking. It seems a good many Karlsruhers take their ruhering seriously.

The sixpack of drinking experiences

Badisch Brauhaus (Stephanienstrasse 38-40). Even if you, like us, haven't got the courage to try the slide that takes you from one floor of this brewery restaurant to another, the place is just plain fun. Running streams in the floor lined with fairy lights, a sliding glass roof, indoor plants, and a view of the funkiest looking hotel we've ever seen make it a great place to drink. Happily the beer is good too; three above-average house beers are led by an exceptionally good Hefeweizen. The food would be worth a visit even if the place were more "normal." Salads are high quality and enormous. If the brewer is there and not too busy, he'll give you an informal tour. Getting there is easy if the trams are running again—they've been torn up for construction for the last three years. The #6 tram will take you down Kaiserstrasse and past the marketplace to Karlstrasse, a couple of blocks away, and the Europaplatz S-Bahn stop works too.

Hoepfner-Burghof (Haid-und-Neu-Strasse 18). Large or regional breweries in the U.S. are often prohibited by state law from selling their own product in an on-premise business, although the brewpub movement has resulted in some changes for the better. But in Germany it's a tradition—even very large operations like Paulaner in Munich operate expansive brewery restaurants and beer halls. Outside Munich, the taps are less imposing, but they're still worth seeking out for above-average food and, usually, a wide range of beer. The Hoepfner is a perfect example. Hoepfner isn't a brand you'll find outside the region, but the brewery is big enough to brew a wide range of softly sweet but clean and professional beers. The garden is beautiful—more intimate than the big expanses in Munich and greener than most. The woody restaurant interior offers comfort when the weather doesn't. Drink there long enough and you're likely to see the semi-trucks delivering the malt through the brewery gates. (Hauptfriedhof tram and S-Bahn stop.)

Gaststätte Kühler Krug (Wilhelm-Baur-Strasse 3) offers a gorgeous setting indoors and out; someone put some serious money into this modern brewpub. A modern copper brewhouse is the centerpiece of this big sprawling place in a park, where some of the outside tables overlook a small brook. It's a "newpub" in its range, but a trio of well-made beers complements a full menu. The service is professional and the food is above average, with particularly good sides and salads. Generally well run, though supplies were short in the restrooms. Getting near it is easy—there's a tram stop of the same name. Actually finding it is slightly more of a challenge, since it's not easily seen from the tramline, but put your back to the city center and head left along the water and you'll find it.

Der Vogelbräu Karlsruhe (Kapellenstrasse 50) is one of a small chain of brewpubs. There's another one you can reach easily by tram in the nearby city of Durlach, Vogel Hausbräu. Der Kleine Vogel, as the Karlsruhe branch was earlier known, was one of Germany's first "newpubs" when it opened in 1985. It still brews a small range of nicely crafted unfiltered beers; it helps if you like yeast. Der Vogel Pils combines hop and yeast bitter, but shows herbal sweetness late. Two small event rooms and a main dining area open up onto a small and crowded but attractive garden in back. It's about a five-minute walk from Durlacher Tor (tram and S-Bahn), near Waldhornstrasse, just inside the town center.

If you want a slick, professional brewpub with lots of beer selections—skip **Knielinger Hausbrauerei König Bräu** (Saarlandstrasse 61, Knielingen). Fewer than a dozen tables inside aren't used in good weather; eight long tables fill the small courtyard of what appears to be the remnants of a farmhouse complex in the middle of a residential neighborhood. The host is as big, genial, and welcoming as any stereotypical German movie character. As far as we could tell, he doesn't speak a word of English, and that doesn't matter at all. The welcome couldn't be warmer, he'll make himself understood, mostly, and you might even get one or two of his jokes. It's a dauntingly simple place; we stayed to eat only because we were writing this book. But a surprisingly ambitious menu foreshadowed a well-cooked, very German meal. The large schnitzel is actually three normal ones piled on a plate.

The beers are clearly made on premise. Yeasty and not altogether consistent, the Pils was a decent session beer—almost more of a Helles in its relatively soft hopping. The Weizen was heavy, but its intense fruitiness made it a reasonable accompaniment to the schnitzel. König Bräu doesn't open until 4:30 PM and can close early if business is slow. Although it's a ways from the center in Knielingen, it's easy to get to. Take the #5 tram west from the market to Knielingen Herweghstrasse, then walk left to Saarlandstrasse and turn right a couple of blocks to number 61. Closed Monday.

Wolfbräu was a small regional brewery that just couldn't compete in a modern market. While they don't brew any more, the brewery tap at **Wirtshaus Wolfbräu** (Werderstrasse 51) remains open, and you might, if you ask nicely, get to see some of the former brewery. We understand that Heidelberger brews the beers now, but supposedly they're still the Wolfbräu formulas. Whatever the source of the formulas, however, some of the Wolf beers are among the best in the city. Wolf was one of our first brewery visits, and the welcome was so sincere that it encouraged us to keep visiting breweries. You'll still get professional beers and solid German cooking.

Other places to explore

Brauhaus Moniger Brauereiausschank (Zeppelinstrasse 17). You should try the Moniger beers while you're in town. Moniger is a significant regional brewery that tends to reach a wider market than its crosstown rival, Hoepfner. The beers are crisper and a bit less sweet than Hoepfner's. We haven't yet managed to get to their outside-the-center location, but it's at the top of our list for next time.

Fortunately, **Cafe Emaille** (Kaiserstraße 142) is a good place to try the Moniger beers if you can't make it to the brewery. Near the Europaplatz, it occupies part of the space of a larger Moniger restaurant that closed about a decade ago. Dozens of old advertising signs make it an interesting place to drink.

Where to stay

Easy recommendation here: the **Allvitalis Traumhotel** at Badisch Brauhaus. Too funky to be included in the tourist office brochure, it nonetheless offers a fine breakfast, house-brewed beer an elevator ride away, and some rather mind-bending décor—a bit of a splurge, but an unforgettable experience. It's a big sprawling hotel, conference center, brewery, and restaurant taking up almost a city block. Some of the themed rooms are, well, geared for honeymooners, but there's nothing tasteless, just different. We got the Sun, Moon and Stars room: stars on the carpet, beautifully carved desk and headboard, a stained glass panel looking in or out of the bathroom, and twinkling star lights in the ceiling (that you can turn off if you can figure out the 20 or so light switches). Rooms open up onto balconies over a big courtyard that appears to be the work of Gaudí on crack. The building's outer walls are all bulges and curves, and at the end of the yard is a two-story joker's head: the eyes open up onto a patio and the mouth is the balcony of the room below. It was one of our most memorable stays ever. The air conditioning works, sometimes.

Traumhotel at Badisch Brauhaus

The big, expensive, and ever so much more conventional hotels line up on Ettlinger Strasse, and maybe by the time you get there the city's construction projects won't be so disruptive. The **Ibis** is a cheap alternative, one tram stop east of the station towards Ettlinger Strasse.

We spent a pleasant night for under $100 including a very good buffet breakfast at the four-star **Hotel Residenz,** which is almost on the Bahnhof parking lot. The rooms with balconies in the back are quiet if you discount the freight trains that come rumbling under your window through the night. There's no air conditioning, so avoid it in a heat wave; Karlsruhe is one of Germany's warmest cities.

What to see

We love the **Tiergarten** zoo in Karlsruhe. It occupies 22 hectares of the center city and contributes significantly to the "ruhe" feel of the town. The 800 animals are amusing enough, but the highlight is a chain-driven boat ride that circulates around the lake that runs down the center.

The **Schloss** and its grounds are a must. If you have kids, then you have to take the small-scale train that takes you around the grounds in a surprisingly extensive run. Like the zoo boat ride, if you don't have kids, pretend you do and take it anyway. The Schloss now contains the **Badisches Landsmuseum.** It's no Louvre, but it does contain a broad range of interesting and old stuff to inform and amuse you when you're not drinking beer.

The **Museum Beim Markt** on the way from the market to the Schloss is worth the low admission price and hour or two it will take you. Changing exhibits on 20th century art and design have been impressive and there are good exhibits about the city as well.

Scams and alerts

The station area serves as a gathering point at night for a variety of people who definitely do not share Karlsruhe's peaceful mindset. It's edgy enough to have a fairly well-armed security squad clearly evident at night, which is why it's safe, but still not ruhe. Change your tram and move on.

Further information

We have read that **Brauhaus 2.0** is a new brewpub complex at Egon-Eiermann-Allee 8, in the same general area as König Bräu. König is emphatic on their website that you not confuse them.

If you're in Karlsruhe in late July, check the Web to time your visit to coincide with the **Mittelalterlich Fantasie Spectaculum** festival (www.spectaculum.de), which stretches over a good deal of the grounds behind the Schloss. Supposedly medieval, but rather like an American Renaissance festival, this is a traveling show that tours Germany over the summer. Enjoy good draft beer and genuinely excellent electrified "medieval" and Irish bands on three stages.

Day trip

Pforzheim

Pforzheim is an easy hop by train or tram; some #5 trams go there and there are plenty of trains from Karlsruhe Hauptbahnhof. The tram is a hoot—it rolls through Karlsruhe like a normal tram to the edge of town, then hops onto the main railway line, becomes a train, and races between a good many stops to Pforzheim at about 70 miles an hour. The town slopes down to several rivers and you can drink your way to the bottom.

The brewery outlet for **Brauhaus Pforzheim** (St.-Georgen-Steige 12) is down a few steps from the Marktplatz. It opens onto a square that commemorates the late February 1945 Allied air raid that destroyed Pforzheim's inner city and killed over 17,000 people just before the end of the war. Despite that unfortunate reminder, it's a lovely place that offers a half dozen well-made beers and very good food: some of the salads are unusually imaginative.

It won't take you long to taste the couple of beers at the **Hopfenschlingel Hausbraueri** (Weiherstrasse 13), an attractive "newpub" near Sedanplatz. Curvy bars and banquettes in a comfortable downstairs area and tables on the second floor overlooking the square offer a pleasant place to drink. It brews a very nice Pils and a sulfury Weizen.

The **Privatbrauerei Ketterer** outlet is close by (Jahnstrasse 10). It closes in the afternoon, so plan on doing it for lunch or dinner. Ketterer brews very nice beers, including a particularly good unfiltered Märzen. The dining room features German specialties, such as genuine fresh Black Forest trout, in a woody quasi-rustic theme with private corners and big gregarious circles. You can also drink Ketterer beers at the **Schlosskeller** across from the Hauptbahnhof (Bahnhofplatz 3) as you wait for your train back to Karlsruhe.

Other than brewing some good beer, Pforzheim has a reputation for producing high-quality watches and other jewelry. There's plenty to do in the afternoons while you wait for Ketterer to open. The **Schmuckmuseum** displays jewelry from around the world. Recreated jewelry workshops hum in the **Technical Museum,** and the **Bäuerliches Museum** features exhibits on peasant life.

Offerings at Brauhaus Pforzheim

Leipzig

Quick orientation

Leipzig's magnificent old Hauptbahnhof claims to be the world's largest in floor area. It boasts 24 platforms and a dizzying amount of modern shopping mall. At the northwest edge of the old town, you can get from there to pretty much anywhere you'd want to go in the city by tram, bus, or the spanking new underground S Bahn City Tunnel.

The shape of the town roughly resembles a not-quite-inflated beach ball. The station was built in 1915 by two railroad companies; each got its own identical entrance. Exit from either one, and the old town lies in front of you to the south across a large expanse of tram lines and an even larger park, Willy Brandt Platz. Cross the park and keep walking away from the station, and you're in the town center in less than 10 minutes. You can get to the spectacular Neues Rathaus on the other side of the old town in less than 20 minutes if you don't stop to drink.

Welcome to Brauerei an der Thomaskirche

Station breaks

The multi-leveled and very modern shopping area that fills the Hauptbahnhof will sell you almost anything—except an interesting beer. Unless we've missed a hidden gem, here are your limited options.

There's a small pils bar opposite Gleis 8 offering a light and dark Hasseröder from nearby Wernigerode and some international brands of draft, in a haze of cigarette smoke. To escape its smelly confines, cross Willy Brandt Platz in front of the station and head into the city center on Nikolaistrasse. On your left and down a set of stairs is the King's Head English Pub (Nikolaistr. 40), which has Newcastle and Guinness and a few others on tap. We found it dark and gloomy, but others might call it atmospheric. It opens at 6 PM most days. On our last trip it was "closed for remodeling." Goodness knows it could use it, but we've encountered too many "temporary" closures that never reopened to be confident about this place. For a more German experience, continue just past our three-block limit to the Gasthaus Alte Nikolaischule; see below.

We try to stay away from America when we're not in America, but if you're homesick, the Champions bar in the Marriott cooks up a good burger and you can wash it down with U.S.-style pitchers of Krostitzer Pils or Schwarz. For other options, walk past the Marriott headed into town, jink right on Brühl and then left onto Reichstrasse, and you'll find a series of bars, all modern and all pretty dull. If you have the time to walk a little farther, skip all of these and head for the Brauhaus at the Thomaskirche. Several trams will take you there easily and the S Bahn drops you at the market in less than five minutes.

History and culture

Leipzig is proud of much of its long past and is better than many cities about openly confronting the nastiness of the 20th century. Commerce and music have come to define the heart of the city. It was a major trading city of the Middle Ages and its stock exchange was one of the premier houses of Saxony. Leipzig retains its character as a commercial city, not only in its extensive (and expensive) shopping areas, but in the myriad trade shows and exhibitions that fill the winter months. Bach played the organ at the Thomaskirche and the street musicians in Leipzig are among the best in Europe.

The Nazi party had a harder time finding traction in Saxony than in some other parts of Germany, but the Third Reich exercised as much control over it as anywhere else. The U.S. Army's 69th Infantry Division occupied Leipzig before the division of Germany that put Saxony into the Soviet zone. In a reaction against the far right, some welcomed the formation of the Communist DDR—although by no means a majority.

Our friend Matthias at the Hopfenspeicher was born in 1958 and grew up in the DDR. He shared his thoughts about the era as we sipped Reudnitzer's excellent (and now, sadly, extinct) Naturtrüb Pilsner.

"I'm not a possession person. I never minded not having things. And we had fun. We could make jokes and enjoy ourselves. But travel—that was what I really wanted. I could go to Poland and Rumania (no one wanted to go there) and Budapest was a little bit like going to the West—they had signs on the stores and advertisements. We could drink beer in Prague—all of us went to U Fleků. But I saw Paris and America on the television and knew I could never go there. 18th of October 1989 was a day of great fortune. I was preparing to leave—I had a wife and a young daughter (she is 24 now) and I knew I would have to leave."

(Were you ever afraid of the secret police?) "Yes. Not all the time, but you always had to think about who you were talking to. I think this person is my friend, but could he be someone who might talk to the police? Still we joked and talked among ourselves."

(And businesses that made it through the DDR era in private hands?) "They were 'private' in name and some small businesses were left alone so the leaders could say anyone could do anything he wanted to in the Republic. But there were larger concerns who really made decisions. Businesses were left alone only when it helped the leaders' image."

Demonstrations in Leipzig in October 1989 were an important part of the peaceful revolution that ended Communist rule here. You can see films of them in the contemporary history museum, but no museum can convey the depth of the shift as well as a conversation with someone who lived through it.

Beer styles and drinking culture

The Gose style of beer originated in Goslar, but spread to Leipzig in the late 17th century and became closely identified with the city over time. We think the Leipziger claims that the style originated in the 14th century are pretty hard to prove.

The 20th century was tough on Leipzig breweries in all sorts of ways. Most stumbled through the Depression and the war, but many were nationalized, "rationalized," and closed during the "worker's paradise." In some ways it's been even worse for the independent brewers since unification. Western capital has poured into the former DDR and bought up and closed down breweries that had somehow maintained independence during the Communist period. Others haven't been able to meet the competition from the big breweries and have given up the ghost. In Leipzig, two major local brands that were easy to find when we started this book have disappeared.

Today most of the larger bars and Gasthäusen are affiliated with one of the big brewing chains. Ur-Krostitzer, a Radeberger brand, dominates the pub scene in the center city. It's local and it's not bad, but it's almost everywhere you turn.

But as in most of Germany, a vibrant brewpub movement enlivened the urban beer scene in the 1990s and 2000s. There's been little movement in more than a decade, but three breweries and a superb beer pub keep Leipzig clinging to our top 24 beer cities. After a significant hiatus, Gose made a phoenix-like rebirth and is now increasingly available even in the youth-oriented center city bars.

Gose brewers managed to get an exemption from the Rheinheitsgebot for this wheat-based beer flavored with coriander and salt. Gose is a genuinely distinctive beer for Germany. It can be almost as tart as Berliner Weisse, with a wheaty, lemony taste; the spices are integral but often subtle, though the salt is pretty evident. For some palates it may take a bit of getting used to, but its extremes don't reach the challenge of some Belgian gueuzes. Despite some flavor and linguistic similarities to gueuze, which have led some of the world's top beer experts to wonder about a connection, the term Gose seems simply to come from the city of Goslar where it originated.

Apart from Gose, you'll find a decent range of other beers, at least for Germany. You're deep in Schwarzbier territory here—the largest Schwarz brewery in the world, Kostritzer (not to be confused with the local Krostitzer), isn't far away, and most local breweries brew a Schwarz. There are pilsners and some of them are quite nice. Hefeweizens, both helles and dunkles, aren't hard to find, and there's even a good chance you might bump into a Berliner Weisse or Kölsch. Landbier is fuller bodied than most styles and can be quite nicely hoppy as well, but is usually only available in bottles at drinks markets. Small breweries and brewpubs usually offer only three beers, some fewer, but many of the larger and regional breweries brew at least four and sometimes seven or eight, though almost none of their restaurants carry more than a small fraction of their range.

The sixpack of drinking experiences

Gosenschenke Ohne Bedenken (Menckestrasse 5) is a reason in itself to come to Leipzig. The owners of the place were intimately connected with the revival and preservation of the Gose style of beer, and this is a great place to try one and sometimes more. "No Worries" serves a small but good range of other beers as well. The 500-seat beer garden can be a great place to eat good German food, but the restaurant inside is nice too, especially if the weather stinks. Service is friendly and unusually cheerful. The bar inside is fairly intimate and you may find yourself drawn into conversation even if you don't speak German. Leipzig's two Gose beers are usually on tap here side by side, Ohne Bedenken's own commissioned version and the one from Bayerischer Bahnhof, but what's interesting is to visit both locations in the same day. Jens the barkeep at Ohne Bendenken swears that every batch of the Bahnhof's Gose is different from the one before it, and if you try it at the brewery and again at Ohne Bedenken, it's hard to disagree.

Bayerischer Bahnhof (Bayerischer Platz 1) used to be one of the main train stations in the city. The façade of the station was restored after the war—it now stands as one of the city's most striking landmarks and one of the world's largest paperweights. The station site was retained as an S Bahn site and now, after several years of construction, trains whiz through the City Tunnel far below the gleaming white arch on the platz. An S Bahn from the Hauptbahnhof takes about five minutes and you can hop off at the market in the old town center in even less time if you wish. A variety of trams and buses will get you there more scenically if less quickly.

Gose options at Bayerischer Bahnhof

The Bayerischer Bahnhof brewery and restaurant is a bit touristy—there's a good chance there will be a tour group there when you are—but they make distinctive beer and they're among the few brewers in the world who depend on Gose sales for success. In addition to the Gose, offered with more syrups and concoctions than you could imagine, Bayerischer Bahnhof brews a chalky, thickly yeasty, almost white pilsner and a similarly unfiltered Schwarz. Despite its abundance the yeast is tasty, and a second half liter goes down easy.

Food is generally well prepared, but be prepared for cream and heavy gravies on dishes for which you do not expect cream and heavy gravies. Portions can be gigantic even for Germany. An English menu is available that does an unusually good job of conveying what you're going to eat.

Brauerei an der Thomaskirche (Thomaskirchhof 3) would be much like any other of hundreds of brewpubs if it were located where those other hundreds of brewpubs are located. But it's not. Directly on a small park overlooking Bach's home church, it's simply a great place to drink. If you sit at the bar, check out the growler filler on your left. They're not uncommon in the States now, but this one was here years earlier.

The beer varies from batch to batch, but at its best the unfiltered Pils can be exceptionally good. The Schwarz was even better on our last visit: nicely chocolaty, softly yeasty, and very, very smooth. Both were moreish. There's also a seasonal—always Hefeweizen in the summer. The restaurant is Italian; the menu is large and imaginative and the pizzas and pasta are pretty good for this part of the world. The barstaff is Italian and everyone speaks English. The service has been without exception welcoming and patient. You'll drink comfortably here.

Brauhaus Kaiser Napoleon (Prager Strasse 233) is fairly typical German modern brewpub, though the Napoleonic theme cutes it up a bit. The Napoleonic reference is to the Völkerschlachtdenkmal monument just down the road, which commemorates the Battle of the Nations (1813), one of the earliest of Napoleon's major defeats. Kaiser Napoleon brews a Helles and a Dunkel, both softly yeasty and pleasant but unremarkable. The Hefeweizen comes from Wickau. The restaurant attracts an upscale and graying crowd, but the advantage is that you can hear yourself think even if it's crowded, which it isn't very often. A good menu suggests they might care more about food than about beer, and an extensive cocktail selection highlighted by house-made schnapps makes you wonder why they bother with the brewery at all. But the brewery, we assume, is something of a draw and they need to provide a range of reasons for people to take the longish trip out from the city. It's easy enough, if not quick, to reach; take tram #2 or #15, get off at Prager/Russenstrasse, and you're virtually there.

Gasthaus Alte Nikolaischule (Nikolaikirchhof 2) isn't really a beer hall, but it's a good place to have a beer on a historic square. The building was a school until it outgrew the space in the late 19th century. Its students included Bach, Schiller, and a host of other names you'll remember from your European history course. The inside is dark and woody and the patio sports a fabulous view of the Nikolaikirche.

Gasthaus Alte Nikolaischule

Krostitzer Schwarz and Pils are on tap. The Krostitzer beers come from Bad Krostitz (*not* Kostritz), just a few kilometers outside of Leipzig, so at least you're drinking local.

Tram 4 reaches the Reudnitzer area a few stops outside the center city; get off at Riebeck/Oststrasse. The former Reudnitzer brewery, a typically beautiful 19th century structure, is on nearby Muehlstrasse, and its former tap is just around the corner at 38 Oststrasse. The **Brauereilokal Hopfenspeicher** was the brewery Gasthof until the Radeberger group shut down the last two local Reudnitzer products in 2012. Today it serves Ur-Krostitzer Pils, Schwarz, and Zwickel, though we hope you can get a bottle of the Sternburg beer that's now produced next door.

The Romanushof (see below) almost knocked this pub off the top six list, but while Hopfenspeicher isn't the beer mecca it was five years ago, we still like the place. It's a type of brewery-owned big pub you don't often find in big cities any more. Hopfenspeicher is typical in many ways, although the bowling alley upstairs gives it a certain distinction, and it keeps later hours than most other similar places. A modest entrance belies its size. Its very pleasant garden backs up to the brewery property, so you have the sense you really are drinking at the brewery if you forget what's being brewed over there. A covered lounge area of the garden is very inviting, with a giant round communal table. Inside, the décor is typical Gasthof with lots of wood and some copper, and some of the tables have their own metered taps. Good if a bit predictable German food is offered; the English menu is one of the few we've seen that is mostly accurate and clear. The Radeberger corporation owns the Hopfenspeicher, though the same family has managed it for over a decade. We hope the big guys leave the management alone—it's still a fine place to drink.

Other places to explore

If you have time before or after your required visit to Ohne Bedenken, a short walk can take you to **Gohliser Wirtschaft** at #20 on Gohliser Strasse. A few years ago, they featured several Gohliser beers from Hartsmannsdorf Brewery. We know it still pours the Gohliser Pils. It also serves Saxon style meals at a fair price. It's an unassuming bit of a pub, but we've always received a warm welcome there.

A few big brewers still compete for attention in Leipzig, and with some leg work you can sample a range of fairly well-known beers. If you're relatively new to Germany, you can find a variety of novel beers in the restaurants and bars in the passages off the market and around the Thomaskirche. The draft Früh Kölsch, for example, at **Johann S.,** almost opposite the church, is disappointing only if you've just come from Cologne.

If you ride the trams and keep an eye out, you'll also find a number of regional beers including Freiberger, Einseidler, and maybe still a few Bauer beers. The Bauer family brewed in Leipzig until 2009 and now contract-brew elsewhere, we think at Hartmannsdorf. The bar scene runs along Barfüsser Strasse, essentially an alley that leads off the market square. On a warm evening the street is crammed with café seating with hardly a spare chair, but there are indoor seats going begging in most of the bars. The young and affluent pack Spizz, but we like the other simpler places like **Bellini's** better. There's some choice of beers and even the Irish Pub serves the local Gose beers.

The area along Karl Liebknecht Strasse south of the center city is an alternative scene that draws crowds on weekends.

Where to eat

Auerbachs Keller (Grimmaische Strasse 2-4) is an atmospheric downstairs cavern and offers a huge menu at prices that make you think you're in Berlin. The **Mephisto Bar** is on the ground floor upstairs in the huge gallery and is a decent place to sip a very expected Krostitzer Pils, or three other usual suspects, on a rainy day. Downstairs looks quite old; the bar is 1920s railroad station décor.

Slightly less atmospheric but much more affordable is **Romanushof,** just down the street from the tourist office at 21-23 Katharinenstrasse. We think it's one of the best things to happen to Leipzig in a while. The Baroque building dates from the early 18th century and was a coffeehouse when Bach, Schiller, and Goethe lived in Leipzig. The Romanushof has the decency not to claim they actually all did indeed have coffee there, but we suppose they could have.

The current restaurant is only a few years old, though the stucco vaulted columns and ceilings give it a much older feel. The downstairs vault feels even older. While it's not a beer destination, it does give you the chance to taste Ur-Krostitzer and Radeberger pilsners side by side. Radeberger was one of the few quality products to come out of the DDR, but other breweries have caught up in quality. When it was time to reorder, we chose Krostitzer's fuller body and better balance.

Food items emphasize Saxon cooking; even the schnitzel featured a distinctive breading with a touch of paprika. Parts of pigs show up in all sorts of interesting ways and there are at least a couple of fish dishes as well. An amuse-bouche of a small pickled cheese salad (much better than it sounds) was an unexpected surprise in a restaurant in this price range. Specials are listed on a meter-tall chalkboard that is brought to your table for your order. Entrees run between 10 and 15 euros. The menu features a range of small dishes specifically designed to be consumed with beer, so you can be adventurously Saxon without risking a fortune.

Where to stay

The Hotel Astoria was once the pride of the downtown, but it's a shell now, so unless you want to get some help from the tourist office to get out of the downtown area, or fork out some serious money on the luxury hotels that remain, you're probably going to have to settle for a chain. The Best Western is across the street from the east end of the Bahnhof, but the rooms are among the smallest in Europe: trust us. Better to exit either of the main portals of the station and walk across the street. The hotels are clustered between there and the Nikolaikirche.

Novotel is on the corner of Strauss and Goethe, which is not as romantic an intersection as it sounds. On the back side of the Novotel is the cheaper but clean Ibis. Continue on Brühl and you'll see the Marriott and the four star Park. If you're there in the summer, even the upscale chains offer good prices. Try to get a rate with breakfast—many European buffet breakfasts will allow you to skip lunch altogether.

The Westin towers high above the city from its location west of the Bahnhof; you can find your way back from town just by looking up at the skyline. The rather charmingly decorated Mercure Art (careful, there's another Mercure far from here) is a long walk north from the Hauptbahnhof, but once you're there at Wilhelm Liebknecht Platz you're staying at an intersection of at least five tram lines.

What to see

Leipzig's center city is mostly traffic free and compact enough to walk easily. Most of it is restored or preserved pretty well. Much of the massive dig required for the City Tunnel (see Bayerischer Bahnhof above) has been covered over and the city is a good deal more walkable than it was a few years ago, though scars remain.

The tourist office has a nice brochure laying out a walking tour of the downtown area. If you find directions at the Bahnhof to the tourist office, ignore them. Walk straight out of the station and down Nikolaistrasse two blocks, turn right on Brühl, and walk past the gigantic eyesore shopping center to Katharinenstrasse. Turn left for a block to #8. You'll see the "i" sign on the left. It's open from 9:30 to 6 PM on weekdays, but closes earlier on weekends. In the winter, it shuts on weekends altogether. Curious.

Keep going on Katharinenstrasse and you'll end up in the old marketplace, where you'll find the old Rathaus and a slew of restaurants. See "Other" below. The Nikolaikirche and school are a few blocks off to the left of the Markt, and Thomaskirche, with its brewery, is straight ahead.

Johann Sebastian Bach was choir director at the Thomaskirche for over a quarter of a century. This gorgeous late-Gothic pile shows little of its over-500-year age, bright and cheery inside, with two magnificent organs. Choirs are allowed to buy "permission to sing" sacred music a capella in front of Bach's grave, so you might get a free mini-concert. Outside, in the church's shadow, is a favorite venue for local musicians (frequently excellent) to busk.

However, our "don't miss" choice for Leipzig, if you have any interest in recent history, is the Zeitgesichtliches Forum, or Contemporary History Museum (Grimmaische Strasse 6, near the Markt). Save at least an hour or two for it. Find it by looking for the statue of a striding man with the red boot of Communism and a fist in a Nazi salute. His outstretched foot is trying to move away from repression into a new and free future. Entry to the museum is free, but photography is forbidden and they clearly hope to help pay the bills by selling souvenir books showing what you couldn't take pictures of. Most of the exhibits are in German only, but you don't have to be a linguist to figure out what's going on. Exhibits range from the table used by the Communist Politburo leadership to a number of films and pictures showing the demonstrations that brought an end to the DDR. A small theater shows portions of anti-Nazi movies, produced by the Communists after the war, that strike at religion and the far right at the same time. Noir has rarely been noirer.

Scams and alerts

It's a city. An above-average number of street beggars inhabit the area across the street from the station, but we haven't seen them cause any particular trouble. Steer clear of the drunken groups at night there, but again we haven't seen anyone threatened.

Perhaps in a futile attempt to limit the drunken action, any shop that sells beer at the station closes early and it's very hard to find a downtown location of any sort that sells alcohol at night. Asian restaurants will sell you beer if you're not particular about the brand. Late night shops exist, but most are away from the downtown area. There is one almost opposite the Bayerischer Bahnhof that stays open until 10 or 10:30. The S Bahn probably gets you there faster than you can find beer near the Hauptbahnhof.

Further information

It's almost universal to greet people with "Hallo" and depart from them with "Tschuss!"

Day trip

Chemnitz

Frequent trains from the Leipzig Hauptbahnhof can take you to Chemnitz. Named Karl Marx Stadt during the DDR period, it's now a monument to capitalism. It thrived as a free Imperial City in the Middle Ages and developed into an industrial powerhouse in the 19th century. Its very success, however, made it a target of Allied bombing in World War II, and not much of the original city remains. After reunification in 1990, Western capital poured into redevelopment. Today Chemnitz has a bustling center, comfortable suburbs, and a respected technical university. And good beer.

If you want to take time away from drinking, the Saxon Museum of Technology offers impressive exhibits and the Villa Esche shows how the rich folks lived before Communism leveled things. A tourist office, which by now may have settled at Markt 1, by the town hall, can give you maps and brochures.

Chemnitz is a great town for a pub crawl because the beer scene ranges from established local-regional breweries to modern spiffy brewpubs to just plain funk. Most are in or near the city center, but we recommend one suburban jaunt before you begin your city crawl.

A tram and a bus will take you to Zwickauerstr. 478 and the **Brauerei Reichenbrand.** Reichenbrand is the sort of place we absolutely love. It's not fancy, the beers won't win a lot of international awards, and the menu is pretty ordinary Gasthaus fare, but it almost defines Gemütlichkeit. The place is clean and inviting, the beers are above average in an above-average country, and the young, friendly staff will make you feel like you've come home. It's the tap for a production brewery—you'll see the delivery trucks squeezing through the courtyard. Somehow the light wood snugs, plastic plants, and the big fake tree inside all work to create an atmosphere that makes us want to stay all day. Clean bathrooms show that someone cares. Smallish independent breweries are closing at a terrifying rate in Germany; we really hope Reichenbrand is here the next time we get to Chemnitz—it's well worth the effort to get there.

On your way back you'll have a chance to see the Braustolz brewery looming over the end of the tram line. We didn't find a tap near the brewery, but you shouldn't have trouble finding the beers in town. The brewery offers tours.

The easiest brewery to find is **Karls Brauhaus** (Brückenstrasse 17), named for the gigantic statue of Karl Marx that still stands across the street. If anyone remembers the DDR days with fondness, we haven't met him, but plenty of Germans feel that it wasn't Marx's fault. Certainly the German Communist reality was a far cry from the workers' paradise Marx envisioned. Free market Karl hasn't fared as well as hoped, either, in this newpub—perhaps the beers we had were rushed to meet the summer demand. The atmosphere was more like a slightly grubby English pub than a German Gasthaus: a bit funky with some battered furniture. The style seemed more out of intention than neglect or insolvency, though, and the bathrooms were fine. The menu was pretty standard German beer-bar fare; you could do worse.

By far the spiffiest brewery in town is **Turm-Brauhaus** (Neumarkt 2), opposite the gorgeous old Rathaus and modern Kaufhof department store. A big wooden staircase leads to an upper level that gives a bird's eye view of the brew house. A wide range of breweriana complements the shining copper to make the inside a somewhat more attractive place to drink than the outside so-typical square with the looming Kaufhof. The beer selection is tiny—a Helles or a copper—but the beers are good: chalky, a bit fizzy, but professionally crafted. We save this for last on a crawl not because it provides a spectacular end of the day, but because it's nearly completely unchallenging—perfect for sitting back and just drinking in beer and atmosphere at the end of a long day.

Finally, if you'd like to fill a suitcase with local and regional beers you haven't tried, the Getränkemarkt in the Ermafa Shopping Mall (Reichstrasse 58) has a great selection, most of them at or near a euro each.

Day trip alert

We were told by a good source that a day trip to the brewery in Rechenberg-Bienemuehle was one of the top brewery-hunting experiences in the area. Rechenberg is a cute, very small town in a nature park with a small local brewery. There's a biker's hotel where you can stay for 8 euros (not a typo).

When Rechenberg modernized its plant, they kept the old one as a museum. It's open only for guided tours. The brewery would make a fine half-hour tour. We found the 2-hour tour numbingly boring, though if a 20-minute lecture—in German—on different spigot sizes is your cup of tea, the multi-train trek could be well worth the time. The Germans on the tour seemed to enjoy it; there were plenty of jokes—in German. If you don't speak German you won't understand any of them. If you speak just enough German, you'll understand most of the jokes are about you.

London

Quick orientation

London is beyond huge it's what New York would love to be if it weren't hemmed in by water. It's what Paris thinks it is. The quick point is that you should look for good pubs relatively near where you're staying, or endure some drink-time-consuming Tube rides.

The city is composed of dozens of postcode districts, each numbered by centrality and compass point, and all addresses include the postcode. W1 is the area near and west of the center. E17 is a long way out to the northeast. All well and good, but while E4 borders E17 it is even further out, so don't make assumptions without actually looking at a map.

If you're there for more than two days, forget the hotel map and buy a copy of *London A to Z*. It also pays to get a bus map from a Tube station; buses are slow

Tower Bridge. No, not Lake Havasu

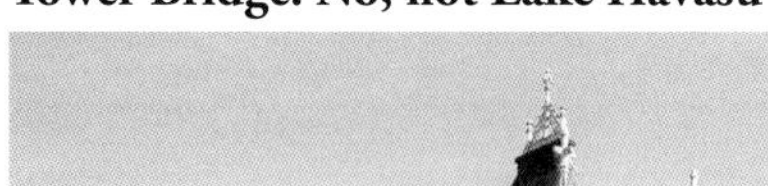

during the day, but they're a good choice if you're going to have to change Tube lines more than once, and at night they move along pretty well. London rivals Paris for the longest distances in allegedly "connecting" subway stations, often involving multiple staircases as well.

We could send you all over town to find great pubs and wonderful beer adventures. But if you're in London long enough to visit more than our dozen picks, get a more detailed guide than ours to assist you. CAMRA publishes several. We've focused our "sixpack" of drinking places on the center area because we think you're most likely to be there and because you can put together a good crawl that will involve more drinking and less Tubing.

Station breaks

London has so many train stations that the Thomas Cook European rail guide, which usually gives a 2-inch-square map to show connections between stations of a city, includes a full-page map of the entire London Underground instead. But a rail center of gravity runs from Euston to Kings Cross and the Eurostar "Chunnel" terminal at St. Pancras. If you're linking London with any of the other cities in this guide, you'll use a rail station in this area.

The neighborhoods south of Euston Road contain a number of typical and comfortable pubs. If you can stand a bit of a crowd, however, right in the forecourt of Euston Station is the Euston Tap, which is not only one of the best train station bars you're going to find, it's one of London's best beer bars. The cider tap directly opposite is sometimes quieter and does feature a few beers.

Good, or at least passable, pubs are steps away from the other rail stations, if not in the station itself. You won't have any trouble finding a decent pint.

History and culture

The history of London is in part the history of England. We assume most readers of this book will know that history better than that of any other of our chosen cities. But in case you missed it, here's the short version.

The Euston Tap

People lived here a long time ago. The Romans came, got sick of the place, and left. Vikings marauded before a particularly persistent Viking descendant, William, sailed over from France in 1066, picked up his "Conqueror" moniker, and moved in for good. Thirty years later, England began the first of eight "crusades" to try to conquer the Mideast. In the midst of them, the 1215 Magna Carta limited the king's power, at least for a while. Following the nasty War of the Roses, which at least gave Pennsylvania two good city names, Tudors ruled long enough to merit a BBC/PBS series. Henry VIII broke with the Catholic Church; his daughter Elizabeth ruled as an absolutist but made Parliament *think* it was important, so after she died they eventually *did* become important. Her successors, the Stuarts, had to take an extended sabbatical in France when Puritans under Oliver Cromwell took power, but returned just in time to rule during 1665 and 1666 when England went to war against the Dutch, the Plague struck with a vengeance, and 373 acres of the city burned to the ground. Londoners naturally blamed the fire on the French.

The Stuarts, however, began in earnest to establish an empire on which the sun did not set. A puny part of that Empire shook free in 1776, but much of it remained in British clutches until the middle of the 20th century. Empire building is a poor way to make friends, and the English found themselves at war with the French for about 500 years until they finally stuck Napoleon on a rock in the middle of the Atlantic Ocean where someone could poison him. After that the British fought the Germans and shivered at the Russians, as issues of empire helped cause the First World War, which led to the Second World War, which set up the Cold War. In the Cold War context, Great Britain decided to stop fighting the rest of Western Europe and join them instead and became part of the Common Market in 1972. It still didn't like the "Frogs" well enough to share a currency with them, though, so you'll still be getting money by the pound in Britain.

The Empire was expensive for the country but profitable for the industrial upper class. The English invented factories, then scooped up minerals from the colonies and sold finished products back to them. This made the air filthy and factory owners filthy rich. While some trading patterns still benefit British business, the factories that cranked out wealth in the colonial days are demolished, vacant, or in "adaptive reuse."

Some of these events had a lasting impact on beer and brewing. The Magna Carta set standard measures for ale, and government regulation of pub hours began not long after. Henry II imposed the first tax on beer to help fund his Crusade; rates rose in almost every war after that. James I's absolute rule included the first laws outlawing drunkenness, and ale houses were burdened with dozens of new regulations that even covered signage. Cromwell's efforts to "purify" London were short lived, hurting the theaters more than the pubs; his moratorium on new licenses only lasted two years. In the early years of industrialization, a campaign against gin drinking benefited the brewing industry; the cost of opening a pub dropped to two guineas. As industry mushroomed, huge London breweries grew to slake the thirst of factory workers. At the start of the 19th century almost half of the beer in England was homemade; less than a hundred years later, virtually all beer was commercially brewed.

Without the Empire, of course, we wouldn't have IPAs or the "Imperial" tag to indicate "strong enough to make you silly." It's taken time for Great Britain's integration into the European Union to have a deep impact on brewing, but it's happening quickly now—brewers now reflect global influences as the styles of beers in London multiply.

Beer styles and drinking culture

A word about British drinking culture is necessary to put London into context. More than anywhere else in the world, the local drinking establishment serves a social purpose well beyond supplying food and booze. The public houses, "pubs," are where people meet to exchange news, solidify old friendships, and make new ones. They're much like the watering holes of the Serengeti except strangers are rarely eaten by lions.

In most cases, you'll order at the bar. If it's crowded there's rarely a line, per se, so try to make eye contact with the bartender, and be patient (and say *please*). It's astounding how often a good bartender can remember who came to the bar when. And how often courtesy crops up: you hear "He was here first" far more often than "I was..." You also usually order your food at the bar. Tipping on food is in a state of flux; no one tipped anyone 30 years ago, but it's changing. You can usually tip about 2/3 of what you tip in the U.S. to get the same kind of smile. Tipping on drinks is still rare, but if you get talking with the barkeep and he (or she) is helpful and things have gone well, it's fine to offer him a drink. He'll thank you graciously, say he'll have it later, and add the price to the round you're buying. It will usually be the cheapest drink that you've ordered and possibly less.

For the better part of a millennium, alehouses have been an important part of London's culture. Beer was one of the reasons the Romans left—they hated the stuff—but the Normans obviously didn't mind. By the early 1300s London had 1,330 "brewshops" selling beer to a population of less than 40,000.

British brewing has mirrored the changes in industry and economy for centuries. Bass claims to have the oldest registered trade mark in the world, and the mark lives on even though Bass, as a brewery, does not. Brewers found huge international markets even before the 19th century. Kent County, south of London, produced—and still produces—some of the best hops in the world, and English beers throughout the country became known as "bitter" because of their ample use.

In the 19th century, water made a huge difference in the taste of the beer. Pale ales thrived on Burton's mineral-rich water, but in London the softer water (and, some wags have maintained, the sewagey Thames) lent itself to dark sweet brown ales. The porter style evolved in the early 18th century to counter the increasing popularity of lighter and cleaner pale ales. It soon was London's favorite style and remained so into the 20th century. The Horse Shoe brewery was the scene of one of the most dramatic events in brewing history. On October 17, 1814, a 22-foot-high vat used for aging porter burst, damaging a second vat as well. Over 600 tons of liquid erupted in a 15-foot-high wall of beer that wrecked the neighborhood and killed eight people. Stories that some of the casualties drowned while trying to dive *into* the flow are apparently apocryphal; reports of the stench days later are not.

The flood didn't even slow the growth of big porter breweries, and a host of other huge producers such as Watneys, Truman, and Courage joined them in the 19th century. Just under the radar, significant regional breweries such as Young's and Fullers managed to make a profit at a more modest size. Scientific advances in water modification meant that London, or virtually any other city in the world, could make any sort of beer, and if you had the patience to look for them, the varieties available were staggering.

The 20th century, however, was tough on larger breweries in most European cities. Traffic, both road and rail, made both receiving materials and exporting beer expensive and slow. Big brewers closed their London locations and shifted production closer to ports or highways. In just a couple of decades, London went from being one of the great beer producers of the world to an output akin to that of Pottsville, Pa. Trumans, the last of the big independent London breweries, closed in 1989, Guinness shifted all production to Ireland in 2005, and InBev shut down the former Watney's plant a few years later.

Until the 1990s, Young's still delivered beer to nearby pubs in horse-drawn wagons, and their mascot ram which roamed the spacious brewery grounds was, like English kings, named and numbered. The land, however, became so valuable that the company at last sold it for redevelopment in 2006. Young's merged with Bedford's Charles Wells, then left brewing altogether. The Young's brands continue, but we don't think their character is what it once was. A project to continue production in a new brewpub at the site of Young's historic Ram Brewery seems endangered after the Chinese (Greenland Group) takeover of redevelopment in 2014. Of the large-scale London breweries, only Fullers remains.

In their glory years, the big guys not only brewed the only beers you could get your hands on, they usually controlled the "local" in which you drank. Brewery policies "tied" publicans—even those who owned their own pub—to beers of a single brand. The "tied estates" of pubs became more important to the financial success of the big brewers than the beer they were making to serve in them. But in 1989, new statutory regulations made it difficult for a brewery to own more than 2,000 pubs. Since then, five of the "big six" British brewers have left the brewing industry, their brands and breweries closed or sold to bigger international companies.

The big brewers could make decent traditional cask beer, but cask was a poor match for pubs appealing to mass market drinkers. A wave of easy-to-maintain lagers—some from the continent and many brewed by the big boys in England—and kegged, pasteurized, dumbed-down ales nearly pushed traditional hand-pulled beer off the market. Quietly at first, signs of a consumer revolt began to appear. In 1971, four Brits on holiday started the "Campaign for Real Ale" to promote cask ale in pubs. Soon several hundred people had joined them, and today CAMRA boasts nearly 170,000 members. The last several years have seen a tidal wave of micros, craft, nanos, and unclassifiable mini-breweries rushing to take up the slack left by the big brewers' retreat.

Today CAMRA finds itself in a tough position as it remains more focused on how the beer is served than how it's brewed, while "craft keg" breweries grab an increasing share of the beer world's attention. Nevertheless, it's impossible to overestimate CAMRA's contributions to the global revolution in good beer.

We know of no other city in the world whose beer scene is changing as fast as London's. More than 50 London breweries are less than six years old, and other casks and crafts pour in from surrounding areas. It's a bit like California in the 1990s: wonderfully innovative creations sit next to taps of genuine misfortune. Part of the joy in this resurgence is a celebration of London's brewing past with some modern improvements. We doubt Truman's in its glory days ever produced a beer as magnificent as its present Eyrie Gold Ale, and the chocolaty goodness of a London Porter from Herefordshire's Red Squirrel Brewery is a sight cleaner and easier to drink than a similar beer would have been a century ago.

The sixpack of London crawls

A "top six" pubs in London is an impossible task; we offer six short crawls here instead that still only scratch the surface. If you have time for only six pubs, do the first two crawls, or choose our top pub (starred) from each crawl.

Our London picks, more than any other city in this book, reflect personal choice—we make no claim that they are "the" best in London. However, most are acclaimed by other writers, they're all reasonably central, and they include historic pubs as well as more modern multi-taps. If you start early and drink late you might be able to do all six mini-crawls in two days. But you won't do anything else. The bars with the best range of beers generally feature a mix of craft keg and cask beer. Many of the historic pubs have been slow to jump on the keg wagon.

The Covent Garden Crawl

These pubs are an easy walk from the theaters of the West End—in the case of Craft, across the street from one. They're near Covent Garden, the historic central market that is now a tourist mecca of shops and street performers. On this ambitious crawl, the distance is very manageable, but you'll need remarkable willpower to move on from one pub to another. Be sure to save time for the Harp, one of London's absolute best.

The Craft Beer Company has several locations in London. We've had wonderful experiences at the Clerkenwell location, but it's a bit out of the way. In July 2014 a new venue on the edge of Covent Garden, a short walk from the Holborn Whippet, brought an even larger selection to an even smaller space. If you're looking to spend a night trying beers, you could just come here. A narrow small pub, it's a wonder they find space for their 45 taps of craft keg and cask beers. After work, crowds jam the roped-off standing area on the sidewalk outside and pack even more densely into the long, cramped bar area. Somehow, service is quick. A downstairs "lounge" was rattling empty when we were last there, but be warned—we visited when the pub was less than a month old. By the time you read this, the lounge may well have been discovered… and filled up.

You'll find some of the expected beers as well as some rarities from local and British breweries, along with some brews you don't expect to see on draft in London. Foreigners range from the Swedish Dugges (see Goteborg chapter) to the adventurous Spanish brewer Naparbier. Be aware a foreign half pint can set you back ten bucks.

This is a company that cares about beer. CAMRA doesn't love them—they serve more craft draft than cask—but there are few places in the UK where you can get a broader view of "what's brewing."

The easiest way to find it is to locate the Shaftesbury Theater on, well, Shaftesbury, and look across to the leisure center across the street. Cowering in the corner is Craft.

To reach **The Harp*** (47 Chandos Place), walk west away from the Covent Garden market buildings. When you hit Bedford, walk downhill and turn right on Chandos; it's down a bit on the right. The Harp can't be beat for a combination of beer selection and history. It dates from 1751 and shows it. The ten cask beers from near and far are served in flawless condition—it was selected CAMRA's national pub of the year in 2011.

The Harp's proximity to the West End and Covent Garden would guarantee a full house for a pub several times its size, but we've somehow managed to find a seat more often than not, sometimes in the somewhat less frantic upstairs area. The downstairs room is long and narrow, and the drinkers spill out into the alley in back. A few mirrors edge their way onto wall space that's mostly lined with portrait after portrait of people mostly obscure to Americans. A good bar game here with friends is for everyone to pick a picture and invent a story to go with the person. The area over the bar is crammed with over 100 square meters of overlapping pump clips that make us dream of buying a flat across the street. The smallish lounge above is plainer, with some soft furniture and low tables and a view of the street. The steep steps that lead to it keep a good many drinkers downstairs, though sooner or later they have to climb most of those stairs to get to the WC.

Retrace your steps and walk back to Bedford. The **Marquis** on the corner might make it into this guide in another city. Read the story on their walls of the local executions. A few casks and a few more crafts offer good choice, and it usually has much more breathing room than the Harp.

Walk back up Bedford past King. The Round House Pub on the left is easy to spot. Rose Street, almost directly across the way, is not as evident. Neither is it much of a street, but more an alley of sorts leading to the **Lamb and Flag.** A Fullers house with several guest casks, the Lamb and Flag is a fine old historical pub that fills with a mix of regulars along with the tourists. The alley in front supposedly featured bare-knuckle fighting, and this is one of several pubs that claim Dickens as a regular. Apparently the author drank more than Washington slept. If we've ever seen a darker interior we don't remember it; even on a sunny day, it's a murky wooden cave of a place. The dining room upstairs is sunnier but much less romantic. Mirrors and prints line the walls. The bar looks like it once sported snob shields, but all are welcome today. We had conversations with four different people before we could even take a seat. Beers are in fine condition.

Euston to British Museum Crawl

A cousin of the York Tap and Sheffield Tap, the **Euston Tap*** features an eclectic assortment of cask and draft. It's a remarkable location—inside one of the gatehouses at the entrance to the Euston railway station. We walked past it several times before we realized it was a pub. Downstairs is a single small, absolutely packed room. Up a terrifying spiral staircase (one hand for yourself, one for your pint) is a lounge with tables and sofas. If you get there near opening, there might be a seat. In good weather they open a small garden next to the park that fronts the station, and fence off a chunk of sidewalk for standees. Businessmen and radicals share the space amicably. The quest for the limited WCs can be challenging—go before you go. If you're into cider, the opposite gatehouse is a second pub serving ciders, perries, and a few good beers.

The Lamb (94 Lambs Conduit Street) is a very personal choice for us, though it does show up on some local press's "top lists." A Grade II listed Victorian showpiece pub, we first encountered it when we knew some of the people at Young's, and we still love it. The Young's beers, while diminished, are still quite respectable, and we love the not-ancient-but-old atmosphere in the Lamb. It's one of the few pubs in London that still have snob shields—engraved glass panels that protected the upper classes from having to watch hoi polloi guzzle ale. From Euston Station, cross Euston Road and jog left to find Upper Woburn Place. Follow that away from Euston a few blocks to the middle of Russell Square and turn left on Guilford Street. Lambs Conduit Street is a few blocks on the right.

Snob shields at The Lamb

Perseverance is a short walk past the Lamb, on the corner of Lambs Conduit and Great Ormond Street. The beer selection is modest but there are good beers, and as we went to press they were establishing themselves as the Bloomsburg Brewing Company with the brewery in the basement. It's been less crowded than many other pubs on our last two visits, and the menu is ambitious and interesting. If you're in London for a while, check early to see if there are any special events; the equivalent of American "tap takeovers" occur from time to time, featuring local breweries.

Holborn and Fleet Crawl

The **Holborn Whippet,** somewhat to our surprise, is headed into its third year. A fantastic location is part of the reason: on the Bloomsbury end of Sicilian Avenue, a tiny pedestrian shopping area. It's pretty easy to spot if you're coming from the Lamb or the Euston Tap. Past Russell Square, Woburn Place becomes Southampton Row. Just past Lloyds Bank on the right, cross Vernon Place, turn right, then look left quick for Sicilian Avenue; the Whippet's on the corner.

The bar is backed by a distinctive square tower of cask and keg dispense systems. Bands of chalkboard above the taps give brief tasting notes as well as the usual required ABV and style information. White walls set off the copper and dark woods of the tap and the bar.

The Whippet is best enjoyed with friends; it's an after-work gathering hole and neither the youthful clientele nor the bar staff are particularly interested in becoming your new best friend. In our visits, the bar staff has been serviceable, pleasant, and sometimes well informed.

The beer selection is generally good: mostly British brewers such as Bristol, Mallinsons, and Dark Star, though a few commercial German lagers are available for the uncritical. The new craft drafts have been well chosen and in fine condition. Our cask samplings, however, while too few to pass definitive judgment, have been inconsistent. Our bartender had no problem serving us a half pint of mud until Bob showed it to a local about to order the same thing. It was quickly replaced with a different—though still buttery and diacetyl-laden—bitter; eh, maybe it was supposed to be like that.

It's a good pub, but move on—there are "can't miss" pubs in the linked Covent Garden crawl, and some fine old places not far in the other direction. Before you head east, a slight detour will take you to the **White Hart,** just south of High Holborn at 191 Drury Lane. Licensed in 1216—the beer selection isn't much of a draw, but the service is very friendly and there's something to be said for having a fresh beer in a place that's been there for 800 years.

Go east to 22 High Holborn. The **Cittie of York** features atmosphere rather than a dazzling selection of beer; it's a stunningly beautiful old pub. More impressive than intimate overall, it nevertheless sports an amazing array of nooks and crannies where you can feel romantically alone. A pub on this spot dates from 1430, though it's not hard to see that this iteration dates from the 1920s. Don't stop in the first hall; of the three main rooms, the farthest back is the most interesting.

Ye Olde Mitre* (on Ely Court in Hatton Garden) would be a tourist trap if it weren't run by a genuine beer enthusiast and curmudgeon who genuinely likes people. Hidden in the core of a giant office block, it's really old, really atmospheric, and really closed except on weekdays. The original 16th century version is gone—you have to settle for the 1772 modern update. Creaky beams and wood benches make you expect to see Ebenezer Scrooge nipping in for a half pint on the way home. Supposedly, Elizabeth I danced around a cherry tree here—ask them the story.

You're just south of the Clerkenwell area if you want to keep drinking. See "Other" below.

Crawling around the Thames

Seven Stars (53-54 Cary Street), one of the few buildings that made it through the Great Fire of 1667, is genuinely charming. Three drinking areas—it would be an exaggeration to call them rooms—cluster around a narrow bar. Near the courts and the London School of Economics, it's jammed except in the middle of weekday afternoons when it's only crowded.

The Cheshire Cheese

If you've come from the Seven Stars, **Ye Olde Cheshire Cheese*** is the new kid on the block—it was rebuilt after the Great Fire. A narrow passageway leading in at 145 Fleet Street takes you to the entry. It's a warren of a pub with numerous small rooms and corridors. The downstairs reflects its monastic origins: down a level, a room has low beamed wood for a ceiling; take a few steps farther to pass a pair of tiny rooms vaulted in white brick, then go still another level down to a larger room that has the feel of a small German beer keller. Supposedly monks brewed on the site before it was a pub; the lower rooms were indeed the beer cellars, and some still are, though off limits to you. Samuel Johnson and Charles Dickens really did drink here. The brews are all from Samuel Smith, but you're not here for the beer. Happily the prices for those beers are exceptionally reasonable for London—a pint will leave you change from £3.

The Viaduct Tavern (126 Newgate) sports beer cellars that once held minor criminals in the Gildspur Prison (Newgate was near, but not near enough). Get there by walking down the Holborn Viaduct, the first raised highway of its kind. The Tavern was an original part of the development of this raised thoroughfare. If you go off-peak when it's not packed, they'll take you down to see the tiny cells. A hole in the cell's ceiling was a lifeline for the incarcerated: the private jail provided no food, so if you wanted to eat, you had to have friends drop provisions down the hole from outside.

In the pub itself, check out the busts of the "hanging judges" from the Old Bailey at the top of the columns. The huge portraits on the wall represent Agriculture, Banking, and the Arts. For some reason a WWI vet had it in for the Arts and attacked it: you have to look carefully but the damage remains. The taps sport a fairly standard range of Fullers beers, but it's still an adventure.

Borough Market area

The iconic **Rake*** (14a Winchester Walk, Borough Market) tops many lists of London's best craft beer venues for good reason. While we've never found it quite as welcoming as Craft Beer, or the range as new to us as that of the Euston Tap, it doesn't miss either by much. Tiny by London standards, it expands onto a partially covered outdoor drinking area in order to handle the mobs that descend south of Tower Bridge after work.

The George Inn (75-77 Borough High Street), the last galleried coaching inn in London, is owned by the National Trust. An easy walk from Borough Market and the Rake, it's a big, rambling bar that makes good use of a couple of stories and a good deal of courtyard. The range of beers is narrow, but Greene King seems to taste better

Pull up your curricle at The George

when you sit at an outside table staring at the centuries-old balconies. Its 300 years don't quite match the Seven Stars or Cheshire Cheese, but if you just want to drink in another century for a while, this is our top pick in London.

The Market Porter (9 Stoney Street) is one of your few chances in London to have a beer at 6 AM. Grandfathered into a license that allows it to serve the market workers (porters) at the end of their night shift, it opens from 6 to 8:30 AM, then reopens at 11 AM. Not the range of the Rake, but some distinctive casks are in excellent condition.

Tower Bridge area

Dean Swift* (10 Gainsford St., Butler's Wharf) is a one-room modern corner pub. An upstairs dining room provides additional space but you can find a table inside downstairs if it's not raining. Dark wood floors contrast nicely with white walls and ceilings. The décor includes a few posters and a couple of fancy chandeliers. A small bar dispenses about ten kegs and four casks, including a house pilsner brewed by London's Portobello Brewery. A bottle collection expands the range considerably. Food runs to burgers, a chorizo Scotch egg, sausages, fish and chips, and a couple of vegetarian dishes, all at London prices. We wouldn't cross the river for this alone, but linked with the Draft House and a brief stop at the Anchor, it's a welcoming and pleasant place to drink. The men's room is, um, intimate, though somewhat redeemed by the really cool faucets.

Draft House (206-208 Tower Bridge Road) is just south of Tower Bridge on the corner of Queen Elizabeth Street. We've had mixed experiences here. It features a good range of cask ales and a wider range of bottles, many of them local. If it's quiet and you get the right bartender you can have a great experience. We think our waitperson was ignorant rather than duplicitous, but on our last visit we were not served the beers we'd ordered, and ultimately no one was quite sure exactly *what* we were drinking. Sit at the bar and watch what's being poured and you'll have a good time. You can get decent burgers with a good smoked cheddar, and there are a variety of sausages, but few other choices. The loos were...well, go before you go.

This area is in the shadow of Courage's now closed Anchor Brewery, the source of some of the best years of Courage Russian Imperial Stout. Offices and apartments occupy the still-recognizable brew house, and you can have a beer in the **Anchor Tap** at 20A Horselydown Lane. Beers aren't special, but you're drinking in a special bit of history here.

Other places to explore

Craft Beer's Clerkenwell location remains our favorite of this small chain of pubs. This aptly named bar has a wide range of cask and draft beers. It's long and crowded; you can find a seat if you're patient or, if the weather is good, join the throngs outside who use the vacated market stalls as makeshift street bars. A knowledgeable staff seems to find a way to make time for you even at the peak of happy hour. Bar snacks are above average; the Scotch egg is a great way to slow the impact of the several pints you're likely to want to sample. Other fine pubs in the neighborhood include the **Crown Tavern** at 43 Clerkenwell Green, where you can share a pint with Lenin's ghost. He drank there when it was the Crown and Anchor; whoever you're drinking next to will be happy to show you where.

Where to stay

In four decades of London visits, our hotel stays have migrated from one section of the city to another, always reveling for a day or two in the unexpected benefits before discovering the inevitable costs. We've gravitated to the Euston area lately—hotel rates are a bit lower than prime, transportation (rail, bus, and Tube) is as good as it gets, and some really nice neighborhood pubs give respite when the superb Euston

Tap is just too crowded. It's also a short stroll to the British Museum, and even the West End is walkable if you're energetic and the weather is good.

Some upscale small hotels and B&Bs congregate around Russell Square (though some in that area are not upscale at all). A tolerable walk from Euston, quite close to the Lamb, and a bottle cap's throw to the back door of the British Museum, they're not cheap, but you can get a level of personal service that even the concierge at a Hilton is not likely to give you.

Budget accommodations, at least by London's price scale, abound in the rows of B&Bs that have taken over the lovely old, middle-class, cheek-by-jowl townhouses near Baker Street and Paddington Station and elsewhere in the city. It's been a few years since we've stayed in the mews and gardens near Paddington—but if you book there, note the name and address of your hotel very carefully. It's usually not on your key, and when you return at night *they all look the same*. You can figure out the story behind this suggestion without need for us to embarrass ourselves further here.

Read a good hotel guidebook if you're going to stay for any length of time. The best of the B&Bs are charming, friendly, and relatively affordable and give you a truly British experience. Conversely, chains offer some confidence that you won't want to move elsewhere on day 2. But a caveat—chains aren't always what they appear to be. Even the big boys like Hilton buy and remodel hotels that probably wouldn't make their grade in other cities (they're fine, but cramped and a bit creaky). Best Western seems to operate simply as a booking service; don't take things like air conditioning and elevators for granted.

What to see

If you're in London for more than a couple of days, invest in a pocket guide that will describe the attractions. Our suggestions are for those on a very tight schedule and include the sights which, if you don't see them, people back home will look at you funny.

❖ **The Tower of London.** Imposing during the day and stunning at night if you see it from Tower Bridge; the tour inside is one of the can't-miss sights. The Crown Jewels have been stolen in hundreds of movies, yet they're still here and offer a bit of an insight into how much wealth flowed into England when the sun never set on its Empire. And, speaking of Tower Bridge—it's not London Bridge. The real London Bridge was sold to a developer and moved brick by brick to Lake Havasu City, Arizona; it now spans the mighty (man-made) Havasu River. The British claim that the developer, Robert McCulloch, thought he was buying the iconic and much larger Tower Bridge; McCulloch reportedly responded that he *meant* to get the little one.

❖ **A play.** Any play, really; there is very little bad theater in London. If you must see a hit, book early online. Otherwise, get to the half-price ticket booth in Leicester Square when it opens (check the tourist guide magazines such as *Time Out* for plot summaries; the ticket booth won't tell you much). Be sure to go to the booth that is in the square itself. The way from the Leicester Square Tube station to the booth is lined with "half-price" ticket shops that aren't always what they appear to be.

❖ **Madame Toussaud's Wax Museum.** There are now so many of these worldwide that the novelty isn't what it used to be, but this is the original and probably the best. Our favorite sections include the French Revolution: Louis XVI and Marie Antoinette were gracious enough to stay very, very quiet for their casting.

❖ **The palaces:**

- The top of most lists is Buckingham Palace, which offers a range of tours with a range of prices. Fifty bucks gets you the grand tour—queens aren't cheap to maintain. Figure on a couple of hours at the very least. If you have 14 friends, the group tickets are much cheaper.
- Our favorite palace is Henry VIII's Hampton Court. It's cheaper than Buckingham and you can get a variety of tours, some with costumed guides. They also offer ghost tours, which are your best chance of actually seeing British royalty.
- Kensington Palace. In one of history's great home remodeling projects, Sir Christopher Wren changed a house into a palace truly fit for a king. A £12 million refurbishment accompanying London's 2012 Olympic extravaganza turned it into a "palace for everyone." You can decide if it includes you.

❖ **The British Museum.** Lord Elgin was only the most notable of the sticky-fingered Imperial antiquarians. To its credit, the museum is doing a lot of fascinating work with the history and display of their thousands of treasures, and you can actually learn stuff.

❖ **The British Library** stands between Euston and Kings Cross/St. Pancras and every year has a different and fascinating summer exhibit, such as original manuscripts of Great Works from Austen to Rowling.

Scams and alerts

This is the city of Oliver Twist and Sherlock Holmes; if there weren't crimes in London, literature would be much poorer. The average Brit is as honest as anyone in the world, but professional thieves are many and skilled. You won't be shot, and probably not hit on the head, but your pocket is going to get picked if you let it.

The British, on the whole, have done better with issues of race and ethnicity than Americans, but tensions sometimes flare, and there are parts of London in which you won't travel comfortably no matter who you are. We visited a brewpub in Brixton several years ago and really didn't notice how out of place we were until we left the pub after dark. A few weeks later, we saw televised accounts of the area burning in riots. But there's a lesson here—we did walk to a bus stop safely. Were we lucky? Maybe, but your physical safety is usually more assured in tough areas of European cities than it is in tough areas of American cities. One reason is that London is probably the most photographed city in the world—and not just by tourists. Published estimates of a half million CCTV cameras seem to be an exaggeration, but there are indeed tens of thousands of them; remember someone is watching you while you're here. That said, use your head and see our comments in the introductory chapter about traveling safely.

Further information

The CAMRA website is a fount of information for cask ale in Britain as well as for any sponsored beer festival in or near the capital, but it's mum about any of the new craft kegs. Fancyapint.com is a good source for other news.

Day trips and excursions

More than any other city in this guide, it can make sense to stay put in London. The world of British beer has come here; you don't have to go looking for it. But if you have cabin fever or want to go hunting on a smaller scale, you can't do better than hopping on a train and heading to one of the other beer cities in this guide. If you're staying in the Kings Cross area, you can do something of a day trip. Birmingham is less than an hour and a half away. Pick your train carefully and Manchester is just over 2 hours away. If you have a full rail pass, leave London at 8:30 in the morning and you'll be in time for lunch at one of our recommended pubs in Glasgow. Trains run as frequently as every 20 minutes, but do your homework: fares vary widely, and routes aren't always direct. You can wind up on a circumnavigation that will flip your 2-hour day trip into an 11-hour excursion. Too, the trains can be excruciatingly expensive if you don't have a rail pass, though you can find some good "cheap returns" online.

Greenwich

If you want to get just outside the city, however, a trip to Greenwich is a fine excursion for sights and for beer. There are some wonderful riverside pubs in London itself, but they can be jammed. In our experiences even the most popular of Greenwich's watering holes—even with views—had plenty of room for us. Greenwich is best known as the location of the Royal Observatory and the Prime Meridian that essentially anchors the world's time zones. There's more to see, however, than a man-made line.

The *Cutty Sark* was built as a tea clipper, able to sail from the Orient with a half ton of priceless tea in only a few months. For years she competed successfully with more capacious steamboats, but in her declining days, she hauled coal under a different name. In the 1920s a retired seaman recognized the once-magnificent sailing ship as she limped into an English port and bought her on the spot. (He had married wisely and well.) In the decades since, *Cutty Sark* served as a training vessel and finally wound up in permanent dry dock on the Thames in Greenwich. An extensive 2012 restoration opened new parts to view; you can roam the four decks on a self-guided tour and see the whole hull from the cafeteria below. Posters, videos, activities, and costumed guides provide a thorough history of the ship and the tea trade of the 18th and 19th century.

Nearby, the National Maritime Museum is a sea-lover's fantasy. Be careful of the people at the Royal Observatory who offer to take your picture for you as you bestride the Prime Meridian—they charge for the "favor."

If you live on the East Coast of the U.S. you may have already encountered the **Meantime** beers that are brewed in Greenwich. Tours of the main brewery are expensive and infrequent except on Saturday, when they're only expensive. Meantime, however, has built a pilot brewery in the "Old Brewery" located within the grounds of the University of Greenwich, and the attached bar serves a range of at least eight of their beers, including some brewed on premise that you can't find anywhere else. A bottle fridge at the end of the bar gives you more options if you need them, and a couple of handpulls dispense guest casks. Beers are in pristine shape, unsurprisingly. Be sure you pass by the "café" to find the bar and restaurant beyond. A very pleasant and good-sized garden adjoins the University grounds; carry your beer out and wait for the food you've ordered at the bar to be delivered to your table. The food ranges far beyond an impressive fish and chips; a whole dressed crab is hard to find this far south. You pay for the quality.

Several other pubs are within walking distance. If you want more Meantime, the **Union** in town serves the full range plus 150 bottles. We prefer a better view. Almost

A welcome sight for a sailor, from aboard the *Cutty Sark*

in the shadow of the *Cutty Sark* is the **Gipsy Moth** gastropub. It's not a beer destination, but it offers several cask and craft draft beers and a magnificent view of the ship through lounge windows or from the small garden. An exquisitely balanced Eyrie, a gold ale from Truman's, ensured a pleasant afternoon. Truman's revival is a heartening story; it's the rough equivalent of a craft brewer reestablishing pre-prohibition Schlitz beers in Milwaukee.

Walk along the Thames downstream from the *Cutty Sark*. On the edge of the large green, the **Trafalgar** offers spectacular views of the Thames and a good range of beers. The **Yacht** next door is a Taylor-Walker house with predictable food, but similarly wonderful views. Go for another several hundred yards, however, for our favorite riverside pub in the area, the **Cutty Sark.** A good range of Young's-Wells beers with an occasional guest seem to taste best in the Crows Nest room with its tiny window two floors up. Inside, you can drink in an atmosphere that exudes nautical and "old." On a good day, drinkers at both the Cutty Sark and the Trafalgar spill out onto the river walk.

Several boat services get you to Greenwich. City Cruises offers an informative narrative; if you're lucky enough to get a live "captain," it's theater in itself. The last boat back is at 5:30, however, and you may well find it hard to leave the gem of a pub you've settled in. A river taxi service runs later. If you get stranded, you can catch the Docklands Light Railway back to the city, or hop a bus that crosses the river to the nearest underground station. Ask at the pub and they'll point you in the right direction.

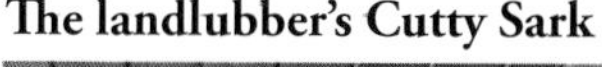

The landlubber's Cutty Sark

Manchester

Quick orientation

The three Manchester railroad stations form a triangle that roughly defines the downtown area. Trains from Piccadilly run to the south and to the airport. Victoria Station serves the north and west. Deansgate is mostly a suburban station. Most of the best beer bars are within walking range of each other if you're energetic, but a free bus shuttle that runs until 7 PM will save drinking time. Frequent trams run between the stations and out to some of the suburbs as well.

Station breaks

You'll probably arrive at Piccadilly Station. If you're changing trains you have lots of options to grab a beer while you're waiting. If you have a half hour or less, the Mayfield Bar upstairs will pour you a cold pint of John Smith's at a fair price—or get you a bottle of Goose Island IPA (see why breweries sell out to AB-InBev?). The décor is modern airport with a few flatscreens and, happily, a TV monitor of departing trains.

If you have any longer, exit, turn right down the station access road to Piccadilly Street, and walk the two blocks to The B Lounge. It's pubbier than it sounds. Modern and comfortable, it sports three handpulls, serves food to 7 PM, and sometimes has live music after that. A block further is the Piccadilly with up to five cask ales in a big rambling setting. Food until 9.

A third option is The Waldorf, a pub that is so much less pretentious than its name. Turn left just past the Malmaison Hotel and it's on your right—you can see it from Piccadilly. The Waldorf is a cozy one-room pub with lots of wood, a coal fire, a few handpulls, and Frank Sinatra on the speakers. Young tattoos and 40-somethings mingle easily. The beer is in good condition. These three pubs are all pleasant places to drink; our edge goes to The Waldorf.

Finally, keep going just past the Piccadilly, cross Newton, and the local Wetherspoon branch is on your right. It can sport up to ten casks, but it's cavernous and we prefer the intimacy of most of the other stops on our list.

Some or all of these pubs can also serve as a way to start the North Quarter Pub Crawl (#6 below).

If you arrive at Victoria, both the Marble Arch and the Angel are within walking distance, but outside our usual 10 minute station break limit. Our bartender at the

Angel assured us that he could get to Victoria in five minutes, but we wouldn't want to race him. In the unlikely event a train drops you at Deansgate, the Knott is under the tracks and Cask is well within range.

History and culture

Like most European cities of any size, Manchester can trace its roots to pre-Roman times. Its modest elevation is well short of a Grand Teton appearance, but was sufficient for the Romans to give it the name of Mamuciam, or "breast-shaped hill." It took centuries for the name to evolve into modern Manchester.

The population grew slowly through medieval and early modern times and was still only a few thousand when the plague of 1603 killed off a quarter of them. Just as the town started to recover, the English Civil War in 1640 and a return of the plague in 1645 knocked it down again. Though small, Manchester developed something of a reputation for its silk and wool weaving businesses, which formed a foundation for the huge growth to come. Until about 1750, cloth production was a cottage industry, with workers laboring in their own homes. That pattern changed dramatically in the last half of the 18th century, and Manchester played a key role in the Industrial Revolution.

Richard Arkwright's water frame mass-produced yarn that was not only stronger, but much cheaper, creating a vastly increased demand for cloth. Just as importantly, Arkwright also developed the concept of building structures designed to hold machinery and attracting workers to something very similar to the company towns of the 19th and 20th centuries. In 1780 he moved to Manchester and established the first true large-scale factory, employing 600 workers in one place.

The early mills were water powered, but when James Watt improved the steam engine, industry no longer had to locate on waterways. Huge factories drew workers in from the countryside, and swelling populations attracted more capital for investment. By 1825 there were over 100 mills spewing cotton; a single factory employing 750 workers could produce as much cotton as 200,000 cottage workers had done a century earlier. Manchester became known as "Cottonopolis" and its population exploded, increasing more than eightfold in 70 years.

Manchester also became an early center of modern capitalism. Up to 11,000 members of its Cotton Exchange met every Tuesday to barter and sell the goods streaming from the factories. The capitalists thrived; workers were not so lucky. While factory profits grew, so did the length of the work day, often exceeding 12 hours in the hot summer months when both daylight and demand for cotton reached their peaks. Frederich Engels's observations of working conditions featured prominently in his *Conditions of the Working Class in England.* His collaboration with Karl Marx in writing the *Communist Manifesto* followed not long after.

Workers became increasingly active, stoning a train carrying the Duke of Wellington because of his opposition to lower-class suffrage. Class tensions reached a climax in 1819 when 60,000 men, women, and children gathered peacefully in St. Peter's Fields in Manchester in support of democratic reforms. Mounted troops charged the crowd, killing several and injuring 600 more. The press dubbed it "Peterloo," a sarcastic reference to the Battle of Waterloo, a decidedly more heroic effort only four years earlier. The result of the deaths of the protesters, ironically, was to set off a conservative demand to reestablish law and order that delayed any chance of reform actually happening. Movements can be delayed but not prevented, however, and some reforms were in place by the end of the 1840s. Still, working conditions remained grim and the working class did not receive the vote until 1888. As in Birmingham and Sheffield, huge working class populations created a demand for cheap mass-produced beer. The 20th century saw Manchester emerge as a major producer of kegged, ordinary bitters.

Manchester's economy continued to rest on its textile production until well into the 1900s, though it never fully recovered from the Depression of the 1930s. By the mid-20th century, however, both population and production had dropped sharply and the city's prospects seemed dim. But a remarkable recovery has reinvigorated the city, and it is again one of England's leaders in technology and finance. Paralleling the upscaling of Manchester's industries, its brewing scene is growing increasingly sophisticated and very much a part of the global craft beer revolution.

Beer styles and drinking culture

Manchester was once home to major regional breweries that dominated the drinking landscape. The decision of these companies to close operations here, along with the breakup of the tied estates (brewery-owned pubs), left a void that dozens of small breweries have begun to fill. Boddington's sales have fallen dramatically since AB-InBev took it over. Holts survives, but it isn't big enough to dominate this good-sized city. Hydes, in nearby Salford, is also a relatively small operation producing cask ales mostly for its own tied houses. As in Sheffield and Birmingham, specialty beer bars have provided a secure outlet for even the smallest breweries. The lack of a dominant brewery or traditional local style means you'll find an amazing range.

While some of the Mancunian craft brewers have jumped on the American hop wagon, more of the local beers are soft-spoken, easy-drinking pleasures. Creamy and milky notes stem from naturally occurring diacetyl and seem to be a bit more evident here than in some other regions. If you can't find a fine under-4% session beer to quaff in Imperial pints, you're not trying.

You can try all you like, by the way, without breaking either your budget or your liver. Almost all of the bars we list will happily offer you a small sample before you buy. But note: if you sample some beers, you have to decide on one and buy it. We generally only take them up on the offer if we know we're going to buy a whole pint.

The sixpack of drinking experiences

You can find good beer in almost any part of Manchester. Our six include selections that are a short walk from three rail stations. The first two are quite near Victoria, the next two close to Deansgate, and the last two are walkable, if you're in good shape, from Piccadilly.

The Marble Arch Pub (73 Rochdale Road) is a fantastical gem with a beautifully kept Victorian décor and a unique, sloping mosaic floor that just naturally guides you down to the bar. The bar staff is exceptionally knowledgeable and eager to help you explore their extensive range of house-brewed and guest beers. The brewery is no longer on premise, but the beers are still plentiful. The Marble Brewery has been a training ground for many of the head brewers in the area and had a sense of adventure long before adventurous beers were common. In truth, the most unusual of their offerings are sometimes easier to find in the States, but you won't be bored while you're here. Besides, we've often found the best of Marble's work to be their simplest brews. Our favorite was the Marble Pint, a 3.9% ordinary bitter that had a remarkable depth from earthy and leafy hops. They're not afraid to bring in beauties from other breweries, either. A Simcoe masterpiece from Hopcraft Brewery in Wales featured in our last visit: wonderfully unbalanced, it was like chewing from a foil pack of pellet hops. A couple other beers were disappointing, but the Marble Arch is such a great place to drink that we'd probably go there if they only served lager.

The extensive menu here is among the best you'll find in a UK brewpub. Gastropub food combined with down-to-earth drinking is a rare treasure. Pan-fried red mullet and hay-roasted lamb featured on our last visit. We'd come back just for the cheese: you can build your own cheese board from 14 artisanal British cheeses and a half a dozen from France and Germany's Allgäu.

The Marble Arch

Marble Arch is about a 10 minute walk from Victoria. To find it, exit the station and walk away from the Manchester Arena on Miller Street. Turn left on Rochdale Road opposite the Crown Plaza. Only a few blocks down Rochdale takes you to to the Marble Arch at #73. It's a longer but manageable walk from Piccadilly: we've done it in a bit less than 20 minutes to get to a train. Exit the station and turn right on Piccadilly (the Big Wheel in the distance), turn right on Newton, and stay left when Port Street bears right. Hang a left at the big, virtually unmarked road (it's Great Ancoats, but you'll have to walk a ways before anyone lets you know; it then becomes Swan Street) and walk until you hit Rochdale. Cross the street, go right, and walk up Rochdale to the Angel and the Marble Arch. You can actually see the Angel and Marble Arch from each other if you know what you're looking for.

As you're walking to Marble Arch on Rochdale, look left at Angel Street; the **Angel** is on the corner. The Angel has been a favorite of ours for years. We were surprised that one of the pub rating websites we've learned to trust over the years rated this solid pub as low as it did, so we returned recently to see if our memories had inflated. We readily understood why not every reviewer falls in love with the place. The tables are sticky and they wobble, the bathrooms could be museum pieces from 19th century Fredonia, the "garden" is a bare plot on a main road with ratty lawn furniture, a good deal of the ceiling paint looks like it might end up in your beer, and most of the accents are the kind that the BBC parodies on their sitcoms. In short, some people coming into this pub would call it a dive.

But the staff works hard to make it clean enough, the furniture doesn't actually collapse, the bathrooms work, sort of, and the paint has stayed put when we've been there. The clientele ranges in ages from children who can hardly walk to pensioners who can hardly walk—and everyone is welcome. A piano welcomes pub-goers to give it a go. The bar staff smiles easily and serves eagerly, and everyone talks to everyone in a British "Cheers" sort of way. Granted they won't know your name, but there's a fair chance they will before you leave.

And it gets better. The kitchen can truly cook and shows careful and skillful preparation of dishes that rarely show on the menus of ordinary pubs. Grilled salmon, baked cod, and a basket of fried whitefish featured along with the required fish and chips on our last visit. A ten pound steak (no, it's the British currency, silly) and a wild boar burger kept carnivores happy, and a vegetarian lasagna and salads added breadth.

Oh, and the beer. There's always an adventure or two to be had. Twelve rotating hand pulls feature some local brews, a few standouts such as Arran, and a couple of ciders. The required bank of drafts is less adventurous, but the casks make your time here worthwhile.

The Deansgate area is a trendy nightclubbing and restaurant area, but it's also home to two fine beer bars. **The Knott** (374 Deansgate) fills one of the arches of the rail line above and is directly across the street from the Deansgate station. Knott's range of beers has gone from good to excellent in recent years and it's now a destination for

Mancunians looking for a fun place to drink very good beers. A wide range of local and regional beers include both drafts and casks, and the staff is friendly and well informed. If you can, try to visit for a meal as well as a beer; they have one of the best kitchens of any pub in the city.

Cask Bar (29 Liverpool Road) is a short walk from Knott: head uphill and turn left on Liverpool opposite the Hilton. Curiously named, the bar has far more draft lines than cask ales, but the four handpulls feature interesting beers that you're not likely to encounter elsewhere. Among the drafts is unfiltered "Yeast Budweiser" from Budweis. The two decent-sized rooms and modest garden in the back can get crowded, but you'll get a truly warm welcome from a staff that cares about good beer. The pub is so well respected that Marble Brewing has done a series of collaborations with it.

The North Quarter pub crawl

The North Quarter is the "hip" area of Manchester and its pubs provide a lovely evening of crawling. They're all within a 10 to 15 minute walk from Piccadilly Station and most are just a minute or two from each other. Only a few have as extensive a range as our other choices, but there are several fun places to drink.

You can start the crawl with our station breaks. The B Lounge and Piccadilly are on your right as you walk along Piccadilly, and The Waldorf is just to your left.

The **Port Street Beer House** (39-41 Port Street) is a relative newcomer to the Manchester beer scene, but tops the list of destinations for many of the city's beer geeks. From Piccadilly, go to Newton Street and turn right. When it splits, follow the right fork along Port Street. The Crown and Anchor is easy to spot on the left, and just past it is the Port Street Beer House. The Crown and Anchor has the feel of a traditional pub and while its range of cask ale is narrow, it serves food, which you'll need before settling in at Port Street.

We've rarely encountered a more beer-focused crowd than at Port Street. It seemed as if most of the conversation was about beer, and the thoroughly knowledgeable bar staff is willing and able to play professor. As with many good beer pubs, they're happy to pour a small sample before you buy, and it's not a bad idea to take advantage of the offer, since if you try all the nearly two dozen casks and drafts you won't be going any farther. It's probably the best place in the city to explore the local beers, including one-offs that don't show up anywhere else.

If you're still standing when you leave Port Street, head back to Hilton Street and follow it to Stevenson Square. Diagonally across on Spear Street (number 31-33) is a relatively unknown gem of the quarter—the **Soup Kitchen** (which apparently it never was), a relatively recent addition to the bustling pub scene. A couple of nicely tended cask ales join a small but lovingly chosen selection of local and unusual bottled beers. It's absolutely jammed on weekends, when the downstairs turns into a popular entertainment mecca. The staff does the best it can to keep up with demand from "the tiniest behind-bar area in the city."

Don't be in a hurry to leave the area. By the time you read this there will almost certainly be another jewel in the North Quarter's crown, even if coffee houses seem to be outpacing beer outlets in the area.

City center crawl to BrewDog

We include BrewDog here because you should visit one somewhere. They are increasingly ubiquitous in England and Scotland and all share the same envelope-pushing oddness. We like the one in Glasgow best, but if you've been to any of them, you don't have to go out of your way to find another.

Despite how it looks on a map, walking to the city center from the Northern Quarter isn't bad. If you mosey down Mosley, you'll pass **The Bank,** a Nicholson pub with five or so casks and an interior that looks more like an actual bank than many of the other bank conversions we've seen. The Bank is known for keeping its beers in exceptionally good condition.

As you reach Princess Street, detour a block or so to the right to find the **Ape and Apple,** a Holt's house. Good Holt's on cask and a warm staff make it a pleasant stop before tracking down the BrewDog. Free comedy features here on Wednesday evenings at 20:30.

To find BrewDog, retrace your steps to Albert Square, go through the square past the buses, and wend your way to Peter Street; look up and aim towards the Radisson. When you reach Peter Street, turn right before you cross, and BrewDog, at number 35, is a few doors down.

As you approach BrewDog, you are standing almost at the spot of the infamous Peterloo Massacre (see "History"). Note the red plaque on the building across the street.

The Manchester **BrewDog** is less of a music venue than the Glasgow outlet, and they don't get all the beers that feature up north, but it still has a funky feel and a range of beers that are so not typical of Scotland or England. It has a roomy industrial interior, six BrewDog taps, and several rotating guest beers, all in keg form. The 25-ml mini-shot of Tactical Nuclear Penguin (32% ABV) will cost you £6—a 20% hike over the Glasgow price. "We had to conform to London prices," they told us. Indeed, we're pretty sure this BrewDog is in a much higher rent district than Glasgow's West End.

To get back to Piccadilly, return to the Town Hall bus area where you can catch the #3 free shuttle route—as long as you do it before 7 PM. The brisk 15 minute walk back to the station takes you through the vibrant Chinatown area around Nicholas and Portland.

Other places to explore

Our friend James at BrewDog recommends a couple of good beer bars that have emerged in recent years. To reach the **The Font** (7-9 New Wakefield Street), turn back along Peter Street—it's about a 10 to 15 minute walk. It used to be a not-so-classy cocktail bar, but the current manager is a big fan of good beer, and as long as

Heineken is always available, the ownership lets him provide it. It's more relaxed and less noisy when the students aren't in town. **The Salisbury,** not far away, is in a similar process of upscaling and may be worth a look.

Where to stay

Hotels abound near Piccadilly Station. Exit right, walk down the service road, and turn right just as you reach Piccadilly to find The Place, a warehouse turned into a four star hotel a decade ago. Spiffiest brick you're likely to find anywhere, at £100 to £200 a night. Premier, Abode, and, across the street, Malmaison are other choices as you walk down Piccadilly.

For bargain alternatives, see the Crown and Anchor above, or check out the more upscale Mitre Hotel (mitrehotel.co.uk). Rooms are en suite and the location is more central; you can still get good beer in the bar or, if you wish, to take to your room.

If you have the cash to spare, the skyscraping Hilton is in the party-hearty Deansgate area and provides spectacular views along with Hilton quality at less-than-London prices. The Radisson is in the central city area and is so close to the BrewDog bar that you can literally crawl back to your room after loading up on the 42% Sink the Bismarck!.

What to see

The Museum of Science and Industry is a must. Five themed buildings include the oldest commercial railroad station in the world. The complex is a celebration of England's Industrial Revolution as well as a local scientific community that included Dalton, Rutherford, and Joule. It's hard to imagine how displays of pumps and pistons could be so interesting, but they are. The guided tour of their full assembly line of operating textile equipment shows more clearly than any textbook can how hard and dangerous life was for factory workers. The museum also contains a water frame from 1775, the machine that really started the Industrial Revolution. A replica steam locomotive runs on Sundays.

Scams and alerts

In our experience, it's a safe and comfortable city. Ask your desk clerk if you intend to go outside well-traveled areas at night.

Day trips

Stockport

You can easily spend a full day at Stockport, only 8 minutes by train from Manchester's Piccadilly Station and not a great deal longer by the bus that claims 18 departures per hour. With half a dozen breweries of its own, it could lay claim to the right to be one of our 24, but neither food nor accommodations are at the level of our other cities. It's quite easy to visit, even on repeated days from Manchester.

Stockport is home to the sizeable **Robinson Brewery,** whose products find their way to good beer shelves in the eastern U.S. A self-proclaimed craft brewery producing 120-barrel batches, it's something of a tweener—too big to be very flexible, but too small to match the big guys' economies of scale.

Robinson recently opened a new visitors' center and gives £9 tours—reserve in advance, for they often fill up. The tour is worth the money, giving you an exceptionally detailed top-to-bottom look at the brewing process (be sure you can manage the 54 steps that start the visit). In 2010, the brewery hired the German Steinecker company to build an entirely new brewhouse that would give them big savings on labor and energy. When they built it, they kept most of the old brewery intact, and on each floor you can see the old copper and new stainless vessels side by side. We've never seen anything quite like it. A few samples are included at the end of the tour; you can buy more beer and quite well-prepared food in the small pub-like tasting room.

In addition to its own vibrant brewing scene, Stockport is something of a magnet for other local breweries, and our recommended pubs come close to matching the best in Manchester, but with the added attraction of a small-town welcome. On our visits, Stockport has been the Lake Wobegon of sixpacking: all the beers are above average.

You can get around in the free (though not as frequent as they claim) shuttle bus, or you can walk to all of the pubs we mention if you're energetic. To save valuable drinking time, however, we usually take a very affordable cab to The Railway and walk back from there. On your way back, don't jaywalk; we want you to be able to read our next chapter.

If you follow our cabsteps, be sure you're taken to **The Railway** on Avenue Street, a tiny alley off Great Portwood Street; there's a similarly named pub with a small selection well out of town. The Railway approaches 20 taps, many of them rotating, featuring a solid mix of local cask ales. A large rectangular horseshoe bar fills the center of the room and hosts remarkably friendly regulars who enjoy swapping beer stories. It's impossible not to get drawn into the conversation by the time you've made your way through your first pint. The "working class" language helps explain why pubs ban children, but it's all good natured. The walls are full of local breweriana and photos, and the wooden floors and traditional furnishings provide an atmosphere that the pubco fakes can only envy.

You could stay all day at The Railway, except you'd miss more of our favorite pubs in the Midlands. A short walk away, the **Arden Arms** (23 Millgate) may be the best place to sample Robinson beers short of the brewery itself. A multi-room maze includes a fine garden with a "Wendy house" (small glassed-in area), a formalish dining area, and a fine compact pub. If you're there for Sunday lunch, the roast lamb and Yorkshire pudding are slowly and beautifully cooked. If the British had Thanksgiving, this would be its meal. But don't dawdle; it sells out early in the afternoon. The pub drips with atmosphere, fortunately only figuratively. It was once used as a morgue for the bodies emerging from the hospital that operated just up the hill. The staff firmly denies rumors of hauntings.

Along the way back toward the station, you'll pass Winters Wine Bar on Little Underbank, down 52 steps from the market. This current Holt pub occupies the former premises of a watchmaker's shop. You can dodge in for a drink if you wish, but in any event take a detour to the second floor to see the inner workings of the performing clock that graces the outside of the building. At the quarter hour, and more extensively on the hour, bells chime outside in a mini-Glockenspiel display. Also on Little Underbank are two or three fish and chips shops, which are increasingly rare. Try them for lunch; the whole area gets pretty quiet late.

Head back toward the rail line, go downhill across the river on Wellington, then left on Heaton Lane to pass under Arch 16 of the railway viaduct, one of England's most magnificent vaulted bridges, to reach **The Crown.** The Crown used to be a Boddington house and the sign is a preserved landmark that misleads Boddington fans into the place on a regular basis. Instead of the bland Boddingtons, the Crown is now an absolutely marvelous free house. A small bar and three or four tiny, squeaky-floored rooms provide enough space to work your way through the more than a dozen distinctive craft ales. If you're there on a Sunday evening, recovering from the Arden Arms's roast Sunday lunch, you'll be treated to some exceptionally good "session" music, and a folk club plays on Tuesday nights. The Crown now serves as a tap for the

Stockport: The Crown and the viaduct

Stockport Brewery, a tiny and brand-new establishment more or less across the street under Arch 14. The brewery is open on weekends for tastings.

If you return to the station by walking uphill on the side of the viaduct away from the city, you'll be rewarded by a few other good, if fairly standard pubs. The loop around that side of the station, however, is farther than it looks. We'd recommend you spend the extra time at the Crown.

Ask directions, get lost, ask directions again, and you can find the **Air Raid Museum,** a distinctive look at the British reaction to German raids of the Second World War. Check online for opening times, but beware: they close earlier than their online information indicates. We recommend getting there well before 4 PM. For a few pounds, an informative audio tour walks you through a part of the massive tunnels that held over 4,000 shelter occupants in the early years of the war. Low on amenities, but big on security, the shelter attracted hordes of people who rode packed trains from Manchester and surrounding areas to wait out the night in safety. A guided tour on the first Wednesday of the month takes you to unlit parts of the tunnels that are otherwise closed.

The other major sight in the city is the **Hat Museum,** whose towering brick smokestack dominates your first view of Stockport from the train. Downstairs, a tour takes you past some original manufacturing machinery that a guide runs for you to see. An impressive hat collection includes a hat form created for Queen Elizabeth and chapeaux belonging to Kylie Minogue and other British notables. Temporary exhibits sometimes highlight new designers. Anyone can try on a myriad of hats; the family section includes lots of costumes for the kids and other interactive exhibits.

Bury

Bury is an easy rail hop and one of several good beer towns in the Greater Manchester area. The real rail adventure, however, begins after you arrive there. A tolerable walk from the main station takes you to the East Lancaster Railway and a steam excursion to Rawtenstall via Ramsbottom. Steam excursion trains aren't hard to find in England, and increasingly both pubs and rail lines are discovering that people who like old trains also like cask ales. We found Leydon Brewery beers at the Railway (2 Bridge Street) in Ramsbottom; a web search on "East Lancs Rail Ale Trail" will take you to descriptions of several other pubs at each of the East Lancs stops. Several of these pubs are attractive, but the star is the starting and ending point—the Trackside Pub.

The Trackside Pub sports a half a dozen tables and a…trackside location on Platform 2. A range of ten cask ales, many of them local, make it a destination in itself. The pub features Lancastrian specialties and seasonal dishes and tries to source locally. The kitchen is open for breakfast and lunch Wednesday through Sunday, but the bar is open late all week. The small space can get packed, especially on folk nights, but we've never had a problem finding a seat during the day when the steam trains are running.

On the way back to the modern station in Bury you'll pass through "The Wylde," the original medieval center of town and the location of several pubs. It apparently got its name from the "wild Irish" who used live in the area. The Two Tubs Inn dates from 1696. The Wyldes Pub serves a good range of the Holt beers from Manchester and will feed you if you get there before the kitchen closes at 6 PM.

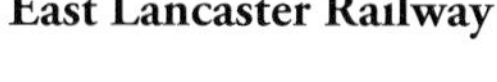

East Lancaster Railway

Milan

Quick orientation

Milan is Italy's New York. Not its capital, but its financial, fashion, and theatrical center and self-appointed Truly Important City. But even as Italy's second largest city, Milan is a fraction of the size of the Big Apple, vastly friendlier, and an easier place to find good beers to drink. It's also an underrated tourist city—the crowds head farther south. Even at some of the good beer bars, the Milanese are rarely swamped by tourists and aren't always used to them; you'll get a particularly warm greeting for a big city.

The Duomo, Milan

Arrive at Milano Centrale. It's nearing the end of construction that has seemed to take longer than that of the cathedral. It's "central" in that it's more or less equidistant from anything you'll want to see, do, or drink, but none of that is very close. The Piazza del Duomo is really the center of town—it's four quick stops on the M3 Yellow Metro line, direction San Donato.

If you're here just for the day, as we were in the 1980s—you need professional help. Find a hotel and settle in for some very fine beer drinking and some magnificent sights as well.

Time matters in Milan. Almost everything closes between 2 PM and 6 PM; often the gap is wider, but it varies widely from bar to bar and store to store. The sights remain open, so midafternoon is a good time to see what you want to see. You won't be able to drink what you want to drink during that time anyway.

Station breaks

We try to pick a station break that will give you good beer, not just beer, but here you'll have to settle for clear and cold beer, somewhat "better 'n Bud," in a nice setting. Not only are the best beer bars scattered in other parts of the city, most of them don't open until 6, 7, or even 8 PM.

So you might just as well stay and drink in the station. Le Goloserie, opposite track 9 in the main hall, will sell you bottles to go if you need them, and there are bars at each end of station at track level, including one inside the Burger King. But look up to see the best places. At the east end of the station is the Sky Bar, overlooking tracks 18-20. It will sell you some food and relatively pricey bottles of predictable imports. Overlooking tracks 6-10, Mokà serves beer on draft. If you want to look at something other than railroad tracks, the Lanzera 2010 Café down at street level has some outdoor tables that overlook the busy square.

History and culture

We learn early in school about ancient Italian history, but modern Italy is a relatively new country—much newer than the United States. In the Middle Ages and well into the Renaissance, the Italian peninsula was home to dozens of usually warring principalities and kingdoms, not to mention the odd Papal state (that is a political, not a religious statement). Giuseppe Mazzini created the "Young Italy" movement in the mid-1800s, hoping to create a nationalist feeling that would unite the country. In the short run, Italy remained divided and its parts continued to be toys for bigger European players, but the stage had been set.

Just about the time of the U.S. Civil War, Giuseppe Garibaldi returned from helping Uruguay become modern Uruguay to lead a band of soldiers up from the south in an attempt to unify the country. At the same time, Count Camilo Benso di Cavour, the Prime Minister of Sardinia-Piedmont, took his army south to try to achieve the same goal. The two forces could have launched a full scale U.S.-style civil war, but Garibaldi yielded, thus getting his face on a U.S. postage stamp a century later.

Finally, Italy was mostly united, though French troops protected the Papal states' independence. In 1870 Otto von Bismarck tricked the French into a very unfortunate war, and the barely decade-old Italy scooped up the Papal lands as well.

Cavour had been the power behind the throne of Sardinia-Piedmont and played a similar role in the Kingdom of Italy. He brought Italy into the modern industrial world, recognizing, for example, that heath care is a right and not a privilege and that people who want to work but can't find work should be helped. Other countries, with less noble leaders, have taken a great deal longer to figure that out.

The First World War hit Italy hard, though the country eventually changed sides enough to come out a winner. But the war's aftermath, combined with a depression that hit a decade before most of the rest of Europe and the U.S., brought Mussolini to power. The word is that he made the trains run on time, a miracle you could only appreciate by traveling by rail in the early 1920s… or mid-1980s. The EU has accomplished Mussolini's miracle *without* having to reduce opposition by force-feeding castor oil to political rivals. Never one to pass up a cheap and easy political trick, Mussolini granted the Vatican City essential independence in the Lateran Treaty of 1929, so if you visit Rome, your "Vatican" experience owes a bit to the mass politics of the north.

Since unification, the north and south of Italy have lived more or less amicably. Tensions remain between the industrial/financial north and the agrarian south in roughly the same way they have lasted in Germany and the U.S. In each of these countries, the northerners are more receptive to other cultures, while people in the south tend to be easier-going and more wedded to tradition. Milan might have a northern tilt, but once you make any effort at all to show you're not an ordinary "take a picture of the Duomo" American tourist, people there will take very good care of you.

The North-South parallels weaken when comparing beer cultures. Brewing flourished especially in the south of Germany but in the north of Italy. Today the Italian south is still more wedded to wine than the north, and while Rome is starting to sprout brewpubs, the serious beer drinker will find it much easier to encounter good beer in the northern third of the country.

Beer styles and drinking culture

Beer is far more an integral part of Italian culture and history than most people think. In 1869, Anton Dreher moved from Vienna to Trieste to open a brewery that became one of the pioneers in developing bottom-fermented styles. The "Vienna Red" style of beer is in some ways as Italian as it is Austrian.

Red ("rossa") beers are stylistically related to Vienna red lagers, although they're usually a good deal stronger. "Rossa" used to be a pretty common name for a strong red lager and several of the craft breweries have returned the name to use. Moretti's "La Rossa" is one of the best known in the world. Buyouts and mergers have put the Dreher legacy in Dutch Heineken hands today, along with the Moretti brands. But Peroni's commercially successful Gran Reserve, a 6.6% attitude changer, is further proof that Italians are ready for different and better beers.

Craft brewing has soared in Italy in the last decade. As we go to press, about 400 breweries are vying for an expanding craft beer market. Today Italian craft brewing has much more in common with Belgium than with Austria. There are no rules, few traditions, and fewer expectations, and the result is a range of really interesting beers. Part of the reason for so much innovation is that craft brewers in Italy have often felt they needed to compete with wine. There is a downside to the winefighting—the effort that Italian brewers put into packaging and vintaging, and the resulting prices, can be noted in any good beer store in the U.S. or UK. Sadly, you won't find many bargains on a bottle of Italian craft beer in Italy either. But in a city where a half liter of Eurofizz can cost you a ten spot, what the heck. Happily, the draft versions of these uberpricey brews can be much more affordable—no more than you'd pay in a city bar in the U.S.—and if you take advantage of the free buffets that many bars offer at opening time, you can have a surprisingly affordable night of exceptionally good beer.

Even in this context, Milan is still a mass market beer city with a small but rapidly growing beer culture. Good bartenders who work within a 15 minute walk of one of Italy's best beer bars have never heard of it, yet it can be hard to find a seat in the best of the brewpubs. Most of the good beer bars are filled by 20- and 30-somethings, though any age is welcome. It's exciting to see this young beer industry appeal so successfully to the young. At least in this northern part of Italy, beer gets respect, and the exploding Italian craft brewing industry has a potential market they are just starting to explore.

Reminder: We've mentioned the late opening hours in some of our selections, but you should inquire about hours even when you find one open during the day. Some of the relatively few bars that are open for lunch shut down altogether in the middle of the afternoon.

The sixpack of drinking experiences

We're giving you a sixpack here because that's what we do, but what we really have is a top five and some lesser alternatives. The choices we give you in #6 are pleasant enough, but the top five would more than hold their own in the top echelon of any city in the world.

Birrificio Lambrate has two locations. We're always drawn to the Via Adelchi (#5) location, in part because that's the one we discovered on our first trip to Milan and in part because Giampaolo welcomes us as regulars even when our visits are years apart. Lambrate is a brewpub that operates as something of a production brewery as well, supplying beers to the best beer bars in the city. They keep an array of about nine on tap, some of them regulars, but several seasonals as well make for a really interesting evening.

Lambrate is one of the top-echelon Italian craft breweries. They're creative enough so that they don't always hit home runs, but they rarely strike out either. The best of the beers are sensational. The Imperial Ghisa was a complete meal of a beer: smoked

The buffet at Lambrate

fish appetizer, salted steak, red wine, and bitter chocolate for dessert, all wrapped up in an 8.5% roasty bomb.

Some guest beers join the house-brewed beer, and you can find good examples of draft, cask, nitro, or bottles. Giampaolo will guide you through the selection, and if you can luck into a time when the bar is not slammed, he can talk wisely about Italian beers in general.

The crowd ranges from rough looking 20ers to families on an outing, and everyone gets along. Come right at opening unless you're planning on coming late. Lambrate follows the wonderful Milanese bar custom of offering free food at the 6:30 PM opening. In Lambrate's case it's a spectacular antipasti buffet. It's dinner.

You can drink outside if it's crowded, but you'll have to put that beautiful beer in a plastic cup to do so.

Isola della Birra (Via Medardo Rosso, 18) was the bar that convinced us that Milan deserved a chapter in this book. Take the 82 bus from Centrale, or walk—it's about 20 minutes. Isola's half dozen draft lines are modest compared to the others in our top five, but you can't miss having a great beer experience here. Max will almost certainly be at the bar. Only slightly curmudgeonly, he might give you a good-humored hard time, but he's a genuinely good guy with a superb knowledge of the beer scene in Milan. Isola has a fine bottle collection in addition to its carefully chosen rotating taps. It opens even later than the others, so save it for after dinner.

A one-room pub with a tented sidewalk patio, **BQ/Birra Artigianale di Qualità** at Via Losanna, 36, has a beer list suited to a much larger establishment. But the owner and the customers understand the value of this gem. The owner is a beer judge, beer festival organizer, and dedicated connoisseur of great beer. He enthusiastically celebrates the great products that have emerged from Italian craft breweries, but he's surprisingly candid about those that don't make the grade. His draft lineup is a carefully balanced combination of brews that he makes himself in a nearby brewery and a wide selection of guest beers. Four hand pulls join nearly twenty taps, but if for some reason that isn't enough for you, the bottle selection is stunningly large. We're thinking we need to find a hotel within walking distance for our next visit.

BQ will feed you some very nice panini made from sourced Italian hams, so you won't go hungry, but you won't have a big Italian dinner either. The Via Losanna location is about a half hour's walk from Isola della Birra; save shoe leather by taking the M2 to Lanza, then tram 14. Having a map with you is a good idea.

BQ has another outlet at Alzaia Naviglio Grande, 44, with more handpulls and a few fewer draft lines. The draft beers at the two branches are not identical, so it can be worth your time to hit both.

"Pazzo" means crazy in Italian, and **PaZZeria** is a crazy good place to drink. A young, energetic, enthusiastic staff handles a youthful, boisterous crowd in this exceptionally good draft beer house. About fifteen taps of Italian and imported beers and a fridge full of bottles provide plenty of drinking choices. Not only is the range of beers exceptional, but they take Belgian care in serving them—each in its own special glass.

A better than average range of food choices is more brewpub than Italian. There are Italian options, but spare ribs and burgers also appear. Good sized portions and well prepared foods aren't that easy to find with really good beer, so if you go for a meal, it makes the fairly long subway ride out of town very much worthwhile. Note the time of the last train back to town. For a city that stays up to wonderfully late hours, the Metro often quits earlier than that in relatively staid Washington, DC.

Despite its distance from the city center, PaZZeria's actually easy to get to, no more than a couple of hundred yards from the Bande Nere metro stop. Officially at Piazzale Giovanni Dalle Bande Nere, 2, it's right on the corner of Bande Nere and Catarina, but it's not all that well signed. Look for the small "open" sign and the usual bar umbrellas on the tables in front.

Birreria Hop's motto is "in beer we trust," and the place can be trusted to provide very good ones. Nine or ten draft lines feature some beers from Lambrate, sometimes including ones you won't even find at the brewery, as well as beers from several other Italian breweries. The Lambrate family connection shows in the selection of 75 cl bottles and in the coasters as well. The atmosphere is wonderfully funky; stucco walls and old wood make it look way older than it is. A young staff is very welcoming—which might involve the waiter giving you a good-natured hard time on the way in. Big smiles, freely offered samples of the beers, and quite functional English will make you want to stay the evening. On a good night you might find a half a dozen breweries represented, and the beers turn often enough to make it worth coming back a day or two later to see what's new.

Get there early to feast on a distinctive free food offering. One of the staff works full time making up fresh mini-pizzas with a creative variety of ingredients that change from day to day. Our second visit featured popcorn on the pizza, and it worked much better than it had any right to. It's another free meal if you're not wedded to a veal extravaganza in a pricey restaurant. A tiny unisex WC inspires us to go before we go, but it's functional if you're dug in for the evening. Tram 16 or tram 9 takes you within a couple of blocks of its Via Regina Margherita, 4/8 address.

Our sixth pick here is something of a coin flip. Consider going to the second BQ and settle into its ten taps and ten handpulls. Barring that, choose one of the three below. The beers are of similar quality, which is to say inconsistent, but at least one or two of the choices are enjoyable enough at each location. Stronger, darker beers tend to be better than the lighter ones. The pubs below provide more extensive menu choices than most of our top five, but we wouldn't skip any of those five to pick up one of these.

❖ **Q Beer** (via Mecenate, 76) is a spiffy newpub built into a warehouse area with a small garden out front and a big dark interior. The gleaming copper kettles are quite evident and pick up on the copper-themed bar. It has five house beers which, if you wish, you can get in huge sizes. Friendly people and a good range of food options from a clean, open kitchen make us look forward to a return visit.

❖ **Il Giardino della Birra** (Via Ortica,10) is a steakhouse that's open for lunch during the week and dinner at 7 PM all days. It's hard to tell from the front that you're actually entering a brewery as well as a restaurant, but it serves three house beers. The beer won't change your life, but we got a warm welcome and a good meal on our visit.

❖ To get to **Fermento,** at Via Camillo Ugoni, 18, take the 82 bus from Centrale station to Via Angiolo Malfucci and walk the three blocks to Ugoni; you'll see it on the left. It's supposedly the city's newest brewpub, but (a) it doesn't brew and (b) it was there in 2007 with a "Fermento" sign over the door and the same picture of the supposed brewery on the same wall. At least the beer names seem to have changed. The house beers are from the Ambrosiana Brewery in Manerbio, not too far away. We like the place: the staff is efficient and the prices are very reasonable for quite good Italian food. A pasta lunch special was 4€ and even large steaks of local beef came in under 20€. Not surprisingly, the place can be jammed at lunchtime. While most of the five beers were pretty ordinary newpub, the Regina Nera dark lager stood out. A clean and roasty beer, it had just enough hints of chocolate and burned sugar to be interesting.

Other places to explore

We haven't been to Ratera, but our friends in Milan rave about it. Via Luigi Ratti, 22.

If you're going to Birreria Hop, you might want to check out **Mom Café** (Viale Monte Nero, 51), which we think opens earlier, just about two blocks away from

Hop toward the tram line. Several draft lines feature big brewery beers, but the happy hour buffet is impressive, and if you're trying to meet anyone under 24 who lives in Milan, they're already here. If you're a fogey, you'll still be treated with respect, but you won't find many kindred souls.

Beer stores. A Tutta Birra at Via Lazzaro Palazzi, 15, near Repubblica, is central and stocks several hundred beers, but most of them are Belgian and other imports. We'd seen most of them in the States. Eataly, a global gourmet chain, has a smaller selection, but the beers are well chosen and it stocks more Italian beers that we haven't seen elsewhere. The prices were surprisingly reasonable and the beers were well inside expiration dates. Eataly has two locations, Piazza 5 Giornate and a brand new one at Piazza XXV Aprile, 10, halfway between the Moscova and P.Ta Garibaldi metro stations. You can piece together a picnic to die for in either place.

Where to stay

The Hilton and the Sheraton Four Points are both 5 minutes' walk from Milano Centrale. If you're a member of either hotel chain, they're perfect, other than the fact they're stuck in high-rise city; no park or Duomo view here. If you're room hunting, cross the square in front of the station and take the diagonal road off to the left past the McDonalds. You'll find three and four star hotels and a few cheap ones with fewer stars. Keep heading toward Repubblica for more options.

The Duomo: upstairs with the saints

What to see

One of the world's great sand castles, the Duomo is absolutely magnificent; its 12 spires and 192 statues dominate the piazza. A tour that includes a walk on the roof will allow you to see the statues up close and personal, as well as a stunning view of the city. You can't appreciate the scale of the thing until you're up in the middle of it.

You have to see Leonardo's "Last Supper" or suffer embarrassment for the rest of your life, but fortunately it lives up to its reputation. Located in the Refectory at the Monastery of Santa Maria delle Grazie, it is stunningly more dramatic today than the dull but still haunting painting we first saw in the 1970s. A 22-year restoration process has restored original colors and revealed details that had been lost for centuries. Go online beforehand to book the limited number of 8€ tickets, or pay through the teeth for a tour when you get there. Be prepared for the fact that you get only 15 minutes gawking time from the minute you step into the room. Read the guidebooks before you go, but go.

The 1877 Galleria Vittorio Emanuele II near the Duomo is similar to those in Brussels and Paris, but a lot bigger: a gloriously ornate old shopping arcade full of fancy plaster, glass roofs, and pricey stores.

La Scala Opera is quiet in the summer, but it has a museum attached and if there are no rehearsals, you'll get a look at the theater itself: phenomenal. Lots of companies will make it part of tours that range from 30€ to 700€ (with hotel included), but 6€ will get you the tour on your own. If you do come for the opera season, get your tickets well in advance.

The water views of the Naviglio Grande canal area are a fine change of pace from the dry downtown. The area teems at night with bars and drinking spots, some of which are fairly beer-friendly. It's calmer, quieter, and still pleasant during the day, although several of the bars won't be open. From Centrale, take the M2 (Green) line to Porta Genova; it's an easy walk from there.

Scams and alerts

Pickpockets. You almost certainly won't get mugged or shot in Milan, but if you aren't alert, you will part with your money or, worse yet, your passport and credit cards. Use your passport pouch without fail, swing the fanny pack to the front, and don't leave anything in your pockets you aren't willing to lose. One quick way to assess the danger of pickpockets is to look at young women in their 20s and 30s and see where they're carrying their backpacks and purses. In Milan, they're universally held in front, and tightly at that. Do the same.

Despite all our caution we got pickpocketed—by a group of young women dressed as nuns. They were not without some decency, however: when one found she had lifted a package of tissues from Bob's wallet pocket… she put it back before dashing out of the Metro car. See our general warning about pickpockets in the Introduction.

Vending assistance. The tram ticket vending machines are very easy to operate; instructions are in English. If someone offers to help you, refuse the offer. If he persists, find another machine. We try to buy day passes a day in advance, so if one station doesn't feel right we can go to another.

Further information

Transportation. Milan is a big city and you can't easily walk from beer bar to beer bar. If you're going to be in the city more than a day or two, make the 2€ investment in a complete tram and bus map, which you'll have to get from an ATM office (Azienda Trasporti Milanese, not a bank machine); there's one in the central station and one at the Duomo. We were able to get one without having to wait for our number to come up by asking at the side desk. Don't bother getting tickets at the ATM office, the vending machines are easy to use and take bills as well as coins—note the maximum amount of change returned, though. 4.50€ gets you a 24 hour pass; a 48 hour pass saves you a bit, but since you only validate the pass when you first use it, two 24 hour passes can get you more, and maybe much more, than 48 hours of use. A single ride is 1.5€, so the passes are bargains.

Day trip

Como

Italy has a boatload of exciting and innovative breweries. In our experience, however, even those that can be reached by public transportation are time-consuming challenges. Unless you're settling in for the long haul, in which case this guide is inadequate anyway, you'll probably be better off finding Italy's best beers in the superb beer emporiums we've listed above.

That said, Lake Como is so different from the urban experience you'll have in Milan that we think it's worth taking the break. Less than an hour from Milan by train, Como combines a pleasant brewery adventure with spectacular scenery.

One of the best of the newpubs, **Malthus,** "Il Birrificio de Como," now ships beers all over the world. The main room is cavernous, wooden beer hall style, but lots of levels and different décors break up the space. A large umbrellified patio-garden is a great place to sample the five house-made beers when the weather cooperates. The Marilyn, an unfiltered lager, typified the well-made but fairly ordinary beers on tap. We've had some bottles the brewery has shipped to the U.S. more recently, and they seem to be becoming more adventurous and more skillful with experience. If you can find the Malthus Baluba, try it—this dark ale starts woody and dry and finishes with some fruit and late chocolate. It's even quite good by the time it gets to the States.

The garden at Malthus, Como

Make time before or after the brewery to drink in some of the scenery. Lake Como, Italy's deepest lake and third largest in area, has become a haven for the rich and famous, but there's plenty to do even if you aren't George Clooney. The Cathedral, some notable churches, and a handful of museums are worth the time, especially if it's raining, but the views are the main attraction. Unfortunately some of the most spectacular views are best seen from places that are only accessible by car, but a funicular railway from the lakeshore whisks you 500 meters up to the town of Brunate in 7 minutes. You can also find those views by booking a bus tour. Inclusive tours from Milan include a cruise on the lake and perhaps just enough free time to hunt up the brewery. You can book the lake cruise separately if you're on your own.

If you're traveling on a rail pass, be warned that a private rail line serves Como as well as the state affiliated F.S. They go to different stations in Como; the private line takes you closer to the brewery, but doesn't take the Eurail pass. In good weather the walk from either station is manageable.

Munich

Quick orientation

You'll arrive at the Hauptbahnhof. The tourist office is accessible only from outside; exit the main (west) entrance and walk right. Train tickets are available from windows on the left side of the main hall as you walk away from the tracks; the ReiseZentrum travel office, for overnight tickets and some reservations, is in the same area.

City transportation includes S Bahn, U Bahn, trams, and buses. Your Eurail pass covers all S Bahns, but nothing else. A 6.50€ daypass (Tageskarte) pays for itself with three trips or a couple of longer ones, and the 3-day pass is an even better deal. Once in the downtown area, almost everything is walkable, and compared to Berlin or London, Munich really is a small town.

Leaving the end of the tracks behind you, walk away from the Hauptbahnhof and in a few minutes you'll be at the huge round fountain that identifies Karlsplatz/Stachus. Go through the tall arched Karlstor to the pedestrian shopping area, and just on the left is Ellie's favorite statue in Munich (see Augustiner Bierhalle below). Follow the main (mostly pedestrian-only) thoroughfare as it changes names. Major beer halls, especially Augustiner's flagship, are on your right as you approach Marienplatz.

Why you're here

Don't mess with Bacchus

The tall, arched tower gate at the end of Marienplatz (past the Rathaus with its famous Glockenspiel) is Am Tal, the end of the major downtown tourist area. The Viktualienmarkt is just past it and to the right, while the Dom, Platzl, and Hofbräuhaus are off to the left. Eight S Bahn lines reach distant suburbs in all directions from Munich, but they all funnel through the core area; a 3-minute wait for a train is a long one in this corridor.

Station breaks

We miss the days when wonderful restaurants flourished in most large Bavarian railroad stations. You can still find beer even early in the morning, but you have to hunt for a civilized place to enjoy it. You can catch a quick beer if you leave the station at the south exit, past the entrance to the S Bahn (to your left as you come in from the tracks). Across the street is an upscale Tegernseer restaurant, if it's open. Ho hum. Better, though you'll have to move fast to stay within our 10-minute limit, is Spaten's smallish beer hall at Marsstrasse 16, within sight of the former brewery. Some of the best beer halls in Munich are an S Bahn stop or two from the station, and if you have a rail pass, it's a quick free trip.

History and culture

Even more than most large cities, Munich means many different things to different people, and not all of the meanings are positive. The origin of the name is religious—München, referring to the Benedictine monastery near the toll bridge that crossed the Isar river. But the city's fortunes have been inextricably linked in secular ways to the Wittelsbach monarchy even into recent times. As the capital of the "free state of Bavaria," Munich long served as a counterbalance to the more Spartan and Prussian Berlin, which eventually dragged Munich into a united Germany. Munich was an early center of Nazi strength; Hitler rose to fame with his "Beer Hall Putsch" (see the note about the Burgerbräu Keller in the beer hall section below). Not long after that, the city became a synonym for appeasement when British Prime Minister Chamberlain returned, promising "peace in our time," from the conference in which the English and French essentially traded Czech independence for a year or two to prepare for an inevitable war. The building in which the agreement was signed is now Arcisstraße 12, on the eastern side of the Königsplatz.

Bombed to bits during the war, Munich became a postwar symbol of a new German spirit, rebuilding its ruined core with Marshall Plan dollars and the dedication that came to be known as the "German miracle." When Munich hosted the 1972

Summer Olympics, it seemed to have fully emerged from its grim past. Mark Spitz and Olga Korbut dominated the news of the games, but a terrorist attack that killed 11 Israeli athletes redefined the Olympic experience for the city. In 2011, Müncheners again thought they had a real shot at redemption with a chance to host the 2018 Winter Olympics, but finished second to Pyeongchang, South Korea. Today Munich tries to present itself as the technological center of Germany and the European Union ("lederhosen and laptops"), a claim that a good many Germans from other parts of the country regard with a measure of skepticism.

Munich, then, remains a city in search of a clear identity. And maybe that's OK, because much of its charm lies in paradox. It claims, with some justification, to be the largest small town in the world. It's a city of remarkably refined art and unrelievedly ugly graffiti (though some of the graffiti belongs quite properly with the art). It's a city where Islamic women showing only their eyes walk through a downtown park where men, and some women, lie on the grass showing everything they were born with (and, often these days, a girth that they were not). It's a remarkably advanced technological city where everything works ... except the up escalators when you're carrying luggage. It's a city of exceptional hospitality and occasional neo-Nazi epithets. It's a city where your expectations can be formed over a decade and reversed in a day.

It's small wonder, then, that Munich is the largest city in the world that defines itself so fully by its beer culture. At the Chinese Tower in the English Garden, businessmen with briefcases sit at tables next to Goths who could set off an airport metal detector at 500 meters. Left and right refer only to which hand you use to pick up the liter Mass of beer; singing is sometimes forbidden, to make sure no one knows which side you're on. Nearly everyone celebrates the existence of seven major breweries, even though only four sites still brew and two of the companies are owned by the Belgian AB-InBev. But there really is a difference between the Hacker Keller and Der Pschorr, even though those two companies have been intertwined almost from their beginning. It's not hard to taste the difference between a Spaten and a Löwenbräu even if they are coming out of the same huge plant. An exhibit in the city museum on brewing spun off to become its own Beer and Oktoberfest Museum, and few cities anywhere treasure a defining beer festival the way Munich does its Oktoberfest.

The Rathaus and Glockenspiel

Trying to capture Munich's beer scene in this chapter is like writing a history of the United States in six pages. It can be done, but only with appalling omissions. Here. as much as any other chapter in the guide, our attempt at a list of six is egregiously incomplete. Nevertheless, perhaps here more than any other chapter you'll find it valuable for someone to limit your options, at least by a bit. Certainly Munich isn't going to do that for you.

Beer styles and drinking culture

Most of the beer cities in this guide are closely associated with a beer style. Munich, really, is just associated with beer. Traditionally Munich beers were dark. Munich water is soft and naturally not well suited to crisp pale lagers; the soft, sweet Münchener Dunkels were a perfect solution. The "Munich" style still means a dark beer. Chewy, with notes of roast and chocolate, it's quite nice when you can find it. Today, the dominant beer for the city is Helles. Gold to rich gold, always malty and sweet and often bready, with a moderate alcoholic strength, it's the beer you'll receive if you just order "ein Bier, bitte." Early in the 20th century, Thomasbräu shocked the Munich beer world by producing a light-bodied and relatively dry pilsner-style beer. Other breweries condemned it as heresy, but the public loved it, and within a few years almost every brewery had a Pils. Löwenbräu Pils was "the" beer on offer when we paid our first visit to the garden at the Chinese Tower, and it was served from 100-liter wooden kegs. In recent years pilsner has diminished to a relatively minor role; it's around if you look, but no brewery really pushes it.

The Munich pilsner's demise mirrors the spectacular growth of Hefeweizen sales in restaurants and gardens. Weizens appeal in part because they're a socially acceptable way for even a male customer to order a half liter, since Hefeweizens were only packaged in bottles until relatively recently. Almost every brewery serves Hefeweizen on draft now, but they're only sold by the liter to tourists. And they are never, ***EVER***, served with a slice of lemon, unless you have stumbled into a place where Americans outnumber Germans by at least 15 to 1.

After World War II, brewers tried to market clear, filtered Weizens (Kristallweizen) that might challenge pilsners in other markets and appeal to women at home. The result, in the words of one of the better Bavarian brewers we've known well, "tasted like [crap]." The answer was to throw a slice of lemon in the glass to augment the natural lemon-citrusy taste of the wheat. (The lime in Mexican lager was likewise introduced to make tasteless, cheap beer interesting, but that's a different book.) On the other hand, the yeasty, flavorful Hefeweizens continue to be served everywhere *without* garnish. Brewers are clever people; if they want a beer to taste a certain way, they'll find a way to do it at the brewery. It took them a while to make Kristallweizen that wasn't "crap," but several current offerings are very pleasant, with plenty of citrus, clove, and even pepper. Today, therefore, not even the Kristalls normally come with lemon slices. If your German restaurant is serving fruit in the beer, walk out.

Even before the recent surge in Hefeweizen's popularity, Müncheners sought it out to pair with Weisswurst—soft, white, gently spiced veal sausages. Weisswurst is almost exclusively eaten at breakfast, so Hefeweizen became something like the orange juice of beers. You can almost hear the commercials: "Weissbier... it's not just for breakfast any more." But it still rules the breakfast table. German beer halls open early (9 or even 7 AM); you owe it to yourself to start a day with Weisswurst and Weissbier at least once.

Müncheners drink nearly everywhere, but the defining experience is the beer garden. Almost 100 gardens in the city fill to capacity on a beautiful day, but somehow leave just enough seats for you to fit in. Nearly all gardens serve food, some of it quite good, but nearly all allow you to bring in picnics. The general rule is that if there is a tablecloth provided, you'll order from the waitstaff; otherwise, buy your own drinks in the garden—you're not allowed to bring them in—and bring your food or buy a feast at the self-service stalls. Be alert for a deposit on your mug—sometimes hefty—and keep the poker chip, if there is one, to redeem it.

The sixpack of beer experiences ... and then some

Munich is one of the cities that defy the premise of this guide; but we promised, and therefore present the following exercise in folly. If we only had two days, these are the places we'd visit (in no particular order). Longer descriptions follow below.

❖ Der Pschorr: the staff make this a "beer theater"—new wooden kegs are tapped on the bar every half hour or so. Superior food. (this page)
❖ Augustiner Bierhalle and Restaurant: good Munich cooking and beer from the wood. (p. 202)
❖ The Hofbräuhaus: because you just have to. Sorry. (p. 203)
❖ Hirschgarten: the largest and possibly best Biergarten in the world. (p. 204)
❖ Augustiner Keller Garten: close to the train station, crowded and deservedly so. (p. 205)
❖ Zum Brunnstein-Maierbräu: a rural Bavarian family-run restaurant in the heart of the city; tourist-free and a short walk from the Ostbahnhof S Bahn stop. (p. 208)

Next is a longer but still woefully abbreviated list of our favorite Munich places, including the above. Munich is most famous for its gardens and beer halls. We recommend you focus your time on them. You won't get much variety in the beer, but the experiences are unlike those in any other city in the world. If you have time, a range of brewpubs large and small give you an opportunity to stretch your palate just a bit.

Big-brewery beer halls and restaurants

Der Pschorr (Viktualienmarkt 15) is a new kid on the block, but although it looks a bit touristy, they've done almost everything right. It's beer theater, but there's good beer and excellent food during the show. The show—in addition to an absolute ballet of waitstaff dashing to and fro, sometimes even pirouetting under fully laden trays of beer and food—is, in fact, the beer. Beer from the wood, in small enough barrels that they have to be changed every 20 minutes or so, which involves someone muscling the new keg up onto the bar and with due ceremony hammering the spigot into the cask and spewing foam into the first half dozen glasses poured. If your wait person really likes you, (s)he'll wait until the beer settles enough to top up your half-liter glass to almost a half liter before she serves you.

The food is carefully prepared, upscale Bavarian beer hall fare. The menu shows imagination, and most of the dishes are well worth the prices that are a cut above other beer halls. They're extremely proud of their local sourcing, from fish to wine to the meats. Der Pschorr doesn't stay open all that late, so go early enough to enjoy a few of the really fresh Pschorr Helles beers from the wood.

Augustiner Bierhalle and Restaurant. Augustiner is, among Müncheners, the most respected of the local breweries, perhaps because they showcase their beers so well. As you walk around Munich, you may see the brewery's delivery truck with racks of "Bier vom Holz" in real wooden barrels that run in size from 10 liters all the way to a mammoth 200 liters.

Augustiner's prime showpiece towers over the city's central pedestrian zone at Neuhauserstrasse 27. Years ago, beer palaces such as this one dominated the entire stretch from the Viktualienmarkt to the Hauptbahnhof; Augustiner is one of the few left today. Exit the Karlsplatz (Stachus) S Bahn station toward Marienkirche, and 200 meters down on your right, side by side, are the Augustiner Restaurant and the Augustiner Bierhalle. Both have the same menu (the restaurant has white tablecloths), and both serve the same beers. Sometimes, for reasons we can't fathom, there are empty tables in the fancier restaurant while the beer hall is packed.

Augustiner's food is showcase beer hall Bavarian, and although the kitchen is a big operation, the food is tasty and well presented. The beer, of course, is fresh and very

Augustiner Bierhalle

Münchenish. They tap a wooden keg in the late afternoon and replace it once. After that you're drinking Augustiner draft from steel kegs—which is not the end of the world, but it's worth getting there for the wood. It doesn't take much of a palate to spot the difference when they shift over to the draft line.

The Augustiner Brewery also runs restaurants Am Dom and Am Platzl, with reliable cooking and beer from the wood. Its gardens are among the city's finest.

Weisses Brauhaus. Just a short walk from the Marienplatz or Isartor S Bahn stops (at Tal 7, doable in the rain) is the official outlet of the Schneider Weissbier Brewery. The building used to house the brewery, but after a 1943 bombing, the company decided to move, not only outside the city walls but away from major bombing targets, to the small town of Kellheim, where it remains today. The brewery still celebrates its Munich roots, however, and the restaurant is one of several in Munich that double as museums. Don't miss the second floor with even more photographs and exhibits. Food is Bavarian: full portions of solid meat and potatoes. Wash it down with a variety of Schneider's world-famous wheat beers.

As much of a museum as a Bierkeller, **Altes Hackerhaus** (Sendlingerstrasse 14) is off the beaten path a bit but worth the effort to find. It's hard to move around in the place without knocking into a sign or tray or other bit of breweriana. Beer and food are more or less what you'd expect, and the service is most welcoming. It's a little daunting, but we like the place. Of course we started in the beer business as can collectors....

The **Löwenbräu Keller** (Nymphenburger Strasse 2) has been one of our favorite Munich destinations for decades. We first encountered the Löwenbräu Keller in the 1980s when recovering from a bout of food poisoning we picked up from a street vendor behind the Iron Curtain. Freedom, fresh Hefeweizen, and German roast chicken were equally comforting. It used to be much bigger before the Allied air force remodeled it in the 1940s, but it's still good sized and gives you the option of a fine, if somewhat urban, garden or a traditional beer hall.

We're not sure the Löwenbräu beers are quite what they were, now that they're brewed by Spaten—they seem sweeter—but we're willing to admit that it's just as likely that our tastes have changed as that the beer has. We took a tour of the Löwenbräu brewery around 1980 and were struck by how proud they were to be using American hops. We don't know if they still are.

The **Hofbräuhaus** has to be on your beer bucket list. (On everyone's city map; turn left outside Am Tal and follow the tourists.) It's the most famous beer hall in the world, and if you're in Munich you have to go there if only to say you have. It's an Experience ... and you may find it's not all that bad. It's one of the few places in the city that you'll hear Blasmusik (oompah band music), though you'll have to check on when and in what part of the massive building it's playing. A smaller Bavarian band relying on strings sometimes plays upstairs. The wooden beer barrels are fakes but pretty clever ones, and the place works really hard on providing a Bavarian atmosphere, corporate style. Downstairs in the Schwemme, tourists scream happily at each other in forty languages over the mandatory one-liter mugs; upstairs is spiffier, more sedate, and more expensive. There's also a small open courtyard just as crammed as the Schwemme in nice weather. But really, once, you should go. The Hofbräu beers are among the best in the city, and the food, albeit mass produced, is well above average Bavarian. In our experience, small kids are not only tolerated but welcome (at least, early). After all, whatever noise they make won't be noticed in the general uproar of the hall. A side entrance to the left of the big square tower out front leads to a backwater of a room where you might be able to find a seat and oxygen, if not music, when the Schwemme is suffocating.

Note: If you're a history buff, you can't visit the beer hall of Hitler's infamous Beer Hall Putsch. The Burgerbräu Keller was demolished a number of years ago, and the Hilton City (Stadt) stands on the site today.

A few of Munich's best beer gardens

If you have only one day in Munich and the weather is good, spend part of it at the **Hirschgarten.** It's not only the largest beer garden in the world, it's arguably the best. Augustiner beer is served from real wood barrels. It can be emptyish at lunchtime; it really hums in the early evening. If you get there early enough, grab a table by the back fence. The eponymous deer come right up to the fence and you can feed them pretzels while you drink your beer. It's OK to bring food into the garden, but the policy strictly requires you to buy your beverages on premise. Why would you want to do anything else?

The food is above average for a beer garden. The charcoal-grilled fish (Steckerlfisch) is especially good. Many of the beer gardens have switched to "grilling" fish in electric or gas-fired ovens, similar to the ones used for chickens. Fish don't drip fat the way chickens do, however, and high heat tends to dry them out. The more gentle heat of a charcoal pit and the experienced and skilled hands of those who run the stalls produce some of the best-tasting fish in the world. Try whatever species they offer; mackerel (Makreln) is the easiest to identify and its oily flesh grills up deliciously.

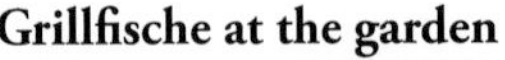
Grillfische at the garden

If you're really strapped for time and are railing in and out of Munich, the **Augustiner Keller** and its beer garden (Arnulfstrasse 52) are a 15-minute stroll from the Hauptbahnhof. If you have a rail pass, you can get there even easier by S Bahn. Get off at Hackerbrücke and go up the stairs to the bridge. Facing the easily visible Hauptbahnhof in the distance, turn left on the bridge, then right on Arnulfstrasse at the bottom of the incline, and the garden entrance is just a few blocks away. The Keller restaurant is impressive, but the garden is exceptional: spacious and handsomely shaded by the traditional chestnut trees. There's a good-sized playground with convenient tables for Mutti and Papa. We've found the food less consistent than most other gardens, but at its best it's quite good. Fischer Vroni is the same grilling company that produces such superb Steckerlfisch at the Hirschgarten.

Even though there are about 3,000 seats, you'll have to be persistent to find two together on a warm evening. Remember that sharing tables is expected in German beer gardens and all but the most formal of restaurants. On a busy weekend, this garden and the Hirschgarten sell over 10,000 liters of Augustiner beer—about two months of production by an American brewpub.

An easy walk from the Marienplatz or Isartor S Bahn stations, the **Viktualienmarkt** is an enormous open market that sells (to locals as well as tourists) everything from meats, fruit and veg, spices, olives, and cheese, to flowers, pot plants, and decorative straw doodads. It's perfect for loading up a garden picnic. On one side, near the meat market, is an unusual urban beer garden that gives you probably the widest choices of food of any of them. The garden is popular and packed at lunchtime, though you can go later and still do well. Many of the food stalls are closed Mondays.

A bit off the beaten path, up on the Nockherberg, the **Paulaner Keller** and garden (formerly the Salvator Keller; Hoch Strasse 77) is one of the newest; its historic predecessor suffered a devastating fire in 1999. Three years of construction and several million dollars have spiffed it up wonderfully. The inside still rocks in strong beer season during Lent, and outside is one of the prettier of Munich's gardens. A central fountain features the Paulaner monk who graces their labels, and a number of fine chestnut trees survived the fire next door. There is a small service section of the garden with a wider menu, but most of the area is self-service with basic beer garden food.

The beer, however, sets this garden apart. To our knowledge, it's the only place in the world where you can buy the Nockherberg Naturtrüb, an unfiltered Paulaner. Not every Naturtrüb turns out really well, but this is one that does. A superbly tasty yeast in well-balanced proportions cuts the sweetness that characterizes Munich lagers and makes for a dangerously smooth beer that disappears as if by magic from your liter mug. The atmosphere is more refined than at many of the big gardens, or maybe it's just more of a "local." One sign of the difference is that it's one of the very few gardens not to charge a deposit on your mug. (The two Augustiner gardens don't either.)

Not far from Max-Weber-Platz is the **Hofbräu Keller,** the oldest beer hall in the city. Not to be confused with the downtown Hofbräuhaus, this is where real fans of the Hofbräu beers make their pilgrimage. A massive warren of six floors of beer halls, dining rooms, dance halls, and theaters lies virtually empty during good weather, when the thousand-seat garden is bursting at the seams. Most but not all of the

Garden life

garden is self-service; part of the section that isn't is a small sand "beach" area. Two unusual features seem paradoxical. First, it has one of the best play areas for children, with an attendant. You can sign your kiddie over to her and go drink worry free. But at 4 PM a rule goes into effect that limits beer sales to a *minimum* of a liter at a time. Ah, well, why not? The kids are safe. Be warned that this garden closes relatively early, with a thud. Pay attention to the time that you have to return your Mass Krugs (mugs) or gain an unwanted and very heavy souvenir.

The **Chinesischer Turm** (Chinese Tower) in the English Garden is touristy, but a one-of-a-kind experience, introducing American and Asian tourists to German beer and music. Food is standard beer garden fare; the spareribs can be very good, and the sauce is distinctive—caraway and curry on our last trip (it changes). The garden can seat about 3,000 and sometimes it seems like every seat is taken. On some afternoons an oompah band plays sporadically from the mid level of the tower. The music can be heard nearly a mile away down the Garden. There's also a fancier restaurant on the premises. Hofbräu beer is served from unusually obvious fake barrels, but the upside of the faux wood is an above-average variety of draft beer styles, including Hofbräu's exceptionally drinkable Hefeweizen.

Brewpubs and small breweries

Forschungsbrauerei and Bräustüberl (Unterhachinger Straße 76), near the Perlach S Bahn station, started as a place where the big boys could experiment. It still serves that purpose during the winter, but in the spring and summer it cranks out distinctive and tasty beers for the general public. Not much variety—a strong Pils and a stronger blond Bock—but both are a bit outside the general Munich style. The modest garden is quite pleasant, with a tiny playground. If you're looking for a friend who is a beer geek and you don't know where he is, this is a good place to start looking. Open daily 11 AM to 11 PM, an hour earlier opening and closing on Sundays; music on some Saturdays.

Airbräu has a Munich address, but it's out at the airport, a good haul on the S Bahn. (A tip: take the S8 rather than the S1. They'll both get you there, but the S8 has fewer than half the stops and takes a more direct route.) Located just upstairs from the S Bahn station, this huge beer hall and indoor beer garden is a prize. The range of three beers plus an occasional seasonal is nouveau urbanbräu: unfiltered and somewhat rough, but more flavorful and better balanced than those of many of the new German brewpubs. The setting is spectacular. Sit indoors at a table with an unobstructed view of the brewhouse, or outdoors in a large covered atrium "garden" complete with live trees. It's a perfect destination for a rainy Munich afternoon.

Paulanerbräu (Kapuzinerplatz 5) occupies the site of the former Thomasbräu brewery that merged with Paulaner in the 1920s. The brews are yeastier than the big commercial versions, but they don't make mistakes. Food is reliable. Paulaner cut its teeth on brewpubbing with this venture. They now have several brewpubs in Asia and one in New York City.

Isartaler Brauhaus (Kreuzeckstrasse 23; Großhesselohe Isartalbahnhof) couldn't be more convenient to for S Bahn travelers—it's in the former station building. It's another new German house brewery, but these guys get it right. The Weissbier compares well to the best of the big brewery efforts.

If you go take a squint at the site of Oktoberfest, you won't be far from the **Hacker-Pschorr Brauhaus** (Theresienhohe 7). It's huge and showy; we think Busch Gardens does it better. Decorations range from brewing equipment to Santa's sleigh, but this cavernous showpiece at least produces drinkable house-brewed beers. The food tasted as prepackaged as the nonstop piped-in oompah music. The same premises feature an Italian restaurant and a sports bar. We didn't return to try either one.

A trip to **Weihenstephan** is almost an excursion, but it's close to a beer bucket must. Take a local train to Freising, exit the station, and look up: that's the brewery, up (and we mean *up*) on the far hill. We've walked it both ways and strongly recommend a taxi, at least "up." The reward is an exceptionally tranquil garden in the shadow of the world's oldest brewery. But don't get your hopes too high—the current buildings are attractive, but hardly date back to the 1040 origin the brewery claims. Weihenstephan is also home to the world's most famous brewing school. Your best chance of a tour is to arrange to join a group in advance.

Other really neat places to drink

If you're not going to take the day trip to visit the Andechs monastery and brewery, **Andechser am Dom** (Weinstrasse 7a) is your chance to sample the beer. We understand that this is the only place other than the abbey that serves the unfiltered Andechs. The bar itself is pretty small scale for Munich and fairly informal, in stark contrast to the touristy Hofbräuhaus around the corner. While you're there, check out Augustiner's entry into the area as well. Andechs has three stories of beer-drinking rooms, the top of which does indeed have a nice view of the Dom. It can get jammed at night.

Unlike most German sausages, Nürnberger Rostbratwurst are the size of U.S. breakfast sausages, with a rich spicy flavor. They're served in pairs, normally four, six, or eight to an order. The **Nürnberger Bratwurst Glöckl am Dom** (Frauenplatz 9) is one of the best places south of Nürnberg to try them. An extra bonus is draft Augustiner beer from the wood.

Wirtshaus Ayinger, Platzl 1A, sits right across from the Hofbräuhaus. The brewery's official name is Inselkamer, but the beers take their name from the small town of Aying where it's located. If you want, you can visit Aying; there's a good beer restaurant at the brewery. But while it's an easy S Bahn ride to the village, it's a long walk to the brewery itself. It's easier to sample the beers here. Aying used to have an establishment on the Platzl that rivaled the Hofbräuhaus. Its centerpiece was a large beer hall that featured, if you can imagine it, a Bavarian version of vaudeville. In its place now stands a Hard Rock Cafe (still featuring the Aying beers) that replaced a failed Planet Hollywood. A far better place to drink the Ayinger beers is at the Wirtshaus restaurant and bar next door. Beer is presented from the wood, though we wouldn't be overly surprised to learn they fill the barrel from a keg in the back. Still, it's a comfortable, traditional-looking place to drink with reliable food.

Zum Brunnstein-Maierbräu isn't in anyone's guidebook, but we think it's a gem. Just a block from the easy-to-reach Ostbahnhof, it's more a slice of rural Bavaria than of Munich. It features mostly Maierbräu beers from the village of Altomünster, although one or two come from Kappelerbräu, the town's other brewery. The atmosphere would be touristy Bavarian, except it's the real thing. Lots of wood, a couple of massive decorative steins, and some critters whose last view of the world was at the wrong end of a gun cover the wall. It's a local for any number of people in the area, but it still feels like a pub in Altomünster. Teenage girls dine there alone, Hans sits at the same table he's occupied for years, and the management makes you feel that on this night, you're part of the village too. Bavarian food with unusually good variety—a "tomato schnitzel," for example, served with pasta, tomato sauce, and cheese. It's pig Parmesan, and you'll never miss the veal.

Augustiner Bräustuben or **Stammhaus,** at Landsberger Strasse 31-35, is a bit out of the way, but a visit lets you see the huge brewery even if you can't get through the door of the brewhouse. A long hall with imaginative seating leads to a stairway to an upper floor garden and more drinking rooms. We like the informality of the place—there aren't peanut shells on the floor, but they wouldn't be out of place. To find it, exit the south side of the Hauptbahnhof and walk or take a tram west (in the direction of the tracks) toward Hackerbrücke; or, more easily, take the S Bahn to Hackerbrücke and instead of turning left to get to the Augustiner garden, turn right across the tracks, then right again when you hit Bayerstrasse.

Our friend Ron Barchet told us about the remarkable Tap-House Munich (Rosenheimer Strasse 108) a few weeks after we returned from our last trip to Munich. It's at the top of our list for our next trip. Over forty taps and hundreds of bottles give the best view we know of into the embryonic brewing revolution going on in Germany today. If you're homesick you'll also find plenty of American IPAs; for some reason the bar seems to have good connections in Pennsylvania. Food is limited, so go after dinner, which is easy enough—although it doesn't open until 5 PM most days, it stays open till after midnight except for Sundays at 11. It's a short walk from the Hilton Stadt, the Rosenheimer Platz S Bahn, and the München Ost U and S Bahn and trams.

Where to stay

Frequent thefts, even though they were minor, got to be so annoying (see "Scams and Alerts" below) that even when we were on a tight budget we started paying a few more bucks to stay at Hilton hotels in Munich. We assume other major chains are as secure. We much prefer the "City" (Hilton Stadt) to the "Park" (Am Tucherpark), though both are quite comfortable. The upper floors of the Park offer exceptional views of the city skyline and the English Garden, and the Chinese Tower beer garden is a 10-minute walk. Buses (line 54) stop across the street and run until 1:30 AM; there's also a tram stop about halfway between the hotel and the beer garden.

But the "City" is often cheaper, and the S Bahn Rosenheimer Platz station is an elevator ride from the lobby, so you're downtown or at the Hauptbahnhof in minutes. Shops and small restaurants abound in this residential area; we've found a laundromat, bakeries, a drugstore, and a cheap Internet shop. It's almost exactly halfway between the Hofbräu and Paulaner gardens, about 15 minutes' walk from each. History buffs: your room is on the site of the Burgerbräukeller, the location of Hitler's Bier Hall Putsch, a fact you'll never learn from the hotel staff. If there is no major conference in town, a room at the "City" can go for under $200 in summer if you book and pay well in advance. If you can get a deal on breakfast, take it; the buffet is so lavish you won't have to spend money on lunch. A Holiday Inn sits directly across the street.

If you're visiting Munich for Oktoberfest, all of the above is moot. Take a room where you can get it, hand over your plastic, and forget it. We've stayed outside of the city and taken the S Bahn into town. Ismaning, Wolfratshausen, and Starnberg are just a few of the many towns with hotels that ring the city. If these are full, Augsburg is less than an hour away, and the new ICE train line has cut the two-hour trip to Nuremberg to just over an hour. The fest grounds are a short and easy tram or S Bahn ride from the Hauptbahnhof.

Scams and alerts

Munich is an unusually safe city, especially by American standards, but it is a city, not the small town it tries to be. Count your change carefully, always, but especially in the good but tourist-oriented restaurants around the Hofbräuhaus. If you're having several beers in a group, your waiter may mark your coaster—make sure the count is accurate. If he doesn't, you should mark your own coaster and be sure that he sees you do it, and everyone stays friends.

Secure your wallet when you walk the intensely busy pedestrian streets between the Marienplatz and Karlsplatz. The main streets are safe even away from tourist areas, but after dark some areas of the English Garden north of the Chinese Tower are not.

We've stayed in more different hotels in Munich than in any other city in the world except London. They've all been comfortable, and they've all had good breakfasts, but in over 40 years of travel all over Europe, about 80% of what we've lost from hotel rooms has gone in Munich. Our many experiences in a very nice family-run budget hotel not far west of the Hauptbahnhof were typical—on almost every trip something disappeared. On one trip it was a keyring with a whistle on it; on another a washcloth; on our final stay there, it was a beat-up copy of *Pocket Guide to Beers*. This last left us deeply puzzled; why would a non-English-speaking housekeeper lift an English beer book? Then we remembered it had been signed by the gloveless Michael Jackson himself. We'll never know if the thief ever realized whose autograph it really was.

Hotel managements have generally been reasonable, if not always gracious, in trying to compensate us. A four star hotel near the Hauptbahnhof replaced (with a gulp) a small plush buffalo with a Steiff pony that cost about as much as a full night at the hotel—but the pony never replaced the buffalo among our daughter's favorites. Oddly, the computers, cameras, and money that we have foolishly left in Munich rooms have stayed put, but repeated annoyances led us to the Hiltons for good.

A petty scam: Some people try to make a living being "helpful" by collecting and returning the liter mugs in beer gardens, especially from tourists unaware that there was a 3-euro mug deposit included in the price of their beer. Gardens have responded by issuing small poker chips with the beers—if you don't produce the chip you can't get the deposit back. Most have also installed large English signs explaining the procedure. (Don't get too smug, Americans, the English language signs aren't really for you; they're for the thousands of Asian tourists who pour money into the European economies.) Hang on to your chip and return your own mug.

It's not exactly a scam, but there are beer bars in Munich and elsewhere in Germany that call themselves names like "House of 188 Beers." We have generally found them to be puberty-pandering palaces of paltriness better called "House of 188 Yawns."

Day trips

We hope we have time to write a book on day trips from Munich. Augsburg, Nuremberg, Ulm, and Innsbruck are an hour or two away, and we've trained to our favorite beer garden in Salzburg, Austria, for dinner and returned the same night. Less obvious, but important for beer drinkers, Aying's Brauereigasthof provides a great meal with a large range of beers. Andechs's monastery brewery would be worth the day's visit for the magnificent Baroque church even if the beer weren't so wonderful. The hikes from public transportation for both of these are manageable in good weather. You can also get to most of our Passau and Regensburg day trips from Munich if you plan carefully or give them an overnight.

We've included the following two suggestions because they're not famous, not very touristy, and not, as far as we know, on anyone else's short list. But they are typical of what Germans mean by their oft repeated and very erroneous statement that "every German town has its own brewery."

Memmingen

Memmingen lies an hour and a half by rail west of Munich. We make no pretense that it's significantly better for beer hunting than any of at least fifty brewing towns within reach of Munich, but it has three advantages that not all the others do. It's relatively cheap, it has a beautiful old town, and it has a tavern where you can try nearly all the Memminger beers without leaving your seat.

Where to stay

If you want to make it an overnight, step out of the Bahnhof and walk right, parallel to the tracks, past the old Postamt which is now a museum. Just past it, turn left on Kalchstrasse toward the Marktplatz. A couple of blocks down on your left is the Weisses Ross, a 16th century brewery and inn that is now a modern hotel. You can get a nice double with bath and breakfast for around $150. Across the street, for about a third less, the Gasthof Zum Schwanen is even older and has a nice beer garden serving Allgäuer beers. No elevator.

Continue along Kalchstrasse to the main square, look right, and you can't miss the Hamptons Café Bar, a restored market hall with the fashionable set drinking small servings of not-beer under umbrellas. Behind it is the Rathaus and just in front is the Stadt information office. You have to look hard to find it. They'll give you a list of hotels and restaurants and a somewhat useful map. Past the Hamptons is Ulmer Strasse; turn right on that and find Drexel's Parkhotel and, if you keep going, a cool city gate. But if you continue straight out of the Marktplatz on Zangmeisterstrasse, you'll pass Martin-Luther-Platz and St. Martin's church and, just past another city gate, the Hotel Engelkeller.

What to see

Sankt Martin Kirche, a Protestant church (which you don't see all that many of in Bavaria), is striking in both its size and simplicity. The chancel is where the budget went: a massive display of silver and gilt dominated by a gigantic dangling crucifixion, but the rest of the church is vast, wooden, and simple. If you're lucky and there's an organ concert, by all means go. The pews are reversible, so you'll face the organ instead of the altar and you can watch the organist at work. (Terry Pratchett's Librarian came irrepressibly to mind.)

If you speak German there are museums, exhibits, and theatrical events. Otherwise, a walk around town requires no language skills. Notice the "seven story house" near Gerberplatz and take time to appreciate the city walls and the tower gates that are still the only way to enter the old city.

Where to drink

You can get Memminger beer in most restaurants and hotels. Allgäuer and Aktien beers from Kaufbeuren also have toeholds in the city. But there are two taverns that make this a good destination for sixpacking.

The **Engelkeller** used to be Memminger's Brauereigasthof. Our oldest notes indicate that the brewery was named Burger and Engel Brauerei and we assume the Engelkeller was Engel's original outlet. But no more. The rather spiffy hotel and restaurant are now in the hands of the Laupheimer family that owns the brewery hotel in Günz. We think the beer may be contracted, but there's no indication of that in the information they give you.

While the Engelkeller still has one Memminger beer on tap (most of their selections are from Ayinger), the best place to drink the local beers is **Zum Strauss,** just up the street from the Parkhotel on Ulmer Strasse. Their sign, mysteriously, is of an ostrich. The place is owned by Memminger and they choose to carry a wide range of the Memminger beers. Not all of them are on the menu, so be sure to ask and keep asking if you want to try them all. Lots of wood, snug-style bar tables, and intriguing lighting fixtures make for a great atmosphere. The locals will mostly leave you alone, but can be chatty if they think you're open to a conversation.

Keep an eye out for special events in Memmingen. It seems to have more than its share of fests, concerts, and celebrations. It's also possible to break your rail trip back to Munich with a stop in Mindelheim to try the Lindenbräu beers. The brewery outlet is about a mile from the station.

Landshut

Landshut is less than an hour from Munich on the train to Passau; trains leave hourly. If you start early enough you might have time to hop off in Freising for a late beer at Weihenstephan (see the list of small breweries above).

Ludwig I (the really early Ludwig, not the crazy one) founded the city in 1204. The "hut" or hat part of the name refers to the steep hill that overshadows the city. Landshut was the seat of government for the combined state of Bavaria-Landshut throughout the 15th century. After a period of economic decline, Landshut has thrived in recent years. It's a quick drive to the new Munich airport and has become a significant business center. It can serve as a good base for exploring Munich, since you might be able to find a hotel at a much better price.

Not far off the "Baroque Trail," the town is dominated by Baroque buildings, but some show hints of their Gothic origins. The town hall was last rebuilt in the Romantic era and is essentially Gothic in style. The pedestrian stretch of Altstadt, the main street in the old city, is a Baroque masterpiece, at least a kilometer of restored and original buildings. At one end is an intricate brick spire, the tallest in Germany, and even ordinary shops seem special in a fairyland décor. Trausnitz Castle on the hilltop is worth a look if you have the time. The tourist office is at the upper end of Altstadt on the right as you head vaguely out of town. Pick up the English language overview of the city and a map for free. Get your exercise climbing the berg to Trausnitz if you have the time and energy, or just have a look around on your way to find the beer.

The Reichardt Bräu brewhouse was one of the most attractive breweries in Europe, but it closed in 1987. Two breweries with long histories remain, however, and each produces an extensive range of beers. To visit them both, avoid Wednesdays and Sunday afternoons when the Wittmann tap is closed. According to our sources, neither brewery actually operates a tap any more, but leases space to others who run the retail establishments. That might explain the Tex-Mex restaurant that takes up a good deal of space in Wittmann's Zollhaus, and the steakhouse and numerous shops that now occupy the footprint of the former Ainmüller beer hall of Landshuter Brauhaus. But never fear, the beers are well represented no matter who's running the show in both places, and if you're tough or with a group you can rack up a dozen and a half beers that are hard to find elsewhere in Bavaria.

To get to the **Zollhaus,** the best place to find Wittmann beers, take a 10€ taxi or walk along the river away from the old town, leaving the Berg behind on your left. Keep your eyes open—the Zollhaus is set on a corner a block or so back from the main road. There's a pleasant garden in the courtyard parking area, and inside is a

View of the Castle from Kathi's

very typical Bavarian beer restaurant. Though undoubtedly reduced from its heyday, it's still a big old square place with dark panels, dark wood tables, and dark wood benches and chairs. An adjoining Saal is a bit brighter, but not quite so atmospheric. Take the time to note the pictures on the wall showing the brewery and the construction of the building. They serve almost the full range of Wittmann beers, which can keep you busy for a while. The menu is small, but the cooking is fine.

When you're done, if you're ridiculously compulsive about trying every Wittmann beer, you can find another one or two at the Getränkemarkt only a block or so on the way back to the city on the road that parallels the river road. Tell the manager the crazy Americans with the computer sent you (that's us) and she might give you a bottle opener for a souvenir.

Then stroll back along the river toward the old town. You absolutely cannot get lost here. Head for the tall brick spire, and when you hit Altstadt turn right and go a short distance to Kathi's Steakhouse. But before you settle in, take the time to drink in the beauty of one of the most attractive streets in southern Bavaria.

Kathi's occupies a portion of what was once the massive outlet for the Fleischmann brewery. Fleischmann merged with Koller years ago to form the Landshuter Brauhaus, and Landshuter downsized its outlet a few years ago. Kathi's has the feel of a steakhouse chain, but it's still the best place to drink Landshuter Brauhaus beers. If Thomas is still there, he'll take good care of you; his English is very good and you can trust his recommendations. If there's just two of you, ask for the small outside corner table where you can see the Castle looming above you on the hill—it's one of the best beer drinking views in the region. Inside is pleasant but unspecial.

The food at Kathi's is upscale carnivore. The degree of doneness is a bit hit or miss, but the meats are high quality and the prices are far lower than an equivalent

American steakhouse. The impressive range of Landshuter Brauhaus beers means you'll find something good to go with whatever you order. Landshuter brought in a new brewmaster a few years ago and apparently gave him some rope. He's having fun. A relatively new Zwickl beer is his creation, and we think he's playing with some of the other recipes as well. In any event, the beers seem a little more lively and a little less formulaic than some others in the area.

Stagger back to the station, a 20-minute walk if you can do it, or take a cab: the taxi stand is almost straight out front of Kathi's. If you have saved time for a stop in Freising, hop off the train, check the Abfahrts for your ride back to Munich, and take a cab to the Bräustüberl at Weihenstephaner Berg 10. A wonderfully scenic courtyard is a dream come true in good weather. You can walk through the town and up the steep hill to the brewery—it's easy to spot—but the hike will put a serious dent in your drinking time. The Bräustüberl is open until midnight, late enough for you to miss the last train to Munich if you don't pay attention.

Passau

Quick orientation

Passau's station is a fair hike from the romantic old town. With the tracks on your right, walk past the ranks of regional and local buses, or take a cab to the center. You're on high ground here; the mostly downhill route to the multi-river intersection that brought Passau early importance is a pleasant stroll if you have plenty of time. Happily the tourist office is much closer, as is one of the best of the city's hotels.

A station break

A station break can be a bit of a challenge, but if the weather is good, you can get to the small Hacklberg garden on Bahnhofstrasse just before you get to the main shopping area. The beer is local, the trees are real, and we wish we had a place like this in our home town. You can sit there and sip a beer and watch everyone hurrying to get

Only part of the organ at Dom St. Stephan

somewhere ... while you're not. If you have time, though, skip it for the city's even better treasures.

History and culture

Passau claims 5,000 years of history, though much of it seems to be more archeological than historical. Still, Passau's location at the confluence of three rivers has attracted settlers for centuries. A settlement stood here even before the Romans took it over, and Passau was a major center of trade and industry in the heyday of the Holy Roman Empire. The church established a presence here in the high Middle Ages and there are still traces of early buildings. At one point, Passau was the center of the largest Church diocese in the Holy Roman Empire. A devastating fire in 1662 wiped out most of the town, so what you see now is mostly Baroque dating from the reconstruction that followed. In contrast to some other cities, therefore, Passau seems sort of new, though for an American, 17th century architecture isn't so bad.

While its economic importance has lagged, Passau celebrates its more industrious past in a number of museums; glass museums in the city and the region bring aficionados from far away. In addition to tourism, today the city's economy rests on the large university whose students make up almost 20% of the city's population. At night, the youngsters take over the Old Town and if you're over 30 you'll find yourself standing out in the crowd. Beer restaurants are more sedate and stay open until 11 or 12 PM; about the only students you find there are the staff.

Beer styles and drinking culture

Passau isn't in this book for a distinctive type of beer, but for the number of wonderful places in and around town to drink whatever they're making. You'll find a full range of the German styles. Hacklberg-Innstadt brews well over a dozen beers and some of the other breweries aren't far behind.

Whatever the style, however, beer lovers in this part of the world like sweet. Many of the local brews have a clean but sugary malt—we're starting to call it cane malt—while floral hops attempt to effect some balance. (Munich beers are sweet, too, but much more malty and less sugary.) That's okay with us; obviously it's what people like and why the big guys have a hard time penetrating this market. You're here to explore regional beers you can only get by traveling to the area, and these are just that. You want hop monsters? Go to San Diego.

Passau still sports a nice range of breweries pouring a good variety of styles. We recommend you go there soon, though; global economics isn't on the side of the regional breweries that float the city. On a visit in the not too distant past, we found five operating breweries, all with associated Gasthäusen. Today there are three breweries, and only two of them serve at the brewery.

You're already too late for Peschl and Innstadt. The Peschl family ran out of resources and patience in 2008, closing the brewery that had been in their hands for 800 years and leaving the city with four breweries. The Peschl tap remains—at least a corner of it for now—as a 30-seat tobacco bar that sells a few beers from Aldersbacher. Missable, unless you want to drink a beer out of one of the old Peschl steins for nostalgia's sake. A beautiful garden overlooking the Danube, that used to be a part of the complex, was full of construction equipment tearing it up when we visited a few years ago, but we believe it's open again and may well be one of the better places to have a beer and a view.

Innstadt gave up in January 2014, only four years shy of its 700th anniversary. The beers are still available—Hacklberg brews them. They're not hard to find; two of our picks below feature them.

One wonders if the local Lowenbräu isn't far behind on the road to the history books; the brewery's Gasthaus closed a few years ago, and its easiest-to-find outlet near the brewery is a take-away sushi stand at the city bus terminal. One can almost hear the hungry Munich Lion waiting to eliminate another of the diminishing number of breweries that have the legal right to the name. As of this writing, though, brewery representatives tell us it's doing just fine. You can still buy bottles at the brewery in the afternoon late in the week. And this is Germany, so you can take them to any of the several parks, or even to the end of the town to drink a few beers with the three rivers.

If Passau isn't what it was 20 years ago, three commercial breweries in a town of 50,000 people and a good range from the surrounding area still make for exceptional drinking experiences.

The sixpack of drinking experiences

The two regional breweries dominate the old town in Passau, but an additional small gem crowns a hill high above the city. The **Arnhofer Weissbierbrauerei** dates from the early 20th century and brews, we believe, exclusively wheat beers, though one of them is a Helles with little of the Weizenbier estery yeast flavor. A bock beer has made it to Philadelphia's Monks Café, but you won't find these beers anywhere else in Germany.

Find Arnhofer by climbing the winding Neuer Rieser Strasse or the more direct Alte Rieser Strasse. If you take the challenge of the latter—and we managed to drag our collective 124 years up that hill, so you can too—continue on the footpath on the other side of Neuer Strasse and it leads almost directly to the brewery. You can follow the road around to the front and get a glimpse of the brewhouse along the way, or climb the stairs that lead up to the garden. Either way, wheezing and gasping, you'll be ready for some of the best Weizenbier in Bavaria and one of the best views in Passau. If you want to wimp out, take the #7 bus signed "Ries" from Am Schanzl (just before you reach the Schanzl bridge across the Danube) and it will drop you off at the brewery. The beer will still be very good, but we'd wager not as good as it tastes after the walk. The 1854 Kellerbier is a superior lager: bready, fresh and yeasty, with a good hop character. The weizen beers are even better. The Leichtes Hefeweizen is one of the best of its kind in the world, wheaty with plenty of chalky yeast, strikingly more-ish. Food is typical German Gasthaus fare; the pretzel was one of the best we've ever had. On a good day you look out over grain fields to Passau and the Danube stretching out below.

Take the easier walk down Alte Rieser and cut off the final curve with steps that lead down on the right to the lower road, then walk upstream parallel to the Danube to find the **Hacklberg Brewery** and the nearby Braustüberl, Gasthaus, and Garten. The address, Brauhausplatz 3, won't do you much good, but it's not hard to find and not too far to walk. Just "Gerade aus," which means "keep going"; if it makes you feel any better, you can ask directions along the way and get told the same thing. Eventually the road opens up and you see the striking Hacklberg brewery. It's a beautiful sight—it appears to be a magnificent residence tucked into the side of the hill—and there's a small museum you can visit during weekdays. The brewery complex features one of the best beer gardens in the city, and the restaurant serves very good food and sells a huge array of Hacklberg beers. Service is friendly and attentive and you won't have to use any more German than you want to. Plan on a full evening.

If Kris is still there, tell him "Hi" for us; we owe him for one of the best of the local beer stories. Supposedly, back in the day, when the brewers at Hacklberg—which still has church connections—wanted to brew a strong Doppelbock, they thought they should get permission from the Pope since they were going to be knocking people off their religious feet. So a couple of emissaries from the brewery packed up a sample of the strong brew in a wagon and hauled it off, up and over the Alps and down through sunny Italy to the Vatican. By the time the beer got to the Holy See, it had thoroughly spoiled. The Pope took one taste and pronounced that since no one could stomach enough of the stuff to get drunk it was perfectly okay for Hacklberg to make it. Good thing the Bavarian brewers use restraint in hopping beers—an IPA might have made it in good shape.

The Hacklberg beers are all quite professional, but a few truly stand out. Unfiltered beers have soared in popularity in the last decade; Hefeweizens paved the way

Brauerei Hacklberg

for a surge in Zwickl, Keller, and Zoigl branded beers. Yeasts differ in taste and add interest to Germany's comparatively narrow range of styles, but some are much better than others. Hacklberg's Zoigl is one of the keepers. It's busy but distinctively tasty. A chalky feel softens the bready malt and shows just a hint of kiwi in a pleasant yeast tartness. The Jakobi Hefeweizen Hell is a chalky, yeasty classic: a full-bodied lemon-wheat malt supports lots of clove and a touch of banana penny candy. Although the beers are sweet, they somehow balance pretty well as they drink. The Festbier is a good example; it has the expected sweet pale malt, but noble hops show enough to sustain a good evening's drinking.

Innstadt has been a local favorite, but there were apparently too few locals to keep it profitable. The brewery was on the far side of the Inn and we believe the tap is still open, a manageable walk from the Old Town. You can cross the Inn on the historic pedestrian bridge just downhill from the Löwenbrauerei, then stay parallel to the river downstream to the brewery site and the brewery Gasthaus at Kapuzinerstrasse 6.

You can save yourself the walk, however, by settling in at the **Bayerische Löwe** on the edge of the Old Town. Follow Bahnhofstrasse as it turns into a pedestrian walkway, and jog right when the pedestrian area goes left. A huge rambling beer hall with a 400-seat garden, the Bayerische Löwe had its own house beer on our last trip, a superbly balanced Zwickl. It also features about 10 other Innstadt beers depending on the season, so take your time or take some friends if you want to try them all. There's an irony about this lion of a beer hall selling Innstadt in the shadow of the Lion Brewery that we're sure has not escaped the latter's management. We hope the Innstadt beers continue to have some separation from Hacklberg's range.

The Lowenbräu brewery employees recommend the **Innsteg** restaurant as a good place to drink their beers, and we heartily agree. Well-above-average cooking combines with some of the best river views in Passau to make it a destination even without beer, but they have a very nice selection of Lowenbrauerei Passau's range. Twenty years ago, Schnitzel vom Kalb (veal schnitzel) was as easy to find as the pork version, but these days it's a specialty that has nearly disappeared due, we suspect, to both cost and concerns about the way veal is raised. It does seem to be making a return, however, and Innsteg does it proud: two slices large enough for either one to fill the plate, and the side dishes are what you'd expect from a good Bavarian restaurant. The view down the River Inn alone is worth the trip.

To find Innsteg, walk down Bahnhofstrasse until it bends left towards the Danube. Turn right instead past the Bayerische Löwe (see above) and up towards the main city bus station. Turn left at the large square and walk past the fountains, then continue downhill past the University church to the last road before the River Inn, Innstrasse. A left turn on Innstrasse takes you past the Innsteg itself, for which the café is named—a pedestrian bridge that used to be a toll bridge (10 Pfennig to walk across, extra if you're pushing a cart). By the way, if you just want a quick beer or snack and a great view of the river, there's a small café at the entrance to the bridge that spreads out to the edge of the river below.

We left Innsteg hoping that Lowenbrauerei Passau has enough such places scattered around the area to survive. Our bus tours showed that it's doing pretty well outside the city, and we've read that they produce beers for other breweries. Still, when we visited the brewery it seemed to have the activity of a brewery a fifth its size.

Finally, though it's a far cry from the great gardens of Munich or Bamberg, our station break, the small **Hacklberg Garten** on Bahnhofstrasse, has a great location, and it's a nice respite from the big store shopping areas that surround it. Operates only in fine weather and serves snacks and cold Hacklberg beer.

Other places to explore

You won't find much else in Passau of great beer interest. Some of the big Munich boys have a few outlets; with only a few exceptions, smaller breweries from the region can't penetrate the market here. But day trip possibilities abound.

If you can, get a copy of the *NeiderBAYERISCHE BIERKULToUR*. If your German is weak you could be fooled into thinking that all of the dozens and dozens of listings have something to do with beer. It's actually just a regional promotional guide that shows you some nice places to visit for sightseeing while you're beer hopping. But it also lists some beer gardens that you might not otherwise find, and it identifies some of the breweries in the region with phone numbers to call for making arrangements for tours. If you decide to rent a car, and designate a driver to avoid the risk of Germany's "no tolerance" DUI laws, much of its content becomes more relevant.

The area has a number of fests throughout the year, with one almost every weekend in the summer. The trick is finding the village of the week, but you can get a good start at www.bayern-und-bier.de. See our section on Festing in the German overview for more information.

Where to stay

If you want to stay a while in the old town area, there are plenty of options of varying tranquility. A few possibilities, including a cheap student hotel, can offer a river view. Our top choice, however, is the **IBB,** a quick hop from the station. We like to drop our bags before exploring and also have the option of catching trains to the myriad drinking destinations within an hour of town. The IBB (four stars) offers clean, comfortable rooms, a better than average breakfast, and a menu of bed pillows, and it may have river views; the atrium rooms are beautifully quiet. The only problem is that it books fully and early. You'll find a room in or near Passau if you show up before the tourist office closes, but this is one of the cities where we strongly recommend some advance planning and a reservation in hand.

What to see

This isn't Munich, you're not going to want to spend a week here wallowing in art and music, but you can fill a couple of days very nicely while you work through the beer halls. The glass museum is worth a look if you fancy such things, and there's a historical museum in the Oberhaus, the large fortress-castle overlooking the city. Frequent buses spare you the walk up the hill.

By far the most famous tourist attraction in the city is the river confluence that brought settlers here in the first place. Down at the end of the old town, at the end of a long wedge-shaped park, it's a genuine three-rivers meeting. Pittsburgh kind of cheats: where only two rivers join, the Allegheny and Monongahela, Pennsylvanians give the merger a new name altogether (the Ohio) and call it three. In Passau, however, there are three distinct rivers that meet almost at the same point, as the Danube is joined by the Inn and the Ilz. The Ilz isn't going to make anyone's first team in the fluvial league, but it's a good-sized, lively creek that charges into the Danube from the left. To see it, go to the Danube side of the peninsula and peer between the cruise liners of staggering length that tie up along the shore. On the other hand, the view where the Danube meets the Inn at the end of the point is unobstructed and fairly dramatic. The Danube is truly blue and shows in strong contrast to the muddy, shallow Inn.

On your way through the old town, don't miss the most impressive structure in the city, Dom St. Stephan, St. Stephen's Cathedral. It's worth the climb. Do all you can to catch an organ concert—weekdays at noon and only 4€. Get there early: though there are over 600 seats, they can fill fast. It's possibly the largest cathedral organ in the world, though the title is as hotly contested as it is ill-defined. The organ is actually five independent but connected instruments that are played from a single console and feature 233 stops and almost 18,000 pipes. St. Stephan is a huge space, but the organ totally fills it with sound. It's hard to identify even where the music is coming from, and the intensity is hard to describe. If you're ever run over by a freight train that plays Bach, these would be the last sounds you heard. The cathedral is worth a look even without the organ. Baroque on its way to Rococo, the ornamentation is symmetrical in overall form, but every detail is individual and exquisite.

Still have time? Try the Domschatz und Diözesanmuseum (Museum of the Cathedral and Diocese), the Museum of Modern Art, the Roman Museum, or the large 19th century Ferdinand Wagner paintings in the Town Hall. And now, surely, it's time for a beer.

Scams

Oh, please. We suppose if you wear plaid shorts and a sign saying "please rip me off" someone will, but you really have to work at it. However, when you book a hotel, check to be sure your room has a window…on the wall.

Day trips

Day tripping out of Passau ranks within the best in Germany. You can tour a brewery, run into more beers than you can comfortably sample in a day, visit the Stiegl beer garden in Linz, Austria, or swill beer in a hall once occupied by monks. Here are our top choices.

The view from Brother Hans's cell

Monastery Aldersbach brewery and hotel

This is our top pick and a must on your beer bucket list. From Passau, take the train to Vilshofen. Frequent buses (especially frequent on schooldays, which stretch into July in Germany) leave from the Bahnhof. Take the bus towards Aidenbach and get off at the Pfarrgarten stop at Aldersbach, where you've called [+49 (0) 85 43/ 96 04-0] and made a reservation for the evening. If you're early enough, head for the 1:30 PM brewery tour—it's the only one of the day. But even if you miss it, you'll still have plenty to do. Your room is a former monk's chamber, plain but surprisingly spacious, the size reduced a bit by the much more recently added toilet and shower. The lines of the ceiling and walls are simple but attractive, and the old wooden floor makes you feel like Brother Hans might have been there last week. Some of the views of the courtyard and church are stunningly beautiful. Open the window and listen. Birds. No cars, no planes, and, if you're lucky, no voices.

Also no telephone, no TV (there's one in a lounge somewhere—pray for directions), no Internet, and no cell phone coverage within the walls. But plenty of beer and good basic food that was good enough for the monks and will be good enough for you.

Take the tour of the place, and take your time. The church is worth giving some time to reflect, meditate, and think about those for whom this is home. Pictures of the current year's confirmation class remind you that this is a parish church for some people who have no idea how lucky they are. If you've missed the tour of the current brewery, no harm. For 5€ you can take your own tour of the previous brewery that is now a museum. It's easy to follow and you can go at your own pace. Somehow even the brewery museum fits the sense of reflection that the entire complex exudes. When you've had your fill of brewery days gone by, it's time to drink 21st century monastery beer.

The beer is best in the Stüberl, a modestly sized, historic beer hall that drips with atmosphere. Beer comes from a wooden keg, and even on a weekday evening you'll be sharing space with lots of locals. You want that company—it keeps the beer fresh. The only food is a big basket of fresh pretzels and breads, but you're allowed to bring your own in. There's a small supermarket directly across the street from the monastery where you can put together a more than adequate picnic.

For a more complete meal, the Café serves three meals a day. It's monk-simple in decoration and atmosphere, but it fits the monastic concept well. The menu is small,

Blessings of St. Gambrinus

but it does feature seasonal specials in addition to the required schnitzels. It's a mom and pop operation (actually it seemed like a daughter and pop operation), but you'll get a good welcome and a good meal before you return to your cell. If you've planned ahead, the gift shop that leads to the museum sells Aldersbacher beers that you can't get in the beer hall or the café. They chill quite well in the cold Bavarian water in the sink in your room.

There's nothing flashy about this place, though it's a little bit touristy. Neither the beers nor the food nor the room are the best we've ever encountered, but all in all, it was one of our very best beer adventures ever. Don't miss it.

Vilshofen

Sometimes we like to just find a small town where tourists don't go and we can get stared at a bit for taking notes on beers—it reminds us of how it felt in the old days before hordes of Beerhunters and Ratebeerers made beer geekdom fashionable. Vilshofen fills the bill beautifully. It's an easy 15-minute train hop from Passau on the hourly express to Munich. Truly a small town, with a brewery healthy enough to operate a few easy-to-find Gasthausen, it's a beautiful place to get away from the English language and soak up some good suds.

To find the beer, go straight out of the station down the hill, turn left on the main road at the McDonald's, and then take a right shortly after, over the bridge and towards the spires of the old town. The **Wolferstetter** brewery, uphill on your first left, is a big enough operation to sell a few beers in Passau itself, but its main focus is in its own back yard. You can drink most days at the brewery Gasthof next to the brewery with a view of the valley below, or take the tiny tunnel-like passage down the hill from the brewery to the main street and settle in to one of the outside tables at the Gastatte Wolferstetter.

Wolferstetter brews good beers with only an occasional misstep. The best are Weizens; the Leichtes Weizen is another good example of the style from a region that does them well and the Dunkles Weizen is a fine blend of roast, clove, banana, and lemon.

As good as the beers are, the best part about this visit is the setting. Busch Gardens couldn't create a "typical German street" any more effectively. Vilshofen is also the gateway for our major expedition to Aldersbach above, and you can catch buses there for other brewing towns as well.

Hutthurm

A pleasant bus ride out of Passau to Hutthurm is a great lunch expedition. Catch the bus in front of the Passau Bahnhof. (There are also buses to Hutthurm from the central terminal, but they are less frequent and not as easy to spot.) Hop off at Marktplatz and wander uphill a bit to the **Hutthurmer Bayerwald Brauerei.** The Bräustübl is another example of the increasingly hard-to-find brewery restaurants that used to be a fixture in every small town. It has recently changed its closing day from Tuesday to Wednesday, so you might want to call and see if this Ruhetag stayed where it was put.

But if you're going to go to Hutthurm, call at least two days before and try to arrange a tour. It's a good example of a local brewery that's making it in a globalized competitive world. Some of the old fermentation tanks attest to the brewery's history, but much of it has been renovated in recent years. The young brewmaster learned to brew at Schneider's big brewery in Kelheim, and he's in charge of a fast-growing operation. Watch for the addition of some Amarillo hops in one or two of the specialty brews—he doesn't use them in American quantities, but you can spot the subtle orange-tangerine Amarillo signature if you look for it. The new fermenting area is a modern wonder. You only see the base of the large conical fermenters, but the pipe work is wondrous. Ellie thought it looked like an old Word Perfect screensaver. Any Hutthurmer beers you can't find at the Gasthaus are probably available in the Getränkemarkt-supermarket across the street. Look for the sign that points you down a small drive. The short bus trip back into Passau will get you there in plenty of time for an evening at a beer garden or hall.

Prague

Quick orientation

Prague stretches on both sides of a big bend of the Vltava River, dominated by the astonishing loom of the Castle. The influx of Western cash in the past 25 years has turned a once shabby downtown only hinting at past elegance into a sparkling and beautiful city (admittedly with a *lot* of Western chain names).

You'll probably arrive at Praha Hlavní Nádraží, the main station. If you walk out the main entrance, you'll be pointed towards the old town. Keep going more or less straight, and you'll cross the river into the area below the castle.

While the station has all the amenities you'd expect, and more, it can be very crowded. The Czech Republic (they prefer to call it just Czech) is not on the euro; if you arrive without cash, you can beat the long lines at the exchange bureau by heading into town and looking for an ATM. Hotels abound beyond the park that stretches downhill in front of the station.

The view from the Castle

Three huge brewing companies dominate the beer scene in Prague. While that limits the variety of beer, the up side is that the beer you do find ranges from pretty good to very good.

Station break

Happily, no more than a 10-minute walk from the station takes you to Ferdinanda, an outlet of a brewery that's an hour or so outside Prague. From the main station exit, go downhill and around the outside of the park on the left side and you'll be on Politických vězňů. Continue past the Wall Street Café (yes, really), turn right on Opletalova, and immediately, at number 24, descend into Ferdinanda.

The menu isn't large, but the food is good and affordable. The Ferdinanda beers come from a brewery in Benešov named for the Archduke Franz Ferdinand, whose assassination triggered the first World War. We found the ordinary beers to be, well, ordinary, but the Ferdinand Sedm Kulí Tmavý 13° was a gem. Sedm Kuli translates to Seven Bullets, the number that killed the Archduke; in this beer they refer to the seven spices used to give it a remarkably distinctive taste. The beauty of the beer is that the spices are very soft, with only a bit of a coriander flavor identifiable. A rich, smooth caramel malt dominates the flavor.

History and culture

Prague lies on the path of several ancient trading routes, but its real history began with the castle's construction near the end of the 9th century. By the late Middle Ages the city had developed into a flourishing commercial and industrial center. Similarities to Dutch society are more than superficial. Like the Dutch, the Czech embraced Protestantism early as a way of distancing themselves from Catholic Hapsburg rule. While Prague recovered fairly quickly from the Hussite wars of the 15th century, the same was not true for the 1618–1648 Thirty Years War.

For some reason, Praguers have attempted to solve a number of political disputes by throwing officials of various sorts out of windows. The first recorded "Defenestration of Prague" occurred in 1419; the most recent was a part of the Communist takeover of 1949. In between was the most famous. In 1618 Bohemians tried to gain more autonomy within the Holy Roman Empire by electing a Protestant king instead of the usual Austrian, Catholic, Hapsburg. Austrian emissaries who were sent to negotiate a settlement were heaved out a window of the castle. Catholic accounts claim angels saved their lives; secular sources give more credit to the dung heap they landed in. The Hapsburgs' military response developed into the Thirty Years War, a conflict that eventually included countries as far away as Spain, France, and Sweden. It didn't last long in Bohemia, though; the Battle of White Mountain (Bílá hora) ended the Czech phase of the war in 1620. The Hapsburgs resettled some of the leaders and killed others, and the era of Bohemian glory was over.

The rise of nationalism in the 19th century led to a revival of the Czech language and Czech customs and paved the way for the creation of Czechoslovakia in 1919.

Russian occupation after World War II established a Communist state, but ultimately the Russians didn't find the Czechs any easier to control than the Hapsburgs had. In 1968 Alexander Dubček led a "Prague Spring" that attempted to create "socialism with a human face." The implication of what *other* kinds of faces socialism wore was more than the Russians were willing to tolerate, and a Warsaw Pact invasion in August ended Dubček's rule.

There were silver linings to even the harshest years of Communist dictatorship, however. Cheap labor made it possible for Pilsner Urquell to use 19th century brewing methods to produce nectar fit for Olympus, but still to compete in a 20th century economy. Communist rulers may have made life tough for Czechs, but Prague was something of a haven for tourists from other Warsaw Pact countries. During a 1979 visit to Pilsen, we were stunned by how subdued the beer halls were. We realized that getting drunk in public posed the risk of saying the wrong thing to the wrong person. At Prague's U Fleků, however, raucous revelers seemed to be an exception to the rule. "Not at all," our English-speaking neighbor informed us. "Listen to them. They're East Germans. The Czech secret police couldn't care less what *they* say about Communism."

The "Velvet Revolution" in 1989 ended Communism and reestablished Czechoslovak independence, though the Slovaks didn't feel so independent and broke away in 1993. The Czech Republic is now part of the European Union.

Beer styles and drinking culture

It is perhaps unsurprising that a people who worked so hard for so long to win political independence would treasure their own distinctive beers. Until the 19th century, though, Czech beers were like most others in Northern Europe: dark, murky brews best served in ceramic or wooden vessels to hide the unpleasant appearance. By the 1840s, however, mass-produced glass and breakthroughs in brewing gave brewers both the incentive and the ability to clean up their acts.

Clearer, bottom-fermented beers emerged from the great brewing centers such as Vienna and Munich, but it was the Czechs of Pilsen who grabbed the gold ring. Recognizing that the city had become known for abysmally poor beer, the leading brewers joined together in 1842 to set and enforce high quality standards. The golden, clear, crisply bitter beer that emerged soon gained recognition around the world as "Pilsner beer." A belated attempt at appellation control failed miserably, and brewers throughout Europe and the United States were brewing up "pilsner beer" by the tun within the decade.

Most Czech breweries produce beers similar in style to Plzeňský Prazdroj, the "original" pilsner. A light beer of average (5% ABV) strength is usually called Světlý Ležák. If you can find a "tank" bar, it means the beer is unpasteurized and delivered in bulk to restaurants that turn it over quickly enough to ensure quality. Don't limit yourself to the light beers, though. Tmavý Ležák refers to a dark lager, with less of a pronounced hop bite than pilsners and all of a lager's evenness. Polotmavý Ležák is a "half dark"—not a black-and-tan mixture, but a purpose brewed dark amber. Rychtář's version is brewed with added sugar and ends with an unusually dry finish.

The sixpack of drinking experiences

The top beer bar in the city is the **Pivovar Club** (Kriikova 17). A short walk from the Florenc metro stop in an undistinguished building in an undistinguished block shines a real gem. They don't brew their own any more, if they ever did, though an apparently functional brew-on-premise kit sits in the window. But the draw is the range of beers from around the country. Six rotating taps is, by Czech standards, a true mega-bar, and if you hang around or return, you're likely to be treated to another choice or two. (Two had changed the day we were there.) It's a small place, so it's advisable to get there early to secure a seat. In the unlikely event that the drafts seem limited, several hundred bottles in the coolers and on the walls provide plenty of additional choice. A good many of the bottles are foreign—they include Sierra Nevada and Sam Adams—but there are more than enough Czech choices to keep you busy for a few days. Carry them back to your hotel or out to the riverbank if you want.

There are several brewpubs in or near the central area of Prague (old and new towns). Our remaining top choices all brew their own beer. Often Czech brewpubs try to lure customers away from the pils pavilions by featuring particularly distinctive beers.

With great reluctance, we admit you probably have to visit the granddaddy of all brewpubs—**U Fleků.** Go there, have a beer, and get the heck out. You'll be drinking with a few Brits, some Americans, a good many Japanese, and scads of Russians. If you can find a Czech in the place, he's with some out-of-town guests. Why don't Czechs go any more? It's vastly more expensive than anywhere else in town, the place could offer a tutorial on swindling, and the atmosphere—with an accordion and tuba—is better suited to a Munich Schwemme than a Prague brewery. But it's an institution, claiming to be the world's oldest brewpub, which perhaps it is. The dark lager isn't bad. We don't think it's particularly special, but people who have spent much longer than we have in the Czech Republic think it's one of the world's best.

(and 3a). So, having paid your dues, go to another brewpub and have a beer with some Czechs. **Pivovar Dům** (Ječná 14) is crowded and certainly interesting. They featured a nettle beer when we were there last. The food comes in your choice of two sizes: regular, meaning huge, and "Lux," meaning enough for a football team. **Novoměstý Pivovar** is another central choice, providing a couple of basic beers that come with a variety of flavors that seem to be added at the bar.

Our top pick for a downtown brewpub is **U Medvídků,** a really old pub that's a really new brewpub. But they take brewing very seriously, aging their strong beer, X-Beer, for better than half a year in wood barrels. They claim it's the strongest beer in the world at 12.6% (33.48 Balling), which doesn't come close to the powerhouses produced by Dogfish Head, Sam Adams, or BrewDog, but it's an exceptional brew and one of the few really good strong beers we encountered in Czech. Deep, dark, and distinctive, it's heavy but interesting, with flavors of figs and surprising orange tones. It has a clean herbal hoppiness as it drinks, truly a beer worth taking some time over. Their 13° Oldgott semidark gets good reviews, but we were disappointed: it was loaded with diacetyl flavors suggesting popcorn butter and, later, butterscotch. We may have just hit an off day. But there's more to enjoy beyond the house beers. Medvídků features several beers from Ceské Budějovice, the "real" Budweiser, including a 16° (6.25% ABV) strong gold lager that certainly isn't your uncle Augie's brew. You have your choice of a really nice bar, several rooms, and a garden out back, but you may not get the same selection in each of the locations.

Public transportation in Prague can take you to several brewpubs; our favorite streetcar excursion is to **U Bulovky Richter Pub** (Bulovka 17), a long ride on Tram 24 or 25 to the Bulovka stop. (Fortunately, most trams have signs that indicate the next stop and some have a changing display that lists the next several.) When you get off, cross the tracks and head down Bulovka past an apartment building to number 17, and you've reached the Richter Brewery. It's Czech, but could be German, both in its wood and brass décor and in its beer: Weizen features prominently. You won't get to speak English here—there isn't even an English menu—but "gulash" is easy enough to spot and you're more likely to be pleasantly surprised than disappointed if you just hold your breath and point to something on the menu. You'll almost certainly be the only tourists there, and the welcoming staff seems to appreciate the effort you've put in to find the place. Best of all, while you're having an evening off from English, you'll be savoring some of the best unfiltered light lager in the Czech Republic. They don't call it a Keller Pils, but that's what it is—dry, chalky, and ultimately bitter with plenty of hop character.

Pivovar u Bulovky / Richter Brewery Pub

A 21st century newcomer to Prague's brewing scene, **Klášterní Pivovar Strahov** (Strahovské nádvoří 301/10) is a bit of a ways outside the central area, but well worth the pilgrimage. New breweries throughout Germany and Czech tend to produce similar yeasty, chalky lagers that are often rushed to the serving tanks to meet demand in high season. All four of the Klášterní beers we tasted, however, were in great condition and a couple of them ranked among the best brewpub beers we've had in Europe. Their Hefeweizen, Sv. Norbert Pšeničné Pivo, was a vibrant, tangy, and estery version of the style with lots of lemon and lemon candy from the wheat malt. Sv. Norbert Specialni Tmavý Pivo is a dark lager, more or less in the Munich style, featuring unusually flavorful dark malts that evoke coffee and chocolate before some herbal hops emerge in the aftertaste. Their India Pale Ale was the beer that Bob dreamed of producing before Ellie insisted on the better balance that characterized Tuppers' Hop Pocket Ale. Nevertheless, an intense caramel foundation provides a good stage for the oily and sweet hops in a beer you just don't expect to find in Prague.

The Tmavý Pivo at Klášterni Šenk

While you're in the area, seek out a couple of other drinking gems. **Klášterni Šenk** (Markétská 1/28) stands on the grounds of a monastery dating back over a thousand years. It features beers from Klášter Hradiště that you won't easily find elsewhere, but probably any decent beer would taste special as you listen to the church bells peal through the small but beautifully kept beer garden. Almost across the street is **U Klášťera,** an affordable and comfortable stop on a cloister crawl. The selection of a half dozen draft beers included three that we had never seen before, including a couple of pleasant Tmavý Ležáks.

Other places to explore

We love floating bars anywhere, but a European river setting is so special that we're willing to put up with some pretty ordinary beers for the pleasure of the view. A number of barges moored along the Vltava's banks provide drinks, accommodations, and even art. One harbors **Kavárna S.p.l.a.v.,** which is easy to spot on the east side of the river near Žofín Palace and Slovanský Ostrov island. You can eat or just drink—the beers are pretty ordinary, but the river view is superb. Be prepared to pay in cash.

If you have time, don't miss Ferdindanda's spiced dark lager (see "Station breaks" above).

Several brewpubs can be reached by a short train trip or extended streetcar run. They include **Pivovar Berounský Medvěd** (see Pilsen day trip below) and the **Bašta Brewpub** well south of town near the Vršovice train station.

Kavárna S.p.l.a.v.: life doesn't get much better

Where to stay

The lines for the hotel booking office at the station can look like bread lines in Moscow in the 1950s. We recommend skipping them and just heading out into the city. Prague is still a bargain for eating and drinking—not so much for sleeping. If you get in early enough and are willing to wear out a bit of shoe leather, however, you should be able to find something that, given the pittance you're going to spend on beer here, leaves your budget intact. Alternatively, go online and find a deal. Be careful with location—don't book "near the station" unless you're quite sure what station they're referring to.

What to see

The Castle is a must. You can buy a variety of packages that get you into various parts of it. Most include the "defenestration window"—they know what they have here. Other buildings are worth the money if you have the time. The grounds are extensive and offer shops and cafés, including some good places to drink if you settle for an ordinary pilsner.

Spend some time exploring the Old Town Square and the surrounding area. From here the Jewish Quarter (Josefov) is an easy walk. Several synagogues are open from 9 to 6 and provide a number of different experiences; a combination ticket makes sense if you plan on seeing most of them. If your time is limited, we recommend you at least try to see the Spanish Synagogue. Better yet, attend one of the frequent concerts; the acoustics are almost as striking as the building itself.

You'll be drawn to the Charles Bridge—the view of the castle is extraordinary. At night when the castle is lit, it's even a more spectacular walk.

The Strahov Monastery would be worth a visit even if it weren't so close to our cloister crawl (experience #6 above). A church has been here since the 13th century, but the lovely current structure is mostly 18th century Baroque. Check the website to avoid visiting on one of its occasional closed days (http://www.strahovskyklaster.cz/).

There's plenty more to fill up days while you wait to begin your nights of drinking. Museums include a museum of miniatures and one describing the Communist experience. The astronomical clock draws crowds to see the Twelve Apostles trot out on the hour. The main tourist office is in the Old Town Hall on the Old Town Square.

Staropramen, an AB InBev-owned company, is the second largest Czech brewer. You'll find the beer all over town, but it's easiest to find the unpasteurized version at the brewery. Two or three English language tours daily can be booked at the company website.

Scams and alerts

Prague is a safe city—for you, if not for your wallet. The Czechs are very good at almost everything they do, and enough of them choose to make money without working for it that it pays to be on guard here.

As mentioned above, U Fleků could hold seminars on skinning customers. The "extra notch on the coaster" trick is one (see "Scams" in Cologne). U Fleků's age-old scheme is to offer shots of schnapps that are "required for the occasion" or "a necessary tradition here" and then charge several times the price of a beer for them. Another is to add a "service charge" for whatever particular part of the restaurant you're in—which is small enough so it's easier to pay it than fight it. If you pay in euros instead of koruna you're going to get socked, far above the standard conversion rate.

Taxis have more ways of scamming you than New York's finest; a hotel clerk advised us that it would be quicker to walk 20 blocks than to try to ride there in a cab that might well travel to your destination via another city. Check the meter to be sure it starts at the correct fare, get an estimate in advance, and whenever possible, call for a cab rather than trying to find one in the street. Even better, use the very good and inexpensive public transportation system. If you have to use a cab, AAA seems to be honest and reliable.

We can't prove this is a setup, but the dial on our scammometer swung pretty hard when two different staff members in our hotel, including the desk clerk (unprompted), told us we "had" to eat in a certain restaurant just down the street. "It will be too crowded for you to get in, so please let *me* make a reservation for you at any time you desire." The restaurant may be fine, the prices may be as good as they say, and maybe, just maybe, both employees really do "frequently eat there [themselves]." We're always suspicious of a recommendation that's made without any idea of what we might be looking for. If a recommender can't show enough empathy to ask a question or two about what we'd like, we're likely to get a canned answer that's no better, and quite probably worse, than an online rating service or what we could find on our own. We've seen a waiter suggest steak to a vegetarian; an unsolicited restaurant recommendation isn't going to be any wiser.

Day trip and excursion

Pilsen

You can visit Pilsen in a day, but you'll have a better experience if you give it an overnight. The main sights are all within walking range, though if the weather is rotten you'll probably want a cab. If you're trying to do it all in a day, check with the brewery for the times of the English-speaking tour.

The Pilsner Urquell tour is our favorite big brewery experience in Europe. The brewery grounds are huge; you'll bus from one part of the tour to another. You'll have a chance to see up close what Western capital has done to transform an aging 19th century brewery into a modern and efficient 21st century business. Beginning in 1993, after its acquisition by the international giant SAB Miller, the brewery began cellaring beer in stainless steel tanks, simplified the fermenting process, and cut the three-month lagering time in half in order to meet global demand. Independent tasting panels failed to find significant differences between the old and new versions of the beer, but purists continue to mourn the loss of the original.

The tour is more informative than most. In addition to the brewing basics, they take the time to explain the triple decoction process that still helps to distinguish Pilsner Urquell from other pilsners. On-premise maltings and exceptionally soft water also contribute to the subtle but distinctive taste. You'll get a good bird's eye view of the vast bottling plant and a good understanding of the "economies of scale" that allow an expensive beer to be obtainable at reasonable prices all over the world.

The highlight of the tour, however, and the reason this tour must be on the beer bucket list, is the trip to the brewery's former aging cellars. Six miles of tunnels below the brewery once held hundreds of huge wooden tuns where the beer was aged for three months or more. You can take an even more extensive tour of the tunnels that ranged under the entire city by booking at the tourist office, but this look is really all you need. At the end of the subterranean ramble you come upon an open wooden fermenter and a couple of the wooden barrels of the type that used to age all Pilsner Urquell. Here in one tiny part of the world is the original "original." You're given a choice of a small cup or a large cup.

The real thing

IMPORTANT: Take the large cup!

The beer from the pitch-lined super barrel is, quite simply, the best lager beer we've ever tasted. The setting had something to do with it—it always does—but the combination of delicacy and depth was unexpected and ambrosial. We wondered to ourselves, as we traveled back to the brewery pub for the end-of-tour samples, why they would allow people to taste this decades-lost definitive example of the style. We realized why a month later in, of all places, Nationals Park in DC. The Pilsner Urquell we bought during that game showed its age a bit, but what struck us was not the predictable differences between this pasteurized import and the elixir we had tasted at the brewery, but the similarities. The brewery is clearly banking that you'll find enough of those similarities to forgive the modern modifications that allow you to drink it at an American baseball game.

Back in town, don't miss the Brewery Museum (Veleslavinova 6), set in an old maltery. An audio guide is hokey beyond words, but provides good information as you make your way through several floors and thousands of artifacts. It's certainly no Smithsonian, but it's substantial enough to take some time. Allow a half a day for the museum and some time in the attached restaurant and beer garden—it's one of the two restaurants in the world where you can sample unfiltered Pilsner Urquell (see below).

There's plenty to see in Pilsen between pilsners. The Cathedral dates to the 13th century and the synagogue is one of the largest in the world. Pilsen is proud of its zoo, and a range of smaller sights includes a museum dedicated to the memory of George Patton.

The beer

Plzeňský Prazdroj is the Czech name for Pilsner Urquell; Prazdroj and Urquell each mean, roughly, "original source." It's the direct descendant of the first pilsner brewed in 1842. The trip to Pilsen allows you to sample the beer in four distinct versions.

The overwhelming majority of the brewery's production is tunnel-pasteurized, a long process that not only kills any bacteria in the beer, but wipes out some of the flavor as well. Some believe the slow pasteurization sets up the beer for oxidation as well, which adds a cardboard-like dullness to what is otherwise a bracingly crisp beer.

If you've had Pilsner Urquell in the U.S., this is what you've had, but it tastes better here before the long boat trip to the States.

Increasingly common is the tank version, sold at bars with "tanková" worked into their names, usually quite prominently. The tank pilsner is unpasteurized and delivered weekly from the brewery. It's not hard to tell the difference between the fresh, crisp tank beer and the stale green bottle you're used to. The lack of pasteurization undoubtedly helps, but another advantage is that the tanks are only installed in bars where the beer turns rapidly, so it's not only better, but fresher than the usual version.

An unfiltered version gives you a chance to get a better idea of what the brewery's proprietary yeast does for the beer. For most of the 20th century, Pilsner Urquell was fermented with a combination of yeasts. One of the 1993 reforms was to replace the blend with a single strain; the brewery claims it is the descendant of the original.

Finally... the brewery tour's brief glimpse of brewing heaven. A crawl that includes all four is a unique liquid educational experience.

Another excursion

You can break your train trip to or from Pilsen with a pleasant stop at **Pivovar Berounský Medvěd** in Beroun. You can see the sign for the brewery from the tracks, but you have to know it's worth getting off the train. A brewery in Beroun started in 1295 and made it to the 1970s. The current operation uses the original names, but is located in a former sugar processing plant. We found the beers exceptionally good for a relatively recent operation. The dark Tmavý may have been the best of a good bunch. It showed a toasted darkness and avoided the caramel flavors that can make a dark beer edgy. Herbal hops balanced well and left the beer amazingly clean. We're impressed with their attention to detail. Double decoction—a two-stage mashing process—is laborious and time-consuming and not really necessary with modern malts, but breweries like this convince us it can still make a difference. The clean, balanced taste is also partly the result of the use of whole flower hops, another expenditure of time and money.

Regensburg

Quick orientation and station breaks

The station is a ways from the center of town. You can catch any of a number of buses, but if you're traveling light, the walk is manageable in decent weather.

A station break isn't obvious here, but if you walk quickly you'll be able to get to the **Kneitinger Keller** just within our 10-minute limit. Find the pedestrian overpass that crosses over the tracks behind the station. On the other side turn left on Friedenstrasse and then a quick right on Galgenbergstrasse and walk uphill. You'll see before you the large former maltery, and the Kneitinger Keller at Galgenbergstrasse 18 is on the right. They have a superb beer garden and it's a fine place to drink the Kneitinger beers we describe below.

The Danube, Stone Bridge, and Dom

History and culture

"Living in Regensburg is like waking up every morning in an amusement park," the fish roaster told us. A better job and duties to his family had taken him to Straubing, about a half hour away, but he said he's never stopped trying to find ways of getting back. Quite a number of tourists who visit the city feel the same way.

Rides at this amusement park are limited to boat trips on the Danube River, but the rich history of the city pours from the walls, squares, and, of course, breweries. A UNESCO World Heritage Site, Regensburg is the oldest city on the Danube, and it shows. A surviving Roman arch bears witness to the city's role as an important Roman outpost from the first century AD. Although the pedestrian "Stone Bridge" has acquired some new stones since it was built about 1,100 years later, one can easily imagine using it to cross the Danube in the early Middle Ages, when Regensburg was the capital of Bavaria. Regensburg reached its zenith in the heyday of the Holy Roman Empire. The city's enormous cathedral is testament to both its former wealth and political influence.

The Holy Roman Empire, as Voltaire noted, wasn't Roman at all, wasn't very holy, and wasn't really an empire either. The Emperor had to get himself elected, and although the Hapsburgs learned how to do that pretty well, the power of local bishops and princes collectively was often much more significant than that of the central government. Religious wars forced the Emperor to allow each prince to choose the religion for his territory, confirming not only the religious power but the political power of local leaders. The situation in Regensburg was even more complicated than most; even as the town became Protestant, the enormously influential Catholic bishopric remained, and three Catholic monasteries preserved Catholicism within the city's territory. The point of all this for beer drinkers is that at a time when many European countries were coming together to form national cultures, Germany was breaking down into smaller component parts. The intense local and regional loyalties that developed have lasted and have slowed the brewing consolidation that has engulfed the rest of the planet over the past 50 years.

With over a hundred thousand residents, Regensburg still has a small-town feel. The local gentry, the Thurn und Taxis family, have been here for centuries. Traditional German taverns have to compete with new ethnic and themed restaurants, but most of the tourists are German and the forces of globalization seem to be on a very short leash.

Beer styles and drinking culture

For much of the relatively recent past, Regenburg's beer scene was dominated by the Thurn und Taxis brewery. T&T was big enough to be an attractive target for Paulaner, which drank it up for breakfast one morning in 1996 and still produces Thurn u. Taxis beers in Munich. Happily, a handful of other regional breweries survived consolidation—we think because they were just small enough not to be high on Paulaner's menu.

Beers in Regensburg are mostly mainstream in character; the styles are those you'll find in much of Bavaria. While you can find some distinctive interpretations and unusual brews, these variations have more to do with the individual breweries than with any particular local influence.

We're not sure why, but towns that preserve their history tend to preserve their breweries, even relatively new ones. Regensburg holds on to its past as well as any city in Germany. It makes our top 24 European beer cities because it features very typically Bavarian breweries and brewery taverns and plenty of them. Three commercial breweries and two fine brew pubs make it a city we love returning to.

The sixpack of drinking experiences

Gaststätte Spitalgarten (St.-Katharinen-Platz 1) is one of our favorite beer gardens in Europe. The garden has been jammed each time we've gone, but patient lurking can secure you a waterside table. Drink in one of the best views of Regensburg: across the sprawling Danube, the spot-lit Cathedral towers over the old town and the ancient Stone Bridge. Nighttime is the best, but the view is always special. If you get there during the day, have a look around; a good deal of the historic hospital complex is visible from the outside, and some of the buildings have been here for a long while. Look in the basement windows that face the Biergarten to catch a dimly lit glimpse of fermenting tanks. The food is pretty standard brewery Gasthof cooking, but competent and tasty. A small range of house brews includes a pleasantly sweet Helles, a softly estery Hefeweizen, and a sweetly leathery and roasty Dunkel. We would love to love the beers more than we do: they're fine if a bit sweet, but unremarkable. Nevertheless, this is our first night's evening next time we return.

All of the mainstream Thurn u. Taxis beers that we know of now come from Munich. Nevertheless, a bit of the early brewery remains and now boasts Regensburg's best brew pub. **Fürstliches Brauhaus Thurn u. Taxis** (Waffnergasse 6-8) is decidedly upscale; you can bust a budget over dinner, but simpler fare is served as well. Try the range of beers in a sampler of cutely appropriate glasses before you splurge on larger portions (see the cover). Most of the beers are solid, though we might have had a more pleasant time of it had we skipped the fruited lager. The Brauhaus Weisse is distinctive, with a soft roast and plenty of hefe esters.

Brauereigaststätte Kneitinger am Arnulfsplatz (Arnulfsplatz 3) sits in the shadow of the Kneitinger brewery downtown and provides a better selection of their beers than the Keller on the hill. A range of rooms include a sort of outside passage, but despite its size, the place is frequently packed. Dinner reservations are recommended, though the two of us have always been able to squeeze in somewhere. Menu choices beyond the basics change daily; this brewery inn would probably make it just as a restaurant on its own. A small range of beers is joined occasionally by a seasonal, but most of what pours is the Pils and Dunkel. Of the two, we prefer the Pils: it's one of southern Bavaria's better examples of the style. The malt shows more than it would across the Czech border but slightly spicy but soft (würzig) hops make it more-ish.

Inside Fürstliches Brauhaus Thurn und Taxis

For the other Kneitinger experience, climb up the hill behind the train station to their **Keller** at Galgenbergstrasse 18. You won't find anything here that you can't get at the brewery, but the experience is wonderfully German. There's a tavern inside and an enormous party hall, but the best part of the complex is a sprawling garden with room for you and 999 of your new best friends. The food is good solid Bavarian fare. Brotzeiten include some local specialties that could feature in the Travel Channel's "Bizarre Foods"—try them if you dare. The Keller specialties are more conventional. If it comes from a pig, they've got it; a turkey schnitzel provides some variety, but we didn't see much for vegetarians. Liters of Kneitinger Pils and Dunkel Export flow freely.

Off the beaten path, but worth the effort to reach, is **Bischofshof Bräustuben** at 50 Dechbettenerstr. Most of the Regensburg breweries produce a small range of beers, but Bischofshof stands as a notable exception. On our last visit to the Bräustüberl Wirtshaus, at the brewery site, the eight beers we had not seen before amused us most of the afternoon. We think they've pulled back their range a bit since then, but you should still find much more choice here than elsewhere in town. The Bischofshof range is further enhanced by the line of beers they brew for Kloster Weltenberg. While the beers specifically labeled "Kloster" are brewed at the monastery, the other "Weltenberger" beers come from Regensburg and are well worth trying. Food is pretty standard and pretty good. If you're going for the food, unless you are vegetarian, try to go on Sunday when a special roast menu features an expanded array of roasted and grilled meats. If you're just there for the beer, you can drink every day from 7 AM to 11 PM.

The **Regensburger Weissbräuhaus** (Schwarze-Bären-Strasse 6) was a part of a small German chain when we first visited, but it has emerged as an independent brewpub with a small but impressive range of beers. The Hell and Dunkel are a cut above new-pub standards, but the Weissbier Hell is exceptional. A full-bodied Hefeweizen features an early creamy clove that joins a soft lemony wheat that increases as it drinks. The Dunkelweizen is almost as good, blending a good roast with clove and lemony wheat. The woody décor makes the restaurant look older than it is, and you can get a good look at the brew kettle from the two levels. Food is good German pub fare. While the building isn't a destination in itself, it is a very comfortable place to drink some of the area's best wheat beers.

Where to stay

The **Hotel Goliath am Dom** came highly recommended and did not disappoint. A rooftop patio gives views of the surrounding hills, and many of the rooms overlook the bustling street below. The old town location is wonderfully central—a stone's throw from the cathedral and a short walk to the river and the historic Stone Bridge that leads to Spital.

Bischofshof's tap, Bischofshof Bräustuben (50 Dechbettenerstr.), has rooms at about 100€ if you plan on drinking yourself to sleep. It's nearly a half hour hike to either the station or the center of town, so plan on some cabbing in bad weather.

If you're using Regensburg as a base for exploring, you might want to consider staying in a less romantic but more convenient hotel near the station. The Star Inn is big and chain-like, with rooms not much larger than those on sleeping cars of the trains it overlooks. Nevertheless, for about 100€ double including a good breakfast, it's a functional base for exploring the area. The Ibis is to the right of the station, up the stairs next to the bridge: slightly farther, but it's crawling distance from the Kneitinger Keller.

What to see

The tourist office is not far from the Cathedral—you pass by the Hotel Goliath on the way. Stop there early to pick up the local guidebook that will give you opening hours of the main sites. The Cathedral is a must, but there are also some very quirky museums (a museum of snuff?) and some art you won't find easily back home. The Thurn und Taxis family traces its ancestry from 12th century Italy to the current Prince Albert II; he and his family still live in the fabulous Schloss Emmeram, which is open for tourists, but at 500+ rooms you're not likely to run into him.

Don't focus so much on the sights, though, that you miss the main sight, and that's the old town itself. One of the best preserved medieval towns in Europe, the city is a UNESCO World Heritage Site for good reason. You can just wander and stare on

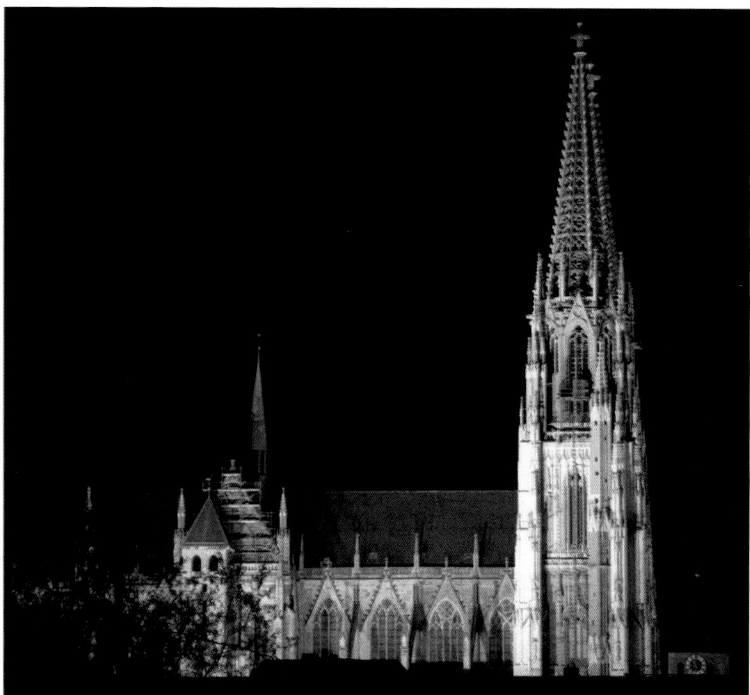

St. Peter Cathedral

your way from pub to pub. Many of the buildings date from the 11th to 13th centuries, and you can see the growth of the city in the architecture spreading out from the oldest areas.

In good weather, head down to the Danube near the Stone Bridge and find Die Historische Wurstkuchl zu Regensburg. The only decision you have to make in this 900-year-old sausage emporium is how many of the small Regensburger links you want; sauerkraut and mustard round out the meal. Most of the tables are out front on the riverside. If you want a quiet time to digest, you can book an afternoon Danube cruise nearby.

Scams and alerts

If you can find a scam, let us know. You may run into a gypsy or three—who probably aren't nearly as poor as they look—but Regensburg still has a small town feel to it.

Day trips and excursions

Regensburg and Passau are just over an hour's rail journey apart. You could make Passau a day trip if there weren't so much to do there. Vilshofen, one of our Passau day trips, is easy to reach from Regensburg. You can also get a direct train to Landshut, one of our Munich day trips, in barely more than a half hour.

Straubing

If you time it right, the Straubing Gäubodenvolksfest, a short railroad hop away, is one of the larger regional fests. It's not Oktoberfest in scope, but it's big enough to give you a good sense of what Oktoberfest is about. At least four brewery tents give you a chance to test your liver as you sample the range of fest and weizen beers. Our favorite is the local Karmeliten Festbier; unsurprisingly, it's sweet, but some late crisp hops provide exceptional balance for the style and keep it appealing as it drinks. The fest runs for 10 days and includes the second week of August. (http://www.volksfest-straubing.de/startseite.html)

Landau

The very typically German town of Landau an der Isar is just over an hour away if you make the tight connection at Plattling. Empty buildings attest to tough economic times, but if you scale the impressive hill the town is perched on, there's an imposing church tower and a fine view over the river and lower town. The good news is that you don't have to mountaineer to get the beer. The **Gasthaus zur Post,** at the foot of the hill, is the main outlet for the Krieger beers that are brewed just down the road. This is another brewery that we would be happily surprised to see still brewing a decade from now, but they're producing very typical beers from the area and the Gasthaus is a pleasant place to eat and drink—and, if you choose, stay—at a genuine bargain price. The center of town is just about a mile from the Bahnhof (not counting *up*): exit the station, turn right along Bahnhofstrasse, parallel to the

Guess who doesn't get any beer

tracks, to Straubingerstrasse—there's a cluster of biggish stores on the left. Turn left, go 500 meters or so, angle left at the traffic circle and across the handsome bridge over the Isar, then follow Hauptstrasse as it wriggles up the hill. It will take you past the brewery and up to the Post, which cuddles into the hill just where the main road kinks right for the *real* climb. Be warned that the Post doesn't open until 5:30 PM and closes altogether on Mondays.

Salzburg

Quick orientation

Our first experience with Salzburg was in 1968. We had seen other European cities, but none like this one. For years after, we said, with the naive assurance of 20-some years of life, it was the most beautiful city on earth. Things change and opinions mature, and now that we realize we haven't been to Kathmandu or Agra, we simply say: this is the most beautiful city we have ever seen.

At a quick (and scenic) 2-hour train hop from Munich, it's possible to make Salzburg a day trip if you only want to see the castle and feast in Europe's best beer garden. But if you're short on time, we suggest you save this city for a time when you can allow at least a few days to breathe in the history and drink in the beer. This is an Imperial city of sessionable beers; savor them.

The Salzach River bisects the city. The newer town, on the northern side, includes the Bahnhof. The Kapuzinerberg squeezes this segment of the city into a narrow band leading to the old town across several bridges, many of them pedestrian only. As you

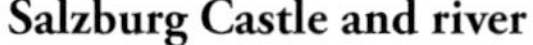

Salzburg Castle and river

face the old town before crossing the river, the castle sits high on one side of Mönchsberg to the left; the Augustiner monastery with Europe's best beer garden under it is to your right, just below that face of Mönchsberg.

It's a wonderfully walkable city, but you'll save some time by getting to know the numerous and frequent buses. A 24 hour pass, which you can get from a machine at the train station, costs 3.30€ (see "Scams" below). Buy passes in advance while you're at the station—they're hard to find elsewhere. Note that your desired route might not run on Sundays.

Station breaks

Outside the station (which may, finally, be finished reconstruction by the time you read this), walk directly away from it past a small grove of trees to a line of modernish stores. "The Corner" is… on the right corner. It has four of the local Stiegl beers on tap and has given us a good welcome.

At the outside edge of our station break limit is Restaurant StieglBräu (Rainerstrasse 14). Gulp Stiegl beers to wash down typical if not memorable food in a place you'd die to find at home. Time how long it takes to get there, so you don't miss your train on the return to the station. To find it, leave the station and walk towards the center of town (you'll see all the buses going by). After a few blocks the road cuts under the railroad tracks, and StieglBräu is on the left as you emerge. You can bypass the line at the tourist office to grab a free map that makes it easy to find.

History and culture

Until the 19th century, Salzburg and the surrounding area, while part of the Holy Roman Empire, had closer ties to Bavaria than to the lands making up the modern state of Austria. Bavarian princes subsidized the growth of the city and it had become a major ecclesiastical center by the late Middle Ages. Even before the Renaissance, Salzburg's archbishops were its political as well as religious rulers.

The Holy Roman Empire was never much more united than today's United Nations, and Salzburg grew in part by waging wars against other member states. Archbishop Wolf Dietrich von Raitenau burned his imperial fingers in a loss to Berchtesgaden in 1611, ending the fun of expansion for good. When he wasn't waging war, however, he redesigned the city and started the beautiful Mirabell Palace. His successor began the new Cathedral and the Heilbronn Palace, and by the mid-17th century, the old town looked much as it does now.

In 1816, roughly day before yesterday in European terms, Salzburg formally joined Austria, but a lasting Bavarian influence remained. Much of Salzburg's history afterwards paralleled that of Vienna. If you're only going to Salzburg, read the history section in our Vienna chapter anyway.

Salzburg was one of Hitler's earliest acquisitions, and the seven years of Nazi occupation weren't the proudest in this proud country's past. The Austrians managed the postwar years bravely and wisely, however. Though occupied by Soviet troops, Austria steered a neutral path in the early years of the Cold War that eventually convinced the Russians they could safely call their men home. Revisionist historians use this example to maintain that Stalin was more flexible in foreign policy than most Americans gave him credit for.

After the war, Austria, though no longer an Empire, reestablished itself as a center of culture and pleasure that gradually made the country a postwar tourist mecca. Salzburg's beers, breweries, and beer gardens featured in the city's revival. People flock to Salzburg now for the music, but the beer is more than good enough to keep them happy once they're here.

History and music intertwine in many ways in Salzburg, but two very different highlights will greet you almost everywhere. Wolfgang Amadeus Mozart was born here in the 18th century, and Salzburg and the surrounding mountains were the setting for "The Sound of Music," based on the true story of the Von Trapp family at the beginning of the Second World War.

Beer styles and drinking culture

Austrian beers are softer than their German equivalents and a good deal sweeter. Pilsners are maltier, and session beers abound. Some of the brewpubs continue a tradition of pushing an envelope established decades ago, but most pubs pour drinkable if sweet gold lagers. The best of them are of exceptional quality. Drinking venues range from wonderful beer halls to more sedate pub-like Gasthausen. Most session-strength beers arrive in half liter portions except for the "liter" beer garden Mass.

Salzburg is a celebration of senses. There's probably more wine than beer in the city, but the beer is good and most of it is more refined than in boozier German cities. Before you dismiss a yellow lager as a yellow lager, take another taste; look for a depth in the sweetness and the just-barely-enough hop balance that allows you to drink it all night.

The larger traditional city-center breweries are gone, though Stern Bräu and Gablerbräu remain as restaurants featuring the Kaltenhausen beers. The Weisse Bräu brewery restaurant continues in good health, however, and Mülln's Augustiner beers are a reason to come to the city. Stiegl, up on a hill well outside the tourist area, is by far the largest local brewery. For a mainstream brewery, it brews good and sometimes very good beers.

The sixpack of drinking experiences

Not only the best in Salzburg, but, if we had our choice, the final kick in our bucket list, the beer hall and garden of **Augustiner Bräu Kloster Mülln** epitomize the best of Germanic drinking. The staff isn't overly friendly—they're too busy—but they'll make sure you get what you need. Find a seat in one of the most welcoming beer gardens on the planet; don't be afraid to ask if space at an occupied table is free. Your experiences with your cross-table associates may vary, but in visits ranging over 45 years, we've always made friends. These friends have ranged from 25 mostly students

The best beer garden ever

passing a guitar around the circle to mere "Prosit" mug-clinking, but Mülln's always been more social than even the best of the German gardens. Oh, and the beer: the Augustinerbräu, named for the monastery that towers above the garden, matches the ambience of the site. It's a bit sweet, but manifests a simple elegance that makes it eminently moreish… and pretty tolerable the next morning.

Pay the cashier for your beer, select a mug from the shelf and give it a rinse in the cold water that pours automatically from the spigots, then hand it and your receipt to the kegman to be "filled." In less fastidious days we all just sloshed mugs in the large stone vat. The rinse is important because it cuts the foaming just a bit and gets you something a bit closer to the liter you think (erroneously) you've paid for. Don't grouse about the underfill, though; the 6€ price is barely more than you'd pay for a half liter elsewhere.

Food stalls occupy various parts of the hall, up the stairs from the garden; get salads, breads, fresh Radi (spiral-sliced giant radish, an essential), and other nosh there. The grills in the garden provide well-above-average Steckerlfisch and spit chicken as well as other choices that now even include fried shrimp.

To get there, cross the river at the Müllner Bridge, climb up to street level, turn right, and look for the signs to the Bierstübe on the left. Conversely, take any of the buses that stop more or less at the Mülln parking lot, or even a commuter train to Mülln-Altstadt from the Hauptbahnhof. We like the entry from the alley above the garden; you walk down through cool marble halls and stairways that seem to be

Augustiner Kloster Mülln

left from the monastic days into the food stall area. In nasty weather, the vast beer hall rooms surrounding the food stalls are open.

For a quiet respite from the garden, or a superior restaurant meal, climb the stairs up through the beer hall, exit onto the alley, walk down to the road, and turn right past the pizza place to Bärenwirt (Müllner Hauptstrasse 8), which has been providing food and remarkable views for the last 350 years. The management will greet you as long-lost cousins and make sure you're well fed and watered. It's owned by the Mülln brewery so the beer is just about as fresh as in the garden. The back patio overlooks the river; even after dark just enough light reflects off the water through gaps in the trees to show the swiftness of the current. Note that to avoid being swamped by several thousand refugees, it shuts off its taps at the same time as the garden—11 PM. Bärenwirt is often filled to its limited capacity, and they recommend you call for reservations: (0662) 422 404.

It's plenty of work to climb up from the old town, but the effort to reach **Restaurant Stieglkeller** (Festungsgasse 10) rewards you with some of the most spectacular beer garden views in Europe. Wedged between the Castle and the old town on the river side of the Mönchsberg, it's made up of several floors that offer a variety of vistas over the city and the mountains beyond. The rambling structure holds over 800 inside and about 1,000 outside; you may have to hunt for a while to find just the right setting.

It's easier to reach if you ride up to the Castle and walk down, but there's still a climb from the entrance to anywhere you'll eat or drink. The beer is Stiegl, of course, which could certainly be worse, but it's the view that brings us back up the hill year after year.

Die Weisse (Rupertgasse 10) isn't why you come to Salzburg, but once you're here it's a must. It could pass for a modern inner city brewpub if it weren't for the fact that it's been around for over 100 years, brewing wheat beers that most Salzburgers don't even know about. It's no secret to those in the neighborhood, though: it's big and crowded, though big enough to find a table if you're not fussy about which one. Huge portions of expertly prepared and typically Austrian food emerge from a kitchen that could probably feed a basketball arena.

We think all their beers are top-fermented wheat beers, but they're not all ordinary Hefeweizens. The light Hefeweizen, a 2.9% ABV masterpiece, sports predictable lemon and clove flavors but achieves an exceptional balance, and the 1901 Original is a roasty garnet Schwarzweizen that balances a molasses sweetness with a spicy clove.

Restaurant Stieglkeller by the Castle

Die Weisse is a friendly place. It's where we first learned about "Fucking Hell Bier." There is really a town in Austria named Fucking and a couple of German businessmen figured if they set up a brewery there to produce a light lager ("Hell") they couldn't be denied the naming rights. They skipped the actual brewing part, commissioned the beer from the German Waldhaus Brewery, and won a hotly contested legal right to use the name in the EU. As far as we know, the U.S. still bans it: Fucking Hell.

Stiegl isn't a massive brewery, but it's big enough to spend money on its image, so the **Stiegl Brauwelt** (Bräuhaustrasse 9) is professional, while stopping short of the amusement-park feel of Heineken. Like most modern "brewery tours," you won't see the current brewery; the "world" is essentially an interesting walk-though museum of brewing located in former brewery buildings, though it does include a stop in the room that contains the small brew house that produces Paracelsus, Stiegl's craft brew. Guided tours at 11 AM and 4 PM might get you more of the brewery itself. A pleasant courtyard gives you a place to digest what you've learned along with several samples of Stiegl beers. Food and more beers are available at reasonable prices. Your bus pass will take you close, and it's clearly marked on most maps.

The name of the **S'Kloane Brauhaus** (Schallmooser Hauptstrasse 27) translates to "smallest brewpub," but it's probably not the smallest brewpub you'll encounter—Isi-Bräu, for example, is smaller. It is, however, definitely petite, and it's a calm and friendly place to drink. Lots of brass—the tiny brewery is behind the bar—and the required wood give it a new-old world feel. A dual-level garden is partly under cover; the chestnut tree outside and the geranium baskets inside contribute to the welcoming atmosphere. The two newpub beers they offer include an unusual "Hefe Gersten," a sort of Hefeweizen without the wheat. Both are yeasty and estery, but pleasant enough to make the visit enjoyable. Consider stopping for a meal here; the food is substantial and some of the items stray from the expected Austrian fare.

Isi-Bräu (Bäckerstrasse 3, Bergheim) is so far off the tourist track that it could almost qualify as a day trip. Your day pass won't be good for the distance—you'll have to buy a ticket at the train station and go to the underground part of the station to find the commuter Toonerville Trolley that takes you to Bergheim. Once there, it's best to ask directions. Then believe them. Over the main road and down into a residential area, you'll walk along cursing the ignoramus who sent you there until… there it is. The minuscule brewery is located in an outbuilding of what is obviously Isidor Brunner's house. And it is his home, except he's running a tiny Gasthaus on the ground floor.

The brewery produces only 200 Hl a year in 200 liter batches. The Hausbrau defies style; it's brown-gold, yeasty, funky, and pretty close to (good) homebrew, which is what it is. He sometimes brews a dunkel and if you're there in the winter you can hope for a bock.

Don't expect any English here, though he's happy to point and let you do the same, and he's as nice as he can be. It helps if you speak a couple of words of Bier. It's a lot of work for a satisfactory, but pretty ordinary beer, but it's one of our favorite days in Salzburg. If you pair the Stiegl experience with this trip, you'll experience the yin and yang of 21st century beer within 24 hours.

Other places to explore

Zwettler's (Kaigasse 3, www.zwettlers.com) is a place to find not only some beers that are not common in Salzburg, but a good meal as well. The Kaiser Karl beers, contract brewed in a variety of places, are well made and served enthusiastically. The Zwickl unfiltered lager is one of the best beers you'll find in Salzburg. The indoor restaurant is downstairs and old; tables outside have a view of Mozartplatz.

It's no beer geek paradise, but the small café on the edge of the Mirabell gardens sells cold beer that you can enjoy while you look at the garden and pretend you're a count. Any beer tastes good in a place like this.

At 1,200 years, **St. Peter Stiftskeller** is the oldest restaurant in Austria. In addition to the historic atmosphere, you'll find much more wine than beer and an ambitious menu with prices to match.

Where to stay

Salzburg is not a cheap overnight, but it's not Stockholm either. You can get a first class room for about 200€ or a very adequate one for about half that. If you arrive late in the day during festival season, which is at least half the summer, let the tourist office find you a room. It's right at the train station, and the people are as friendly, honest, and helpful as they can be.

However, Salzburg has so many options it's hard to judge from tourist office descriptions what you're going to get. If you arrive early enough in the day and you have the patience, get a map and a copy of "Hotels in und um Salzburg" from the station tourist office, leave your bags with your traveling companion, take a bus into the center, and knock on doors. If your efforts don't pay off, you can see what the other tourist office in Mozartplatz can get for you.

If you're in town for only a night or two, the Ramada is practically attached to the station and the Austria Trend Hotel Europa Salzburg is right across the street. Either will give you an adequate room at a fair price and you might get a very nice view. For a longer stay, we think it's worth the effort to book in advance at the Stein (info@hotelstein.at) to get a river view. The first class Sheraton gives you a pleasant, if uphill, cross-the-river walk to the Augustiner Keller, and it backs up to the Mirabell gardens—though you'll pay for the peace and quiet. The building that housed the Gablerbräu Brewery is now a hotel.

The view from the catacombs

What to see

The tourist office will give you plenty of options. Our list here barely scratches the surface.

Festung Hohensalzburg towers over the city and quite rightly draws hordes of tourists. The castle's interior tour is worth the time and money. A "Fortress Card" gets you a lift on the funicular railway that can spare you a cardiac calamity, plus an audio guide tour that gets you into the inner rooms (you don't want to miss the torture chamber, after all) and admission to other rooms and museums. You can eat up there and get some pretty stunning views, but we'd suggest you finish up and walk down to the Stieglkeller instead.

We asked our Austrian friend Hannah to take us somewhere tourists often miss; her choice of the catacombs (as well as Zwettler's, above) was a spectacular success. Carved out of the steep stone cliffs hundreds of years ago, worn steps take you up to rooms that heard Mass when Columbus was learning to tie his shoes. Tour groups are banned on the narrow and uneven steps, so you get a few moments of quiet reflection in midst of the crowded city. The rooms range several stories above the monastery and quaint cemetery below; the view is spectacular. Hang on to the rail on the way down.

The Mirabell gardens are truly beautiful and, if you're not staying in the old town, probably very close to your hotel. We thought the entrance price at the Mozart house was a bit much to see some dead guy's view of the river; Austrians we asked hadn't been inside either. Three floors of exhibits include manuscripts and original instruments, however, and, if you're a Mozart fan, may be worth the time and expense. A 17€ combination ticket will get you into his birthplace and the now fully restored residence, where his family lived for decades.

A long bus ride takes you to the base of Untersberg. Take the cable car to the top (you thought the aerial segment in the "Sound of Music" credits was breathtaking? *ha!*) and get an unmatched view of the surrounding area. Try to pick a clear day or your vista will be mostly white and fluffy.

We love the Salzburg zoo. It's not as flashy as many, but makes good use of its mountainside location and has enough of a range of fauna to amuse more than just the kids in the group. We think it's recovered from flood damage in 2013. The bus back from Untersberg stops right in front of the entrance; the same route takes you back to the center of town after your visit.

If you're there in high summer, you're likely to encounter Salzburg Festival events. The festival makes your hotel harder to find and more expensive, so you might as well see if you can take in a performance or two. Some are quite affordable.

Scams and alerts

Salzburg deals with hundreds of thousands of tourists in a short season; watch your wallet in the crowded streets, but overall it's a safe and welcoming city.

We did encounter one scam, tiny but a scam nonetheless. The official helpers at the bus station in the central station will give you generally good advice on getting around. One eager young lady explained to us clearly and correctly the advantage of the 24 hour transit pass and then offered to sell one to us. When we asked if we could get future passes from the machine she said, "Yes, but we're *much* nicer." But on every transaction the change was incorrect—in their favor. All in all, the laugh might have been worth the 30 cents it cost us the first time, but the new math got old after a couple of days.

Day trip

Hallein

Hallein is an easy 25 minute train ride from the main station; more or less hourly trains are even more frequent during the week. A tour of the salt mines is a must. The highlight is donning miner's overalls and sliding down one of the world's longest banisters to the mining area. It's thoroughly commercialized, and a wide range of ages and weights manage the slide without mishap. You can book a tour from your hotel in Salzburg or ride out and get help from the information office in Hallein. There are taxis waiting at the station to take you up the hill to the mine. Don't try to walk it unless you're in really good shape.

If you're not jammed on a tourist bus from Salzburg, you can spend some time in the village. It has a Celtic museum (how did *they* get there?!) and a house where Franz Gruber lived after he wrote "Silent Night"; it features the guitar Father Mohr used to accompany the song for the first time.

It's not hard to find a village with local beer in Austria, but not all have as long a tradition as Kaltenhausen Hofbräu, which started brewing in 1475. It now has Kaiser (Heineken group) money behind it, but brews exceptionally good beer. The Zwickl beer is one of Austria's best, and one-off specialties included a candy-sweet coffee lager, which you have to admit is different for this part of the world. The Braugasthof offers large portions of very good food in a dressily charming interior and spacious courtyard.

Finding it is half the fun. From the station, cross the river into town (check out the amazing views upstream), then turn right and keep an eye out down to your immediate right for a pedestrian path close to the water. About a kilometer of path and small road takes you to a sign for the Braugasthof Kaltenhausen, pointing you back up toward the main road. The brewery's easy to spot from there. If the weather's ugly, take a cab: the address, 69 Salzburger Strasse, is misleading since the "69" is in Kaltenhausen, the next town over.

Once on the river path, it's a beautiful walk, much of it on a residential street, so you'll see how some Austrians live along the way. We passed by a family hosting a small party on their river-view terrace, with what sounded like the soundtrack from the "Sound of Music"; almost too much.

The Hof at Kaltenhausen Hofbräu

Sheffield

Quick orientation

As we've retraced our steps in the final months before publication, we've often told publicans and bartenders that their city will be included in this guide. More often than you'd think, they don't even feign surprise, already assuming they're part of a brewing Valhalla. In Sheffield, the shrug was so "of course it is" that we stepped it up, calling Sheffield the best city for beer drinkers in Europe. Same shrug. But after a moment, they'd always take the time to be sure we *really* understood why it is. And as we approach publication, danged if we don't think they well may be right.

Station break

You don't have to leave the station to have a complete day of beer drinking. Right on Platform 1 is the Sheffield Tap free house that features a range of at least 10 cask ales, even more kegs, and a huge range of bottles we've never seen anywhere else. If you want to stretch your legs and have a couple of halves in a bit of a pub tour, you can

Narrowboats at Victoria Quays

go on our junior varsity Sheffield tour. It counts as a station break because it involves no more than 15 to 20 minutes of walking total, though how much time you spend drinking is up to you.

The station area is right in the shadow of Hallam University. Most of these places get crowded and not quite as peaceful at night when students are in town. BUT—this is the JV tour, here only because of proximity to the station. With a few more blocks of walking you can hit the varsity places…though if you have a train to catch, we promise you'll miss it.

Start at the Howard. It's straight uphill, across the street from the station; you really can't miss it (remember, we miss most things that can't be missed). Four taps, reasonably varied, food until 7, pubby.

If you want to divert from the JV tour, walk down the street from the Howard to the Rutland Arms's 10 taps. But to stay on our station break tour, walk a short way further uphill to the Globe Pub. The "Scream" sign out front is intimidating, but the pub is not. Three handpulls. Next, go up to the Millennium Galleries, turn right and head up the ramp that takes you to the right of the Galleries. The Graduate is clearly a student hangout, but has a few cask ales and lots of space. A pretty good menu goes until 10 PM; the décor seems late 20th century—maybe the '60s?—Crosby, Stills, Nash and Young on the sound system, anyway. The tourist office is next door if you've already realized you're not going to change trains after all.

Take a gawk at the Winter Garden. You'll be back later (see below).

Opposite the Winter Garden is the Crucible Theater. Head towards it, and on the left is the Old Monk. Its appealing exterior is even more appealing a block further along on Norfolk Street. If you crave sub-zero Heineken it's perfect, but better, turn around and have another pint at the Graduate. Retrace your steps down Surrey and Howard to get back to the station. Try to figure out why you left the Sheffield Tap in the first place.

History and culture

People have lived where Sheffield sits for more than two and a half millennia. The Romans came and went, and it showed up in the 1086 Domesday Book, but was little more than a minor market town until the Industrial Revolution. Even in the early 19th century, Sheffield was pretty sleepy, but even so, the very small population in 1831 supported no fewer than 1,500 pubs. There aren't that many now, but we believe the pub-to-person ratio is still astonishingly favorable.

Thomas Rawston established the first major brewery in Sheffield in 1758, but most of the big breweries opened during the industrialization of the 19th century. By mid-century, rail and canal connections made Sheffield a major industrial center. Factories were hot and dirty, which encouraged their workers to drink even more—and centered their tastes on clean, rather bland ales and lagers. The first lager brewery was built by a Scot, surprisingly, but the booming market attracted all sorts of capital. The Exchange Brewery was Sheffield's largest until the middle of the 20th century; Gilmour (see New Barrack Tavern, below) was a solid second.

The growth of huge corporations in the 20th century changed Sheffield and its brewing scene. Consolidation and "rationalization" cut the number of breweries to around 30 by the end of the 1800s. Stones and Wards lasted into the 1980s, cranking out rivers of mass market beers. They tried to jump on the CAMRA cask wagon in the early '80s, but it was too little and too late. Just as big steel corporations shifted to cheaper and newer plants, the big Sheffield breweries became redundant arms of Britain's "big six" brewing corporations.

Beer styles and drinking culture

When we first started collecting beers, quite a few came from Sheffield. Those four major regional breweries made the town a rival to Burton-on-Trent. But few would have said the pub culture was special enough to settle in for a prolonged visit. Drinking a beer from a Sheffield brewery wasn't much different from drinking one of the big boys from out of town: Beer. Eh.

We mourn the passing of regional breweries, whose pubs, if they aren't simply closed, often become mere outlets for big conglomerate brewers whose key executives sometimes seem hard pressed to tell the difference between mild ale and mulled. But Sheffield shows, more clearly than any other city we know, why the figurative glass of brewery consolidation is, perhaps, more than half full. As the last of the big Sheffield breweries went on the real estate listings for adaptive reuse, some residents were determined that something local had to take their place. (The same story is playing out in cities from Zurich to London to Milwaukee. As local but unremarkable beers have died out, smaller breweries have learned to thrive on developing niche markets.)

In Sheffield, David Wicket broke the trail. In 1990 he set up the Kelham Island Brewery and the adjacent Fat Cat pub, which remains one of Sheffield's best watering holes. When he started, Sheffield's brewing giants allowed the newbie only a tiny role in the market, but barely more than a decade later the big four stood shuttered and Kelham Island was the city's largest brewery. Kelham not only brewed good and interesting beers, but the Fat Cat highlighted guest beers as well, and in doing so encouraged future competition. Very smart small brewers from Sheffield to Binghamton, New York, realize that competition enlarges the niche rather than divides it—Wicket got it right years ago. There are now about a dozen breweries in Sheffield, every one of them providing distinctive, innovative, and thoughtfully made beers. Nearly all the brewpubs feature guests. Beer specialty bars provide a guaranteed market for the smallest players, and the result is a theme park for beer drinkers. There is no particular style linked to the city—the culture is one of choice.

Most of the pubs here and in Derby celebrate the brewing revolution. Staff are knowledgeable and enthusiastic advocates of flavorful beer. Nearly all the places we list are happy to pour you a small sample before you commit to a pint.

The sixpack of drinking experiences

We asked a friend who lives in Sheffield to name the six best pubs in town. When he stopped laughing, we suggested throwing darts to make a choice. "No," he snickered, "spin the bottle." It's true: you just can't pick a "top six." So here's a top six...and another top six. The order here is more in the sequence of a pub crawl than one of preference. Because we promised, we've starred the six we like best, but that ranking changes with every visit.

The first sixpack

A Kelham Island pub crawl can include all of this group except the Sheffield Tap. Start at the Harlequin and end at the Shakespeare, or vice versa. If the weather is good, you might stop between the Harlequin and the Gardeners Rest at the Riverside, listed in "Another" below, not so much for the beer but for the fine river view.

We sometimes start this crawl with the **Harlequin*** on Nursery Street, a very manageable walk to the Kelham Island gems that follow. The 53 bus will take you quite close; ask the driver—Harlequin is near the top of an uphill grade on the right. More than a dozen rotating beers are in perfect condition and served with a Yorkshire sparkler to enhance the head. When we visited, eclectic music ranged from Buddy Holly to soft disco and gospel; we don't think there was a single selection we didn't like. The upscale décor is traditional enough to make it a very comfortable place to drink. Not so upscale are the crude postcards in the loo, but we think they add to the atmosphere. The Harlequin is set off a bit by large roads and apartments, but it's little more than a ten minute walk from Kelham Island, or you can take the 53 bus onward. We love this pub.

To take an abbreviated Kelham crawl, stay on the 53 bus to Neepsend Road. Get ready to hit the stop request when you see the Kelham Island Museum. Keep an eye out on your left for the **Gardener's Rest***—if you're lucky, the driver won't go flying

At the Gardeners Rest

by it. The 53 continues on to the Hillsborough area, but be warned, Hillsborough is a big area and is characterized by …hills. The 53 route can take you close enough to walk to the New Barrack Tavern and from there to the Hillsborough Hotel, but only if the weather is good.

The Gardeners Rest was refurbished after the floods of 2009 and is the brewery tap for Sheffield Brewery beers. In addition to a fine pub bar, it has a sun room and a garden out back that overlooks the River Don. About a dozen cask ales in fine condition make this a great place to start—or finish—a pub crawl. The bar staff is wonderfully understanding about those who end their crawl here, though they can't quite hide their preference that you *start* here instead. This is one of our favorites in the UK. The beer and the view would be enough, but we've always received the sort of warm welcome here that you dream about back home, but don't always receive in the real world. Sheffield, however, is likely to make that welcoming dream come true; it's still a small town even if it's outgrown its clothes. An interest in beer will make you new best friends with remarkable speed.

When you leave the Gardeners Rest, turn right along Neepsend and bend right at the fork, jog right to follow the river, and walk along behind the once-factories-now-residences. When you come to the bridge, cross over. The Milestone, a very nice restaurant with a couple of interesting beers, will be on your right. If you want to eat there, and we advise you do, make reservations. Go left, ask directions if necessary, and you'll see the **Fat Cat***. Cousin to the Devonshire Cat (see below), it's the brewery tap for the Kelham Island brewery and as good a beer bar as you could wish for. Multiple taps feature the Kelham Island beers as well as stars from around the UK.

The **Kelham Island Tavern** is nearby. Anyone at the Fat Cat will be happy to direct you. It's another first class beer bar featuring local beers as well as those from around the country. If you can time your visit to a "session" night, you'll be rewarded with music you'd pay a ransom for in a fancier venue. The house regulars are high quality professionals, but the best folk musicians in England stop by unannounced to join the group.

A relatively new entry is the **Shakespeare,** which is visible from Kelham Island, though not on it. It's easiest just to get someone to point at it across the parking lot. It has an early to mid-20th century feel to it, though its current incarnation is only a few years old. It sports a fine range of beer in excellent condition and a very knowledgeable staff—the author of the CAMRA guide to Sheffield pubs works there. From here you can hike uphill back to the town center, or take a bus or, if it's late, hail a cab.

Well away from Kelham Island, the station's **Sheffield Tap*** has a selection of beer that puts it into our top six. At peak times it's best if you are good at entertaining yourself; the Tap is bustling and relatively impersonal for Sheffield, where most pubs welcome you like a long-lost cousin. But if you show up in the quieter afternoon, even here the bartender can be your new best friend. It's still one of the best station bars in the world. Not only are there about 30 casks and drafts, but on our last trip they focused on a handful of local and relatively obscure breweries. You could get on the train and go visit some of them…or just stay put and spend more time sampling them. "Tap" clones in York and London are similarly rewarding. They'll sell bottles to go, but be ready to part with a good piece of your purse.

The second sixpack

From the center of the city and stretching west to Hillsborough, a range of pubs can provide very special experiences. Like our first six, these can be done in a busy day, but we hope you have time for a more leisurely approach. We've listed them more or less in crawling order rather than by preference.

The Rutland Arms (86 Brown Street) topped the favorites list of some of the younger bartenders we talked to. It's pretty noisy and pretty crowded, but very lively, and if you don't wind up in a conversation with someone, it's you, not them. The beers are in good condition and there's a good range of them. Food is very respectable British pub grub.

The Museum isn't far away and has a convenient town center location in the pedestrian Orchard Square. We don't know why you'd be in Sheffield if you were primarily interested in shopping, but if you are, the Museum is close to the big stores and a variety of shops. On our visits, it's been quieter than many of our other choices. The barstaff is predictably friendly and there are several cask ales in good condition. It's an almost stereotypical pub in the best sense of the word: a great place to have a conversation or read the day's paper while you sip a really good pint of ale.

When we first found the **Devonshire Cat*** (49 Wellington Street), it was one of England's very best. It seemed to get a bit lost in the explosion of great Sheffield pubs in the years thereafter, but in January 2014 the Abbeydale Brewery took it over and breathed new life into it, and it now serves as the brewery's in-town tap. A majority of its twelve handpulls are usually guest beers, with an expanded range of craft keg beers from Sheffield and beyond. The bottle selection is enormous. Take a good look through the window into the bottle room, which sometimes harbors a gravity-pour cask of something exotic. On our last visit, a single cask of Sheffield's Abbeydale stout had been conditioned in a whiskey barrel from America that had been shipped to England in pieces and reassembled by one of the last of the independent British coopers. The whiskey flavor was faint compared to American barrel-aged beers, but that just allowed the stout and wood to show in a way they often can't. The other special was a strong ale collaboration brewed at Abbeydale with Michigan's Founders brewers. The name, 3712, referred to the distance in miles between the two breweries. The big citrusy flavors were no surprise.

The history of the Devonshire Cat goes back hundreds of years; during most of the last century the pub was a Wards Brewery outlet and operated for a time as the Alma Hotel. When it opened as the Devonshire Cat in 1981 to supply cask ale, it was a curiosity. Now it's simply a classic.

It's a fine place to drink. Beers are poured in superb condition, with tight creamy heads that last much longer than you'll let them. Dark woods and several shades of red ooze atmosphere, but the furnishings are newer and the effect is trad but cheery. The place is surprisingly good-sized but, not surprisingly, gets jammed in the evenings. A range of music is soft enough for conversation. There are no screens or fruit machines—just a place engineered for groups to spend some time together.

It's also one of our first stops in the city for its food. Locally sourced meats and produce, with fish and chips that you'd be hard pressed to find at a first-rate chippie, reflect a kitchen that knows how to make the most of prime ingredients; it's enough to make you think you're in an upscale restaurant rather than an affordable pub. The burger is the best we've tasted outside the U.S.

A short walk from Devonshire Cat, on Fitzwilliam Street just short of West Street, **The Hop** is a big atrium-like beer pavilion dedicated to selling a great deal of Osset's beer. Twenty- and thirty-somethings with some money to spend fill the place at night, though it's pretty sedate early on. Draft beers, though in good condition, contribute to a sense that this bar could as easily be in Berlin or New York as Sheffield. Still, the brewery produces quite respectable beers and if you fit the demographic, it's a "go to" place. Not a destination, but a fair enough part of this crawl.

The Red Deer (18 Pitt Street) has, by Sheffield standards, a modest range of cask ales, but odds are its nine handpulls will include something you haven't tried in the other Sheffield pubs. The food is made in-house, and the atmosphere can't be beat. Quintessentially pubby, it frequently made the top five when we asked bartenders in other pubs to name their favorites. Sometimes you'll run into live music; at other times it can be a nice calm place a few blocks from the noisy city center.

A tram can save you a long walk uphill and west to 54-58 Langsett Road and **The Hillsborough*** with its associated Woodstreet Brewery. The Hillsborough features a number of guest beers as well as a good range from the house brewery. Their hilltop location means their back garden and sunroom offer a superb view out over Sheffield, and reminds you of how grateful you are that the tram stops almost in front of the brewery. If you go at an uncrowded time and get to know the bartender, you might be able to nip downstairs for a quick look at the brewery and cellar.

A longish walk downhill (which you will retrace with greater effort) takes you to the **New Barrack Tavern** (601 Peniston Road). It's an outlet for Nottingham's Castle Rock brewery, which produces very pleasant ales, but you'll find some good guest beers as well. If you look closely, especially around your feet, you'll see reminders that this was a Gilmours house before Sheffield's second largest brewery closed in 1954. If the pub isn't busy, you'll probably have a chat with the managers, Steph and Kevin, who have put their own distinctive stamp on the place. Their award-winning garden is one of the most beautiful in the city and there's solid pub food. It's a mom-and-pop establishment, with the personal commitment to making you welcome that is more common in the UK than anywhere, and—when there's not a football match at the nearby stadium—is a peaceful place to drink.

Another favorite pub

Although it's not going to make the list of the top craft attractions in Sheffield, we've spent some lovely afternoons in **The Riverside's** waterside garden. Right on the River Don, at 1 Mowbray Street, it's a short walk from Kelham Island's pubs and only a couple minutes' scamper from the Harlequin. The last time we were there, the beer

The Riverside Pub

was less reliable than at the Harlequin, but new management held the promise of improvement. We think the atmosphere is worth an "adequate" pint; in another city it might make our top list.

Still on our Sheffield beer bucket list

As much time as we've spent in Sheffield, we still haven't seen all we'd like. Partly it's because our exploring time is limited by the need to return to favorites like the Devonshire Cat and Harlequin, and partly because the scene is still evolving. You may get to the two places below before we do.

A **BrewDog** outlet has opened up with a splash in the downtown area. Our hotel clerk apparently thought it was a brewpub, alas (they'll learn). We like BrewDog's spirit of adventure and have enjoyed their outlets, but Sheffield's local bars are so many and so good, we save BrewDog for another time in another city. The beers are interesting at the least and sometimes dramatic, and they hire good people, but they're not close to indigenous. If you haven't had the BrewDog experience and you're here for a while, it might make sense to stop in, but don't skip the local winners we've listed to do it.

A bus ride to the outskirts of town will take you to **Abbeydale Brewery.** Their beers show up in good pubs throughout the region and increasingly make it as far as London. We've never been able to tear ourselves away from the more central pubs long enough to get there. Named for the Beauchief Abbey, which lies in ruins nearby, Abbeydale does a number of religiously titled beers that sometimes venture outside conventional boundaries. You'll find their beers all over Sheffield, especially in the Devonshire Cat.

Where to eat

We had a phenomenal meal at the Milestone in Kelham Island one year; returning on another visit, without reservations, they couldn't seat us at all, so apparently they're still superb. Pub grub was no longer an option at that hour (many pubs still only serve food at lunch) and we were contemplating making dinner out of crisps when a clever barmaid suggested Indian. An easy walk from the Shakespeare, the 7 Spices Balti Restaurant treated us like royalty and the food was first rate. (See the discussion of Balti cuisine in the Birmingham chapter.) If you don't eat Indian food in England, you're missing what might be the only good justification for the Empire.

On another late return from a neighboring city, we knew we had missed even the 7 Spices' late hours and thought we might go hungry that night. Happily, however, it's not hard to find super-late-night shops that can deliver a reasonably full meal to your hotel at a more than reasonable price until two or three in the morning.

Keep your eyes out downhill from West Street and you'll find a true fish and chip shop. They're an endangered species. Some pubs' fish and chips are very good now (and some aren't), but a real greasy-paper chippie is still an experience to be savored.

Where to stay

For a chance to stay at a brewery, you could try the Hillsborough, which has six rooms, all en suite. Our sources say it's comfortable and very reasonable. They advertise that they are "biker friendly" and they are not on the tourist office's list of approved places—frankly we think this last is a point in their favor.

For more conventional accommodation, the Novotel is straight up the hill in front of the station. Behind it is the Mercure, which has the advantage of a lobby that opens onto the Winter Garden. The tourist office, on Surrey Street in the shadow of the Millennium Gallery, can give you recommendations.

The Hilton is a relatively low-lying brick edifice on one of Sheffield's old canals. It has lovely views of a marina full of old narrowboats, but it's a ten-minute uphill climb to the center of town. Still, there's a nice waterside pub open in the afternoons right underneath it. From the station it's a twelve-minute walk if you figure out the right route. Even with a £5 cab ride, strikingly low summer rates can make it a good option, especially if you can get a rate that includes the exceptionally good (even for Hilton) buffet breakfast.

What to see

Kelham Island Museum gives a sense of Sheffield's role in the industrial revolution. Exhibits include a brewing gallery and some striking industrial displays. Just wandering around the museum grounds is an experience in itself. We'd recommend you go even if it were a major excursion, but it's right on the #53 bus line and only yards away from a start to our Island pub crawl. The River Don Engine is the most powerful surviving steam engine in Britain, powering an enormous rolling mill for most of the 20th century until it was finally retired in 1978. It roars to life again at the museum two or three times a day, several days a week, a truly awesome sight. Machine enthusiasts travel from around the world to see it run, and you can experience it just because you're here for the beer. Important: Check with the museum in advance; maintenance and funding issues sometimes restrict the operating schedule.

One of the joys of sixpacking is that it takes you to places and sights that local people really treasure, but which never make the "best of Europe" guidebooks. The Millennium Galleries aren't the Smithsonian, but they're much more intimate and just about as eclectic. John Ruskin, the noted 19th century writer and all-around celebrity, started a collection of beautiful things with the intention of letting the ordinary workers, who saw so little of beauty, enjoy them. Included in the collection is a thousand-year-old book of sermons and an 11th century psalter, both lavishly illustrated. Ruskin seemed to be more interested in the fanciful creatures that adorned the book than in the contents. Don't miss the late 19th century painting of San Marco, Venice.

The Millennium Galleries open out to the Sheffield Winter Garden or Peace Garden, one of Europe's largest botanical glasshouses. Exotic plants fill this spectacular structure as a bit of tropical Yorkshire. The only problem is that you can't get a beer here, though there's a nice tea stand that plays some great British acoustic music. However, if you go into the Mercure hotel, the bar features one cask ale that you can drink in the hotel lobby whose glass walls form one wall of the garden. For a free 20 minute audio tour, ask at Fancie (opposite side of the garden from the Mercure).

Uphill from the railroad station and opposite the Graduate Pub, the Graves Gallery Art Museum has a well-displayed exhibit of minor masterpieces. It's certainly not the Louvre or the Prado, but it's a good low-key stroll though the past few centuries of European art.

A couple of local historians offer walking tours, including a "ghost tour." You can find out how to book them at the tourist office. The tourist office also can provide you with a brochure for a self-guided two-hour stroll around the city that will give you a good sense of Sheffield's industrial past.

The old police and fire station has become a museum of emergency services; sometimes on weekends they'll take you for a short ride on one of their "appliances." It's on West Bar—opening hours are limited, so be sure to check.

Scams and alerts

The once somewhat dicey neighborhood between the center city and the Victoria Quays (Hilton and Holiday Inn, among others) has improved markedly in the last three years, and we don't know of anything to worry about in Sheffield. Tattooed journeymen workers have repeatedly stopped what they were doing to escort us to the next intersection to be sure we wouldn't get lost.

Further information

There are a few transit centers and they're not all that easy to find. Get directions and a rather poor photocopied map from the tourist office. They may or may not be able to find a transit map for you. You can buy a day pass good on both bus and trams and it's well worth the investment.

Day trip/excursion: the twelve hour Derby crawl

Arguably, the Midlands and South Yorkshire have the densest concentration of really cool beer-drinking towns on the planet. We've agonized over which to include as primary cities in this book, which to relegate to day trip status, and which—worst of all—to omit.

From Sheffield, you can visit at least half a dozen cities within a couple of hours by rail that can make you question our choices. The one we've settled on is Derby, which claims to have more and better beer than Sheffield. It doesn't, but doesn't miss by much. Trains to Derby run several times an hour and you can get back after the pubs close.

Derby (pronounced "Darby") has more good pubs than you can reasonably visit in a day. The ones below are among our favorites, but they're also on something of a straight shot to or from the station. The entire route is walkable in a bit over a half hour if you don't stop. To our knowledge, that has never been done. To preserve valuable drinking time, we usually take a cab to the Furnace and walk our way back, and that's the way we'll guide you here. For a brief day trip, you could just visit the railway pubs, the Alexandra and the Brunswick Inn. You wouldn't see Derby itself, but you could taste nearly a couple dozen local beers.

Our extended tour starts at the farthest point, with the **Furnace Inn** on Duke Street. It's a bit out of the way, above the town center, so if you're in a hurry you can skip it and start with the Flower Pot, but it's a lovely pub that brews its own "Shiny" range of good beers. Three distinct drinking areas open up to a wood-paneled bar featuring seven casks and four craft kegs as well as a couple of dozen bottled beers we hadn't seen before. You'll get a warm welcome at the bar and be welcomed into conversation with those at the table next to you if you look like you'd like to be. A concrete garden in the back isn't the most scenic you'll ever visit, but it's functional and has a good-sized covered area for showery days, which is to say much of the time. There's an acoustic open mike on Mondays.

From the Furnace take River Road (it's almost in front of it) to the right until it turns into Edward Street, and when that meets King Street look left across the street to spot the tiny **Seven Stars.** It's one of the oldest pubs in Derby and its slightly below-ground layout is wonderfully historic and attractive. Alas, the beers are not. Once a good real ale destination, it now offers just a couple of unremarkable national beers. You may want to stop for half a pint just to drink in the atmosphere, but don't let it preclude the gems that lie ahead on your walk back to the station.

Look down the street from the Seven Stars and you can spot the **Flower Pot.** If you time your visit for a Derby beer festival, you won't actually have to go to the festival. On our last visit the Flower Pot poured well over 20 real ales on handpull and gravity. The gravity beers are served from their "cellar"—a temperature-controlled glass chamber that you can view from both the pub and the street. A warren of connecting

The Flower Pot (and tall friend)

rooms with wooden floors and varied, comfortable furnishings, the Flower Pot is more open and better lit than the Seven Stars, yet still has an atmosphere that sings of old and authentic. A connected venue offers an amazing range of live music. A good-sized "garden" in back is stoned; if you try all their beers, you will be as well.

Follow King Street briefly and turn right when you can get a glimpse of the Cathedral. Just past it is **Ye Olde Dolphin Inne.** You have to forgive the extra e's—it dates from 1530 and looks it. Four tiny rooms include a cute snug, and they have a fine little garden out back with a view of the Cathedral. There's an upstairs dining room on weekends that you reach by creaky stairs off a tiny uneven passage that gives you a sense of just how old the building is. The beer list is not extensive, but they've always had a beer or two for us that were new and enjoyable. Occasional beer festivals provide a wider range. The food is affordable and much better than the big chain pubs down the road. Those cavernous establishments, a Wetherspoons and a clone, do have some casks and serve food until 11 PM.

If you look downhill past the Dolphin's garden, you'll see the **Silk Mill** on the left at the bottom of the hill. Named for the historic silk mill (now a notable museum) nearby, it has a nice trad-modern atmosphere and a very pretty garden and, apparently, ties to the Exeter Inn across the river. Eight handpulls pour several beers we haven't seen anywhere else in town.

From the Silk Mill, head down along Full Street, then cross the river to your left on Derwent Street to reach two of Derby's best pubs. If you bear right on Exeter Place after the river, you'll find the **Exeter Arms,** home to the Dancing Duck brewery. It's

Ye Olde Dolphin Inne

a fine brew pub that also sends a good deal of beer to the trade. We've sampled their beers in good condition in Birmingham and London, but this is where you want to try them. They brew a huge range. If you're lucky enough to get a version of their gold, try it; we liked the nice balance of ale fruit, nutty biscuity malt, and gentle balancing hops. The pub is what you'd want if you could build one back home: multiple woody rooms, with a sense that people who brew beer and love beer drink here. We understand from people who live in Derby that the Exeter Arms has the best food in town—actual gourmet quality. Consider booking, as tables fill fast.

Exit the Exeter and walk back towards the river, where you passed the **Brewery Tap** at the fork in the road. The Tap, outlet for the Derby Brewing Company, is a lot more modern inside than its lovely old brick exterior promises, but it's a great place to really look and think about the house-brewed beers. Their Business As Usual, an amber bitter, shows toasted malt and a hint of grilled flavor, with sweet burned sugars and diacetyl on a leash. It's a nicely balanced 4.4% brew that you could drink for a long time and still find your feet.

The last stops of the trip are just minutes from the station but a bit of a hike from the Brewery Tap. Go back across the river and take a left on Cropton. Keep the huge Derby Theatre center on your right and make your way via Morledge to Siddals Road on the other side of the big intersection. Where Siddals ends at Railway Terrace, about half a mile, you'll see the **Alexandra Hotel** on the right. You probably spotted it from the train from Sheffield just before it pulled into the station. Alexandra is a traditional, rather dusty two-room boozer, a Castle Rock outlet, but with a nice range of guests. Most of the handpulls, and the conversation, are in the pub bar. If you want to actually sit down, choose the lounge or the tiny "Wendy house" (sunroom) in the garden—but you'll have to go find your own beer and friends. The narrow bar features nine handpulls, railroad memorabilia on the walls, and very welcoming service. Our bartender was eager to talk about the beers, including an unusual and subtle vanilla porter. You could spend the better part of an evening here perusing the pictures of locomotives or the shelves of second-hand books (on sale for charity, if you want to take one with you). But save time and liver for a final stop at The Brunswick Inn, which is a can't-miss Derby gem.

From the Alexandra, walk toward the tracks on Siddals and turn right on Railway Terrace. The **Brunswick Inn** is on your right, only a few minutes from the station. Railway Terrace was a planned community built by the railroad for its workers in 1842, and the plan included a "local" pub and hotel, the Brunswick. In the late 1970s the pub was slated for demolition, but it was saved by a citizens' coalition which rescued not only the inn but the entire complex. The lovely reconditioned rowhouses are now tiny but choice private cottages, and the Brunswick continues to function as one of several locals within a five minute walk of the station. Four very attractive rooms (including a nice "family" room) mean you can hear yourself think except at the very busiest of times. A small bricked-in garden at the rear looks out on the communal courtyard of the Terrace. Sixteen handpulls feature local and regional beers including a half dozen of their house-brewed casks. An extensive range of ciders are on cask and draft. The house beers are solid; if you're having just one, we recommend the porter: notes of molasses and even tobacco blend with a cherry fruit sweetness, and at 4.3% you can drink almost all you want. The inn is proud of its locally sourced food. Take time to read the walls; the place is a small museum.

There are a few pubs clustered around the station and some of them serve cask. But really, if you have time for them, you had time to linger at the Brunswick.

Stockholm

Quick orientation

Stockholm is a paradise for beer drinking, sightseeing, and just enjoying life. For those who can afford it. When the weather permits. Even in a cold summer rain or nasty winter snow, however, you'll get a warm welcome in a place where "everyone" really does speak English and seems glad to have you there. Stockholm can be a great first destination for new travelers, but we still find new experiences and just-enough-foreign to be fun 35 years after our first visit.

Stockholm spreads out over several islands in a beautifully scenic but hilly archipelago. You'll arrive in Norrmalm, the modern city center that includes the train station and many of the largest stores. Gamla Stan, the old town, lies a couple of subway (they call it the T) stops to the south. From there the increasingly fashionable Södermalm, once home to over a dozen breweries and now the location of the city's best pubs, is another stop or an easy walk farther south. Other islands are accessible by buses, trains, trams, and a small network of ferries.

Gamla Stan and Flyt

We'll mention prices now because we, and every tourist we've met in Sweden, can't help it. Sweden is *expensive*. The bottom line for your bottom line is that if you are on a tight budget, go somewhere else to drink. The Swedes, for instance, go to Denmark, which is no bargain either. If you can afford to be here, when you go to a bar think of kronor as funny money and just spend them.

Station breaks

Stockholms Centralstation is a multi-floored labyrinth that can leave you totally bewildered. Take it easy, look at the wall maps, and you can find an exit leading to most of the places you want to go. We can't imagine why you'd only be there long enough to change trains, but if you're waiting for a departure, the Bishops Arms (Vasagatan 7) is a good choice for a quick beer. The Bishops Arms sits directly atop one of the entrances to T Centralen, a major tube stop linked to the Central rail station. If Columbus had tried to find that specific entrance, however, he would have discovered Finland first, so we suggest you write down the address, look at the exit maps to get close, then show the address to someone to get directions once you get to a street. Happily, our other pubs are much easier to find.

History and culture

Sweden is so closely associated with neutrality and pacifism today that it's easy to forget that Swedes were among the most feared warriors in early European history. Supposedly Rurik, a Swedish Viking, founded the first Russian dynasty, and his bloodline lives on in the pretender who still claims to be the rightful Emperor of Russia. While some historians cast doubt on that story today, there's no doubt that while Norwegian and Danish Vikings were out discovering places like Greenland and America in the first millennium, the Swedish Viking traders headed east, deep into the regions that later became Russia. In the 17th century, Gustav II Adolf spent most of his reign fighting in the Thirty Years War. His troops marched into battle singing Lutheran hymns, which apparently scared the devil out of their Catholic foes, and if he hadn't been accidentally killed by his own men in 1632, he might well have achieved his goal of dominating the Baltic region. Even without him, Sweden became one of the great powers of Europe.

The Soviet dissident author Alexander Solzhenitsyn blames the troubles of his country and the corresponding success of Scandinavia on the Great Northern War (1700–1721). While most European countries were playing armed chess farther south in the War of Spanish Succession, Peter the Great was involved in an enormously costly 20-year marathon against Sweden. Both countries developed absolutist governments to fund and fight the war, and kept them once it was over. Wars increase government control and decrease personal freedom. By the time the gunpowder clouds cleared, both Swedes and Russians had become accustomed to a state that took an active interest in the lives of ordinary people. The Russians went on to use the power of the state to involve themselves in European politics, while Sweden, reluctantly, gave up its dream of turning the Baltic into a Swedish lake and turned inward to deal with its own problems. Thirty years later, Sweden sat out the Seven Years War while Russia invested men and money in a key role. Had the positions been reversed, Solzhenitsyn implies, Russia would have developed the socialist workers' paradise that the Communists promised and never delivered.

It's remarkable to think that people so closely identified with stealing, pillaging, and warring all over Europe developed a society that now takes care of its less fortunate citizens as well as any in the world and hosts the presentation of the Nobel Peace Prize. The goal of a relatively small gap between rich and poor has its roots in a long-standing egalitarian ethos, and Sweden often serves as a model of the modern welfare state. But this development wasn't as smooth as many think. The economist Paul Krugman observed, "The Swedes themselves are unsure what they have done right," and the government has sidled to the right since the heyday of truly democratic socialism. Nevertheless, Sweden maintains one of the most generous social welfare systems in the world, and its vibrant economy thrives even in the context of one of the highest tax structures in the world. It helped that Sweden was blessed with natural resources and its people embraced a strong work ethic. Sweden's century of the world's fastest economic expansion also stemmed from heavy government investment in education, communication, and infrastructure. In short, a combination of government policy and capitalism made Sweden rich enough to afford state socialism.

From our perspective, however, the workers' paradise seemed to come at a cost. Despite the best effort of the Swedish Nanny to rein in underage drinking, when we first visited Stockholm we'd rarely seen a city with more drunken youths, and drunks of all ages littered the streets.

When we think someone else is taking care of things, we all tend to shrug off some of the responsibility that we owe to each other, and the anonymity of big cities isolates us. Any of us who have spent time in New York have seen people walk around someone lying on a sidewalk. On our visits to Stockholm in the late 1970s and early '80s, however, we were struck by how many bodies had passed out on the streets, and how many people simply *stepped over* them rather than even walking around. We were also struck by how quickly an ambulance arrived out of nowhere to cart off someone who had fallen in some sort of stupor; it seemed like more of a street cleaning operation than a rescue. (However, if we had a choice of cities in which to collapse, we would lean to Stockholm.)

In our last two visits, however, we've seen far less public drunkenness. Maybe the kids have learned to binge at home, or maybe it's just too expensive, but aside from some street beggars, who are almost never Swedish, you'll find little evidence of human suffering in Sweden. Public areas are safe and comfortable. The welfare state survives, but seems a bit less oppressive and intrusive; restrictions on freedom, including drinking, continue to annoy occasionally, but overall Stockholm is one of the most pleasant places to eat and drink on the Continent.

Beer styles and drinking culture

When we first started traveling, no one would have picked Stockholm as a brewing destination except perhaps the long-deceased Mr. and Mrs. Pripps. In the 1980s it was a desert of mass market beer and watered-down supermarket brews pitched to teenaged lager louts. But a couple of years ago we met some people who were so passionate and articulate about the virtues of Akkurat Bar, we reconfigured summer plans (admittedly with lingering skepticism) to make the time-consuming detour to Stockholm.

Our friends were right. The beer culture in Stockholm began to change in 1993. House of Ale Oliver Twist broke new ground in introducing a range of flavorful beers to the city, and when its owners opened the larger Akkurat a few blocks away, Stockholm became a serious beer destination. Today an explosion of new craft brewers, battling some of the most restrictive regulations in Europe, have propelled Sweden to rival Italy and Denmark as superb and dynamic brewing centers. Craft brewing is a global movement, but Oliver Twist and Akkurat have done as much to develop a beer culture in Stockholm as the Brickskeller did in Washington in the 1970s and '80s. An unusual spirit of community among the dozens of good beer bars prevails; the best of them will cheerfully recommend and steer you to the others.

Today, Akkurat and Oliver Twist no longer share ownership, but they remain the top beer bars in Sweden; their rivalry is a friendly one. You'll find good pubs in almost every part of Stockholm. They're less numerous than those of San Diego, Philadelphia, or Brussels, but at least a couple of dozen establishments celebrate the burgeoning Swedish craft brewing scene. If you want a bigger pub crawl than our suggestions, get a copy of "Pubguide Stockholm" (we found ours at Akkurat) and follow its maps.

When we were there last, Stockholm's only actual brewery was Monks Café and brewery, which operates one of the biggest draft houses (Monks Porter House in Gamla Stan) and a small handful of other outlets. They close much of their operation in the summer, though, leaving Stockholm without serious brewing of its own. However, that changed in the spring of 2014 with the opening of Nya Carnegiebryggeriet, the brainchild of Brooklyn Brewery (whose beers are more prevalent in Stockholm than those of any of the Swedish craft breweries), Carlsberg Sweden, and D. Carnegie & Co., the historic brewers of Carnegie Stout. On the Stockholm harbor, at Ljusslingan 17, it's a production brewery which anticipates an eventual production of a million liters of beer a year in small batches. A good-sized restaurant, the New Carnegie Mill, is attached. We haven't gotten there yet but you should. Note the relatively short opening hours: it's closed Monday and Tuesday, and opens at 5 PM during the rest of the week and at 1 PM on weekends.

Most pubs serve draft ("fat") beer in .4 or .5 liter glasses. Some will cheerfully serve half portions if you're tasting several, and many of the others will do the same with some reluctance on a slow night. Strong beers routinely come in smaller portions. Expect to pay between 70 and 95 crowns for most beers, which will leave your bank account at home diminished by $11 to $15 each.

The tight regulation of alcohol, stemming from the state's effort to keep everyone healthy, may or may not be slowly curbing teen drinking, but it definitely puts a damper on your ability to sample the myriad excellent Swedish beers. Swedish label tsars are so inflexible they make American TTB officials look like advocates of free love. In 2012 the Train Station brewery wasn't allowed to use a label with a cowboy walking along a railroad track because beer labels are not allowed to show people "working."

On a practical level, supermarket big-brewery beers, easily available to those 20 and older, top out at 3.5% ABV. While low-alcohol versions of good Czech beers are interesting, there aren't many. The "monopoly"—as the Swedes refer to Systembolaget, the system that distributes everything stronger—means craft brewers face a nearly insurmountable challenge in selling their beers if they can't get listed in the System catalog. A few have managed to survive by entering into (surprisingly legal) arrangements to sell beer directly to restaurants. For an example of this successful strategy, try the wide range of excellent Nynäshamns Ångbryggeri beers at Akkurat.

For craft beers outside the bars, ask directions to the nearest Systembolaget. The good news is that—as with so many other things in Sweden—the government does take its task fairly seriously. The main System store in downtown Stockholm pales beside the best bottle shops of Belgium or the United Kingdom, but always yields treasures for us. Even some of the lesser System stores might offer you beers you haven't tried, and for Stockholm, the prices are as reasonable as they get. You'll pay a modest premium for a vintage Baltic porter, but some interesting beers are priced well below bar levels.

Included among the government's regulations is a ban on "bars," businesses whose sole function is to sell alcohol, so every drinking place in Stockholm has to be also a restaurant serving full meals in a sit-down setting. The connected drinking areas are absolutely indistinguishable from "bars," however you define the term, and the regulations seem to be more annoying than functional. The up side is that you can get a good dinner quite late at night; pubs staying open until 11 PM or midnight have to keep their kitchens open until very nearly last call.

The sixpack of drinking experiences

Akkurat (Hornsgatan 18) sells more beer than most sports bars: 130,000 liters of it every year. Yet the throngs that can make it a challenge to find a table are there to drink beer and whisky seriously. No TVs or games distract them; a double blackboard of ever-changing guest beers dominates the dark, woody, and very pubby décor. Akkurat does whatever is necessary to give an opportunity for new Swedish brewers to showcase beers at their best. Not only are the beers in pristine condition, but we've never seen a bar staff that made more of an effort to serve each beer with care. Don't be in a hurry; the wait is worth it.

While we think Akkurat provides good value for money, you won't find bargains there. Expect to pay what you would in the most exclusive craft beer houses in New York. But pretend your kronor are Monopoly bills and enjoy one of the most carefully selected ranges anywhere. Don't ignore the extensive bottle menu, either. If you've won the lottery, ask for the vintage menu that lists dozens of otherwise unobtainable beers, including a range of Westvleteren vintages at prices that can leave you taking a vow of poverty.

In addition to showcasing some of Sweden's best new breweries, Akkurat offers a range of imports from the relatively mundane Erdinger Weissbier to Cantillon beers you can't find in Belgium. We've also seen American beers there that we've never seen in the States. Akkurat's owners and Cantillon's Jean Van Roy are friends, and Cantillon produces occasional special one-off beers that Akkurat cellars for years and prices accordingly. If you're in a group of four or five you can split them and share the cost. But even if your budget doesn't allow you to explore those cellared treasures, there will be a Cantillon presence among the drafts at normal prices.

Akkurat's range of 400 single malt whiskies is among the most extensive in Scandinavia; a heaven-favored dedicated manager samples each one before adding it to the list. In our next lives, or when the price of livers on the black market becomes more reasonable, we'll go back to try them.

The menu is modest, but the kitchen knows what it's doing. Akkurat steams over 15 tons of mussels a year, most of them sourced from Swedish purveyors who ensure superb quality. They are at least on the level of the best of the Brussels mussel houses. Most of the mussel dishes favor cream, but the kitchen will usually hold it on request.

Akurat's draft offerings change frequently. Go early and leave late if you're in Stockholm for more than a day or two. There's almost always some beer from Nynäshamns Ångbryggeri, a local craft that manages to be adventurous without making mistakes.

Akkurat is a short walk from the Slussen T stop. Exit the station on the market square, turn left on Hornsgatan, and walk uphill a couple of short blocks. If you can tear yourself away, find Oliver Twist by crossing to the other side of Hornsgatan, retreat a half block towards Slussen, then go uphill for two blocks, ending with a set of stairs that takes you up to Oliver Twist on the corner. Akkurat's staff will be happy to point you in the right direction.

House of Ale Oliver Twist is the bar that started the Swedish beer revolution in 1993. In 2001, it became the first bar outside the UK to achieve Cask Marque accreditation. Since then Oliver Twist, or OT, has achieved such world recognition that a host of breweries in Sweden, the UK, and the U.S. brewed one-off batches to celebrate its 20th anniversary in 2013.

About half of the two dozen taps rotate and, as with many of the best Stockholm bars, you'll probably find something that is exclusive to the OT. The range of beer signs and banners that adorn the dark wood walls and ceilings attests to the international flair of this not-at-all-ordinary local. Food is a bit more than pub grub, fine if you're here for the evening, though the kitchen at Akkurat has a defter touch.

Oliver Twist is smaller than Akkurat, and while it may not be as flashy, it has more of a "local" feel to it. Regulars, invariably friendly, populate the bar and sometimes hug the staff as they leave as if they were related. It's less likely to be crowded and can be a good alternative when you can't get in the door of Akkurat.

Ardbeg Embassy (Västerlänggaten 68—formerly Glenfiddich Warehouse 68) is a long, narrow bar with a restaurant seating area, on a touristy shopping street in the heart of Gamla Stan. Ardbeg features a couple of dozen Swedish craft beers on tap and around 300 whiskies. On an earlier visit, the beers showed the effects of a heat wave, but recently they were in good condition and served with care. The beers rotate, as they do in most of Stockholm's star pubs; on our last visit, eight of the Gotlands Bryggeri beers were on tap along with several seasonals from a variety of other Swedish craft breweries. If you're under 55 years old, you can obtain a vintage whiskey cooked up before you were, though a one-centiliter mini-encounter can set you back a few hundred bucks. Happily, most whiskies are newer and less devastatingly expensive. The beers, for Stockholm, are relative bargains.

The cordial bartenders all speak English, of course, but many of the customers don't, and Ardbeg feels like an escape from the heavily touristed old town. The menu includes venison and moose (not a dessert). Entrees run from a vegetarian dish or salmon for $25 to the $50 moose. Feeling raw? Reindeer and moose tartare with roe is just $20.

Flyt (Trangravsvej 5). The same people who created Akkurat and Oliver Twist had one more card up their sleeve with this floating playpen. Moored at the base of Gamla Stan, less than a 10-minute walk from Akkurat, Flyt isn't intended to be anything other than a fun place to eat and drink, but does that superbly. Excellent food from a simple menu, a very limited range of very drinkable beers, and some other more stultifying drinks provide all you need while you bob pleasantly in the harbor. Tables and sofas on deck let you loll in the sun, and a snug brown interior comforts in bad weather. There are floating bars with better views, but none with better food and drink. The delicately fried soft-shell crabs rival any you'll find in Maryland, and the head-on roe-laden rakor (shrimp) are virtually unobtainable in the States. There's an art to the shrimp: separate the head and the tail and suck the juices out of the head for an amazing flavor experience. Then run your thumb between the spiny legs and scoop out a teaspoonful of roe that you'd pay an arm and a spine for in a sushi house. The actual shrimp is almost a pleasant afterthought. The two house beers, Hell and Heaven, are exceptionally well crafted brews from Jämtlands brewery, another of Ruben Bolen's projects. We wonder why they don't blend the two and offer a "Purgatory," but about 1/3 dark and 2/3 light gives you a beer that will put you on a path to

Flyt

heaven on earth. There's usually another well-chosen Swedish craft beer at the outside bar. When you've had your fill, you have about a four minute walk into Gamla Stan to reach Ardbeg and a host of fine Swedish craft beers.

Taylors & Jones with the Twist (Hantverkargatan 12) may be the world's best shopping mall food stand. Tucked into the entrance to one of Stockholm's labyrinthine shopping areas, Taylors & Jones specializes in house-made sausages and a carefully selected range of a half dozen or so local beers. Sit at the bar or the tall tables, or take a break at the sidewalk café tables outside; the atmosphere is lunch counter, but the experience is first rate pub. A small but imaginative menu supplements the sausages. You can find it by walking out of Akkurat, turning right and walking "to the end of the street," about two miles. Happily there are buses, and the nearby Hornstull T stop is just a quick couple of stops from Slussen. Your best bet is to follow the advice we received from several of the barkeeps—once you've arrived more or less at the intersection, ask anyone where it is. "The Twist," by the way, is a shout-out to House of Ale Oliver Twist, which inspired this and so many other good drinking places.

While many of its best outdoor drinking venues float, Stockholm has some more conventional beer gardens as well. By far the best is the **Mosebacke** beer terrace (Mosebacke Torg 3), next to the Södra Theater, which sits on top of a bluff in Södermalm, overlooking the harbor and the cruise ships far below. It's a true German style beer garden stretching out along the top of the hill with separate stands for food and drink, picnic tables, and strings of cheerful lights at night. Best of all, there's one kiosk, on the right as you enter, that offers dozens of craft beers—served in proper glassware—that are hard to find even in the good beer pubs. Finding the garden is a challenge, but can be a hoot. From Slussen, down by the water, look for the gigantic almost free-standing Katarina elevator. Built in 1881 to get commuters back and forth to the top of Södermalm, it's closed now, but the skyscraper it's attached to has another elevator to get to the swanky night club on its roof. Get up there, then go along the bridge to reach the high ground. Continue straight ahead a block or so, then turn left in front of the Södra Theater. The garden is ahead, up more steps and through a stone arch. Alternatively, you can climb Götgatan and turn left on Hökansgatan to the theater and garden. The walk is fine if you don't mind *up*. Be advised that the kiosk may not be open at all times, and the whole place will be empty in poor weather.

Other places to explore

Most of the entries that follow were in our top six in the first draft of this guide. The explosion of genuine craft beer venues has pushed them out of the top, but they remain among the most pleasant drinking experiences in Scandinavia.

The Bishops Arms has a few outlets around town, and more in many other Swedish cities. The concept reminds us of the JD Wetherspoon chain in the UK—enough mainline beers to make money, and enough managerial freedom to make each bar a unique experience. Expat Brits with a vivid imagination can cure a bout of homesickness. The long leash on the management means that the beer selection is decent and sometimes very good. The Bellmansgatan branch (Bellmansgatan 12) can be a fine part of a Södermalm pub crawl, and the Vasagatan location (Vasagatan 7) provides a good lunch if you're shopping or waiting for a train. Food ranges from well-fried cod and chips to an exceptional veal filet with white asparagus and herb butter. Warning: a real pub in the UK will offer session beers of 4% ABV that allow even moderate hopping to stand out. However, some of the beers you find at the Bishops Arms, while lovely and almost affordable, are of American IPA strength. You can end up as dazed by both hops and alcohol as you would be in a long night in San Diego.

One of several Monks outlets, **Monks Porter House/Café** in Gamla Stan (Munkbron 11) features over 50 drafts and hundreds of bottles. During the summer, however, it turns into a "Summer Camp" of a lightweight among the city's best bars. Fewer than half a dozen draft beers remain, whole sections of the place are shuttered, and the menu shrinks. The bottle selection is still available, and if you're not going to Amsterdam or Belgium you might want to consider paddling through a few of the dozens of de Molen beers. We're told that Monks is one of the best experiences in the city in the winter snows.

Strandbryggan Sea Club (Strandvägskajen 27), one of a handful of floating bars in the city, made our top six in the original draft of this guide. The beers are ordinary but the experience is extraordinary. Only the explosion of first rate taps in so many pubs and the memorable food at the floating Flyt push the Sea Club to the also-ran section. A short tram ride from Skansen or the *Vasa* museum brings you to a sunny day's paradise. You're not in Portland; some of Stockholm's iconic drinking experiences come with pretty mediocre mass market beer. On a warm afternoon, though, we'll cope with an ordinary Swedish lager to bask in one of the best places in the city for shaking off stress and getting away from it all within sight of downtown. Stretch

Picnic options at Hötorget

out on a lounge chair on the deck softly rocking in the harbor, sip a cold lager, and power up the Kindle. For us, life doesn't get much better than this.

Hötorget and other markets. Kungs Hallen at Hötorget is the most central of several city markets. It seems to us to have diminished in size and increased in commercialism in recent years; dwindling stalls have made way for over a dozen restaurants. Shellfish can be worth the splurge at the seafood stall, especially if you're there late in the summer for kraftor (crawfish) season. The rest of the year, shrimp, as at Flyt, are a freshly steamed, unforgettable head-sucking experience. The markets are also a great place to stock up on picnic supplies for a Systembolaget "exbeerience." If you're pubbing or staying in Södermalm, the market there is smaller, but nearly as rewarding, and contains a better-than-average "Irish" pub.

Systembolaget and a picnic. Grab picnic fare at the nearest market. A few food stores sell (expensive) ice cubes; the small store at the T exit to Gamla Stan is one. Alternatively, get some sturdy string and find a comfy dock to dangle bottles into Scandinavia's natural refrigeration system. Even at the height of summer, it won't take long to bring a beer to perfect serving temperature. Remember you're not in Munich, so find a spot away from heavy foot traffic and use a paper bag to cover the bottle unless you've found a nicely isolated place to linger. We've used sweater sleeves (obvious, much?) and never had a problem.

The English Crawl

An "English Pub" crawl in Stockholm can rival a similar adventure in an English town; the most striking difference is the malnutrition of your wallet at the end of the night. Happily the "British" pubs vary enough to make an interesting evening. The Bishops Arms pubs around town are a good start; here a few other more or less British pubs we liked.

One of our favorites, **Black & Brown Inn** (Hornsgatan 50), is just a short walk uphill from Akkurat and even closer to the Bellmansgatan Bishops Arms. The range is modest, but it almost always has a few beers you can't find in other pubs. The service is exceptionally welcoming, even by Stockholm's normal friendly standards. Michael, the barkeep, knows his beers well and enjoys talking about them. Don't ignore the bottle fridge—it holds some of the most unusual finds. The dark woods, fireplace, and armchair snug give it a particularly comfortable pub-like feel. Most of the dishes seem to involve garlic (though they do have good fish & chips) and are served on wooden trenchers with a good deal of garnish and style. The music tracks tend to Irish folk-rock and seem to fit the place well. It's unusually child friendly.

The **Queens Head** (Drottninggatan 108) is a big sprawling boozer up near the university section. The large L-shaped bar held a huge number of taps and casks on our last visit, but a closer look showed that many were duplicates. Some of those were unusual, however, and it was a pleasant and quiet student-free interlude at the height of summer. A limited menu features a few entrées and some snacks. Check out the bathrooms with the glowing handles. We're told the pub rocks when school is in session.

The **Half Way Inn** (Swedenborgsgatan 6) is near the Queens Head in the university area, at the Mariatorget T stop. Looking at the map, you'd think of using that stop for the Queens Head too, but remember this is Stockholm: the Queen is several flights *upstairs* from Half Way.

Where to stay

If you can find budget accommodations outside of a hostel, please email us. As in many European cities, however, summer rates at the hotel chains can approach a relative bargain. One summer we booked a room at the Hilton with a water view for just over $200; a different trip cost us nearly twice that. The Hilton's location is perfect: only a short block from Akkurat and close to numerous other Södermalm pubs, stores, and markets. The waterfront rooms offer a remarkable view over the water to Norrmalm and Gamla Stan (and Flyt) and are well worth some extra crowns. If you can wangle a rate that includes breakfast, grab it; the buffet is a notch above even Hilton's usual high standards. Other major chains cluster in the city center, and some of them offer water views as well (water is *everywhere* in Stockholm). A few smaller hotels are tucked away in Gamla Stan.

What to see

Drottningholm

If the Swedes' role in European politics decreased after the Great Northern War ended in 1721 (see "History" above), they didn't completely retreat to isolation. Like many of Europe's most sumptuous palaces, Drottningholm had humble beginnings, but in a conscious or subconscious attempt to rival the palatially extravagant Louis XIV, the Swedish royalty poured money into an upgrade that eventually mimicked the style of Louis XV more than that of the Sun King. Imitating the palaces that had so much to do with bankrupting the French government had much the same effect on the Swedish royal family. Originally the private property of Swedish royalty, Drottningholm ended up as a state palace when Gustav III had to hold a fire sale to pay off his debts. Your admission fee helps fund it now (about $15, but more if you want to see all the parts). It's one of Europe's most impressive palaces and a good reminder of how much a "player" on the world scene Sweden was at the height of its power.

The best way to get there is by boat. A historic canal boat can take you over and back, about an hour each way, for a fairly reasonable $30; combination tickets are available. (http://www.stromma.se/en/Skargard/Stromma-Kanalbolaget/)

Tivoli Grona Lund

It's not as beautiful or as central as Copenhagen's Tivoli, and the biggest of the roller coasters measures about three and a half flags on a Six Flags scale. However, Tivoli is a fine place for a half liter or two in the midst of the noise and thrills of a good-for-European amusement park. Each time we've returned, it's seemed they've added a new coaster—to the same small area. There are now four coasters so interwoven that you really can only tell which is which by the shape of the cars whizzing by. If you can't find something to amuse you here, you've spent too much of your life at Busch Gardens. If you're over 65 it's free; otherwise it'll cost you about $15 to look around, and have access to the food and drink. Some of the cafes in the park have lovely water views. Virtually all the draft beer is the mundane Norrlands Guld, though there are a few more interesting brews in bottles if you search for them.

Skansen

Ellie's favorite European museum, Skansen is the most accessible and rewarding of Scandinavia's several outdoor museums. Original structures reassembled here include homes, barns, artisan workshops, and churches that can teach you much about post-Viking society, while the zoo that it sort of merges into on the hilltop is good fun for children well into their 60s. Benches allow breaks in the fair amount of climbing up and downhill that it takes to see everything. The folk music performances can be well worth adjusting your schedule to see.

The Mint Museum

No need to guess which of us spent half a day here. Bob's an "easy date" for unusual history museums. This one's a gem. Tracing the history of money is almost as useful as tracing the history of beer if you want to find out what really happened to whom. The museum starts with the first western "coin" from Lydia over 2,500 years ago. We've read about it and seen it on television, but have never gotten up close and personal. The exhibits follow, more or less sequentially, the various stages from "intrinsic" coins (valuable for their metal or other content) to "credit" coins (an artificial, agreed-upon value to facilitate trade). The museum includes the first "euro," which originated in Athens and was used all over the Mediterranean, and a later "euro" from Charlemagne. We've seen bills from the German inflation of the 1920s (an ordeal that still shapes Eurozone policies today), but never so many and so richly (sorry) displayed.

One of the reasons this museum works is that the Swedes minted early and often; Viking currency was sort of the dollar of its day—and even the term "dollar" stems from the Swedish original. You don't have to fill in much to show both Swedish monetary history and that of the western world at the same time. Don't miss the displays on counterfeiting—including a Swedish king who counterfeited his own currency to finance a war.

The *Vasa* Museum

In 1628, at the height of the Thirty Years War, Gustav II Adolf commissioned what was meant to be one of the premier war machines of the world, a massive 64-gun warship capable of carrying 300 troops to mop up whatever the guns hadn't destroyed. Soaring 50-foot masts and hundreds of gilded wooden decorations made the ship as beautiful as she was deadly. They also made her fatally top-heavy; on her first launch, *Vasa* staggered down the harbor for about half a mile before she heeled over, took in water through the carelessly open gun ports, and sank like a rock. And there she sat until 1961. Remarkably, the ship held together as salvagers hauled her out of the

Nordiska Museet

mud, and she became the centerpiece of a museum that not only celebrates the *Vasa* herself, but gives intriguing insights into the 17th century world that created her. A fascinating exhibit in the basement chronicles the technology of *Vasa*'s restoration and preservation, a continuing process of success and setback even after 53 years. The museum's huge roof is easy to spot in the museum area near Grona Lund, and it's a manageable hike or a trolley ride from the ferry stop. A *don't*-miss.

The Nordiska Museet

The Nordic Museum features centuries of Nordic home and public design with some quirky exhibits among the more usual costume and pottery displays. An exhibit on the history of hair (Did You Know: human hair was ideal for braiding into horse reins because it never freezes) and an exquisite doll house collection were among the girly items Ellie enjoyed. The museum's grand Gothic architecture itself belongs in a museum.

ABBA Museum

For $40 you can dress up like Swedish musicians for a souvenir picture. Or save the money and buy three superb Swedish craft beers back in town. The choice for us was an easy one.

Ferry ride

You can get to the museum area by bus, but a ferry ride is more fun and it's included on your transit day pass. Board across from the edge of Gamla Stan and disembark a stone's throw from Grona Lund's entrance and an easy walk to other nearby attractions. A tram runs from Skansen past the *Vasa* and the Nordiska Museet and on into town. Just past the museum area, the tram passes near the Strandbryggan Sea Club.

Scams and alerts

Copenhagen redux. Bring a credit card with a big limit.

The only "scam" is government operated: taxes so high they could make a Republican out of Barack Obama, albeit with government services to match. While you're in Sweden, you'll be funding universal education, universal health care, and decent housing for people who would be in shanties in other countries. Think of the cost of Stockholm as a nondeductible charitable contribution, and you might find it easier to part with such an inordinate amount of your trip's budget.

The Swedes aren't going to steal from you—they already have your money. We have noticed on recent visits, however, a ubiquitous campaign warning about pickpockets;

easier travel within EU countries means people come here to steal. Remember, the most skilled real-life Artful Dodgers recruit real-life Oliver Twists who operate in groups and rarely look seedy.

Further information

The "Stockholm Card" gets you into 80 museums, including some of the pricey ones, and gives you transportation as well. Prices range from nearly $70 for a one-day pass to a more reasonable $30 a day for the five-day version. Make a careful study of how much you'll use it; to get value from most of the passes, you'd have to go on the wagon and do nothing but sights.

Although Sweden is part of the EU, Swedes rejected the opportunity to join the Eurozone and resolutely maintain their own currency (kronor, or crowns). "Bankomats" are plentiful; as always, guard your PIN and keep your money is a safe place.

Restaurant and bar service charges are included—and itemized—in the bill, but if your server has done anything more than throw food in your general direction, he'll expect a "tip," a separate and sort of voluntary addition to the check. Average service gets about 5%; for a personal connection we leave about 10%, an amount that doesn't shock the bartender, but does clearly make him grateful.

Day trips and excursions

Our friend Christian at Oliver Twist speaks like a native Brit, but he's a thoroughly Swedish beer geek. When we asked about what other cities to visit, he looked at us with a "Why would you want to leave Stockholm?" expression that made us doubt the wisdom of this section in this chapter. But on reflection he suggested Göteborg and Malmö as towns with good pubs. They both turned out to far exceed our expectations and, we suspect, his.

Göteborg is very much an excursion rather than a day trip. Plan at least one overnight; you'll be happy if you give it two. Malmö can be an excursion from Stockholm too, but we've listed it as a day trip from Copenhagen (see the chapter), since it's only a quick hop from the Danish capital.

Göteborg

When we try to tell people just how pervasive the global craft beer revolution has become, we often cite Göteborg. (The local pronunciation is roughly "Yer-te-borya" but fortunately "Goat-aborg" will be recognized.) We visited the city decades ago when one large local and a handful of national brands were all you could get. It was a paradise for beer can collectors, since some of the Swedish breweries produced series of half liter cans picturing great works of art or scenes of Sweden's stunning natural beauty, but the beer in those cans was always the same yellow stuff.

Today Göteborg has a thriving beer culture based on beers rather than containers. At least a half dozen breweries lie within 25 kilometers of the city, and they all get good representation at the city's many specialty beer bars. Some of the new brewers play with outrageous ideas and sometimes produce beers that aren't really very beerful, while others strive to achieve excellence in traditional styles. It's all just as it should be for a splendid beer-centered short break.

We recommend giving Göteborg at least two nights. You still won't get to everything, but you'll get a sense of the city and be able to visit the gold star pubs. If you stay longer it isn't hard to find more winners on your own.

You'll arrive at a wonderful combination of old and new at the train station. Exit to the right, cross the street, and you're in the midst of a huge modern shopping center. Exit to the left and you're in a grand square framed by large and not always expensive hotels. The Clarion spreads new rooms around the old Post Office and their rate includes a vast if somewhat mass-produced breakfast. Radisson and Best Western offer plenty of range of price and accommodation. Göteborg is walkable, but buses and trams that leave from the square can take you almost anywhere. If you're lucky, you'll ride in a vintage streetcar of the sort that's now usually only found in museums. In a pinch, if you're careful, the plentiful cabs are affordable; to be safe, negotiate the rate in advance.

Ölstugan Tullen (Andra Långgatan 13) is not far from the old town, the center of the beer bar district. It's a great bar with glowing taps and funky furniture and friendly, knowledgeable staff. It would be a good place to drink no matter what it served. Tullen, however, is the only bar we know that dedicates all of its 20 or so taps to Swedish beers. You'll find great beers from tiny breweries that just can't fight their way into "the System" or onto the taps of bars that are as interested in carrying beers from Escondido, California, as they are in showing off what's being brewed next door. A limited menu features Swedish "home cooking" that looks better than it sounds and tastes better than it looks. Tullen is one of Europe's great beer bars and in itself justifies the trip to Göteborg.

But tear yourself away, for there's much more to be savored. Across the street at the corner is **The Rover** (Andra Långgatan 12), reportedly one of Göteborg's best beer

The bar at Haket

emporiums. It boasts a wide range of imports including fairly unusual beers from the U.S. and the UK. It was closed on our last visit, but by the time you read this, renovations should have returned it to its place of honor.

If you walk north to Järntorget you'll see one of Sweden's many Bishops Arms. A large, remarkably British single-room pub, it includes a sizeable and very popular sidewalk garden. The manager knows and cares about beer, and while some of the draft taps are pretty ordinary, he keeps a range of local beers as well. His enthusiastic recommendations of other local bars ensured that we'd return to his, but if you want to chat about the local brewing scene, get there in the afternoons before the crowds descend. The menu is small but good: the fish and shellfish soup is a triumph.

From the Bishops Arms, walk a block or two to the #3 tram line and take it two stops to a bit before it begins its climb uphill. From there an energetic 15 minute walk gets you to **Haket** (Första Långgatan 32) faster than the tram, which overshoots it. Haket has a reputation not only for serving a great selection of local beer, but for offering some of it at prices the nearby students can afford. It's kind of punky, but welcoming even to codgers, and the beer selection is exceptional. Predictably crowded at night, it's a great place to stop in for a chat about beers and breweries during the day. Don't miss the refrigerator of one-off bottles almost hidden to the left of the bar.

If you have time, there's much more here. On the way to Tullen, you'll pass **Jerntorgets Brygghus.** It looks like it might be, or have been, a brewery, but it's just a bar. A young, mostly 20ish crowd piles in late at night, though the place can rattle empty in the afternoon. Many of the taps are pretty ordinary, but you'll find a few, like some

Lunch at the Fish Church

from the nearby Ocean Brewery, that are local and distinctive, as well as some beers from outside Sweden that you might have trouble finding in their native land.

Worth a visit, but not at the cost of the top spots near the old town, **Ölrepubliken** is an expansive drinker with interesting wall displays and some good beers to drink while you're there. It's a bit off the beer-beaten track, though an easy bus ride to or from the train station.

Feskekörka, or Fish Church, is the city's most famous market. It looks like a church, but once inside you'll mostly pray for more time in Göteborg. Pick up a carryout seafood plate and take it outside to the tables that overlook the canal. You'll have to put up with very ordinary beer here, but the experience is worth the break in your beer questing. A short walk from the Feskekörka, **Lager Huset** overlooks the water and puts you back on the craft beer path. A nautically themed, dark wood, pubby interior provides a good atmosphere in which to drink with friends. The beer list can't rival Tullen or Haket, but it has enough of interest to provide a relaxed alternative to the crowds of the town center drinkeries. The Systembolaget store in the huge mall opposite the station has a decent collection that includes some locals, plenty enough to fortify the train ride to Copenhagen, Stockholm, or Oslo. If you get there within a half hour of closing, bring a copy of *The Girl with the Dragon Tattoo* (set in Stockholm; you can look up all the settings in Södermalm); you'll have time to read the whole thing while you're in line waiting to check out.

Vienna

Quick orientation

Vienna is smaller than London, Paris, or Berlin, but it's been a major European capital for centuries and takes up enough space to prove it. It is possible to walk from one side of the old town to the other, but a bus-tram pass will save you time and shoe leather. You can buy passes from multi-language vending machines in subway stations or from transit office windows. The machines take bills and give change.

The old parts of Vienna are enclosed by ring roads that follow the space once occupied by city walls. The #1 tram follows the ring road route and usually takes you fairly close to wherever you're going. Some bus routes cross the old town during the day and early evening; at night you're underground or on foot.

Station breaks

Vienna has had more train stations than some cities have trains. The good news is that the train network is part of an excellent transportation system. The bad news is that you have to be as careful as you are in London or Paris to be sure you're at the right station. Complicating a tricky situation are the construction projects that are overhauling and realigning several of the stations in anticipation of the full opening of the new

Schönbrunn Palace rivals Versailles

Hauptbahnhof. As a result, some trains now come into different stations than they did a few years ago.

The new Hauptbahnhof should lead to less confusion for international travelers, but delays continue. For now it's mostly a regional and local station, and probably won't be much more until the end of 2015 at the earliest. The new station will have 100 shops and restaurants. We hope at least one of them will serve good beer. In the meantime you can grab an eponymous beer at Restaurant Puntigamerhof at Wiedner Gürtel 12, a couple of long blocks away.

A number of routes shifted to the Meidling station, but it's hard to guess if they'll be there by the time you are. If you do find yourself at Meidling, you can get S Bahn trains to Mitte and Hauptbahnhof easily. If you're switching trains during the week, there's a fine beer bar a couple of blocks away. Follow the signs to the Euro Center, walk up the hill, and Zobel is on the corner. They have half a dozen drafts, good food options, and some sofas outside for lounging with your beer.

If you find yourself at Westbahnhof, you're near some great places to drink. Several are listed below. Bauernbräu is a bit far for a station break, though it's only about five blocks downhill, and it keeps odd hours in the summer. Känguruh Pub is closer but doesn't open until 6 PM. 7Stern Bräu is a bit of a hike.

History and culture

The first settlements at what is now Vienna date from Roman times, but aside from some restored walls, little remains. Reduced to insignificance by the collapse of Rome and the threat of nearby Magyars, Vienna rose anew in the 13th century. The decision of the Babenberg royalty to locate in the growing city ensured its prominence. It took the Hapsburgs almost 150 years to consolidate their power, but they ruled over the golden age of the Austrian-dominated Holy Roman Empire.

In 1529 Ottoman Turks besieged the city. Vienna's successful defense, coordinated by the aged German mercenary Nicholas, Count of Salm, saved not only the city itself, but perhaps much of the rest of Europe as well. With Vienna more or less secure for the moment, the city prospered and grew. The historic silk and diamond districts that remain attest to an economy strong enough to afford to support expensive public and imperial buildings.

Tensions between the Hapsburg and Ottoman powers continued until the Turks attempted another siege in 1683. This time it was a Polish army rather than German that saved the city. The final battle, however, was the last word, and the city soared into the 18th century as Vienna took its place among the great capitals of Europe. The dissolution of monasteries opened up new land in the inner city, and the unusual tolerance granted to Protestants attracted craftsmen and business. A visit to Schönbrunn Palace shows how seriously the Austrians tried to be Imperial French.

The 19th century was a time of paradox: industrial eyesores, child labor, and cholera outbreaks tarnished the glory of Viennese music and arts. The revolutions of 1848 rocked the empire and nearly brought national liberation and liberal democracy to much of Austria. The collapse of the revolutions, in part because the middle class and peasants both feared change, returned the conservative Hapsburgs to power for the rest of the century. But the fundamental forces of change lurked beneath the surface among the subject nationalities of this neither Holy nor Roman Empire.

The Hapsburg attempt to cling to empire and emperor in the face of rising nationalism gave us the First World War. The Empire paid for its folly with its life: a new Austria emerged as a shrunken shell of its former self. It might have been the best thing that ever happened to Vienna, though, as the city left behind its imperial ambitions to focus instead on its long-standing tradition of shrewd business dealings. The road wasn't always smooth. Although Austria's annexation to Hitler's Germany wasn't voluntary, it wasn't universally unpopular either. The country had to deal with rebuilding and recovery from significant damage during the Second World War while enduring a period of post-war Soviet occupation. Still, on the whole, the 20th century was a good one for Austria in general and Vienna specifically. Today Austrians enjoy a high standard of living, blessed with fine schools, a good health care system, and...very good beer.

Beer styles and drinking culture

While fundamentally a wine city, Vienna also has a rich brewing tradition. Its role as imperial capital linked it to the local Bohemian brewing culture, and the lack of a Reinheitsgebot allowed Austrian brewers to be more creative than their Bavarian counterparts. Vienna had a long history of monastic brewing, but none of those breweries survive. Commercial breweries grew as the city expanded after the final defeat of the Turks, and one of them gave us an important and distinctive beer style.

Some accounts claim that bottom-fermented beers existed in Vienna in the 18th century, but we doubt it. We know that Anton Dreher, after an unspectacular attempt to brew a Burton style pale ale, turned for advice to his friend, Spaten Brewery's Gabriel Sedlmayr, who convinced him to give bottom fermentation a try. Beginning in the 1840s, Dreher brewed with a malt lighter than the darks of Munich and darker than the pale of Pilsen. The result was an amber beer—the classic Vienna Lager. Lager beers take time to condition; amber lager that was brewed in March and served the following fall came to be known as March beer, or Märzenbier.

Thomas Friedman calls the 19th century the beginning of the second of three "eras of globalization." Governments at these times were dominated by business interests, and sometimes the companies themselves spurred imperialism throughout the globe. During the 19th century this worldwide commercial development also led to mass migration of people from Europe and Asia to the Americas. The immigrants included brewers, and their beers followed their flags. Only a decade after Dreher's breakthrough, Württemburg-trained Charles Stegmaier was brewing lagers in the Wyoming Valley area of northeast Pennsylvania. Brewers brought the Vienna amber lager to Mexico, where its tradition remains in brands such as the amber version of Dos Equis.

Closer to home, a stronger-than-average version of Dreher's Vienna Märzen became the hallmark of the Oktoberfest in Munich. Today many of the Oktoberfest beers have taken the yellow brick road, and light beers dominate the fest. But both

Spaten and Hofbräu continue to brew a dark Märzen, largely because that's what the export market wants. A handful of brewpubs in Europe, and a much larger number in the U.S., produce amber Märzens. However, neither the European nor American brewers usually have the tank space to lager the beer for the months required to produce it at its best, where Spaten and Hofbräu do.

In Vienna, the style lost some of its character as tastes shifted to lighter beers. While Viennese and Austrian beers remained sweeter than most of their Czech counterparts, they lightened in color. Today a "Märzen" in Vienna is a sweet gold lager.

In other ways, Viennese brewing followed the same pattern as in many cities in Europe. Monastery and small tavern breweries yielded to the economies of scale of larger factories. These bigger breweries cannibalized each other's markets and lost ground to even bigger international conglomerations with even larger economies of scale. Today Dreher's brewery survives in a corporately vestigial form in Italy. In Vienna only Ottakringer, a relative newcomer dating to 1837, survives. It produces mostly sweet but clean lagers, well-aged and smooth if undramatic; Gösser, Stiegl, Zipfer, and other Austrian regionals are similar.

A ray of flavorful hope comes in the increasing popularity of unfiltered beers. A Zwickl just means unfiltered, though it's usually a light lager. Wheat beers aren't automatically made with the yeast that makes German wheat ales taste like clove and banana, but they can be. A "Spezial" usually isn't that special, but it is a bit stronger than an ordinary lager. The city of Pilsen was a part of the Holy Roman/Austrian Empire when it invented the Pils style, and Austrian pilsners have close cultural ties to the original. Again, an Austrian pils is likely to be sweeter than its Czech counterpart, but clean and sessionable.

Two important words to know: a Krügel is a half-liter mug, while a Seidel is a little less than 12 U.S. fluid ounces.

The sixpack of drinking experiences

Despite the blandness of the larger breweries' products, or perhaps because of it, a flourishing brewpub scene has emerged in Vienna in the last decade or so and Vienna's best beer bars offer far more variety than you'll find in most German drinkeries. A few of the brewpubs rush lagers in season—you'll notice the sulfur—but most produce respectable beers. Picking the top six is now, happily, a tough call; our also-rans in Vienna are also really nice places to drink. We've chosen these six for beer, ambience, and food but also convenience to the center.

1516 (Schwarzenbergstrasse 2/Krugerstrasse 18) was the first brewpub in Vienna we visited after we started writing this book, and it almost qualified Vienna's inclusion on the spot. We were stunned to see Victory's Hop Devil on tap, and even more stunned to see that they claimed to have brewed it. It turns out that Bill Covaleski, one of the two founders of the Downingtown, PA, brewery, had visited the pub, got talking, and the next thing you know was stirring up a batch of the beer. 1516 has brewed it under license since, and the fact that one of their regular beers is an American IPA says much about the philosophy of the place. You'll find a wide range of not-necessarily-Austrian beers and people who love talking about beer and brewing—in English. It feels a bit un-Austrian, but when you talk to other brewers and beer geeks in Vienna, 1516 is the first name that arises.

Tables outside are an extension of a long inside bar that curves a bit to provide some individual spaces, and the standing room has a bit of a British pub feel to it. Another drinking area fills the second floor. It's woody and welcoming, with the beers calling to you from a long chalkboard above the bar. Plan on a long and pleasant visit. The location is an easy walk from Stephansplatz.

While you're in the area, **Stadtbrauerei Schwarzenberg** is barely a block away at Schellinggasse 14. It's one of the newest of Vienna's brewpubs and brews good if not very distinctive beers. One of the tables has a tap to pour your own beer.

Salm Bräu (Rennweg 6) makes brewing equipment, and you can see a showpiece example of their work at the back of the bar area. They also make above-average new-pub beers, including a fine Hefeweizen, a respectable Pils, and a very nice Dunkel, but the atmosphere and food are more memorable than the beer. It's a big, sprawling, multi-floored place: without a reservation, you'll end up out in the courtyard, which is very nice unless it's raining, or in the cellar room, which does give you a sense of the history of the place. Salm's downstairs room was the wine cellar of the monastery next door and it's been spiffed up nicely. Unfortunately it can get smoky and overheated; if the weather's good we opt for the garden. Crowds swarm here for the huge platters of spareribs, for good reason. Ribs in European restaurants often look better than they taste, but here they don't disappoint. A huge menu offers plenty of other choices that include some from "family" recipes. Tram 71 drops you out front.

7Stern Bräu ("Seven Stars"; Siebensterngasse 19) is modern, but feels older. The brewhouse stands within a big center-of-the-room bar, and the walls are bright and cheery. A fair-sized patio garden is a fine place to drink if the weather's good. The range of beers is exceptional for an Austrian brewpub—there were, appropriately, seven on our last visit, and they were making a chili beer long before the recent craze. The Dunkles is very sweet, but picks up some nice chocolate and a whiff of vanilla as it drinks; the Rauch was shockingly smoky but quite professional, and a hemp lager was a good deal better than most other hemp beers we've had. We won't be ordering the chili beer again. Much of the menu is traditional Austrian—gulash, sausage, and potatoes—but the tenderloin is exceptional.

Many of Vienna's brewpubs and bars are big enough to host an imperial party in this imperial capital. **Känguruh,** located in an artsy area of town at Bürgerspitalgasse 20, is more intimate. Its size makes it hard to find a seat even late in the evening, but also creates the intimate atmosphere that almost ensures a conversation with your neighbor or bartender. Some tables ring the sometimes packed, almost circular bar; you might have to stand for a while, but a seat will open up if you're patient. A street-side drinking deck provides more space in good weather.

Seven taps pour a thoughtful range of beers, many of them from Austrian breweries that you won't see elsewhere. Don't ignore the extensive bottle list that can introduce you to even more local and regional specialties. This is a bar that invites you to settle in for a long evening of beer exploration. Accept the invitation.

It's a bit of a trip from the center city, but we think it's Vienna's best beer bar. Make it part of an evening's crawl—it doesn't open until 6 PM and is closed altogether on Sundays. To find it, walk south from Westbahnhof on the major road Mariahilfer Gürtel, cross Mariahilfer Strasse (which is different), and as it bears left, look for Bürgerspitalgasse. It's less than a 10 minute walk from the station. Plan on dinner elsewhere unless you think that man can indeed live on bread alone.

To get a great sense of this artistic neighborhood and taste a handful of other hard-to-find beers, head south from Westbahnhof along the left-hand side of Mariahilfer Gürtel. The easiest, if not the shortest, route is to turn left on Mittelgasse, then right on Wallgasse past the historic Raimund Theater. Take a left on Gumpendorfer Strasse and **Bauernbräu** is less than a block more at 134-136. The building is the work of artist, musician, and architecht Arik Brauer and it's worth a look even if you don't stop in. But do stop. The Kunstbar (Arts bar) features more of Brauer's art; if your companion seems to take a loooong time in the bathroom, you'll understand why when it's your turn to go. Four beers from the Gratzer brewery in Kaindorf range from acceptable to superb. The Hopfinger Hohann was not only an exceptionally well-balanced gold lager, it was one of the best organic beers we've had anywhere. They open at 4 PM and close at midnight, so you can have dinner here before Känguruh opens, or grab a late night meal if you're still standing when the Kangaroo is finished with you. The Gumpendorfer Strasse U Bahn is a block away.

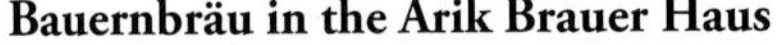
Bauernbräu in the Arik Brauer Haus

The PUB (Schottengasse 2). We know places like this make beer purists cringe, but we can't help being drawn to the bells and whistles of this youth-oriented chain. Sprawling multiple levels near the former Schottenstift monastery offer a conventional beer garden, a sedate pub, a good-sized restaurant, and a 21st century drinking playground. The associated beer garden goes under the name of Zattl and is a pleasant stop in itself. "The PUB" is a long room on the lowest level with some conventional tables, but more that have pour-it-yourself taps. You get a card, insert it in the meter, and draw as much as you want from the several spigots in the middle of the table. Unpasteurized "tank" Pilsner Urquel was an easy choice for us. The gimmick here is that your consumption is posted on a TV screen at the end of the room for all to admire. The same screen compares how many liters this branch of the chain is downing compared to nearly 20 other branches around Germany, Czech, and Austria. Where was this when we were 22?

Fischer-Highlander-University crawl. Vienna's dozen or so breweries ensure fine brewing adventures beyond the scope of this book. We're pretty confident about our first choices in this chapter, but this far down the list we could almost throw darts. If you're staying nearer to a brewpub other than our selection here, skip ours and go to yours. We chose these because, if you expend a bit of energy, they form an ambitious but doable crawl. Get started on it early.

Fischerbräu (17-23 Billrothstrasse) is an average kind of brewpub with kind of average beers. The beers are yeasty and sometimes the yeast tastes really good. It's a good place to eat, however, especially if you're hungry. Big portions give good value for what you spend, and the beer is plenty good enough to pair with the food. The best part of Fischerbräu is the place itself. An old style, many-roomed beer hall, it's a fine place to dwell inside, but the garden is even better. You can hear some road noise, but in general it's well shielded and you drink with a view of the fermentors through the windows of the brewery. Tram 35A runs in front or the U4 gets you close.

The **Highlander Pub** (Sobieskiplatz 4) does pretty well with their tiny brewhouse; the beers are quite yeasty and generally tasty. The chalky, yeasty, softly lemony Zwickl was the best of the bunch, but the others were fine. Imaginative seasonal menus make it a good food destination. In our experiences the service has been exceptionally good, and while the atmosphere would bring us back wherever it was located, its proximity to other good drinking spots makes it easy to add to a crawl.

The entire area is clearly university centered, but the University itself has several good drinking spots. **Stiegl Ambulanz** (4 Alser Strasse) is a well-funded beer palace. It's remarkably hard to spot. The whole block of Alser Strasse is a single blank wall; the only hint at your destination is a smallish doorway halfway down, flanked by small banners that read "Essen" and "Trinken." But this unprepossessing entry leads into a huge block-square enclosed park; it wouldn't surprise us to see a large white rabbit dashing through the gate. Among the trees and lawns stand a handful of restaurants, the biggest of them being Stiegl's. Ambulanz is big and shiny, in stark contrast to the area's brewpubs, but we didn't feel the same sense of personal connection. It's business, well done, but just a bit chilly. A small on-site brewery produces an acceptable house beer, though with not quite the character we'd been having elsewhere. The rest of the beers are from Salzburg's Stiegl brewery, and if you're going to Salzburg we'd suggest you spend your Vienna time elsewhere. But if this is your sole Austrian stop, the Stiegl beers are well worth trying on their home soil. You might find the professionalism of the Salzberg commercial brew refreshing in contrast to the yeasty beers above.

In this same Wonderland courtyard, **Universitätsbräuhaus** features house beers brewed by Stiftsbrauerei Schlägl in Aigen, but you won't find most of them anywhere else but here. We were disappointed in several of them, although the sweetish pils was pretty tasty. The menu shows a university imaginativeness with curries and seasonal specials, but the execution was inconsistent. Lots of wood inside and an attractive garden out in the park give you plenty of choices of where to drink. They finally banned smoking in the dining rooms in the summer of 2014, but expect Rauch, and not in your beer, in the cellar and the garden.

Other places to explore

In good weather the Volksgarten has great atmosphere and good food. The beer is pretty ordinary, but the setting is definitely not.

Where to stay

Like most cities, Vienna offers a huge range of hotels. If you're on a budget, you'll find some nice options online or you can get help from the tourist office. In summer, Vienna is one of the cities where big hotels have trouble filling up and will offer serious discounts. We got 40% off on our last visit to the Hilton am Stadtpark, plus a view of St. Stephen's spire and a location virtually on top of two U lines, an S Bahn, and several bus and tram lines, all within walking distance to the 1516 brewpub and the city center. Some of the other big chains are even more central. Several budget hotels congregate around the Westbahnhof.

What to see

You can't do "all" of Vienna. The map called "Stadtplan & Museen" is available for free at the tourist office and many hotels. It lists well over 100 major sights and museums and lets you follow your own interests.

It's easy to get palace fatigue on a trip to Europe and decide to skip a few of them. Don't skip Schönbrunn. It's the Hapsburgs' attempt to show that they were just as classy and powerful as Louis XIV. They might have been as classy—after all, Louis XVI married the Hapsburg Marie Antoinette—but they weren't as rich or powerful, so it isn't Versailles. But it's pretty awesomely close. As long as you've made the effort to get there, get the big tour and get a sense of how big the place really is.

If you have the strength after Schönbrunn, the zoo isn't far away.

Scams and alerts

Vienna's a big city and normal caution is in order. Still, we've never experienced anything other than welcoming professionalism.

Further information

Eight euros can get you an hour-long tour of the Ottakringer brewery, 9 AM to 2 PM weekdays. Take tram 2 or 44 to Johann-Nepomuk-Berger-Platz or tram 46 to Thaliastrasse/Festgasse. Be sure to call for reservations, as tours must reach a minimum size to run. Tel. (+43 1) 491 00-2904. You may be able to make arrangements by email at michael.neureiter@ottakringer.at.

Day trip

Bratislava

Just over an hour by train, or a more leisurely float by boat down the Danube, takes you to the largest city in Slovakia. Be sure to note departure times back to Vienna, and especially the last one, because you may spend more time here than you expect. *Important*: Buy the 6€ map at the station or when you land.

A bus from the train station will take you close to the **Patrónsky Pivovar** (Brnianska 3732/57). A modern-rustic sort of a place with a big glassed-in sun porch and more garden tables in good weather, it offers an upscale atmosphere and some of the best newpub beers we've found. The prime drinking area evokes an American diner with a copper-clad, wood-topped bar. The tiny copper brewhouse is easy to see near the front door. The menu is huge with lots of starters, six soups, and more ducks than you'll find in Long Island. The trout is exceptional.

Nearby, but you may have to ask for directions, you can catch the 204 tram which both terminates and originates in a hamlet just below Patrónsky. It will take you back to town and drop you within a couple blocks of **Starosloviensky Pivovar** (Vysoká 15). You can't help but love this place: a drawbridge-style boardwalk takes you past arched windows to an interior with stone floors and throne-like seating. Very medieval, 21st century style. The brewhouse is one of the smallest we've seen since Sam Calagione crafted beer in soup pots in Rehoboth Beach, Delaware. Unfortunately these guys can't brew as well as Sam did. But go for the place, not the thick, yeasty, roughly metallic beer. Order the smallest size before you commit to a big one. It isn't easy to churn out consistent gems from a brewery this tiny; you may have better luck than we did.

Return to the big intersection and catch the 2 or 4 tram to **Hostinec Richtár Jakub** (Moskovská 2652/16). This "beer club" is Bratislava's star. Step down into the long and narrow bar that parallels the street. A dozen taps, an almost unheard-of number for this part of the world, pour three or four of their own along with guest beers that include outright aliens like BrewDog. The house beers would be run of the mill in Portland, Oregon, but they're exceptional in a Slovak context. A relatively limited menu will feed you if you need it to. You'll almost always find people who speak

Starosloviensky Pivovar: mind the portcullis

good English in places that celebrate beer culture as much as they do here; expect to stay longer than the beer requires. Breweriana buffs will dwell on the vast bottle, glass, and coaster collection. If you just came here on your trip to Bratislava, your day would not be wasted—but you might well be.

If you can tear yourself away from Richtár Jakub, take the 207 Electrobus up the castle hill and then walk back downhill. Don't be daunted by the medieval house numbering system, just keep walking down Zámocká and you'll see **Zámocký Pivovar** (Castle Brewery) at 794/13, a long block before the bridge over the highway. Enter from the main road and you'll see a good-sized hotel-type bar that serves the three-star pension upstairs. If you hunt around for the rustic stairs to the side, however, they'll take you down to a very attractive garden-patio out back. Plastic curtains keep it pleasant in marginal weather. Four or five house beers can amuse you while you enjoy the atmosphere. The wheat beer had a bit of a Lemon Pledge edge, but the others were very good brewpub beers. The star was the Zámocký Světlé 10°, a difficult style to make well; here the flavors are clean and well balanced. The evident yeast is tasty and less assertive than in some other beers in the city. An extensive menu makes this a good food destination.

From here you can walk to the old town. Along the way is **Bratislavský Meštiansky Pivovar** at Drevna Street 8, down a small street behind the Crown Plaza hotel. Our friend Aidan at Vienna's 1516 brewpub calls it a factory, and he's right. Three levels of eateries, drinkeries, nooks, halls, and…stairs. The servers here have big calves. Despite its size it can be so jammed on weekends that even a couple can have trouble finding seats. The beer menu is limited to a pair of house beers, but one of them, the Bratislavský Bubák Tmave 12°, was a dark red gem balancing roasted sweet malts with some finishing dryness and some notes of bitter chocolate as it drank.

As you leave Meštiansky you're on the edge of the old town. Try to leave some time to explore. There are a number of decent bars serving pretty good commercial but local beer, and the patios and gardens offer spectacular views of history. When we first visited Bratislava it was part of Communist Czechoslovakia and we were struck by how dull and lifeless the old town was. Buildings were in poor repair, and you had to almost guess whether a door led to a shop, restaurant, or private house. No longer; you could just as easily be in Nuremberg, Germany, or any other continental town joyfully celebrating its centuries-old past.

❦ *Zurich*

Quick orientation

Switzerland has a romantic image—William Tell, Heidi, and nearly as many cows as Wisconsin—but Zurich's magical gnomes are bankers and the city is business oriented. Swiss independence includes their currency: you'll find no euros here. As a result, Zurich is one of Europe's most expensive cities. Distressingly, the near parity between the dollar and the Swiss franc makes it really difficult to pretend you're not spending as much as you are.

It's unlikely that Zurich could claw its way into our top 24 cities on the strength of its beers alone. If you augment your time there with our suggested trips down the lake and into the hills, however, you'll get adventurous beers and lots of absolutely beautiful places to drink them. When we win the lottery, Zurich will be one of the first cities we'll go back to.

You'll arrive at the central Hauptbahnhof, which is on the Limmat River close to the lake and sort of south and east of most of what you'll want to see. Cross the river and turn right to wander through the old town to the lakeshore; turn right out of the station and follow Bahnhofstrasse to find stores that you need to be a Trump to patronize. Many of our top six are further afield; buy a tram pass and get a map with the tram lines on it.

The Swiss speak four languages, five if you count English, but few of them speak all of them. Zurich is in the allegedly German section of the country, but if you have trouble understanding the Schwyzerdütsch commonly spoken in Zurich, don't worry, so do the Germans. One key term to know: draft beer is "offen bier."

Summer is the rainy season; in this cranny of the mountains, the sky can go from blazing sun to blazing lightning in a blink. If your hotel offers a loaner umbrella, take it.

Station break

Easy call here. The Federal, smack in the middle of the main hall of the Hauptbahnhof, is one of our top six choices for drinking. It's one of the best train station bars we've ever encountered, but note the "friendliness" (i.e., *not*) caveat below.

History and culture

Zurich is an old place. Settlements grew around the Limmat in prehistoric times. The Celts popped in but left pretty quickly; the Romans built a fort and moved in for a 400-year stay. If you visit the site up top of the Lindenhof, you'll see why the spot was a perfect place to fortify. The area was Church property after the Romans left, until a general economic revival brought commerce to Zurich that led to its wrenching itself free of Church control by 1218. By the 15th century the trade guilds, spiritual ancestors of today's gnomes, were in full control.

Ulrich Zwingli brought the Protestant Reformation to Zurich and with it the usual religious civil wars, but Zurich emerged as a center of Protestantism and served as a haven for French Huguenots and other European dissidents. The influx of population strengthened the city's economy and spurred the growth of a cottage textile industry. Collected somewhat against its will into the Swiss Confederation of the late 18th century, Zurich endured some years of decline before gradually establishing itself as a force within the new federal state.

Zurich reached a population of nearly a half million in the 1960s, but the Swiss had both the money and the inclination to seek less crowded abodes and moved in significant numbers to the outlying areas. The population today is about a third of a million, which is big enough to support a rich urban life, but small enough that you will rarely feel too crowded to breathe.

Zurich may be best known abroad for its banks, which have been repositories for more or less legitimate assets over the years. The term "gnome" as applied to a Zurich banker is relatively new, coined by British politicians during a currency crisis in the 1960s. Although the name was intended to be disparaging, some Zurich bankers began answering the phone, "Hello, gnome speaking." In recent decades, Zurich's role in the world's financial dealings has been of less than Alpine stature, as global finance has focused within large conglomerate banks in the West and Far East. Nevertheless, the gnomes are still there, and still very secretive about what they do and for whom.

Despite their reduced role in global money decisions, the Swiss have done better than most European countries in keeping inflation in check. Investors regard the Swiss franc as a safety. The result is that the exchange rate has led to soaring prices for traveling Americans. For a while in the 1980s Americans could buy a Swiss franc for less than forty cents; now it costs more than a buck. So remember, when you feel like your restaurant is gouging you, they are only asking you for about the same number of francs they did a decade ago—you're just paying over twice as much for those pretty bills.

Beer styles and drinking culture

While Zürchers have brewed beer for centuries, the beverage of choice for most of the city's population was wine. The sap-sucking phylloxera bug all but wiped out European vineyards in the late 19th century, however, allowing brewers to step in with a more dependable alternative. As in many other European countries, large regional breweries developed to slake the thirst of an increasingly industrial population.

Hürlimann surged into the lead not only in Zurich, but in all of Switzerland, by making use of an early "ice machine" to lager increasingly larger batches of clean beer. Zurich's Lowenbräu—no relation to the Munich brewery of the same name—was a close second.

The late 20th century put the same economic strain on large-scale brewing in Zurich as it did in cities all over Europe. Transportation that once enabled large breweries to thrive in city centers eventually grew too expensive to sustain and drove the big boys into more rural settings. Company mergers attempted to achieve greater economies of scale. None of the big Swiss brewers, however, was able to attain a size that could withstand the predatory giants of the north.

Poor marketing strategies doomed Swiss Lowenbräu. We had the chance to talk to the corporate head in 1977. He was ecstatic that his Lowenbräu light had bested Miller and Bud in blind taste tests, and he was ramping up production to "take over the state of Florida." We tried to tell him that, without dropping more millions into marketing than his brewery was worth, he was likely to get clobbered in Miami. Unfortunately, we were right, and Hürlimann bought him out not long after.

But Hürlimann's takeover of Swiss Lowenbräu in 1984 failed to give it the traction it hoped for, and it merged with Feldschlösschen a decade later; Hürlimann's Zurich site brewed its last beer in 1996. Feldschlösschen's independent run ended soon after, when it in turn fell into Carlsberg's clutches. The brewery in Rheinfelden still operates, turning out Feldschlösschen and Hürlimann brands that most people would be pretty hard pressed to distinguish from Carlsberg without looking. The most iconic major Swiss brand, Hürlimann's Samichlaus, is now brewed in Austria.

Zurich joined the craft revolution almost as soon as Feldschlösschen hauled Hürlimann out of town, when local investors created Turbinen Bräu. The brewing scene today is in flux. Most Swiss in this area still like clean, vaguely German lagers, and it's hard for the little guys to make a dent in the biggest part of the market. Nevertheless, there's enough foreign influence in Switzerland as a whole to allow some of the Italian and Belgian spirit of innovation to gain a toehold. You'll find these daredevils at Federal and Les Halles as well as on the shelves of Drinks of the World.

Otherwise you'll make do with clean lagers that at least give you a break the next morning. For the most part the styles will be familiar, although "Spezial" isn't very. It's got a bit more oomph, running to 5.2% ABV rather than the 4.8% Helles. Some small breweries—Rapperswil for example—use corn (maize) proudly and well. We note with pleasure that beers made from corn don't usually taste like corn.

The sixpack of drinking experiences

When Hürlimann transferred production to the Feldschlösschen brewery in Rheinfelden and shut down the Zurich facility, three Zürchers set up the tiny **Turbinen Bräu** to replace it. The brewery caught hold and now supplies over 100 local outlets. Turbinen Bräu enthusiastically and correctly claims to be the largest brewery in the Canton of Zurich, but its 17,000 hl is a small fraction of either of the two giants in their heyday.

"Turbinenhalle" is a good brewpub, sort of industrial-chic motif. It's not cheap, but the menu is imaginative and decidedly not Swiss, with offerings such as chickpea curry and ostrich filets. Asian-oriented options are designed to go with an Asian-themed beer they brew. If the weather's good, you can sit outside. Entrees can run towards forty bucks, but you may be used to that if you've been in Zurich a few days. Beers are good enough; you can taste the Perle hops in their Sprint, and the Hefe-Weizen is a pleasant Swiss surprise.

It's not central, but not all that hard to get to either. Take tram #2 to Kappeli and walk back two blocks to 571 Badenerstrasse. It's closed Sunday and Monday evenings.

Steinfels sits downstairs from a huge dance club in the party district, at 267 Heinrichstrasse in the Escher-Wyss Platz-Hardbrücke area. Formerly Back und Brau, it's very modern and cavernous, yet warm, with curvy red couches and lots of light wood paneling. The spiffy copper brewery sparkles behind glass walls and produces four mostly commendable beers: the seasonals are hit or miss, but the Pils and Weizen are both quality beers. The service is pretty friendly given the fact that you're sometimes sharing it with several hundred other friends. Sushi and Thai curry ribs join pizza and burgers on the menu. In good weather there are tables outside from which you can watch the young and happening crowd try to figure out where to get drinks with far less character than yours has.

Bauschänzli (Stadthausquai 2) isn't going to make anyone's list of craft beer outlets, but the bustling garden atmosphere, fantastic water views, and (for Zurich) very reasonable prices make it one of our favorite destinations in good Zurich weather. It sits

Bauschänzli garden on the river

on the site of a Baroque fortification jutting into the Limmat River, just above the bridge and a long football punt from where the river empties into the lake. The first beer garden here dates from 1907; a significant renovation in 2006 provided its current look. Zurich's month-long Oktoberfest is held here, and a winter circus sets up as well.

Head away from the station down the west side of the Limmat toward the lake, and you'll know you're getting close when you see the tourists straining to gawk at the topless women at the Frauenbad river beach next door. Pavilions dispense mostly tasty Germanic food. It's self-service, but when it's not crowded they cook a number of items to order rather than let them shrivel on a steam table. A dozen or so beers include some that are interesting, and if you're persistent and/or lucky you can move in on a table by the edge of the river with a view of the lake. We've heard that on a clear day you can see the Alps. Yep, that's what we've heard.

Nearby, on the lake at Bürkliplatz, is Hermann Hubacher's statue of Ganymede, featuring a Swiss take on the ancient story. The Greek legend of Ganymede was about an abduction, but here Ganymede pleads with his hand outstretched to Zeus (in eagle form) to help him ascend to Mount Olympus (read: the Alps).

At **Les Halles,** a self-service restaurant, specialty beer bar, beer shop, artists' hangout, and joyfully funky marketplace all somehow successfully combine. This cleverly reused warehouse is vast, cement floored, wallpapered with ragged posters, and cluttered with food and beer stands and insanely mismatched seating. Les Halles is a principal outlet for the Erusbacher & Paul beers from just outside the city limits and is counted by local beer drinkers as one of Zurich's breweries. The beer shop features beers from Swiss breweries that even Beers of the World (see below) doesn't carry, and it's a good place to explore the Belgian and Italian influence on some of the small Swiss breweries. It's an incredibly cool place to hang out and, for Zurich, a real bargain. Order somewhat limited food options from a variety of separate counters. Note our salad bar caution in "Where to eat" below. Find it at Pfingstweidstrasse 6, in the same industrial district as Steinfels.

Located in the great hall of Zurich's Hauptbahnhof, **Federal** offers a hundred Swiss beers in several draft lines and a bounty of bottles. The Hauptbahnhof hall is so enormous that the benches and tables around Federal's doors have an open, garden feel in any kind of weather. You can sit for hours watching people dashing off to get someplace that isn't as nice as where you're sitting. So what's not to like? Gruff, overworked, and underattentive servers and an apoplectically cranky manager. Don't even think about taking out your camera here.

Reinfelder Bierhalle (Niederdorfstrasse 76) is in the old town, across the Limmat from most of Zurich's action. There are other beer halls in the area, but this seems to be the classic. The crowded, long tables are typical, but Reinfelder differs from Bavarian Bierkellers in that it is a good deal smaller, it serves beer but doesn't particularly celebrate it, and they absolutely expect you to eat, considering themselves much more a restaurant than a drinking place. The Feldschlösschen and Eichhof beers aren't bad and the food is surprisingly good. The place held up its reputation for gruff servers on our last visit: Aunt Gretchen strongly disapproved of us at first, but by the end (and after compliments on the dinner) grew positively genial.

Other places to explore

LaSalle Restaurant and Bar (Schiffbaustrasse, 8005 Zürich) is an upscale restaurant built into a theater/art complex within a huge structure once used for shipbuilding. It makes no pretension of being a beer bar, but it's worth seeing for its great use of space, and it's one of the few bars in the area to serve a range of the local Turbinen Bräu.

Pay a visit to **Drinks of the World** in the lower level of the Hauptbahnhof, pick up a picnic from one of the carryout stands (or if you're lucky and it's Wednesday, the amazing market that fills the main hall), and have your own festival in a park. The store carries over 300 different beers, including some of the smaller Swiss breweries that don't show up around town. You'll pay less than bar prices for the beers, though that will still be small comfort at the checkout counter.

The **Coop** near the station has some interesting beers including ones from Serbia and Liechtenstein that we had not seen elsewhere.

Where to eat

If you're expecting Swiss fondue you may be disappointed. The Swiss think of it as a winter dish—or a tourist dish. There are a couple of places that offer it year round, and we've heard they do it pretty well. But if you're going to go to Appenzell (see our excursion suggestion below), save your fondue famishment for the real thing up in the hills. Another local specialty is Rösti, shredded potatoes fried into a crisp mat and often topped with cheese or other diet-busting goodies.

Most of the time the places where you want to drink are places where you'll want to eat; you'll be fed well, and occasionally not too expensively, in any of our sixpack of drinking spots above.

Remember "that look" you got from your parents that made you wish they'd just spanked you instead? You can experience it anew if you pile more than a reasonable amount of stuff on your plate at the one-trip-only salad bars in Zurich.

Where to stay

The tourist office in the station has good hours and a computer that can supposedly show every vacant room in the city. But sometimes the hotels themselves don't even know what they've sourced out to the Internet that might actually be available. Zurich can often be a place where you can find rooms on weekends and during school holidays, but special events sometimes fill the place up.

In the movie "White Christmas" Bing Crosby describes the cost of moving his Broadway show as "somewhere between ouch and *boiiiiingg*." Like everything else in

Zurich and Switzerland, hotel prices are *boiingg* or beyond. If you're on a really tight budget, sorry, just don't go. You'll do a little better in small towns, but you'll still feel like you've been hit in the breadbasket by an Alpine horn.

If space is tight, the **Limmathof,** just across the Limmat River from the train station, is cheap (for Zurich) and the location can't be beat. Our room was a "Whose-Liner," a reference to the television improv game in which one person stands while another lies down. One of us actually did have to climb onto the bed if the other wanted to move around the room. The management told us they had other bigger rooms, but if you're at the Limmathof because Zurich is full of people, those larger rooms are full too.

One of the best upper-mid-level hotels in the city is the **Hotel Krone Unterstrass** (Schaffhauserstrasse 1). We paid more than twice what we have paid for a Hilton room in Munich, but for Zurich, that's about the best you can do. This business hotel offers several attractive "studio" rooms that use the wardrobe as a room divider between the bed and kitchen areas, and there's a coin-op laundry for guests in the basement. An excellent breakfast will cost you an additional 19 CHF per person. We recommend you pay it, eat all you can, and minimize or eliminate the cost of lunch. On weekends some of the better hotels on Bahnhofstrasse a few blocks from the station have vacancies with very attractive rates, but watch for a big increase on weekdays.

Sleep in a brew kettle? Not quite, but as long as you're going to pay through the nose for a place to stay you might consider sacrificing both nostrils for a splurge at **B2** (Brandschenkestrasse 152). Hürlimann's old brewery tower, high on a hill above the town, has been converted to a modern-funky boutique resort and spa. They've kept some brewery theme: the old machine room looms behind the front desk, and the bar is in the old brewhouse, with all fifty vertical feet of its walls lined with old books. The room décor is imaginative, wood and glass with industrial bits and some awesome views, and the spa features a variety of fizzy or flowing pools. For Zurich, all this spiff is almost reasonable at a bit more than $400 a night for one of the larger doubles. Pay in advance for a smaller room and you can drive the price down closer to $300.

B2's location isn't central—about 20 minutes' hike to the center and seriously *up*, though once you learn about the secret back entrance it's a short train hop from the Hauptbahnhof. Food in the area isn't particularly special, but there are a few relative highlights. Don Leone is 5 minutes away and serves good—and large—pizzas: cross the Hürlimann Areal (warehouse complex), trundle down the four flights of steps to the main street below, turn right for a long block, cross Bederstrasse, and look for the burgundy awning down on the left. There's also a restaurant in the plaza below the Areal where you can drink comfortably and eat adequately.

We'd suggest you drop the 20€ on a cab to get to the hotel and then find out how to use the elevator in the back that can save you the 57½ steps up to the place. But here's how to get there by train if you want to save the cash. Take the S4 to the Giesshübel stop (it's only a few minutes) then walk back in the direction you came across the river and look for a small set of stairs on the right leading to the elevator. When you get to the top just walk through the (level) courtyard.

What to see

If you plan on more than a couple of sights, consider the museum pass.

The Uetliberg gives you one of the best views of Zurich. Take the S10 tram to the end of the line and then puff uphill for another 15 minutes if you're in good shape (the Swiss call it "an easy 10 minute walk"). There are a couple of places to have an ordinary Swiss beer in an extraordinary setting. Even with some moderate haze, you can see the Alps looming in the distance. The tram ride itself is something of an adventure: it's hard to believe it will actually make it up that hill, and harder yet to believe it will be able to stop itself on the way down.

For an unusual view of the industrial past, visit the Mühlerama (Seefeldtrasse 231), the Mill Museum. The oldest equipment is made from wood and some of it is still operational. The building housed a brewery in the late 19th century and milled malt for much longer than that.

The Kunsthaus (Heimplatz 1) has a marvelous range of genuine masters and includes works by Veronese, Breughel, Van Gogh, Degas, Picasso, and many more. Don't miss the London scenes by Monet. We've rarely seen a museum that can take you on as extensive a historical journey without leaving you almost too weak to find good beers at night. It's not small by any means, but it's more manageable than some of the huge museums of other major cities. The #5 tram stops in front.

The Landesmuseum Swiss history museum is across the street from the side entrance to the Hauptbahnhof. It's a good place for history buffs with exhibits on the Reformation, Enlightenment, and the development of the Swiss government and some nice religious art.

Scams and alerts

Alert: Just as the Swiss won't use anyone else's currency, they often won't use anyone else's electrical sockets as well. Be prepared to get your hands on a Swiss adapter if you're not staying in a first class hotel. But scams? At Swiss prices they don't need to scam you.

Day trips and an excursion

Wädenswil

You can find the Wädenswil beers in Zurich, but it's very easy to try them on site. The S Bahn will take you there; in fact, finding the S Bahn in the Hauptbahnhof is the hardest part of the trip—it's to the far left and then down the tracks a ways. When you arrive in Wädenswil, take a picture of the local map in the station with your phone, then walk the five blocks up to the brewery. If it's not clear, ask anyone.

Options at Wädenswil

The Wädi Bräu Huus (spellings seem to vary) brewpub is nestled into lush shrubbery that could make you think it was in suburban

Atlanta rather than in chilly Switzerland. Lots of wood-framed glass gives a clear view of the brewery, and the good-sized brewpub is a fine place to drink. The sampler sizes are relatively generous, certainly sufficient to give you a pretty good idea of their fairly extensive range of beer styles. The brewery claims their Wädenswiler Hanf is the first hemp beer in the world and it's actually quite good. Strong pepper aroma leads into charred sugar-malt with milder toasted rope and an herbal aftertaste. We assume the bit of a buzz comes from the 5% alcohol.

A pleasant walk through town takes you back to the Havn where you can catch the steamer to Rapperswil if you wish.

Rapperswil

A more extensive day trip than Wädenswil, Rapperswil can still easily be done in a day. Steamers down Lake Zurich are easy to catch, and the voyage is long enough to enjoy a surprisingly tasty Eichhof Braugold Premium from Lucerne and some remarkably good snacks. Note: if you're traveling on a Eurail pass, it's good on the steamer—and good for the first class lounge, which is well worth seeking out on board.

We first visited Rapperswil in 1968 and fell in love with it long before it even had a brewery. The Swiss are almost always good to Americans, but they seemed especially glad to see us then, perhaps because we were there on the 4th of July. A recent trip on a more mundane day confirmed that memory, however.

The welcome for English speakers is warm enough to draw New Zealand ex-pat Steve Hart to this village to open his small brewery. It's not a short trip to the **Bier Factory Rapperswil,** but it's a pleasant walk in good weather. To get there, start by the dock with your back to the lake and walk right along the water on Seequai. Take a left fork on Seetrasse and follow it until it dead ends at Fischmarktstrasse. Go left, bend right at the next fork onto Rathausstrasse, which becomes Neue Jonastrasse,

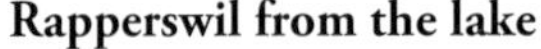
Rapperswil from the lake

and keep going for about a kilometer. Turn right on Schönbodenstrasse and look for #3 in a low old industrial-parky area. If you make an appointment, you can take a two-hour tour of the brewery a few long blocks away for a price. You can taste the beers and get simple food at the brewery tap room, although if you want something extensive you'll have to find it elsewhere. There are plenty of good Swiss restaurants along the way.

Steve balances skill and adventure as if he were a Dane. He doesn't always hit it out of the park, and he's pretty honest about admitting mistakes. His Linth Maisbier, however, is the best corn ale we have ever tasted. It didn't taste at all like corn, though the Alpful of hops he dropped in might have distracted us. The superb Rappi XXA Xtrra Bitter Strong Ale, essentially an IPA, would be right at home in San Diego, though the hops tend to show floral more than citrus flavors. Even the Rappigold has enough hops to strike a fine balance with the pale malt.

Try to leave time to explore the town—it's a beauty, with a magnificent castle looming over it, gorgeous wall paintings, and the occasional steep vineyard tucked between buildings. Rapperswil is called the "Town of Roses" from the over 180 varieties that dot the town. Sixteen thousand rosebushes fill many of the public gardens, especially at the Capuchin monastery and the Duftrosengarten, the latter a garden designed for the blind with interactive fountains and particularly fragrant varieties.

The **Nautic Pub,** on Seequai, features beers from the Falcon brewery. It's a nice place to drink and wait for the boat. For both beer and food, you might do better farther in town. If you run late, you can take the train back to Zurich, though you might spend some time looking for the station.

An excursion: Appenzell

As long as you're in Switzerland, you might as well spend a day or two in a town that looks like it belongs in a Shirley Temple movie. Nestled among the hills, with real Alps a short trip away, Appenzell works hard to be the Swiss city of your dreams and succeeds more often than it disappoints.

We list Appenzell under day trips, but it's not. You'll need to spend at least a night, maybe two, to appreciate it.

You'll arrive by a train that at a distance looks like something out of a model railroad setup. If you're lucky, by the time you go, the rail construction that made our journey here an unexpected adventure will be done; if not, just keep your ears open and follow directions. Someone will make sure you make the rail-bus-rail connections.

There are some hotels near the station. Walk past them downhill to the main part of town. The tourist office is on Hauptgasse and it's one of the more helpful ones you'll find.

History and culture

Appenzell is the main town of Appenzeller Innerrhoden (Appenzeller Inner Rhodes in English), which began as one of the properties of the abbey at St. Gallen. It finally broke free of Church and, later, Austrian control and joined the Swiss Confederation in the 15th century. The Appenzellers' struggles to determine their political fate apparently ingrained a fierce independence they still value today. For a while Appenzell seemed on its way to becoming a significant force in Europe. Its troops ranged as far as Swabia in Germany and into upper Italy, until a nasty defeat or two reordered their priorities.

The Reformation and Counter-Reformation tore Switzerland apart, and Appenzell avoided bloodshed only by allowing each parish to choose its own religion. The "Inner" remained Catholic, under strict control of the church authorities, who mandated church attendance and other behaviors. Eventually both Protestants in the "Outer Rhodes" and Catholics in the Inner became so fed up with renewed interference from St. Gallen that they put aside their differences to regain independence as separate cantons within the Swiss Federation.

The closely held traditions that make Appenzell so charming come at a price. Independence doesn't always mean forward thinking, and Appenzellers repeatedly voted down women's suffrage until the Swiss National Court made them accept it in 1990. Some still are none too pleased about it. But you probably don't speak enough Schwyzerdütsch to talk politics, so simply relax and enjoy. Traditions live on with only some commercial trappings, and you'll be well treated by these people who welcome your visit, not just make their living from it.

Beer styles and drinking culture

All this could be enough reason to visit Appenzell, but **Brauerei Locher** (Appenzeller) offers more beer styles than any other brewery in Switzerland and quite possibly in Europe. So take a day to enjoy Appenzell, take a ride to an Alp or poke around town, and enjoy these beers while you're there. A huge range of spices and herbs grace a number of the generally successful Locher offerings. Moreover, when breweries all over Germany were selling off their wooden barrels, Locher was scooping them up at bargain prices. They now have one of the most extensive barrel aging programs anywhere.

You'll find several of the Appenzeller beers in restaurants and bars around town. For more, go to the brewery visitor center and load up your suitcase with a dozen or more other styles. If it's closed, the drinks market just down the road from the Coop carries a wide range of the Appenzeller beers, including some rare ones such as the 11% Bavik, as well as the much harder to find Lager Hell from Gossau.

The visitor center is a new addition to the Locher brewery and well worth the visit. You'll get a good AV presentation and see a number of displays and pieces of equipment in their small museum. There are some scheduled tours, and you might be able to join a group tour if you call ahead. If you go as part of a tour, you'll get to taste some of the beers there; otherwise check for one of the infrequent public tastings. The bottle shop sports nearly every beer currently in production.

As you walk out of the visitors center laden with bottles, you'll remember why you chose to pay more for a hotel with a good ice machine in the kitchen.

Where to eat

Appenzell is justly famous for its cheese. Although there are several dozen producers, each with their own individual processes, the general style is Swiss for grownups: slightly funky, but not too challenging. Don't miss trying it in one way or another.

Unless you really don't like cheese, find a fondue or raclette (toasted cheese scraped off onto bread).

For a genuine fondue or raclette experience it's hard to beat **Zur Bäumli,** where manager, chef, waitstaff, busboy, and owner Josef Cicini couldn't be nicer. His son has won Iron Man competitions in Florida so he likes Americans—and adores American cars, which he can afford with his Swiss francs better than you can. His open kitchen is a destination in its own, and his style in making a fondue is sheer ballet. Locovore central: the salad, beer, bread, butter, and every ingredient in the fondue (cheese, wine, schnapps) are *all* from Appenzell: "Immer Appenzell!" Appenzeller fondue is amazing with the Locher Quollfrisch Naturtrüb or Appenzeller Dunkel. We'd recommend the Naturtrüb—the yeast helps cut the richness of the cheese. Take your time; eat slowly. You won't finish it all anyway, but pacing gives you your best shot of avoiding the chef's good natured ribbing when you quit with a quarter pound of Appenzeller cheese still in the pot.

There's a range of prices and menus in the rest of the town. Other than the fact that in Switzerland those traveling on U.S. dollars never get what they pay for, you generally get what you pay for. Scam free; but do remember that in Switzerland when a restaurant is open until 10, they mean you have to get your check paid and your keister out the door by 9:55. You often won't be fed if you're not there by 9. Do we sound like we learned this the hard way? Twice.

Where to stay

Nowhere in Appenzell is more than a 15 minute walk from anywhere else, but it's remarkable how much they pack into the place. A dozen hotels and twice as many restaurants vie for the tourist bucks. The tourist office will give you a descriptive book on the hotels and let you know which of them have rooms free.

The **Hotel Appenzell** is in the upper price range but has some large rooms and unusually good views. Room 302 is almost a suite and looks up at the hills on the other side of the railroad. You can watch the toy train (the one you came in on) cut up across the green hill and disappear in the distance. One of the advantages of a three star like the Appenzell is that they do have a good ice machine. If you ask nicely and firmly they'll fill your three liter plastic bag several times a day. Don't trust the opening hours of the restaurant; get there well before "closing." The breakfast is simple but exceptionally well executed. If you want an omelet, just ask, but fresh fruit and an excellent selection of cheeses—including, of course, Appenzeller—make it unnecessary. They have their own bakery and the breads and rolls are superb.

Gasthof Hof, right behind the Appenzell, is simpler at half the price. The nearby **Traube** is another budget choice (by Swiss standards). **Santis** across the square is the class joint of the town and you'll pay for it. **Adler** has some nice views and is really close to the brewery, but it's on a main road.

What to see

Just wandering around town is time well spent, but if you have the time, there are some true adventures to be had.

St. Mauritius church in Appenzell

We recommend a trip to the Ebenalp. It's a short rail hop to the base of the mountain, and from there a cable car will take you near the summit. There's a good bar or two near the base station, but save your drinking time and money for the Gasthaus that looms above the landing station near the top. Clambering up there through movie set décor (cows with huge clonking bells around their necks) makes the good soup and cold beer taste even better. Fortified, you can walk a path beyond that takes you closer to the summit. Fortified fully, you might try it, but don't do it without adequate time (maps show how long the various trails take) and very good shoes. If the day is clear you can see for miles and miles, but even in nastier weather, the experience of soaring through the clouds and just missing the jagged edges of the mountain as you rise is one you will not soon forget.

Safely back in town, check to see if there is a performance of traditional local music. The venue in the town hall can be almost as interesting as the performance. The St. Mauritius church is Rococo glorious, with an old-style graveyard full of beautiful wrought iron markers.

Other attractions include visits to the distillery that makes the Alpenbitter and Santis Cream herbal liqueurs, a cheese producer, and a local sausage maker. Get details from the tourist office.

Glossary

"i" The international symbol for the local tourist office, often in red.

Abfahrt [Ankunft] The list of all train departure times from the station you're in, posted throughout the station. Printed on yellow paper, the Abfahrts poster is usually easy to spot (Ankunft, or Arrivals, is on white). For each train it shows all the stops on that route, with arrival times; codes indicate further information such as days of the week that train runs, or doesn't, and amenities on board.

antipodean hops Hops grown in the Southern Hemisphere, usually Australia or New Zealand; often have a crisper, woodsy flavor.

bahn.comfort A special semi-reserved seat class in German trains; see p. 3.

bottom fermentation Beer fermentation using a yeast that works best at a slow rate and low temperature and usually drops to the bottom of the tank when finished.

Brotzeit[en] Literally "bread time," "menu" German for snacks.

diacetyl A chemical compound formed during fermentation that gives a taste of butter, cream, or butterscotch. It may or may not be desirable; see p. 13.

en suite hotel room With private bath.

fat øl Swedish for draft beer.

Festgelende, Festplatz The field or park where a German festival is set up.

Fokker A German World War II fighter aircraft.

free house In Britain, a pub that is not commercially tied to a specific brewery.

Gasthaus, Gaststätte, Gasthof "Gast" means guest in German; different forms of inns, restaurants, and pubs.

gemütlich / Gemütlichkeit Gemütlichkeit means comfort, good times; gemütlich is the adjective.

Getränkemarkt Store that sells beer and soft drinks.

ggf freiegaben A special seating class in German trains; see p. 3.

handpull In Britain, a system of drawing beer up from unpressurized casks using a distinctive, tall hand-pulled pump handle.

Hax'n [Haxen] A fresh pork hock, usually roasted or grilled on a spit; crisp, greasy, complicated to eat, and a favorite beer hall meal.

Holzfass German for a wooden beer keg.

ice cubes Eiswürfel, glaçons.

Kellerbier German unfiltered lager style.

left luggage room A place in a hotel where luggage can be stored before the room is ready or after checkout. Usually it's quite secure; see p. 6.

Mass German one-liter glass or clay mug, which is never filled to the top, so don't complain.

moreish Describes a beer whose flavor leads you to take another sip.

newpub Our term for a modern brewpub serving unfiltered beers.

noble hops A categorization of five varieties of hops traditionally grown in Germany and the Czech Republic and used more for aroma than bittering.

Pfand Deposit paid on your mug, which is returned when you bring it back.

Prosit or Prost! German "cheers!" shared with pretty much anyone around you.

queue British for lining up for anything.

Radi Daikon; Germans spiral-slice these huge white radishes and serve them with salt as a beer snack. Salt the radish plentifully and wait ten minutes for the salt to "weep" out the heat.

Rathaus German town hall.

Rauchbier Beer style made with smoked malt ("Rauch" means smoke; also in "Nichtraucher" non-smoking areas).

schnitzel Pork (Schwein) or veal (Kalb) cutlet, pounded thin and fried in a crisp crust.

Scotch egg Hard-boiled egg wrapped in sausage, breaded, and deep fried. Served with "brown" or steak sauce or Worcestershire sauce.

session beer/ale A brew of relatively low alcohol and usually not very aggressive flavor, that can be consumed all evening with not too ill effect.

skunk Undesirable beer flavor; see p. 13.

sparkler (Yorkshire sparkler) A device placed on a tap head that serves cask ale. It restricts flow and results in a creamier head and softer carbonation. Lower carbonation can make the beer less bitter.

Steckerlfisch In Germany, whole fish grilled on sticks over open coals, available at large fests and gardens.

tall font Traditional means of dispense of cask ale in Scotland. Beer is pulled by air pressure rather than pushed by CO_2 gas, thus preserving cask ale's low levels of carbonation.

tied house A pub in the UK owned by a particular brewery. It can serve some guest beers as well. Large breweries are limited in the number of tied houses they may own, and "pubcos," pub-owning companies, have largely replaced the large tied house estates. Punch Taverns, the largest pubco, controls over 3,500 pubs.

top fermentation Beer fermentation using a yeast that ferments fairly quickly at relatively warm temperatures and usually rises to the top of the tank when finished.

TTB "Tax and Trade Bureau," a unit of the U.S. Treasury Department tasked, among other things, with making sure beer labels conform to government regulations.

Wirtshaus Literally "host's house," German for a brewery outlet.

wort The sugar-loaded liquid resulting from steeping malt in hot water, the first step in brewing, before the yeast is added for fermentation.

Chronology

Years	Events	Beer and Brewing
1st millennium AD	43 to 410 Roman Empire in Britain 800 Coronation of Charlemagne	620 Weltenburg Monastery founded. Brewing may have occurred 768 Hop garden near Weihenstephan 822 Earliest documented link between hops and brewing (France)
11th century	High Middle Ages 1066 Norman Conquest of Britain	Rise of monastic brewing 1015 Founding of the Michaelsberg brewery in Bamberg, Germany 1040 Weihenstephan began to brew 1050 Weltenburg definitely brewing
12th century	High Middle Ages 1150 Approximate end of the Viking Era Gothic architecture began in France	1100s English pubs increasingly carried names and pub signs became more common
13th century	High Middle Ages 1215 Magna Carta began the path to Parliamentarianism in Britain 1280s Creation of the Hanseatic League that promoted North European trade	1200s Government began to take a more active role in regulating beer and pubs
14th century	1337 Start of the 100 Years War (to 1453) Beginning of the Renaissance 1348 Beginning of the "Black Death" plague in Europe	1302 Gaffel began brewing 1360s Increasing number of hop suppliers in Holland
15th century	High point of the Renaissance 1431 Joan of Arc 1455 Gutenberg revolutionized printing with movable type 1485 The Tudors began ruling in England (to 1603)	1412 First hopped beer in England 1492 Stiegl began brewing in Salzburg, Austria
16th century	End of Gothic architecture 1517 Luther started the Protestant Reformation 1522 Zwingli began the Swiss Reformation in Zurich 1555 The Peace of Augsburg ended the German Religious Wars Dutch "Golden Age" 1682 The French court moved to Versailles; the age of the Great Palaces began	1678 Heller began brewing Schlenkerla in Bamburg

(time marches on, next page)

Years	Events	Beer and Brewing
17th century	1600s (early) End of the period of Renaissance architecture; beginning of Baroque 1607 English founded Virginia 1618–1648 The 30 Years War (the Dutch War of Independence, the 80 Years War, began in 1568) 1620 The Pilgrims ran out of beer and settled in Plymouth 1637 Peak of the "Tulip Mania" in Holland 1662 The Great Fire of Passau 1665 Last major outbreak of the bubonic plague in England 1666 The Great Fire of London 1669 Last meeting of the Diet of the Hanseatic League	1637 English pubs banned by royal decree from brewing their own beer (production breweries were easier to tax)
18th century	1702–1715 The War of Spanish Succession, Louis XIV's last attempt to control all of Europe 1740–1748 and 1756–1763 France and England led rival coalitions in the world wars of the 18th century 1740 (to 1789) Peak of the Enlightenment, the "Age of Reason" 1750–1780 Art evolved from Baroque to Rococo 1789 French Revolution 1798 Peasants War, Belgian popular uprising against French occupation	1758 A brewery opened in Tadcaster, UK, which later became Samuel Smiths 1759 Arthur Guinness signed a 9,000-year lease on the property for the St James Gate Brewery in Dublin 1777 Bass Brewery established 1785 Budvar Brewery established
19th century	1803 Napoleon crowned emperor 1806 Francis II, the last Holy Roman Emperor, abdicated 1815 Napoleon defeated at Waterloo 1848 Revolutions throughout Europe undermined monarchies 1848 Publication of *The Communist Manifesto* 1848 The Seneca Falls Convention began a path to women's suffrage in the U.S. 1871 Unification of Germany 1874 Woman's Christian Temperance Union founded in Cleveland, Ohio	1814 The "Great Porter Flood" in London 1829 Yuengling began brewing in the U.S. 1842 Schaeffer began brewing lagers in the U.S. 1876 British trademark system established. Bass, waiting at the office door, grabbed the first one 1878 British hop growing peaked at 71,789 acres (less than 10,000 today) 1879 Beginnings of Weyermann Malt Factory in Bamberg, Germany 1888 Emil Christian Hansen at Carlsberg Brewery published a method for propagating pure brewer's yeast. *Saccharomyces carlsbergensis* became a world standard

(and on, next page)

Years	Events	Beer and Brewing
20th century	1914–1918 World War I 1917 The Russian Revolution created the Communist Soviet Union 1929 Wall Street crash set off worldwide depression 1933 Roosevelt and Hitler both came to power 1939–1945 World War II 1948 The Marshall Plan jump-started European postwar economic recovery 1948 Start of an 11-month airlift to Berlin that saved the city from Communism 1951 European Coal and Steel Community established, precursor to the European Union 1989 Fall of the Berlin Wall and the end of Communist control of Eastern Europe 1990 German reunification 1999 The euro became the standard currency in some members of the European Community	1919 The 18th Amendment established Prohibition. U.S. breweries produced sodas and other products, brewed illegally, or closed 1933 The 21st Amendment repealed the 18th Amendment. Budweiser and Yuengling delivered beer to the White House in gratitude 1969 Fritz Maytag finalized control of Anchor Brewery. Anchor Steam Beer became an early craft classic 1977 Michael Jackson's *World Guide to Beer* introduced millions to the history and culture of beer 1982 Bert Grant opened Yakima Brewing, the first modern American brewpub 1983 The number of brewing companies in the U.S. dropped to near 50
21st century	2004 The European Union admitted 10 new members, eight of them former Communist countries 2014 Referendum kept Scotland part of the United Kingdom. Glasgow voted for independence	2007 Michael Jackson died of complications from Parkinson's disease 2008 InBev acquired Anheuser-Busch to form the world's largest brewery 2014 Number of breweries in the U.S. exceeds 3,000 for the first time since 1873

Index